Principled Diplomacy

**Recent Titles in
Contributions in Political Science**

Public Authorities and Public Policy: The Business of Government
Jerry Mitchell, editor

Shepherd of Democracy? America and Germany in the Twentieth Century
Carl C. Hodge and Cathal J. Nolan, editors

Gerald R. Ford and the Politics of Post-Watergate America
Bernard J. Firestone and Alexej Ugrinsky, editors

The Democratic System in the Eastern Caribbean
Donald C. Peters

The Third World and South Africa: Post-Apartheid Challenges
Richard J. Payne

The Brazilian Legislature and Political System
Abdo I. Baaklini

Self-Determination in Western Democracies: Aboriginal Politics in a Comparative Perspective
Guntram F.A. Werther

United States Electoral Systems: Their Impact on Women and Minorities
Wilma Rule and Joseph F. Zimmerman, editors

Comparative Judicial Review and Public Policy
Donald W. Jackson and C. Neal Tate, editors

American Ambassadors in a Troubled World: Interviews with Senior Diplomats
Dayton Mak and Charles Stuart Kennedy

Moving the Earth: Cooperative Federalism and Implementation of the Surface Mining Act
Uday Desai, editor

Assessing Governmental Performance: An Analytical Framework
Eugene J. Meehan

PRINCIPLED DIPLOMACY

Security and Rights in U.S. Foreign Policy

CATHAL J. NOLAN

Contributions in Political Science, Number 313
Bernard K. Johnpoll, Series Adviser

Greenwood Press
Westport, Connecticut • London

Library of Congress Cataloging-in-Publication Data

Nolan, Cathal J.
　　Principled diplomacy : security and rights in U.S. foreign policy
／Cathal J. Nolan.
　　　p. cm. — (Contributions in political science, ISSN 0147-1066
; no. 313)
　　Includes bibliographical references and index.
　　ISBN 0-313-28006-1 (alk. paper)
　　1. United States—Foreign relations—20th century. 2. Security,
International. 3. Human rights. 4. United States—Foreign
relations—Soviet Union. 5. Soviet Union—Foreign relations—United
States. 6. United Nations—United States. I. Title. II. Series.
JX1417.N64   1993
327.73′09′04—dc20　　　92-30006

British Library Cataloguing in Publication Data is available.

Copyright © 1993 by Cathal J. Nolan

All rights reserved. No portion of this book may be
reproduced, by any process or technique, without the
express written consent of the publisher.

Library of Congress Catalog Card Number: 92-30006
ISBN:　0-313-28006-1
ISSN:　0147-1066

First published in 1993

Greenwood Press, 88 Post Road West, Westport, CT 06881
An imprint of Greenwood Publishing Group, Inc.

Printed in the United States of America

The paper used in this book complies with the
Permanent Paper Standard issued by the National
Information Standards Organization (Z39.48-1984).
10 9 8 7 6 5 4 3 2 1

Copyright Acknowledgments

The author and publisher gratefully acknowledge permission to use the following:

Cathal J. Nolan. 1992. "The Last Hurrah of Conservative Isolationism? Eisenhower, Congress and the Bricker Amendment," *Presidential Studies Quarterly*. Vol. 22, No. 2. Permission granted by the Center for the Study of the Presidency, publisher of *Presidential Studies Quarterly*.

Cathal J. Nolan. 1991. "La liberté est-elle divisible? Comment rapprocher les concepts de mission et de sécurité dans la politique étrangère Américaine," *Études Internationales*. Vol. 22, No. 3.

Cathal J. Nolan. 1990. "Americans in the Gulag: Detention of U.S. Citizens by Russia and the Onset of the Cold War, 1944–1949." *Journal of Contemporary History*. Vol. 25, No. 4.

Cathal J. Nolan. 1989. "Road to the Charter: America, Liberty, and the Founding of the United Nations," *Paradigms: The Kent Journal of International Relations*. Vol. 3, No. 1.

"Who would treat politics and morality apart will never understand the one or the other." Viscount John Morley, *Rousseau* (1876).

For
Valerie, Ryan Casey, and Genevieve Michelle

CONTENTS

Preface	ix
Abbreviations	xi
Abbreviations Used in the Notes	xiii
Introduction	1

Part I: *The Soviet Union*

1. Responding to Revolution	13
2. From Recognition to Alliance	45
3. The Great Divide	73
4. Rhetoric and Realism	103
5. Human Rights and Détente	127
6. Beyond Containment	155

Part II: *The United Nations*

7. Active at the Creation — 181
8. An End to Leadership — 207
9. Congress vs. the President — 237
    Conclusions — 263
    Select Bibliography — 273
    Index — 283

PREFACE

In an interpretive survey of this type it is next to impossible to single out all one's intellectual debts. In many respects, the path I traveled was well-worn before me. Here and there I came upon a new bend or twist, but I was often aware of a host of companion minds traveling with me through diplomatic and political history. Where a particularly salient scholarly debt is recognized as owed, I have acknowledged that fact in the footnotes. The purpose of this preface, then, is to render thanks to those who most directly aided and influenced me in the course of writing this book.

My thanks to the Associates of the University of Toronto and the Center for International Studies, for research grants that enabled me to visit archives in Washington; the Connaught Foundation and SSHRC, who funded interviews in Geneva; the Human Rights Foundation for the Judge Harry Batshaw Fellowship; and the Department of Political Science at the University of British Columbia, which provided funding for completion of the study and a friendly and professional working atmosphere in a spectacularly beautiful natural setting. I am grateful to Jean Edward Smith of the University of Toronto. His clipped, trenchant criticisms were made (and received) in a spirit of friendly respect and genuine interest in improving the study. Thanks also to James Barros and Richard Gregor of the

University of Toronto, for their sage counsel and constancy of support. Delmar Smyth of York University has been of similar, inestimable help in recent years. And I am grateful to Kenneth W. Thompson, Director of the Miller Center at the University of Virginia, for his guidance and professional encouragement. I also appreciate the continuing support of Inis Claude, emeritus of the University of Virginia, whose balanced writings on international organization I have long admired.

My thanks to Mildred Vasan, Lisa Reichbach, and the staff at Greenwood for their professional excellence and prompt responses to my queries. Thanks are also due to Robin Stearns, production editor. I wish also to thank others who read the manuscript in whole or in part, and from whose comments and criticisms I have benefited: Aurel Braun and Patrick White of the University of Toronto; R. Gordon Hoxie, of the Center for the Study of the Presidency; Arthur S. Link of the Firestone Library and Princeton University; Charles Pentland of Queen's University; Carl Hodge, Okanagan College, who was also an understanding collaborator on another book that competed for time and attention with this one; Frank Sherman of American University, for his scholarly input and his friendship; Rusty Coneybeare, whose suggestions gave me pause on more than one occasion; the reviewers for Greenwood, and other reviewers at Boston University.

I want to thank students in my graduate and senior American foreign policy courses at Miami University. I was moved by the teaching award they bestowed. I would like them to know that I learned much from their keen inquiries and sceptical challenges, enthusiasm, and interest. Particular mention to my graduate assistant Larry Clark, to Jeff Dafler (now with the State Department), and to Brian Hallahan and Douglas Hosier, all of whom like myself have since moved on to greater challenges at other institutions. I also enjoyed lively and rewarding exchanges with many undergraduates, among them Matt Duchene, Lee Gillette, Patrick Jakeway, Leslie Ann Klaus, and Kristin Wold.

Above all, I am grateful for the constancy of support, understanding, and affection of my wife, Valerie. My debt to her is permanent and ineffable. The tasks of writing and revision also have been eased by the playful interruptions of my two-year-old son, Ryan Casey.

ABBREVIATIONS

ABA	American Bar Association
ARA	American Relief Administration
CFE	Conventional Forces in Europe
CIA	Central Intelligence Agency
CSCE	Conference on Security and Cooperation in Europe
EC	European Community
ECOSOC	Economic and Social Council
ILO	International Labor Organization
INF	Intermediate Nuclear Force
KGB	Committee of State Security
MFN	Most-Favored-Nation
NATO	North Atlantic Treaty Organization
NKVD	People's Commissariat of Internal Affairs
NSC	National Security Council

OECD	Organization of Economic Cooperation and Development
OGPU	United State Political Administration
POW	Prisoner of War
SALT	Strategic Arms Limitation Talks (I and II)
SDI	Strategic Defense Initiative
SHAEF	Supreme Headquarters, Allied Expeditionary Force
START	Strategic Arms Reduction Treaty
U.N.	United Nations
UNHRC	United Nations Human Rights Commission
U.S.	United States
U.S.S.R.	Union of Soviet Socialist Republics
WTO	Warsaw Treaty Organization

ABBREVIATIONS USED IN THE NOTES

ADAJ	*American Diplomatic Action Affecting Jews*
AFPBD	*American Foreign Policy: Basic Documents*
AFPCD	*American Foreign Policy: Current Documents*
AJIL	*American Journal of International Law*
BDHR	*Basic Documents on Human Rights*
CMPP	*A Compilation of the Messages and Papers of the Presidents*
DAH	*Documents of American History*
DRAR	*Documents on Russian-American Relations*
FRUS	*Papers Relating to the Foreign Relations of the United States*
GPO	Government Printing Office, Washington, D.C.
NPP	*National Party Platforms*
NYT	*New York Times*
PWW	*Papers Of Woodrow Wilson*
SAL	*Statutes at Large of the United States*

SDFP	*Soviet Documents on Foreign Policy*
SHAFR	Society for Historians of American Foreign Relations
S/S	Secretary of State
TIAS	*Treaties and Other International Acts Series* (U.S.)
U.K.	United Kingdom
U.N.	United Nations
UNGA	United Nations General Assembly
UNGAOR	United Nations General Assembly, Official Records
UNTS	*United Nations Treaty Series*
USFP	*United States Foreign Policy*
WWI	World War I
WWII	World War II
YUN	*Yearbook of the United Nations*

Principled Diplomacy

INTRODUCTION

> Politics will, to the end of history, be an area where conscience and power meet, where the ethical and coercive factors of human life will interpenetrate and work out their tentative and uneasy compromises.
> —Reinhold Niebuhr, *Moral Man And Immoral Society* (1932).

The main purpose of diplomacy is to achieve security for the nation to ensure the survival of its particular values. Liberal-democratic states are further obliged by public opinion, and by certain key assumptions about how to sustain international order, to be concerned in foreign policy with support for liberty and human rights abroad. The resulting interplay of national security and liberal and humanitarian concerns forms one of the persistent patterns of democratic diplomacy. Moreover, with the spread of democratic ideas and institutions to most major industrial powers in recent decades, a development often shepherded by American diplomacy, that tension has been widely felt in contemporary world politics as well. These themes are of special interest now that the Cold War has ended with overwhelming political victory for the democratic nations. While it is going much too far to proclaim, as some have, that 1989 ushered in the ultimate philosophical ascendancy of liberalism in history and world affairs, there clearly has been a historic shift of enormous proportions and significance for the future of international relations.[1] The collapse of most of the communist world has, at least potentially, left the major democratic powers collectively capable of building a new world order based on principles of liberal-internationalism.

This study assesses some problems of reconciling concern for liberty with interests of national security in democratic diplomacy through their examination in U.S. foreign policy. An interpretive survey of the importance in U.S. policy of a set of key ideas about international order, it examines how these ideas became manifest in two specific policy settings: first, regarding the Soviet Union, a preeminent bilateral relationship until the collapse of that state in December 1991; and second, toward the United Nations, a major multilateral relationship and forum for human rights diplomacy. The book is thus centrally concerned with governing ideas in U.S. diplomacy—how such ideas arose; how they have been sustained as well as challenged by different forces and events; how they have been slowly disseminated among and accepted by allies (and several former adversaries); and how they are now imbedded in the structures of international organization and even the international system as a whole. The book is therefore not a history *per se* of U.S. diplomacy concerning this cluster of issues, although it is historical in approach. Nor is it directly concerned with the ongoing theoretical debate among political scientists over whether democracies are inherently more peaceful than other types of states, though it draws upon elements of that debate and may have implications for it.[2]

Conceived in Enlightenment Europe but first enacted and realized in revolutionary America, liberal-democratic ideas have spread widely, and not just concerning domestic affairs.[3] Identification of long-term national security with the establishment and success of liberty in other lands, or the idea that liberty is indivisible, has had powerful, though not constant, resonance in U.S. foreign policy. That is most fundamentally the case because the idea of a liberalizing mission constitutes the core of American national identity and expansive nationalism. It is argued here that, in good measure as a consequence of U.S. diplomacy, ideas about representation, liberty, and a direct connection between human rights and international security have become increasingly important in defining and perhaps sustaining world order in the modern era. Today, liberal notions about political organization and the underlying supports of peace are central to considerations of global order (and justice), sometimes competing with, other times seen as reinforcing the balance of power. It has been the United States, *primus inter pares* among the democracies, that sought to bring about this liberal-internationalist reconstitution of world politics, albeit inconsistently. At its most idealistic, U.S. diplomacy has tried to create a community of like-minded states bound by trade and respect for the rule of law between and within nations. It has not been without its successes.

The United States has pursued this Kantian vision largely out of commercial self-interest: demands for "free trade" and the "Open Door" have closely followed (and sometimes preceded) intervention or engagement abroad. But American statesmen have also tended to assume that democratic states are mostly pacific, and therefore that a progressive expansion of the zone of liberal-international peace, usually seen as coterminous with the territory and power of liberal democracies, was in America's long-term self-interest. They have led the way in this century in promoting revolutionary change in the structures and operation of international order and organization, away from established notions about absolute sovereignty and non-intervention in internal affairs. Moreover, by virtue of geopolitical pre-eminence in the aftermaths of the Cold War and the Gulf War, the United States is well positioned to continue to lead in world affairs, should it choose to do so, for some time to come.[4]

As a western power, the United States has fundamental security interests in common with other democratic nations, and since 1945 has jointly participated in an extensive network of multilateral security relationships. However, America has a very different history of interest in promoting liberty abroad from most other democracies, despite similar values and traditions. It has not always agreed with its allies on how to establish lasting international security, the extent of the obligation of democratic nations to promote liberty overseas, or the theoretical nature of the relationship between national security and foreign suppression of individual rights and freedoms. The United States usually has been the more forceful in pursuing the connections among liberty, human rights standards, and security, albeit, narrowly defined and selectively applied. In addition, the influence on Washington's foreign policy decision-making process of domestic groups—primarily ethnic and religious—concerned with human rights has varied in scope and effectiveness according to time and issue. That has led to a pattern of intermittent U.S. intervention on matters of rights and security, further complicated by the distorted filtering of domestic impulses through Congress.

The first part of this book focuses on human rights policy toward the Soviet Union. Chapter One picks up the checkered tale of American concern for individual and national liberties in Russia just as the outbreak of World War I made such indulgences most problematic. It recounts popular and official reactions to the March and November Revolutions, outlining the change at both levels from joyful embrace to a sense of bitter betrayal. In discussing the Allied intervention in the Russian Civil War that followed, the emphasis is on the moderating role played by Woodrow Wilson. Still, the intervention signaled that relations between the United States and the suspicious and hostile successor regime to the Tsars seldom would proceed smoothly. Successive administrations refused to extend formal recognition to the bolsheviks, although they did not discourage trade or prevent private contacts.[5] In addition to ideological animosity on both sides, other irritants in the relationship reflected the fact that the bolsheviks carried over practices from tsarist times that exhibited an utter disdain for the rights of individuals, including foreigners. Caught up in that net of indifference and suspicion was a fair number of luckless U.S. citizens. Also engaging the sympathies of organized opinion in the United States was the victimization of clergy, under a policy of renewed persecution of religious believers. That led to large and important segments of the U.S. population becoming quite agitated, and to a lobby of Washington for humanitarian relief, as well as sanctions.

During the 1930s the Soviet Union also cleaved to an old tsarist policy of rejection of a right of expatriation (or naturalization). Chapter Two recounts how the United States sought—somewhat disingenuously—to tie resolution of these and other outstanding issues to a change in its recognition policy. It then points to the purge trials of the 1930s as a source of difficulty in improving bilateral relations, and more importantly, as a major influence on the perceptions of not only key U.S. analysts and policy-makers, but the American public as well. It relates how American catholics as well as certain ethnic groups strongly opposed any further openings to, or expanded relations with Moscow. The role of public, and particularly catholic, opinion on individual and religious rights in the Soviet Union proved to be an important obstacle to providing Lend-Lease to Russia early in World War II. Such frustrations led Franklin Roosevelt into making imaginative but dubious claims about the prospects for liberal and religious reform in Russia to follow victory in the war. That was to have deleterious effects on later public perceptions of the costs of the war, and the prospects for a cooperative peace with the Soviet Union.

For most Americans, almost everything about the Soviets appeared to change when they became somewhat reluctant allies in a common war against Nazi Germany.[6] It was thought even at the highest levels of government that a new relationship might be worked out with Moscow. But that hope breathed through the thin reed of basic reform of Marshall Joseph Stalin's repressive regime, an end to opportunistic Russian expansion, and agreement over the political character and control of defeated Germany. And so, beginning during the German collapse in 1945, Moscow's relations with the democratic West underwent another rapid deterioration. Soviet armies, then Soviet political influence, and lastly Soviet-style regimes spread across eastern and central Europe. The original shocking encounter with nazism, followed by the establishment of Soviet hegemony over half the European continent, raised with a new urgency the old question about the relationship between international security and national and individual liberties. Just as those events were developing, and related to them, the Soviets moved harshly against hundreds of American citizens trapped behind the moving boundaries of Stalin's territorial ambitions and security fears. No amount of protest or pleading could move Moscow from its determination not to permit the departure of these unfortunates, an attitude that helped harden opinion in the West. Chapter Three focuses on this little-known episode, tying it to the origins of the Cold War and underlying American assumptions about repression as an indicator of likely Soviet foreign policy behavior.

During the Cold War, U.S. diplomacy was subject to fierce pressure from key ethnic populations demanding a wide range of intervention in support of erstwhile countrymen (or co-religionists) still within the Soviet sphere, or inside the Union itself. Since 1945, U.S. policy toward Moscow has been almost constantly subjected to intense popular and congressional pressure for intervention on behalf of individual or national liberties. Both placed considerable strain on the country's national security policy and underlay it in important respects—in a complex relationship that caused confusion about the moral content of Cold War policy. Demands for liberation of eastern Europe played an important role in the 1952 election campaign, leaving the Eisenhower administration rhetorically supporting "rollback" and "liberation," a stance well out in front of what it hoped or intended to fulfill. As a result, U.S. policy became locked in by a rhetoric of idealism, even crusade; it was therefore unable to take advantage of and help widen growing divisions within the Soviet bloc, and between the Soviets and China. Successive administrations knew this, yet for domestic political reasons and because of the deepening involvement in Vietnam still played to the ethnic and ideological galleries. This overall drift in policy and dishonesty with the public is the main theme of Chapter Four.

Chapter Five deals with the role of human rights issues in the demise of *détente*. After Richard Nixon wound down the war in Vietnam, refocused attention on events in Europe and the Asian mainland, and arranged a *rapprochement* with Moscow, an important example of how liberal and humanitarian ideas have at times undercut, rather than supported, national security interests occurred. During the early 1970s, human rights issues were resorted to by neo-isolationists as a means of restricting foreign entanglements. This time the initiative came from the left, as opponents of Cold War commitments used human rights legislation to limit military and foreign assistance obligations. Conservatives then seized upon the issue to undermine *détente* by linking a major trade agreement to Soviet guarantees of liberalized emigration. Further complicating matters, well-organized lobbies continued to pressure U.S. policy-makers to initiate sanctions. The result was a period of incoherence during the Ford and Carter years, in which congressional and executive branch factions warred over the use of human rights issues to limit the conflict with the Soviets or, alternatively, to wage ideological warfare against Moscow.

Although facing a badly divided foreign policy constituency, the Reagan administration set out to take the offensive against the peripheries of Soviet power, while engaging in renewed economic and political struggle at the center of the Cold War in and over Europe. Chapter Six begins with a review of this administration's underlying assumptions about the Soviet threat. It then traces continuities from these themes into the second Reagan term, when genuine change occurred in the Soviet Union. In their eventual promise these were fundamental, potentially liberal-democratic reforms. After initial suspicions about sincerity, the West rushed to endorse these reforms and embrace the man who had opened the floodgates of change in the East, Mikhail Gorbachev. Americans rejoiced at the end of the Cold War; events in Russia signaled no less an historic event than that.[7] However, the ability of the United States to respond positively and imaginatively during the first Bush years was hobbled by legislative leftovers of the fierce debates of the 1960s and 1970s as well as the massive deficits left over from the 1980s. Linkage of jewish emigration to access to trade and investment credits thus continued to hamper U.S. response to the Soviet crisis into 1991. Deficits and neo-isolationism constrained direct aid to rescue, if ever rescue was possible, Gorbachev's faltering *perestroika* (restructuring) programs.

Americans are used to viewing the preservation (and ultimately, extension) of the democratic sphere as intimately connected with their own long-term national security. At first, this was a passive concern in which the realities of national weakness overwhelmed most impulses toward foreign policy idealism. But once the United States emerged as a world power that passive stance could not be maintained. The twin goals of security and promotion of national and individual liberty were linked at American behest in the twentieth century experiment with international organization. The launching of the League of Nations therefore witnessed U.S. proposals on national self-determination, labor rights, and new legal protections for religious minorities, in addition to its overall challenge to the old structures and mechanisms of international order. However, foreign and domestic resistance, such as the rejection by Japan and India of Wilson's efforts at Versailles on behalf of political rights for women, were also encountered; and reflected in Wilson's own rejection of a racial equality clause owing to pressures from southern segregationists.[8]

With the advent of the United Nations, international organizations made explicit these early, liberal assumptions about the connection between respect for liberty and international security. Undertakings on human rights in the U.N. Charter constituted something of a quiet revolution in law and interstate relations.[9] They were put there under paramount American pressure, a fact not always appreciated later by critics or proponents of internationalizing human rights. Made more detailed in the Universal Declaration adopted at Paris by the General Assembly in 1948, and in numerous subsequent covenants and conventions, concern for international action to secure respect for human rights remained unusually high on the U.N. agenda. It also migrated into numerous international organizations concerned with establishing the social and economic preconditions thought necessary for lasting peace and security. The second part of the book explains the paradox of American involvement with human rights in the multilateral sphere. For in the U.N. arena, the United States has drifted from being the major power backing such initiatives, toward an erratic and nearsighted diplomacy that has confused and angered allies, and needlessly undermined its wider claims to international leadership.

The United Nations was conceived by its sponsoring powers (the United States, the Soviet Union, Great Britain, and China) primarily as a security organization. From its inception, however, democratic countries have tried to reconcile an interest in the possible contribution of international organization to peace and security with their formal obligation to promote human rights and basic freedoms. That tension resulted from an American initiative taken at the founding conferences at Dumbarton Oaks and San Francisco. The United States was the prime mover behind insertion of reference to fundamental rights and freedoms as a main purpose of the organization in the U.N. Charter. In 1945, still feeling the deep psychological effects of the Depression and World War II, the majority of Americans (in government and out) wanted to believe that U.N. coordination of political, social, and economic programs would serve as a long-term support for peace and security.[10] Drawing rather innocently on their own country's experience with a written Bill of Rights, U.S. planners provided much of the inspiration and language of the Charter provisions and Universal Declaration. Influential Americans as politically diverse as Eleanor Roosevelt and John Foster Dulles endorsed efforts to make individual rights and fundamental freedoms a major concern of postwar international institutions, and pushed for the United States to lead on such issues. Chapter Seven details the key U.S. role on human rights issues at the Dumbarton Oaks and San Francisco conferences.

Interest and involvement in promoting human rights and liberties through the mechanism of international organization quickly waxed and then waned among legislators and the American public. Popular support for the United Nations and in particular for programs which purported to advance "international" conceptions of human rights and social justice, fell precipitously from the high-water mark of the late 1940s. Indeed, the early 1950s witnessed an all-out assault on the burgeoning network of U.N. institutions and conventions, led by an influential portion of the congressional wing of the Republican party. Opposition focused on the idea that the United Nations should have no role whatever in promoting or defining human rights and social welfare. Conservative opponents of an internationalist foreign policy and New Deal domestic policy marshaled their efforts around a proposed constitutional amendment that was intended to severely limit the president's ability to conduct foreign affairs, ostensibly to forestall U.N. interference with domestic legislation. It is argued here that behind what appeared to be an ideological attack by the political right on the idea of international conceptions of human rights was a much deeper, and older, isolationist rejection of America's new international leadership role. Beyond that, conservative-isolationists tapped into growing fear of the inevitable effects that role was beginning to have on the country's previously protected, even provincial, domestic life. Chapter Eight deals with this struggle, which had lasting effects on policy within the U.N., and on the U.S. reputation as a respecter and champion of human rights.

The conservative-isolationist reaction to America's elevated role in world affairs was narrowly defeated and, in time, receded, although it has never entirely disappeared as an influence on U.S. policy toward the United Nations. Although it is widely recognized that a divergence subsequently developed between Congress and the executive branch over U.N. involvement with individual rights, this study argues that the shape of the pattern of divergence is not as described in the received interpretation of recent years. Where recent literature stresses the lead role of Congress on human rights in the 1970s and 1980s,[11] the evidence from the U.N. suggests that the executive branch rather than Congress has been consistently more supportive of a U.S. leadership role to promote rights and fundamental freedoms. Chapter Nine relates the frustrations of successive chief executives after Eisenhower when faced with Senate indifference or even hostility to multilateral human rights initiatives. It concludes with an appraisal of the efforts at a balanced, prudent internationalism on the part of George Bush within the United Nations, which currently enjoys more public support than at any time in recent decades.

NOTES

1. Francis Fukuyama, "The End of History?" *The National Interest* (Summer 1989): pp. 3–18; and *idem, The End of History and the Last Man* (Free Press, 1992). The best reply to date from the point of view of international relations is Samuel P.

Huntington, "No Exit: the Errors of Endism," *The National Interest* (Summer 1989): pp. 3–11.

2. See Michael W. Doyle, "Liberal-Internationalism," in *Shepherd of Democracy? America and Germany in the 20th Century*, Carl Hodge and Cathal Nolan, eds. (Greenwood, 1992): pp. 1–19; and W.B. Gallie, *Philosophers of Peace and War* (Cambridge University Press, 1978): pp. 8–36.

3. That idea is nicely developed by Henry Steele Commager in his insightful study *Jefferson, Nationalism, and the Enlightenment* (George Braziller, 1975): p. 3.

4. For a contrary view, see Paul Kennedy, *The Rise and Fall of the Great Powers* (Random House, 1987). But cf. Joseph Nye, *Bound to Lead* (Basic Books, 1990); and Samuel Huntington, "The U.S.—Decline or Renewal?" *Foreign Affairs* #67 (Winter 1988–1989): pp. 76–96.

5. Isolationism should not be taken to imply that the United States disengaged economically in the interwar years, for it did not. An excellent general study is Manfred Jonas, *Isolationism in America, 1935–1941* (Cornell University Press, 1966; University of Chicago Press, 1990).

6. See the poll results in *Public Opinion Quarterly* (Winter 1944–Spring 1945): pp. 513–22; p. 103.

7. A remarkable document, the Charter of Paris, was signed by 34 nations in 1990, which followed a nonaggression agreement between NATO and the Warsaw Pact. This may be taken as a definitive date for the end of the Cold War. See the report on the conference, with text, in *New York Times*, November 22, 1990 [hereafter *NYT*].

8. Japan was the principal proponent of a clause on the equality of races, but with India was the principal opponent of Wilson's effort to secure political rights for women. "Notes of a Meeting of the Council of Ten, February 13, 1919," in Arthur S. Link *et al.*, eds., *The Papers of Woodrow Wilson*, Vol. 55 (Princeton University Press, 1986): pp. 145–47 [hereafter cited as *PWW*].

9. Article 1 (3), Charter of the United Nations.

10. See poll results on evolving public attitudes toward the United Nations in *Public Opinion Quarterly* (Spring 1945).

11. Cf. Arthur Schlesinger Jr., "Human Rights and the American Tradition," *Foreign Affairs* (1978): pp. 503–26; David Heaps, *Human Rights and U.S. Foreign Policy* (AAICJ, 1984); David Forsythe, "Congress and Human Rights in U.S. Foreign Policy," *Human Rights Quarterly* (August 1987): pp. 382–404; and Sandra Vogelgesang, "Domestic Politics Behind Human Rights Diplomacy," in *Toward a Humanitarian Diplomacy*, Tom Farer, ed. (NYU Press, 1980): pp. 52–64.

Part I
The Soviet Union

1 RESPONDING TO REVOLUTION

Russian-American relations were at a low point in 1914. Before the outbreak of war in Europe, relations had steadily deteriorated over a clash of national ambitions in the far east. Mutual animosity also developed over U.S. insistence in 1912 on abrogation of a seventy-two-year-old Commercial Treaty owing to tsarist discrimination against American jews, and popular perceptions of the repressive character of Russian society.[1] But the war now powerfully redirected the course of relations toward increased linkages. U.S. goods poured into Europe in supply of the wartime demands of the *Entente* powers, including Russia. Also, the search for markets to replace those lost in Germany meant that trade levels rose sharply.[2] Yet even as the United States was steadily being drawn into the *Entente* camp, animosity toward tsarism intruded into calculations of foreign policy. Those who led the crusade to abrogate the Commercial Treaty saw little reason to ease the pressure. Arguing that Russia's difficulty was liberty's opportunity, leaders of the American jewish community protested granting any commercial credits to St. Petersburg, and individually refused to authorize war loans. The efforts of President Woodrow Wilson to secure a revised Commercial Treaty to facilitate expanding wartime trade thus ran into old arguments about tsarist repression and anti-semitism.[3] As a result, no new agreement was signed. Instead, the growing trade was handled through a sequence of executive agreements that studiously avoided redefining the troublesome prewar issues in favor of strict technical provisions.[4]

THE MARCH REVOLUTION

The abdication of Nicholas II in March 1917 was welcomed with widespread enthusiasm and even rejoicing in the United States.[5] An experiment in freedom appeared to be underway in Petrograd (the renamed wartime capital) in the first months of 1917, and Americans applauded this departure in liberty. The Provisional government implemented wholesale reform measures that informed Americans had long wished the Russian people might enjoy. Among the more important reforms was a promise of respect for basic civil liberties; expanded participation in a variety of representative bodies and greatly extended suffrage; eased restrictions on national and religious minorities; return of thousands of political dissenters from exile or imprisonment; Poland was given its independence and Finland granted broad autonomy.[6] The old U.S. agitation for intervention on behalf of Russian jews also declined sharply after the March Revolution, when laws discriminating against jews were repealed. Americans who heard of these measures were pleased; those of jewish faith were elated, and some rushed financial aid to the revolution.[7] This outpouring of sympathy and praise in the United States sprang both from the personal sympathies of generations of refugees from tsarism who had found sanctuary in America, and the fact that U.S. support for democratic reform in Russia had remained at relatively high levels on the electoral agenda since the early 1890s. Additionally, war with Germany looked ever more likely in the spring of 1917, and many had already come to see the war as a contest between *Entente* democracies and Central Power autocracies.

The Wilson administration was equally approving of the end of autocracy and apparent triumph of democracy in Russia. Shortly after the Tsar's abdication, Ambassador David Francis cabled from Petrograd: "This revolution is the practical realization of that principle of government which we have championed and advocated, I mean government by consent of the governed."[8] Secretary of the Navy Josephus Daniels wrote in his diary that on March 20th, Wilson spoke to his cabinet of "the glorious act of the Russians."[9] Three days later, with the worsening, unrestricted submarine warfare crisis with

Germany foremost in his thoughts, Wilson again spoke approvingly to the cabinet about events in Russia. Daniels recorded: "Hope was expressed that [the] Russian revolution would be permanent.... He seemed—in fact—stated his pleasure—that America was the first nation to recognize the new Russian government."[10] There is no reason to doubt the sincerity of these expressions of hope for the success of representative government following the March Revolution. Yet it was not these early, vague sentiments that ultimately guided policy, for crucial national security interests were at stake as well.

Given the U.S. declaration of war against Germany on April 6, 1917, Wilson's immediate concern was to encourage the Provisional government in Petrograd to continue active military operations so the Germans might be pressured on two fronts at once.[11] There was little consideration in Washington of the negative impact of all the revolutionary turmoil on the Russian war effort—a huge oversight, considering the opposite observation had been made of the effects of the 1905 Revolution. Instead, it was quite inaccurately assumed that U.S. and Allied interests should view the weakening and final collapse of tsarism as aiding successful prosecution of the war.[12] Surely, it was thought, free Russians can be counted on to fight against German militarism and autocracy with even greater zeal.

Upon America's entry into the war, Wilson's appreciation of the March Revolution turned into effusive public praise. In May, he wrote that he had "the greatest sympathy" for the revolution. Two months later, he greeted the first ambassador from the Provisional government with congratulations on representing a nation "actuated by the same lofty motives" as the United States.[13] He saw the changes as reinforcing Russia's war effort and making it a more acceptable partner of western democracies in the campaign against Prussian autocracy. This optimistic view of the impact of the March Revolution on Allied fortunes was laid out in Wilson's appeal for a formal declaration of war against Germany. He announced his central war aim as the "vindication of right, of human right, of which we are only a single champion." In the most famous phrase of his presidency, he proclaimed: "The world must be made safe for democracy. Its peace must be planted upon the tested foundations of political liberty." As for Russia, it:

was known by those who knew her best to have been always in fact democratic at heart.... The autocracy that crowned the summit of her political structure, long as it had stood and terrible as was the reality of its power, was not in fact Russian in origin, character, or purpose; and now it has been shaken off and the great, generous Russian people have been added in all their naive majesty and might to the forces that are fighting for freedom in the world, for justice, and for peace. Here is a fit partner for a League of Honor.[14]

Almost nothing of Wilson's depiction of a natural Russian propensity to democracy had any basis in historical fact. Nor was it clear that Russia was staying in the war for similar reasons to those Wilson proclaimed as just and appropriate cause for America to embark upon hostilities. But the high-sounding rhetoric should not obscure the fact that he understood that overriding U.S. interest involved keeping Russia in the war. That is why through the summer of 1917, while affirming belief in "the ultimate triumph of ideas of democracy and self-government" in Russia, Wilson's more basic policy was to offer to extend "every material and moral assistance . . . in the promotion of the common cause [war with Germany] in which the two nations are unselfishly united."[15]

Still, the Revolution relieved Wilson of prosecuting a crusade to end autocracy in Germany, and restore the balance of power, in association with an even more autocratic regime in Petrograd than that in Berlin.[16] He admitted as much in June 1917, explaining that the presence of tsarist Russia among the Allies had been the "one element to confuse the issue" of a war to rid the world of autocracy and imperialism. Russia, he claimed, had "long been hostile to free institutions; it had been a stronghold of tyrannies reaching far back into the past; and its presence among the Allies had seemed to be in disaccord with the great liberal principles they were upholding in this war. Russia had been a source of doubt."

Happily, this anachronism of an autocratic ally in a war publicly described as a crusade against autocracy and for self-determination was eliminated just at the point of U.S. entry into the conflict. "Free men of all the world," said Wilson, "were thrilled and heartened by the news that the people of Russia had risen to throw off their Government and found a new democracy." What did this mean for Americans preparing to take on the Central Powers? "The conviction was finally crystallized in American minds and hearts that this war across the sea was no mere conflict between dynasties, but a stupendous Civil war [sic] of all the world; a new campaign in the age-old war, the prize of which is liberty."[17] What it meant, then, was that

Americans were told they could and should embrace as a crusade for human and national rights, for a noble and wholly American conception of peace and world order, a conflict that for two-and-one-half years they had been told was none of their affair.

Wilson's rhetoric was not merely effusive propaganda designed solely to raise the fighting morale of a hitherto isolationist nation.[18] Nor was it the whole of his policy. He sincerely believed that America brought to the struggle in Europe distinctively liberal interests and war aims; and by basing policy partly on that belief, he went a long way toward making his rhetoric a political reality. Although not a view necessarily shared by all the top foreign policy figures in his administration, the liberal-internationalist component of Wilson's war aims was also believed in by his trusted counselor on foreign affairs, Colonel Edward House.[19] Yet however sincere Wilson was, and however he worked to fulfill the principles he set out, by repeatedly using such powerful, exaggerated rhetoric he helped sow great expectations for a harvest of liberty and representative government in Russia. When the bolsheviks brutally and unexpectedly dashed those hopes within a few months, he and a great majority of Americans reaped a barren sense of bitterness and even betrayal that had implications for future relations, and not just with Russia. Notwithstanding the sacrifices of the Great War, genuinely fought on at least one level to make the world safe for self-determination and democracy, as well as from autocracy and German imperialism, in anger and frustration the country would watch helplessly as a new concentration of tyrannical power arose in the east, in the lands of the old Russian Empire.

THE ROAD TO BREST-LITOVSK

By contrast to the administration's support for the democratic revolution in Russia in the spring of 1917, it reacted sharply to the Bolshevik Revolution eight months later. Secretary of State Robert Lansing suggested a draft declaration on policy that expressed "disappointment and amazement" at the "rise of class despotism in Petrograd." Wilson concurred with Lansing in principle, but thought a public statement inopportune.[20] Beyond that, at this early stage Wilson appears not to have fully understood the radically different nature of the new regime in Petrograd. Daniels recorded him as saying, about the possibility the bolsheviks might make a separate peace with Germany: " [the] action of Lenin & Trotsky sounded like *opera bouffe*, talking of armistice with Germany when a child would know Germany would control & dominate & destroy any chance for the democracy they desire."[21]

Recognition of the bolshevik regime was withheld in the hope and with the expectation that it would not long survive. That was a course the United States took in the company of other nations, among whom it was, at first, the most moderate. No Allied power dealt officially with the bolsheviks, who repudiated Russia's foreign commitments (including its massive war debts), began negotiating a separate peace with Germany, published secret treaties of the *Entente*, and openly promised to foment world revolution. Besides, it was unclear which of many factions would prevail in the fierce civil war that soon broke out in Russia.[22] The initial U.S. stance of nonrecognition hence was both a policy common to the Allied powers, and a reasonable response to an unclear political and military situation in Russia. Only later would the nonrecognition policy be permitted to ossify into a pretense of principle, and become an excuse for inaction and isolation from the problems of Russian and European postwar reconstruction.

The relatively passive initial U.S. response to the advent of bolshevism derived largely from central preoccupation with the war effort against Germany. Yet it was also a product of Wilson's firm conviction that principles of noninterference and self-determination, acting in support of the balance of power, were sound foundations upon which to build a lasting peace. He therefore emphatically rejected a proposal that the United States guarantee to preserve Russia from a bolshevik despotism that promised to be worse than that of the Tsars. He wrote privately in February 1918 that those who supported such a proposition:

entirely misinterpreted the spirit and principles of this Government if [it is thought] possible for it to interfere with the form of government in any other government [*sic*. country?]. That would be in violent contradiction of the principles we have always held, earnestly as we should wish to lend every moral influence to the support of democratic institutions in Russia and earnestly as we pray that they may survive there and become permanent.[23]

Wilson must be taken seriously on this point: he believed as much in self-determination for Russia as for the several subject nationalities of the Austro-Hungarian Empire.[24] He made that conviction explicit in his justly famous "Fourteen Points" address, although the offer was heavily influenced by the need to directly respond to the threat of a separate Russian peace with Germany.[25] Point VI promised Russia "an unhampered and unembarrassed opportunity for the independent determination of her own political development and national policy," and extended "a sincere welcome into the society of free nations under institutions of her own choosing; and, more than a welcome, assistance also of every kind that she may need and may herself desire."[26] That offer of assistance was, of course, contingent upon Russia remaining in the war on the Allied side.

Bolshevik agreement to a separate, and carthaginian, peace with Germany at Brest-Litovsk in March 1918 ended any slim chance that might have remained of early recognition by the United States or the Allies, because that treaty dramatically endangered the *Entente* powers by permitting Germany to effect a mass transfer of troops from the eastern front to the West. Even so, Lenin used this very occasion to appeal to the Allies for help, fearing that the Germans might contest the weak bolshevik hold on power.[27] There was great bitterness and fear in Allied quarters when the treaty was announced and its implications realized. However, the United States was slower to anger over bolshevik tactics than its European counterparts. In mortal fear over the sudden shift toward Germany in the military balance in the war, the western Allies pressed for U.S. participation in a military excursion to reinforce the rapidly crumbling eastern front; some even wanted to support the "Whites" in Russia's burgeoning civil war. This quicker, more hostile, and interventionist Allied response to the Bolshevik Revolution certainly occurred because France and Britain had been in the war longer; lost vastly more men and national treasure than America (which at that point was hardly even engaged in the land war); and been placed in grave, imminent, and mortal danger by Brest-Litovsk.

INTERVENTION AND THE PEACE SETTLEMENT

The exigencies of war make the strangest of bedfellows. Bolshevik and Allied interests also momentarily coincided around Brest-Litovsk, leading to Allied acceptance of Lenin's and Trotsky's request for intervention to protect stores in Murmansk from falling into German hands.[28] Wilson had determined, as a precondition of U.S. participation, that an invitation should come from Russia; and he acted only after receiving assurances that Lenin and Trotsky had consented to the Murmansk operation.[29] Moreover, the United States for months resisted fierce British and French pressure to approve the use of

Japanese troops (the only sizable force then available that might possibly have shored up the eastern front) through Siberia.[30] But the pressure could not be resisted forever, especially given the early success of the German "spring offensive" in the West and growing desperation among the Allies. Within four months of Brest-Litovsk, Wilson reluctantly agreed to send small numbers of troops into Russia. It was principally this Allied pressure in response to Brest-Litovsk, and not opposition to the Bolshevik Revolution *per se*, that brought about American "intervention" in North Russia in August 1918.[31]

Throughout the exercise, Wilson placed heavy constraints on use of U.S. troops. Specifically, he ordered that they were not to be used to fight the bolsheviks or otherwise interfere with Russian internal affairs. Skirmishes nevertheless took place, partly as a result of the general chaos in Russia, and partly because Francis deliberately misinterpreted his orders and authorized minor participation of U.S. troops in aggressive British operations against the bolsheviks.[32] With this exception, the United States participated reluctantly and half-heartedly in what Wilson considered at best an ill-advised excursion.[33] Similarly, it was not hostility to bolshevism but opposition to Japan's ambitions in the Far East, particularly in China, that led to a second small U.S. force of 7,000 men being sent to Siberia. That unit was ordered to help rescue a trapped Czech Legion and guard against unilateral actions by the Japanese, but otherwise refrain from active participation in the ongoing civil war.[34] It thus is no exaggeration to conclude, as does Arthur S. Link, that Wilson was in fact "the one person who prevented large scale military intervention" by the Allies and Japan.[35] To his credit, Wilson absolutely insisted on this despite his belief that the bolsheviks were unrepresentative of the peoples of the Russian Empire, and were in fact preventing that part of the world from achieving genuine self-determination.[36] The key to understanding this paradox is to appreciate that he hoped and believed the Soviet system would soon collapse of its own accord: he sought to preserve Russia not for the bolsheviks, but for their anticipated and inevitable successors who would fulfill the promise of democracy and self-determination held out for them in the Fourteen Points.

For example, in mid-1918 a female revolutionary's botched attempt at assassinating Lenin provoked a campaign of bloody reprisals by the bolsheviks. Tens of thousands died in what became known as the "Red Terror," a brutal excess marked by mass arrests and summary executions. Wilson considered intervening to restore order, but ultimately responded to the violence simply with expressions of "horror" at the "state of terrorism," and a caution that "military intervention in Russia would be more likely to add to the present sad confusion there than to cure it."[37]

This policy of non-interference in Russian internal affairs was maintained in the face of emotional pleas from consular officials to use available U.S. troops to stop the bloodshed. In early September, Consul DeWitt Poole advised Washington that the "truly efficacious course" to stop the Terror "is a rapid military advance from the north. Our present halfway action is cruel in the extreme." He argued, inaccurately, that the Allied landing at Archangel "has set up the bolshevik death agony. It is now our moral duty to shield the numberless innocents who are exposed to its [the regime's] hateful reprisals."[38] Three weeks later came another plea for armed intervention.[39] Yet, in spite of his personal sympathies, Wilson refused to use the military to stop the "Red Terror" in Petrograd. He instead orchestrated an international diplomatic protest to "inform the bolsheviks that the whole world . . . is revolted by the present inhuman and purposeless slaughter," and to warn that they would be held "jointly and severally responsible for their present deeds."[40] Bolshevik leaders dismissed Wilson's warning, replying with the coldhearted explanation that "violence in Russia is used only in the holy [sic] interests for [of?] the liberation of the masses."[41]

Germany's unexpectedly abrupt capitulation in November 1918 thrust Russian issues further into the background of Allied concern. German and central European questions captured most of the attention of American and Allied policymakers until the end of their meetings at Paris (Versailles) from January to June, 1919. In fact, evident in the documentary record is a general disarray among the Allies at the Versailles conference over how to resolve the problem of bolshevism.[42] In contrast, Wilson's position was clear. Even before the conference began, he was disposed to end the interventions. Rather than overthrow the bolsheviks, he hoped to arrange a peace settlement that included a reasonable accommodation of their demands and the entry of Russia into the League of Nations. He adopted that position not mainly for reasons of sentiment, but in the belief that remedy of grievances between nations would reinforce the peace settlement by underwriting the balance of power.[43] During the Paris talks, U.S. delegates opposed extending or expanding military intervention in Russia.[44] The Americans debated the extent to which the principle of self-determination ought to apply to the subordinate nationalities of the old Russian Empire, but did so with an emphasis on preserving Russia's territorial integrity against Polish and other ambitions and in accordance with Point VI of the Fourteen Points.[45]

The main initiative of the conference at Versailles to arrange a negotiated Russian peace, dubbed the "Prinkipo" proposal, was drawn up by Wilson personally. It called for all factions fighting in the Russian civil war to meet on the Prinkipo Islands in the Sea of Marmora to work out a settlement, and thereby to facilitate withdrawal of all Allied expeditionary forces. However, only the bolsheviks among the combatants agreed to the proposal, and since even they refused to respect the precondition of a cease-fire, the initiative came to naught.[46] The United States also made the other notable approach to linking a Russian settlement to the general peace agreement for Europe. In February 1919, Colonel House sent an emissary to Russia, William C. Bullitt, in an effort to obtain a statement from the bolsheviks on the terms by which they would agree to cease fighting and deal with outside powers. In March, Bullitt cabled to Wilson, House, and Lansing the highly encouraging report that the bolshevik leaders were "full of a sense of Russia's need for peace, and therefore, disposed to be most conciliatory." However, the statement Bullitt attached to his cable, drafted by the top bolshevik leaders and which he had obtained from Lenin after some difficulty, somewhat belied his optimistic assessment. It was shrouded in numerous and difficult preconditions and prior demands—concerning such matters as repayment of debts, concessions, and territorial compensation—and couched in language that either had been deliberately calculated to offend or was foolishly brash. Consequently, the bolshevik note was not supported or acted upon by the United States and the Allies.[47]

In contrast with these efforts, French Prime Minister Georges Clemenceau supported the creation of a so-called *cordon sanitaire* of small, independent countries around the bolsheviks.[48] Similarly, Britain's Secretary of War, Winston Churchill, startled Wilson (then returning to the United States from Versailles) and the rest of the American delegation by pressing for extensive military intervention in what would have amounted to a crusade to crush bolshevism. Caught somewhat off-guard by what appeared to be a change in British policy away from the more moderate stance of Prime Minister Lloyd George, Wilson cabled the U.S. Commissioners: "[I] am greatly surprised by Churchill's Russian suggestion. . . . [I would] not be in favor of any course which would not mean the earliest practicable withdrawal of military forces. It would be fatal to be led further into the Russian chaos."[49] During a direct exchange with Churchill a week earlier at a meeting of the Supreme War Council, Wilson had already bluntly stated that U.S. troops could not be used to support "reactionaries" in Russia, and would have to be pulled out eventually even if that meant "many Russians might lose their lives" following bolshevik victory.[50] He saw no need to deviate from that position, and a good many reasons to hasten the withdrawal of U.S. troops as soon as easing of the Russian winter permitted.[51]

Despite the importance of the issue, little more was done to draw Russia into general European security arrangements. Therefore, when the Versailles conference ended, it did so without Allied or American agreement on what to do about a host of issues left over when an erstwhile ally, the old Russian Empire, was displaced by an avowedly hostile new power, the Soviet Union. Two of the great nations of Europe, Germany and Russia, hence entered the 1920s deeply and dangerously hostile to the peace settlement, with *revanchist* ambitions concerning their adjusted borders, and harboring grudges against the putative betrayal of wartime, liberal-internationalist promises made by Wilson.[52] In time, these two powers would locate common ground in opposition to the Versailles settlement. In particular, they shared antagonism toward the weak and quarrelsome states—some carved out of their prewar territory—set up between them. Clemenceau had championed that arrangement, but it would prove more a temptation than a barrier to revisionists and nationalists in Berlin and Moscow alike.[53]

Clearly, it was not Wilson and liberal-internationalism alone that failed at Versailles. "Realists" did not fare much better in their proposed solution to the problem of bolshevism. Overall, western initiatives toward Russia died of half-measures. Clemenceau's dream of a *cordon sanitaire* would never be sufficiently reinforced by Anglo-French and American political commitment or military power to be effective, and was further and fatally undermined by German *revanchism*. Meanwhile, Wilson's vision of an equitable, balanced peace based on the principle of self-determination did not take sufficient account of east European *irredentist* movements (such as led to the Polish-Soviet war of 1920), nor that democracy and self-rule was ultimately incompatible with Great Russian (now Soviet) imperialism.

Wilson's best intentions notwithstanding, the course of U.S. relations with the young Soviet Union was obscured for a while longer by continuing chaos in those vast lands, and by the lingering and directionless Allied excursions in North Russia and Siberia. The main reason for the North Russian expedition, to hold off the Germans and try to keep open the eastern front, was invalid after Germany's surrender. In February 1919, Wilson therefore ordered the American contingent home from North Russia, over the objections of the British and the French.[54] Participation in the Siberian expedition continued until 1920, however. The attempt to limit that effort was hampered by several complicating factors. These included a desire to assist the trapped Czech legion (former allies to whom there was a strongly felt moral obligation) and the rumored presence of great numbers of former German and Austrian prisoners of war (at least 700,000, and perhaps as many as 1.5 million) loose in Siberia. Most important and problematic, Tokyo's large-scale military operations in Russia merited continued observation, as they reflected imperial intentions to exploit the chaotic situation to enhance Japan's strategic position in northern Manchuria, and possibly gain control of parts of eastern Siberia itself.[55] In all of this, Wilson was guided by a belief in the principle of self-determination as a support for long-term world order, and hence acted to preserve the integrity of even a sovietized Russia, hoping the bolsheviks might yet be overthrown by internal resistance to their oppressive measures.

Still, Wilson was exasperated over the failure to arrange a common policy, and he faced mounting domestic opposition to keeping American soldiers overseas long after the defeat of Germany.[56] By the end of 1919, he also could see that bolshevism was entrenched in Russia, dashing his hopes for democracy. He lamented that the bolsheviks represented "nobody but themselves," concluding bitterly: "There is a closer monopoly of power in Petrograd and Moscow than there was in Berlin, and the thing that is intolerable is, not that the Russian people are having their way, but that another group of men more cruel than the Tsar himself is controlling the destinies of that great people."[57] For just a moment he allowed his anti-bolshevism to overcome his caution and suspicion of Allied and Japanese intentions. He let American troops be drawn indirectly into the Russian civil war through an Allied railroad construction project, which he hoped would serve the Open Door principles and stabilize commercial life in Siberia. The project was implicitly anti-bolshevik, however, as the railway helped secure and improve transport infrastructure in the strategic rear of Admiral Kolchak's White forces.[58] Yet the indiscretion was not fatal, and it did not last. When all was said and done, and the last U.S. troops left Siberia in early 1920, Wilson had successfully upheld an important principle of his liberal-internationalist diplomacy: through firm resistance to British and French (and even some American) entreaties to intervene on the side of the Whites and against bolshevism, and through stiff opposition to Japan's ambitions in Siberia, he had done much to ensure that the territorial integrity of Soviet Russia would be maintained.[59] That defense of principle in diplomacy would now influence the post-civil war Russian policy of the United States in several unexpected ways.

NONRECOGNITION

The United States devised a systematic response to the reality of the bolshevik regime only after the Russian civil war finally ended in 1920. At that time, the United States moved from a reasonable, *ad hoc* withholding of recognition to a more ideologically inspired and hostile policy of diplomatic rejection of the Soviet government.[60] Wilson was by then too ill to participate in framing policy. It was Secretary of State Bainbridge Colby who indicated, in response to an Italian request for clarification of U.S. policy toward the Polish-Soviet war, that nonrecognition was to be a set policy. He asserted his faith that a "restored, free and united Russia will again take a leading role in the world, joining with the other free nations in upholding peace and orderly justice." Until then, there could be no normalization of relations:

There cannot be any common ground upon which [the United States] can stand with a Power whose conception of international relations are [*sic*] so entirely alien to its own, so utterly repugnant to its moral sense. . . . We cannot recognize, hold official relations with, or give friendly reception to the agents of a government which is determined and bound to conspire against our institutions; whose diplomats will be agitators of dangerous revolt; [and] whose spokesmen say that they sign agreements with no intention of keeping them.[61]

That was a most significant departure, not just in Russian policy but in general recognition practice. For only the second time in American diplomatic history, a government was not recognized *de jure* because of its revolutionary antecedents, despite exercising undisputed *de facto* control over a sovereign country.[62]

Even so, this policy was conceived as anti-bolshevik, not anti-Russian: the administration upheld a distinction between the Russian people and their bolshevik masters. That is why the United States refused to recognize the independence of the Baltic States, and although recognizing Poland and Finland as established facts, cautioned them against seeking annexations at Soviet expense.[63] The main features of policy thus were set for the next dozen years: the United States acknowledged the existence of the bolshevik regime, but claimed to have no interests in common with it and withheld legal recognition in protest against its promotion of subversion through activities of the COMINTERN. Then, in 1921, the United States issued a formal declaration objecting to further military intervention in the Soviet Union. With the need to defend Russian territorial integrity made obsolete by the Japanese withdrawal, this declaration represented the ascendancy of a post-Versailles, isolationist wind in America against which even the outgoing Wilson administration had to bend. In addition, as one keen contemporary observer put it:

The frontier disputes arising out of Russia's revolution and civil war were now settled. In favoring their settlement on a basis which would keep Russia a united nation, the American Government felt that it had in part repaid to the Russian state an old debt of friendship, even though Russia's new government was regarded as one with which amicable relations could not be maintained.[64]

Henceforth, as it moved into a more "sullen and selfish" political era at home and abroad, the United States would mostly hold itself aloof from active concern with Soviet affairs.

Wilson's Republican successors, Warren Harding, Calvin Coolidge, and Herbert Hoover, all would maintain essentially intact the policy toward Russia framed during Wilson's last year in office, a policy that had widespread public and congressional support, and that never became a partisan political issue.[65] Thus, when in 1921 Soviet envoy Maxim Litvinov appealed for recognition, he was rebuffed by Harding's Secretary of State, Charles Evans Hughes.[66] The only substantial change in emphasis the Republicans made to the basic policy laid out by Colby was absolute insistence that the Soviet Union repay Imperial Russia's outstanding war debts.[67] More generally, during the 1920s, the United States withdrew from a host of international political and security commitments. Most famously, of course, the United States, along with the Soviet Union, failed to join the League of Nations. Among other important political and security issues in the 1920s (that did not concern hemispheric problems, where the United States remained quite active and engaged) were the continuing dispute with Japan over its efforts to close the "Open

Door" in the Far East; the naval rivalry with Japan, and even Britain, which led to the Washington Treaties on naval limitation of 1921 and 1922, and the London Naval Treaty of 1930; a drawn-out debate over U.S. adherence to the World Court; and the question of participation in the Geneva Protocol of 1924, which called for compulsory arbitration of disputes and joint military action against aggressor powers. Yet, all the while the United States was abandoning its security and political leadership interests and obligations, it still sought to maintain and expand commercial ties, and maintained a very active economic diplomacy in all theaters.[68]

Hence, passivity regarding bolshevism by successive Republican administrations was part of the more general isolationist recoil of the United States from the bloody World War I contact with Europe's political quarrels, and it followed the same pattern of formal aloofness from political contacts coupled with an abiding interest in trade. This general postwar American inclination to isolationism was strengthened concerning Russia by significant opposition provoked by Wilson's dispatch of troops to Murmansk and Siberia, without achieving any foreign policy gain discernible by the general public. Furthermore, the Republicans shared Wilson's tendency to rely on legal and moral norms as supports of international order, without accepting his concomitant commitment to collective security and preservation of the balance of power. As a result, they often framed policy toward Russia in distant, moralistic terms. And while on the one hand, they did not go so far as to make transformation of Soviet society toward democracy a precondition of recognition, they were at best ambiguous about how to deal with reports of repression. As a result, rhetorical concern for civil and political rights became blended with real insistence on respect for property rights, especially those of U.S. citizens who had suffered expropriation by the Soviets.

Harding made this connection explicit in a 1923 address he prepared on recognition of the Soviet Union, that was never delivered due to his fatal illness:

I prefer to safeguard our interests and hold unsullied the seemingly proven principles under which human rights and property rights are blended in the supreme inspiration to human endeavor. If there are no property rights, there is little, if any, foundation for national rights, which we are ever being called upon to safeguard. The whole fabric of international commerce and righteous international relationship will fall if any great nation like ours will abandon the underlying principles relating to sanctity of contract and the honor involved in respected rights.[69]

Later that year, Harding's successor Coolidge told Congress, where there was some interest in recognition: "Our Government offers no objection to the carrying on of commerce by our citizens with the people of Russia.... [However,] I do not propose to barter away for the privilege of trade any of the cherished rights of humanity. I do not propose to make merchandise of any American principles. These rights and principles must go wherever the sanctions of our Government go."[70] The Soviets responded positively to the implicit suggestion of expanded commercial relations, but disdainfully rejected preconditions to recognition pertaining to propaganda activities of the COMINTERN and questions of war debts and property confiscations, and so the *status quo* remained. Most other western states, including the Baltic States themselves, moved after 1924 to break the diplomatic stalemate and extend *de jure* recognition. Yet not even that moved the United States from the essentials of the Colby note.[71] In fact, once it became clear that recognition had not led to settlement of outstanding debt, compensation, and subversion issues for several other powers (including Britain, which broke relations again in 1927), U.S. officials became even more convinced of the moral rectitude and legal soundness of their position.[72]

In sum, American failure in the 1920s to formally recognize that a bolshevik government was in power in the Soviet Union rested on, first, a certain policy inertia retained from the Wilson years, long after the expectation that bolshevik rule might collapse had ceased to have merit as a basis for policy; second, real and important disagreements over war debts and the principle of compensation; next, a fierce hostility to the continuing propaganda and other subversive aspects of Soviet foreign policy; fourth, a growing isolationist reaction in American politics that meant correspondingly few domestic political reasons to change the policy of nonrecognition; and lastly, a debilitating habit among U.S. policymakers of thinking about international affairs in rather complacent and overly legalistic and moral terms.[73]

The dominant attitude of the U.S. government toward the Soviet Union in the 1920s therefore can be characterized as one of mere latent hostility, and might be more accurately described as largely apathetic.[74] Throughout the decade, American statesmen sincerely believed they could do little to improve relations with what they saw as an inappeasably hostile regime in control of the Soviet Union. For the most part, therefore, they were content to settle into official near-insensibility to Soviet internal affairs. Even regarding commerce, while willing to permit and occasionally encourage private contacts, there was no perception of a need for formal treaty arrangements to facilitate trade.

FAMINE RELIEF AND CIVIL RIGHTS

In spite of a lack of formal relations, the United States did have several semi-official contacts with the Soviet Union during the 1920s. The most significant developed as a result of a great famine in Russia, arising from the successive dislocations of World War I, the revolution and civil war, ideologically inspired mismanagement of the rural economy, or "War Communism," and a serious drought.[75] The shortage of food and seed threatened between 10 and 30 million lives beginning in 1919.[76] When news of the budding crisis leaked out of Russia, the American Relief Administration (ARA) quickly positioned itself to address the problem, which it had been established to deal with elsewhere in war-torn Europe. ARA operations were overseen by Herbert Hoover, who served as Director of European Relief at the end of World War I and would the following year become Harding's Secretary of Commerce.[77] Hoover offered ARA relief as early as 1919, but bolshevik leaders insisted on prior cessation of hostilities in the civil war, an end to all Allied intervention, and diplomatic recognition of themselves as the sole legitimate Soviet government. The United States of course did not control the various White armies, had already pulled out of North Russia and was acting to restrain the Japanese in Siberia, and regarded diplomatic recognition and state-to-state relations as a wholly separate issue from humanitarian assistance. When Hoover therefore replied that the ARA could not meet Soviet demands, Moscow flatly rejected the offer of assistance.[78]

In January 1921, Hoover managed to get some aid through to the affected population in Russia without bolshevik approval, using an American Friends Service Committee relief program operating out of Moscow. Through the Quakers, he made a second offer of massive relief to the Soviet Government, this time contingent upon its agreement to release all American citizens then held in Russian jails or being refused permission to leave the country. For reasons of their own, bolshevik leaders still were unwilling to admit the scope of starvation in the country, and stayed profoundly suspicious of the ARA proposal.[79] Indeed, rather than accept the proffered humanitarian assistance, Lenin again attempted to turn the question of U.S. relief to his political advantage. Hoover was told, through the Quakers, that American prisoners could be released only if the U.S. government would directly negotiate the terms of famine relief, rather than insist that arrangements be made with the privately organized ARA. The issue turned on the fact that although Hoover was a member of the cabinet, in his capacity as Director of the ARA he did not represent the United States, and therefore no formal relations were implied or established on either side. Secretary Hughes rejected Lenin's demand on the ground that the bolsheviks were trying to use direct negotiations over humanitarian aid to prise formal recognition out of the United States (which they clearly were), when that issue should have been considered unconnected to humanitarian aid.[80]

The situation in Russia grew increasingly desperate in the first half of 1921. Faced with enormous shortfalls in agricultural production, peasant disturbances and riots in Petrograd and Kronstadt, and the prospect that seed grains were being rapidly consumed by the starving population, in March the Soviet leadership decided on drastic measures. They at last dropped more doctrinaire economic policies and, while not easing off food confiscations in the countryside to feed their urban political base, moved to adopt Lenin's "New Economic Policy" proposals on reintroducing private incentives and ownership. Externally, they also put on a new, more expedient face. In July, an appeal for outside help to stave off the famine finally was made, delivered for greatest international effect not by Lenin but by Maxim Gorky. Hoover immediately reiterated his offer of major ARA assistance, yet the offer was still conditioned by his government's requirement that Americans held prisoner in the Soviet Union be released.[81] Hughes sent an ARA envoy to Riga under explicit instructions that he must obtain agreement for release of all Americans before negotiations on relief could begin.[82] Lenin accepted this condition, which he had rejected six months previously, and personally ordered the expedited freeing of U.S. citizens.[83] The arrangement was formalized in a treaty-like agreement in which the ARA insisted on the twin stipulations that assistance be distributed "to the children and sick without regard to race, religion or social or political status," and that "as the absolute *sine qua non* of any assistance," all Americans detained in Russia would be released.[84]

Over the next two years, the ARA distributed 48 million dollars' worth of donated food, seed grain, clothing, medicine, and other goods directly to the affected Soviet population. Individuals and social agencies in the United States contributed 24 million dollars of the total, Congress added 20 million, and the War Department donated another 4 million dollars' worth of surplus medical supplies. The ARA also distributed another 12 million dollars' worth of goods purchased with gold reserves supplied by the Soviet government.[85] ARA officials went directly into the Soviet countryside, ensuring that relief supplies were mainly distributed on a humanitarian basis, and not used to support friends or withheld to punish foes of the government. The ARA program was also by far the largest foreign assistance effort, ending in July 1923, when defeat of the famine was signaled by a resumption of Soviet grain exports.[86] Ironically, given the never-absent suspicion about Hoover on the part of top bolsheviks, in George F. Kennan's estimation, ARA relief not only "saved several million people from starvation," it may well have also "saved the Soviet regime itself from utter failure and collapse."[87] In an additional irony, and entirely indicative of the humanitarian motive of both individual donors and Congress, insistence on prior release of American citizens was the most criticized aspect of the relief. It was widely held that no conditions whatever should have been attached to the offer of humanitarian relief.[88]

A more convoluted criticism came from Americans sympathetic to the bolshevik cause, persons who "clung tenaciously to the thesis that Hoover and the ARA were bent on the destruction of the Soviet Government and injury to Russia." Yet as a contemporary observer noted, such critics changed with the skill of a chameleon their explanation of how these ends were being sought: "First . . . it was by withholding relief; next, by delivering relief; then by sabotaging relief and by misrepresenting the capacity of Russian transport; and finally, by minimizing the need of relief in 1922–1923."[89] The essence of that thesis would be repeated several decades later by the senior revisionist historian William Appleman Williams, who argued "the entire [ARA] operation" run by Hoover "was an important phase of his broad plan to effect the ultimate Americanization of the Russian economy."[90] At most, however, the available evidence shows that Hoover conceived of food aid to Europe as a buffer against the further spread of bolshevism. Moreover, he personally regarded the Russian Revolution as a partly understandable overreaction to the tyranny and unjust social conditions which had existed in tsarist Russia.[91]

It is in any event more important to understand that very few Americans seemed bothered that a senior cabinet official had negotiated with an unrecognized and unfriendly government in order to provide massive assistance, in large part funded by Congress and the War Department. Why, U.S. destroyers were even used to deliver essential foodstuffs, personnel, and equipment to Soviet Black Sea ports! Nor were Americans in or out of government upset that U.S. aid was likely to strengthen—and in fact, did strengthen—the hold on power of that hostile regime. In short, Harding, Hoover, and other members of the administration did not cynically welcome the famine as eroding support for a regime they otherwise would have preferred to see fall from power. Nor did they, as did several European governments, seize upon the desperate situation in Russia as presenting an opportunity to extract financial and other concessions from Soviet leaders on a host of unresolved problems, especially unpaid debts.[92] Instead, throughout the crisis the Harding administration evinced an overriding interest in distributing relief directly to the Russian population, with only the prior condition that U.S. citizens be released from Soviet custody. Although also importantly concerned not to deal with the bolsheviks on an official level, this technical aspect of policy took a distinctly secondary place to the principle of humane relief.

After the ARA completed its work in 1923, American-Soviet relations settled into a dismal pattern of aloof and distant sparring that continued for nearly ten years. There was little domestic impulse to recognition, although the business community would have preferred it, and as yet no international threat sufficient to wake Americans and Soviets alike to their common geostrategic interests.[93] Nevertheless, two problems that did surface are worthy of brief note, not least because they represented problems of principle and interest that had bedeviled relations with Imperial Russia for decades, and would continue to irritate relations with the Soviet Union in decades to come. The first issue concerned a continuation of America's long-standing struggle with Russia over a right of expatriation. In the absence of a bilateral convention on naturalization law, the ARA arrangement that led to the release of prisoners and reunification of families of naturalized citizens quickly proved to be a temporary victory for the United States. The second long-term problem in American-Russian relations that resurfaced in the 1920s concerned the interest of large segments of the U.S. public in aiding victims of religious persecution in the Soviet Union.

In 1926, the State Department sought to ascertain the Soviet government's attitude toward three U.S. citizens imprisoned subsequent to the ARA-negotiated release of Americans in 1921. Litvinov, then Chief of Soviet Foreign Legations, assured a Norwegian go-between that he "did not wish American citizens to be treated with injustice." Upon glancing at the relevant files, however, he noticed that two of the prisoners were Russian-born, and advised that such naturalized Americans "would be regarded and treated as Russian citizens" for as long as they remained in the Soviet Union. In a most unrevolutionary-like turn, he next cited tsarist practice as precedent for the peculiar idea that citizenship resumed when a naturalized expatriate *re-crossed* the Soviet border. He told the Norwegian interlocutor that such regulations were not new, and had "applied in Russia before the revolution." Litvinov then concluded, without ever exploring the merits of the individual cases and apparently without a thought to their humanitarian aspects, that although the native-born American could be set free, nothing would be done for the two naturalized U.S. citizens born in Russia.[94] It thus became clear that Soviet commissars were going to be as impatient as the Tsars of persons renouncing citizenship and departing their empire. It was equally clear that the United States had no intention of abandoning either its citizens or a principle for which it had stood as international champion since the American Civil War. That clash of principle, of fundamentally different theories of the legitimate relationship of the individual to the state, ensured a festering quarrel that would continue between the Soviet Union and the United States over the struggle for respect of a right of expatriation.

Repression of jews had been a thorn in the side of U.S. relations with tsarist Russia prior to World War I. But the reformers behind the March Revolution had abolished most anti-semitic laws, an advance formally confirmed by the bolsheviks in their "Declaration of the Rights of Nationalities" issued in November 1917.[95] As Cyrus Adler and Aaron Margalith put it, with fine irony, the new masters of Russia treated jews "not as confessors of one or another religion, but as members of the economic class to which they belonged. If they were persecuted, imprisoned, or even executed, it was because they were employers or capitalists, and as such were considered 'exploiters' and 'enemies of the state.'"[96] The American jewish community's attention to Russia also had been lessened by the postwar independence of Poland. An upsurge of horrific anti-semitic violence in that country and across eastern Europe claimed tens of thousands of lives in the first years after the war. American jewish efforts consequently focused on the specifically jewish clauses in the Minorities Treaties worked out at Versailles, and paid less attention to happenings within the Soviet Union.[97] With this shift in attention by an influential religious lobby in the United States, and given overall legal, theoretical, and political innovations concerning belief introduced by the bolsheviks, the problem of persecution of religious minorities was to take a more general form in the Soviet Union than it had in tsarist Russia.

The bolsheviks—with their policy of official atheism—were of course ideologically hostile to all forms of organized religion, and early on made a concerted effort to break its hold over the Russian population. They were especially eager to rein in the orthodox church, which they correctly regarded as a main support of Old Russia and a cardinal obstacle to control over the hearts and minds of the peasantry.[98] In May 1922, the Russian hierarchy appealed to daughter congregations of the orthodox diaspora for assistance to forestall a trial of Patriarch Tikhon and some fifty other clerics. A petition for intercession from orthodox dioceses all over America was sent to the State Department. Secretary Hughes considered the petition, and then advised Harding that: "The general situation to which the appeal relates is undoubtedly one of the most important recent developments in Russia." However, he was forced to admit that he could "not perceive that there is anything which this Government can do" about the impending trials. Harding concurred, as was his habit on matters of foreign policy, adding that "acknowledgement of the petition is the only action which may be taken."[99] Tikhon eventually was released, after being stripped of his office and demoted to layman status by the so-called "Living Church," a radical schismatic group that seized control of orthodox institutions with the tacit approval of bolshevik leaders.[100] The Moscow Patriarchate would not rise again for another twenty years, until Stalin discovered its utility for raising morale during World War II. Inside a year of Tikhon's being defrocked, however, the Harding administration would learn that such passivity regarding religious persecution in Russia did not sit well with large segments of the American public.

In March 1923, the bolsheviks moved against the catholic church, which had a much larger American and international constituency than the orthodox. They arrested and condemned to death a catholic Archbishop and a number of catholic clergy.[101] The sentence on the Archbishop was commuted to imprisonment following a huge international outcry, but the Soviet state pressed ahead with execution of the Vicar-General of the catholic church in Russia, Monsignor Buckavich, and warned of additional executions of clerics to come.[102]

Hughes knew that in view of anguished protests and petitions flooding into his office he would have to make some gesture, even though he believed it was "doubtful whether any representations which we might make would have any effect." He asked for permission to make known "how deeply the action which has been taken against these ecclesiastics has stirred public opinion in the United States." Harding, forever out of touch with popular feeling, replied: "I know nothing of the merits of the cases of Russian ecclesiastics but [representations] can do no harm and may be helpful."[103]

The President's diffidence was matched by that of U.S. consular officials in Germany charged with communicating to the Soviets America's objection to the pending executions: they delayed, on the assurance of a minor official that the punishment had been postponed. When the death sentences were in fact carried out shortly thereafter, the public outcry was great, and the administration acted quickly and with more circumspection. It revoked a visitor's visa promised to Madame Kalinin, wife of the Soviet President, "as a protest against the action of the Soviet authorities in connection with the condemnation of the Roman catholic ecclesiastics." Later, the unofficial Soviet representative in Washington, Boris Skvirsky, confessed to the State Department that he was greatly dejected because the depth of anti-Soviet feeling aroused by the executions meant that all his work for recognition had been "undone by a single act."[104]

Religious persecution in Russia continued to significantly affect U.S. public opinion throughout the late 1920s, further weakening the case of those arguing for breaking the recognition logjam on grounds of trade or simple realism. During 1928 and 1929, Stalin issued a series of decrees aimed at draconian suppression of most organized, and even private, religious activity.[105] In February 1930, Pope Pius XI responded with a call for three days of prayer for all victims of religious persecution in the Soviet Union. The Pope's initiative sparked huge demonstrations in America.[106] The agitation intruded into cabinet deliberations. Secretary of the Interior Ray Wilbur inquired of Acting Secretary of State Joseph P. Cotton whether the United States might do something to relieve the situation. Cotton replied that although the "religious situation in Russia sounds outrageous ... this government as a government must keep its hands off. The President [Hoover] must make that answer to any delegation [of citizens] if he sees them."[107] Besides, Hoover had bigger domestic problems to worry about just then.

Over the next three years, however, the suffering born of the Great

Depression and a radically altered and more dangerous international situation would force Americans to rethink their stance toward the world, including the self-indulgent policy of nonrecognition. Making that reassessment in the first instance was Herbert Hoover, that overly maligned and often caricatured architect of much that was sound and successful in U.S. foreign policy in the 1920s and early 1930s.[108] The inertia of the nonrecognition policy was great, however. It would take an initiative that was at once realistic about national interests and aware of national prejudices to make a change acceptable. It might even require a little creative deceit to overcome the strong emotions raised by antagonism to the Soviet system's repressive internal character and its subversive activities abroad. Hoover would begin to provide a necessary adjustment to the shifting balance of power, most notably in the Far East. But he was to prove unable to overcome attitudes toward the Soviet Union that weighed against the possibility of change. Not until 1933 would a president be elected with just the right mixture of geopolitical insight, personal flair, and Tammany Hall duplicity to get the whole job done.

NOTES

1. On pre-Civil War relations see Norman Saul's masterful *Distant Friends: The United States and Russia, 1763–1867* (University of Kansas Press, 1991). On the Far East see Howard K. Beale, *Theodore Roosevelt and the Rise of America to World Power* (Collier, 1968): pp. 159–289; and R. Esthus, *Theodore Roosevelt and the International Rivalries* (Regina, 1970). On perceptions of tsarist repression see George Kennan, *Siberia and the Exile System* (Century, 1891); and Frederick Travis, *George Kennan and the American-Russian Relationship, 1865–1924* (Ohio University Press, 1990).

2. James K. Libbey, *American-Russian Economic Relations, 1790s to 1990s* (Regina, 1989): pp. 16–20; and John L. Gaddis, *Russia, the Soviet Union, and the United States* (John Wiley, 1978): pp. 46–52; cf. Benson Lee Grayson, *Russian-American Relations in World War I* (Ungar, 1979); on American public opinion and the 1905 revolution see Arthur Thompson and Robert Hart, *Uncertain Crusade* (University of Massachusetts Press, 1970).

3. *NYT*, September 29 and October 2, 1915. In 1916, both parties made their toughest declarations on tying a commercial treaty with Russia to recognition of "the absolute right of expatriation and prevent[ion of] discrimination of whatever kind between American citizens." Kirk Porter and Donald Johnson, eds., *National Party Platforms, 1840–1972* (University of Illinois Press, 1973): pp. 194–207 [hereafter *NPP*]. Also see the author's "The United States and Tsarist Anti-Semitism, 1865–1914" *Diplomacy and Statecraft* (November 1992): pp. 438–67; Naomi Cohen, "Abrogation of the Russo-American Treaty of 1832," *Jewish Social Studies* (January 1963): pp. 3–41; and Gary Dean Best, *To Free a People* (Greenwood, 1982). The

issue broadened in 1914 when thousands of naturalized Americans were trapped overseas by competing claims to their citizenship and military obligations.

4. For example, see "Protocol of Agreement," 23 September 1915, *Statutes at Large of the United States of America* (GPO: 1851–1936), Vol. 39: pp. 1638–40 [henceforth *SAL*]; also available in Stanley Jados, ed., *Documents on Russian-American Relations* (Catholic University Press, 1965): pp. 55–56 [henceforth *DRAR*].

5. Peter Filene nicely surveys responses to the March Revolution in *Americans and the Soviet Experiment, 1917–1933* (Harvard University Press, 1967): pp. 9–21. Also see Travis, *George Kennan*: pp. 328–29.

6. A concise account is Richard Pipes, *The Russian Revolution* (Vintage, 1990): pp. 272–337.

7. Jacob Schiff, a prominent jewish activist and banker who earlier opposed loans to the Tsar and financed the Japanese during the Russo-Japanese War, now reversed course and urged credits for Russia. Best, *To Free a People*: pp. 214–15; and see Cyrus Adler, ed., *Jacob Schiff: Life and Letters*, Vol. II (Doubleday, 1928): p. 257.

8. Department of State, *Papers Relating to the Foreign Relations of the United States, 1918: Russia, Vol. I*: p. 6 [hereafter *FRUS*].

9. *The Cabinet Diaries of Josephus Daniels, 1913–1921*, E. David Cronon, ed. (University of Nebraska Press, 1963): p. 117.

10. Entry for March 23, 1917, *ibid.*, pp. 119–20. American recognition came a mere four hours before French and British, but that did not dampen Francis' or Wilson's enthusiasm. *FRUS*, 1917: pp. 1205–12.

11. See Daniels' entries for December 4, 1917, and April 30, 1918, in *Cabinet Diaries*: p. 246, 301.

12. The United States never became an Allied Power in World War I. Instead, it insisted on the term "Associated Power" in a vain effort to uphold a tradition of forebearance from "entangling alliances." In the conduct of the war and negotiation of the peace, the distinction meant almost nothing.

13. May 8 and July 5, 1917, *Woodrow Wilson: Life And Letters*, Vol. VII, Ray Stannard Baker, ed. (Doubleday, 1939): pp. 57, 148.

14. "Message to the Congress," April 2, 1917, in Henry S. Commager, ed. *Documents of American History*, 7th ed. (Meredith, 1963), Vol. II: pp. 128–32 [hereafter *DAH*].

15. "President of the United States to the President of the Russian National Council Assembly," August 24, 1917, *DRAR*: p. 49. On the dichotomy between this declaration and the facts, see George F. Kennan, *Russia and the West Under Lenin and Stalin* (Little, Brown, 1961): pp. 18–19.

16. On Wilson's ideas about democracy as a support for the balance of power see the author's "Woodrow Wilson, German Democracy, and World Order," in Hodge and Nolan, eds. *Shepherd of Democracy?, op. cit.*, pp. 21–39.

17. "Address by Woodrow Wilson," June 25, 1917, *DRAR*: p. 43. He later depicted the war as "the culminating and final war for human liberty." "Fourteen Points Address," January 8, 1918, *DAH*: Vol. II: p. 139. Also, see "Message to the Russian Government," June 8, 1917, *Compilation of the Messages and Papers of the Presidents* (1923; 1932), Vol. XVII: pp. 8270–72 [hereafter *CMPP*].

18. See Francis' remarks to that effect in his *Russia from the American Embassy, April, 1916–November, 1918* (Scribner's, 1921): pp. 90–94.

19. Exchanges between Wilson and House from May through August, 1917, in *The Intimate Papers of Colonel House*, Vol. III, Charles Seymour, ed. (Houghton Mifflin, 1928): pp. 125–48.

20. December 4, 1917, *Wilson: Letters*, Vol. VII: p. 391. And *inter alia* see Robert V. Daniels, *Red October* (Scribner's, 1967); the first three volumes of E. H. Carr's *The Bolshevik Revolution* (Macmillan, 1956; Pellican, 1971); Adam Ulam, *The Bolsheviks* (Macmillan, 1965; Collier, 1976); and *idem, Russia's Failed Revolutions* (Basic Books, 1981).

21. Entry for November 17, 1917, Daniels, *Cabinet Diaries:* p. 243. As late as 1919, Wilson still mused vaguely about the democratic ideals of the bolsheviks. See "Diary of Dr. Grayson," entry for March 9, 1919, excerpted in *PWW,* 55: p. 471.

22. *NYT,* January 18, 1818.

23. February 23, 1918, *Woodrow Wilson: Letters,* Vol. VII: pp. 564–65. He earlier declined to aid the Provisional government to secure greater rights for women, agreeing simply to attach to an observer mission men (led by Elihu Root) with reputations for "popular sympathies and [a] catholic view of human rights." *Ibid.,* Vol. VII: p. 59. Also see Elihu Root, *The United States and the War: The Mission to Russia,* Robert Bacon and James Brown, eds. (Harvard University Press, 1918).

24. The best treatment of this aspect of Wilson's Russian policy is Betty Miller Unterberger, "Woodrow Wilson and the Bolsheviks," *Diplomatic History* (Spring 1987): pp. 71–90.

25. See Lloyd E. Ambrosius, *Wilsonian Statecraft* (Scholarly Resources, 1991): pp. 109–12.

26. "Fourteen Points Address," January 8, 1918, *DAH*: Vol. II: pp. 137–39. Colonel House played a key role in drafting Point VI. See his *Intimate Papers:* Vol. III: p. 331.

27. Pipes, *Russian Revolution*: pp. 590–98. Also see the classic study by J. Wheeler-Bennett, *Brest-Litovsk* (London, 1956); and Department of State, *Proceedings of the Brest-Litovsk Peace Conference* (GPO, 1918).

28. Pipes, *Russian Revolution*: pp. 598–99. Also see Richard H. Ullman, *Anglo-Soviet Relations 1917–1921*, Vol. I: *Intervention and the War* [Princeton University Press, 1961): pp. 113–19; Francis, *From the American Embassy*: pp. 264-65; George F. Kennan, *The Decision to Intervene* (Princeton University Press, 1958): pp. 46–49; and Brian Pearce, *How Haig Saved Lenin* (Macmillan, 1988). On U.S. differences with the Allies see Edward B. Parsons, *Wilsonian Diplomacy* (Forum, 1978).

29. Unterberger, "Wilson and the Bolsheviks, " pp. 76–79.

30. Ullman, *Intervention and the War*: pp. 128–30; also see John Silverlight, *Victors' Dilemma* (Weybright and Talley, 1971).

31. Ullman, *Intervention and the War*: pp. 130–257, *passim*: and John W. Long, "American Intervention in Russia: The North Russian Expedition, 1918–1919," *Diplomatic History* (Winter 1982): pp. 45–67. Also see Francis, *From the American Embassy*: pp. 306–12.

32. Unterberger, "Wilson and the Bolsheviks," p. 86.

33. See the *aide-mémoire* of July 17, 1918, in *FRUS,* 1918: *Russia,* Vol. II: pp.

287–90; and "Francis to Robert Lansing," February 23, 1919, *PWW*, 55: pp. 234–35. Among studies that argue, in contrast, that Wilson aggressively sought to incorporate Russia into a " liberal-capitalist world order," see N. Gordon Levin, *Woodrow Wilson and World Politics* (Oxford University Press, 1968): pp. 123–57; and William A. Williams, "The American Intervention in Russia, 1917–1920," *Studies on the Left* (Fall 1963): pp. 24–48. A realist critique is Lloyd E. Ambrosius, "The Orthodoxy of Revisionism," *Diplomatic History* (Summer 1977): pp. 199–214.

34. The literature on the interventions is vast and disputatious. An excellent review article is Eugene Trani, "Woodrow Wilson and the Decision to Intervene in Russia: A Reconsideration," *Journal of Modern History* (September 1976): pp. 440–61. Among the major works on this topic, see for emphasis on the Open Door and Wilson's anti-imperialism, Betty Miller Unterberger, *American Intervention in the Russian Civil War* (Heath, 1969); and *idem*, "Woodrow Wilson and the Russian Revolution," in Arthur S. Link, ed., *Woodrow Wilson and a Revolutionary World* (University of North Carolina Press, 1982). A critical treatment of the Open Door idea is Levin, *War and Revolution*: pp. 123–53; on anti-Japanese aspects of the Siberian intervention see Kennan, *Decision to Intervene: passim.*

35. Arthur S. Link, *Woodrow Wilson: Revolution, War, and Peace* (AHM Publishing, 1979): p. 97. Other studies sharing this view include Betty Miller Unterberger, *The United States, Revolutionary Russia, and the Rise of Czechoslovakia* (University of North Carolina Press, 1989); Linda Killen, *The Russian Bureau* (University of Kentucky Press, 1983); and *idem*, "Self-Determination vs. Territorial Integrity," *Nationalist Papers* (Spring 1982): pp. 65–78.

36. *PWW*, 55: pp. 317–20.

37. "Executive Orders," August 3 and September 6, 1918, *DRAR*: p. 44; and "Reply by Chicherin to the Neutral Powers on the Red Terror," (September 12, 1918) *Soviet Documents on Foreign Policy*, Jane Degras, ed. (Oxford University Press, 1951), Vol. I: pp. 105–9 [hereafter *SDFP*]. Litvinov cabled a cynical offer to moderate the Terror in exchange for diplomatic concessions. "Telegram from Litvinov to President Wilson on Intervention," *ibid.*, pp. 129–32. More generally, see George Leggett, *The CHEKA* (Clarendon, 1981); and the older study by S.P. Melgunov, *The Red Terror in Russia* (J.M. Dent and Sons, 1926). Frederick Schuman notes that comparable acts by Whites went mostly unremarked in the U.S. press. *American Policy Toward Russia Since 1917* (International Publishers, 1928): pp. 151–57.

38. *FRUS*, 1918: *Russia*, Vol. I: p. 682.

39. *Ibid.*, p. 691.

40. *Ibid.*, p. 682. On the vague but mostly favorable international response to the initiative, see the dispatches in *ibid.*, pp. 692–704.

41. The Soviet reply is in *FRUS*, 1918: *Russia*, Vol. I: pp. 707–8. U.S. troops once threatened to intervene in order to prevent wholesale executions without trial, but against *White forces* in Siberia in 1919. "Memo from Newton Baker, with Enclosure from General William Graves," December 29, 1918 and March 3, 1919, *PWW*, 55: pp. 399–403; and see "Polk to Lansing," *ibid.*, pp. 493–94.

42. See the richly documented study by John M. Thompson, *Russia, Bolshevism and the Versailles Peace* (Princeton University Press, 1966). This work is both

the best and most comprehensive account of Allied policy toward Russia at the Paris Conference.

43. *Ibid.*, p. 50. Also see Link, *Revolution*: pp. 95–98; Kendrick Clements, *Woodrow Wilson* (Twayne, 1987): pp. 199–212; and Robert Ferrell, *Woodrow Wilson and WWI* (Harper and Row, 1985): pp. 144-47. A cursory dismissal of Wilson's policy, which argues he had no regard for the balance of power, is Ambrosius, *Wilsonian Statecraft*: pp. 100–1. Cf. Edward Buehrig, *Woodrow Wilson and the Balance of Power* (University of Indiana Press, 1955); and Note #16 *supra*.

44. For example, see the memoranda by Lansing and House, February 17, 1919, in *PWW*, 55: pp. 202–4.

45. Poland attacked bolshevik Russia in alliance with Whites from the Ukraine in an effort to push its eastern border back to the old 1772 boundary. On the strong U.S. opposition to Polish *revanchism* see Schuman, *American Policy*: pp. 175–79. On the interplay of jewish issues with the complex question of relations with the new Poland see Frank W. Brecher, *Reluctant Ally* (Greenwood, 1991): pp. 25–41.

46. The tough Soviet reply is in *FRUS*, 1919, *Russia*: pp. 39–42. Also see Thompson, *Russia and Versailles*: pp. 82–130.

47. "From William Bullitt," March 16, 1919, *PWW*, 55: pp. 540–45; "Notes of a Meeting of the Supreme War Council," February 14, 1919, *PWW*, 55: pp. 180–83; "Proposals for Peace Submitted by Lenin Through Bullitt to the Paris Peace Conference," March 12, 1919, *SDFP*, Vol. I: pp. 147–50; William C. Bullitt, *The Bullitt Mission to Russia* (New York: 1919); and Bullitt cable in *FRUS*, 1919, *Russia*: pp. 74–98. Also see Thompson, *Russia and Versailles*: pp. 131–77, 252–56; and Beatrice Farnsworth, *William C. Bullitt and the Soviet Union* (University of Indiana Press, 1967): pp. 32–54.

48. Thompson, *Russia and Versailles*: pp. 33–61, 376–98.

49. "Wilson to the American Commissioners," February 19, 1919, *PWW*, 55: p. 208; and Martin Gilbert, *Churchill* (Henry Holt, 1991): pp. 407–12.

50. "Notes of a Meeting of the Supreme War Council," February 14, 1919, *ibid.*, pp. 180–83.

51. "Bliss to Baker and March," February 13, 1919, *PWW*, 55: p. 150.

52. Italy also left Versailles dissatisfied, convinced that Wilson had betrayed his own principles and Italian claims to certain territories given to the new Yugoslav state. But Italian dissatisfaction just did not pose the same threat to the peace as did German or Russian. See Alexander DeConde, *History of American Foreign Policy*, 3rd ed. (Scribner's, 1978), Vol. II: pp. 68–69; and more generally, Rene Albrect-Carrie, *Italy at the Peace Conference* (Archon, 1966).

53. Of course, the main evidence for this conclusion has to be the Nazi-Soviet Pact of 1939, repartitioning Poland between Germany and Russia, and dispensing altogether with the Baltic States. On the important German-Soviet *rapprochement* during the 1920s see R.H. Haigh *et al.*, *German-Soviet Relations in the Weimar Era* (Barnes and Noble, 1985).

54. February 14, 1919, *PWW*, 55: pp. 188–92; and Long, "The North Russian Expedition," especially pp. 65–67.

55. On Japan, see Kennan, *Decision to Intervene*: pp. 84–106, 406–17. Cf. Ullman, *Intervention and the War:* pp. 258–336. On relations with Admiral Alexandre Kolchak see Linda Killen, "The Search for a Democratic Russia," *Diplomatic History* (Summer 1978): pp. 249–53.

56. "From the Secretary of War," February 11, 1919, *PWW*, 55: pp. 81–82.

57. "Address at Kansas City," September 6, 1919, *DRAR*: p. 43.

58. *FRUS*, 1919, *Russia*: pp. 345–47, 494.

59. That point is very nicely made in Unterberger, "Wilson and the Bolsheviks," pp. 89–90.

60. On the peculiar diplomatic position in which the United States for four years continued to recognize the Provisional Ambassador and reject the bolsheviks, see Killen, "Search for a Democratic Russia," pp. 237–56.

61. "Note of Department of State on Polish Situation," August 10, 1920, text in *CMPP*, Vol. XVIII: pp. 8862–67; partly reproduced in *DRAR*: pp. 47–48; also see Department of State, *Notes Exchanged on the Russian-Polish Situation by the United States, France, and Poland*, International Conciliation Pamphlets, October 1920, #155.

62. In 1913 the United States refused to recognize the revolutionary government in Mexico. Lincoln and Seward of course did not recognize the Confederacy, but that was a central issue under contest in the Civil War. A useful contemporary study is "The Recognition Policy of the United States: With Special Reference to Soviet Russia," *Foreign Policy Reports*, Supplement #3, (November 1926): pp. 5–29; on legal implications of the decision see Schuman, *American Policy*: pp. 262–79.

63. *Congressional Record*, 66th Cong., 1st Sess., Senate Doc. #105, *The Baltic Provinces* (1919); Linda Killen, *The Russian Bureau*; *idem*, "Dusting Off an Old Document: Colby's 1920 Russian Policy Revisited," *SHAFR Newsletter* (June 1991): pp. 32–41; Ronald Radosh, "John Spargo and Wilson's Russian Policy, 1920," *Journal of American History* (December 1965): pp. 548–65; John Spargo, *Russia as an American Problem* (Harper and Bros., 1920); and Albert N. Tarulis, *American-Baltic Relations* (Catholic University Press, 1965).

64. Schuman, *American Policy*: pp. 177–99, 216; and *Current History*, Vol. XIII, Pt. 2: pp. 338–40, 515–19. This policy received extensive public and congressional support. See *Congressional Record*, House, 66th Cong., 3rd Sess., Hearing Before the Committee on Foreign Affairs, H. Res. #635, *Conditions in Russia*, January 27–March 1, 1921; and *ibid.*, Senate, Hearings Before the Committee on Foreign Relations, S.J. Res. #164, *Relations With Russia*, January 26, 1921.

65. On Republican foreign policy see Warren I. Cohen, *Empire Without Tears* (Temple University Press, 1987); Lewis Ethan Ellis, *Republican Foreign Policy, 1921–1933* (Rutgers University Press, 1968); and *idem*, *Frank B. Kellogg and American Foreign Relations, 1925–1929* (Rutgers University Press, 1961). More generally, see Selig Adler, *The Isolationist Impulse* (Free Press, 1957; 1966); Arthur M. Schlesinger, Jr., *The Age of Roosevelt*, Vol. I, *Crisis of the Old Order, 1919–1933* (Houghton Mifflin, 1957); and John D. Hicks, *Republican Ascendancy* (Harper, 1960). Also see *NPP*: pp. 213–42.

66. *Current History*, Vol. XIV: pp. 189–90.

67. For instance, see Secretary of the Treasury, *Obligations of Foreign Governments and World War Foreign Debt Commission*, fiscal years 1922–1925 (GPO, 1925).

68. See the fine review essay by Brian McKercher, "Reaching for the Brass Ring," *Diplomatic History* (Fall 1991): pp. 565–98. On interest in trade with the Soviet Union, see *FRUS*, 1922, Vol. II: pp. 825–35.

69. *NYT*, August 1, 1923; also quoted in Schuman, *American Policy*: pp. 233–34.

70. "Coolidge: Message to the Congress," December 6, 1923," *DRAR*: p. 61. Ironically, William Borah, *doyen* of the political isolationists in the Senate, led the campaign to recognize the Soviet Union and thereby expand trade. Schuman, *American Policy*: pp. 220–23; and *Congressional Record*, Vol. 62, Pt. 7, pp. 6945–48, 7439–41.

71. The Baltic States, Poland, and Finland had exchanged recognition with the Soviets in 1920. The real breakthrough for the Soviets was the Rapallo Treaty with Germany, signed in 1922. Britain led the way among the erstwhile Allies in 1924, followed by France and Italy.

72. See Secretary of State Frank B. Kellogg's memorandum, "Policy of the U.S. Toward the Soviet Regime," February 23, 1928, *DRAR*: pp. 63–65.

73. See the discussion in Edward M. Bennett, *Recognition of Russia* (Blaisdell, 1970): pp. 49 ff.

74. An insightful treatment of this theme is Robert Browder, *Origins of Soviet-American Diplomacy* (Princeton University Press, 1953): pp. 19-24.

75. Carr, *The Bolshevik Revolution, 1917–1923*, Vol. II: pp. 147–72. Lenin also ruthlessly applied food levies, including use against the countryside of armed gangs and even the CHEKA. "Telegram to the Zadonsk Soviet," in Warren B. Walsh, ed., *Readings in Russian History* (Syracuse University Press, 1963), Vol. II: p. 728–30.

76. See Secretariat of the League of Nations, *Report on Economic Conditions in Russia with Special Reference to the Famine of 1921–1922 and the State of Agriculture* (World Peace Foundation, 1922).

77. Hoover's reputation for rigidity often is overdone. For example, see his first reaction to bolshevism in Daniels, *Cabinet Diaries*: p. 252.

78. An excellent contemporary account of the ARA is H.H. Fisher, *The Famine in Soviet Russia, 1919–1923* (Macmillan, 1927); on Hoover's first exchange with the bolshevik leadership see especially pp. 10–27.

79. Bolshevik suspicion of ARA relief as hostile is also documented in Benjamin Weissman, *Herbert Hoover and Famine Relief to Soviet Russia: 1921–1923* (Hoover Institution, 1974): pp. 40, 157–71, 182–83.

80. *FRUS*, 1921: Vol. II: p. 797.

81. "Reply to Gorky," in Fisher, *Famine in Soviet Russia*: pp. 52–53.

82. *Current History*, Vol. XIV: pp. 1030–33.

83. Weissman, *Hoover And Famine Relief*: p. 48.

84. "Agreement Between the American Relief Administration and the Soviet Authorities in Russia," August 20, 1921, text in *FRUS*, 1921, Vol. II: pp. 813–17; and *NYT*, August 21, 1921. A liaison office of the ARA was established that acted on behalf of the State Department in arrangements concerning U.S. citizens. Just under 800 (many of them women and children, and many also jews) were released. E.S. Brown, "Some Unofficial Relations with Soviet Russia," *Michigan Law Review* (March 1924): pp. 421–36; ARA, *Annual Report of the Executive Committee, 1923*; and Schuman, *American Policy*: pp. 206–7.

85. ARA, *Annual Report: 1923*; *Current History*, Vol. XV: pp. 134–36; *Congressional Record*, Vol. 61, Pt. 5, p. 4854; Vol. 62, Pt. 1, p. 565; and Fisher, *Famine in Soviet Russia*: pp. 138–72.

86. Schuman, *American Policy*: p. 206.

87. George F. Kennan, "The U.S. and the Soviet Union, 1917–1976," *Foreign Affairs* (July 1976): p. 675; also see Commission on Russian Relief. *The Russian Famines: 1921–22, 1922–23* (National Information Bureau, 1923).

88. Weissman, *Hoover and Famine Relief*: pp. 48–49.

89. Fisher, *Famine in Soviet Russia*: p. 48.

90. W.A. Williams, *American-Russian Relations, 1781–1947* (Rinehart, 1952): p. 201.

91. See Hoover's original proposal to Wilson in Fisher, *Famine in Soviet Russia*: pp. 10–23; Thompson, *Russia and Versailles*: pp. 222–67; and cf. Weissman's discussion of Hoover's motives and agenda, in *Hoover and Famine Relief*: passim.

92. "Note from Chicherin on the Brussels Conference, Famine Relief, and Debts," October 28, 1921, *SDFP*, Vol. I: pp. 270–72; and see Selig Adler, *Uncertain Giant, 1921–1941* (Macmillan, 1965): p. 53.

93. A representative sampling of the range of opinion on U.S. policy can be found in testimony and debate in *Congressional Record*, Senate, 68th Cong., 1st Sess., S. Res. #50, *Recognition of Russia, 1924*. The main ARA effort ended in 1923, but it quietly continued relief efforts in outlying Soviet areas for several years more. W. Averell Harriman recalled that during a 1926 trip to Tiflis (Tiblisi) the ARA still was active in the area. W. Averell Harriman, *America and Russia in a Changing World* (Doubleday, 1971): p. 6.

94. *FRUS*, 1927, Vol. III: p. 650. For earlier examples of friction over this issue see *ibid.*, 1919, *Russia*: pp. 148–49; 167–91; and *ibid.*, 1920, Vol. III: pp. 668–700.

95. On the ambiguous bolshevik attitude toward jews as both a religious minority and a separate national minority, see Salo W. Baron, *The Russian Jew Under Tsars and Soviets*, 2nd ed. (Schocken Books, 1987): pp. 168–204.

96. Cyrus Adler and Aaron Margalith, *With Firmness in the Right: American Diplomatic Action Affecting Jews, 1840–1945* (American Jewish Committee, 1946): p. 294 [hereafter *ADAJ*].

97. *PWW*, Vol. 55: pp. 368–81; and Brecher, *Reluctant Ally*: pp. 25–30.

98. Dimity Pospielovsky, *The Russian Church Under the Soviet Regime, 1917–1982* (St. Vladimir's, 1984), Vol. I: *passim*. Cf. William Fletcher, *The Russian Orthodox Church Underground, 1917–1970* (Oxford University Press, 1971): pp. 16–79. A contemporary U.S. account is William Emhardt, *Religion in Soviet Russia* (Morehouse, 1929).

99. *FRUS*, 1922, Vol. II: pp. 835–40.

100. Fletcher, *The Orthodox Church Underground*: pp. 31–40.

101. A partisan account is the contemporary treatment by Francis McCullagh, *Bolshevik Persecution of Christianity* (E.P. Dutton, 1924).

102. *FRUS*, 1923, Vol. II: pp. 815–16; *NYT*, March 29 and April 4, 1923.

103. FRUS, 1923, Vol. II: pp. 815–16.

104. *Ibid.*, pp. 817–22; and *NYT*, April 11, 1923.

105. Fletcher, *The Orthodox Church Underground*: pp. 79–122.

106. See Filene, *Americans and the Soviet Experiment*: pp. 248 ff.

107. Quoted in Donald G. Bishop, *The Roosevelt-Litvinov Agreements* (Syracuse University Press, 1965): p. 62. Religious persecution in Russia was regularly reported on by the Russian Section, set up in Riga to compensate for the lack of an

embassy in Moscow. See the table in Natalie Grant, "The Russian Section," *Diplomatic History* (Winter 1978): pp. 107–115; and Daniel Yergin, *Shattered Peace* (Houghton Mifflin, 1978): pp. 3–21.

108. See the essay by DeConde in Mark M. Dodge, ed., *Herbert Hoover and the Historians* (Hoover Library Association, 1989): pp. 87–116.

2 FROM RECOGNITION TO ALLIANCE

Strong support for an opening to Moscow had existed for years within specific sectors of the American business community, handicapped in relation to European competitors for Soviet trade by a lack of diplomatic and commercial treaty support.[1] Additional economic pressures for a change in policy had built up since the onset of the Depression. As traditional foreign markets closed out U.S. goods, the lure of trade with Soviet Russia convinced many in labor, business, and Congress of the wisdom of recognition.[2] Also, steadily worsening relations between Japan and the Soviet Union, combined with Japanese pressure on U.S. interests in China, suggested to some in the State Department that a concert of interests with Moscow existed in the Far East. Secretary of State Henry L. Stimson considered a revived relationship in the early 1930s, though primarily in terms of these national security interests in Asia rather than trade. As the situation in China worsened, he grew increasingly unhappy with Hoover's reluctant leadership, but was unable to shift U.S. policy toward Russia in face of twelve years of inertia.[3] On the other hand, the Russian Section in the Riga embassy was mostly skeptical about the merits of an opening, as were other top career officers.[4] A real move was going to require leadership from a different administration, with a broad mandate for change.

RECOGNITION

Worldwide depression, Japanese moves against China, and Adolf Hitler's ascension to power in Germany in January 1933 made apparent to President Franklin Roosevelt the need for greater U.S. engagement in world affairs. The need to address domestic economic recovery was of course primary, yet the New Deal also required a rollback of protectionist barriers with major trading partners and a search for secure export markets. With established markets in Europe moving under protectionist barriers that suggested an opening to the relatively untapped Soviet market. Economics dovetailed nicely with strategic concerns as well. Relations with Japan were already badly strained during the Hoover years. The United States objected to Tokyo's effort to slam the "Open Door" in Manchuria and Shantung province; to the 1931 invasion of Manchuria; and to Japanese pressure leading to a naval arms race in the Pacific, extant despite the Washington (1922) and London (1930) naval conferences regulating capital shipbuilding. In turn, Japan was bitter over U.S. refusal to recognize its League mandate over Yap Island (in the Carolines); revival of a statutory ban on oriental immigration; and Washington's nonrecognition of the puppet state of "Manchukuo" established and maintained to the north of China by force of Japanese arms. Concerning Germany, while Roosevelt kept a low policy profile in the early years, he recognized earlier than some others that Hitler's challenge to the Versailles settlement was a fundamental threat to U.S. interests in the postwar *status quo* in Europe.[5]

Roosevelt faced a clear dilemma as he moved to repair the sinews and bone of American capitalism: success at home might prove a chimera if world order collapsed in the meantime. Yet the public—through Congress—would not permit him sufficient latitude to commit the country in ways that really constituted support for international peace and security. How then was he to prevent the aggressor nations from destroying the peace? The answer was to prop up the balance of power in Europe and Asia by obtaining support of *other nations* for collective security. There was the rub. During these critical years all Roosevelt had to offer—or felt he could risk—were words of encouragement, symbolic gestures, and vague promises that if others stood up to the fascist powers, a U.S. commitment would follow. To this end he waged a sustained rhetorical campaign, aimed mostly at Britain and France but also at the Soviet Union. He was realistic enough to see that the anti-German alliance of 1914 (if not 1917) was the only way security could be guaranteed in Europe; and that in Asia, the Soviets and Americans would either have to stand together against Japan or fall separately. But before he could join Moscow to the security camp of the western democracies, he had to convince his countrymen to give up their posturing over nonrecognition.

Not all Americans agreed that it was time to deal directly with the Soviets. Some were unpersuaded by the economic arguments; many more, mired in isolationism, disregarded concerns over security in Asia. Important opposition came from religious groups, concerned generally with the atheistic character of the Soviet state and particularly with persecution of co-religionists. The strongest opposition came from the Christian churches, and especially from catholics.[6] That was considered in the earliest ruminations on recognition, as was a long-standing dispute over protections for American citizens. Secretary of State Cordell Hull identified to Roosevelt what he considered the four main stumbling blocks to reversing the policy of nonrecognition: "(1) operations carried on in this country under the direction of the Communist International at Moscow, (2) freedom of religion for American citizens in Russia, (3) fair treatment of Americans in Russia, and (4) satisfactory settlement of governmental and private indebtedness."[7] Others in the State Department confirmed that opposition by religious groups made it advisable to extract guarantees on freedom of religion prior to recognition. Roosevelt then met with church leaders to make clear that he intended to emphasize matters of religious freedom, and would also work to free clerics imprisoned in Russia.[8] He had hoped to place relations on a realistic basis, and send a subtle signal to Germany and Japan that the United States might support collective security measures against their revisionist policies. Yet, to carry an important element of American opinion it was necessary to promise that guarantees of religious and individual liberty would be sought in advance—from an atheist, police state. Domestic symbolism, electoral politics, and moral posturing were already starting to erode the intended effects of his diplomatic initiative.

Maxim Litvinov (Commissar for Foreign Affairs since 1930) arrived in Washington to discuss recognition in November 1933, delighted at the chance to secure U.S. support against the Japanese at least, and perhaps even within Europe.[9] According to Hull, the cabinet agreed that of all advance agreements necessary for recognition, "the two most important were precautions against Soviet propaganda and illegal activities in the United States and freedom of worship for Americans in Russia."[10] Secretary of the Treasury Henry Morgenthau recorded that Hull described the religious question to Litvinov as the single most important one under discussion. In fact, Hull sought to impress the importance of the religious question upon Litvinov by warning that if an agreement on religious freedom was not forthcoming, Roosevelt would be thrown out of office at the next election.[11] A sharp exchange took place. Litvinov objected that it was impossible to guarantee freedom of religion, while the Americans protested vehemently that such a pledge was an essential precondition of recognition. Hull later wrote: "It shortly developed that, although [Litvinov] spoke English quite well, he had misunderstood our objective to be freedom of religion for Russians as well as Americans." After that confusion was cleared up, Litvinov brightened and relaxed. He assured the Secretary that Soviet law already provided comprehensive protections to believers, and hence a guarantee of religious freedom to American residents would not be a problem. Hull apparently did not notice the contradiction between the commissar's objection to what he thought was a request for religious freedom for Russians, and a guarantee of similar rights for Americans on an assurance that Soviet law already protected religious liberty.[12] Litvinov later gave the same easy assurances to Roosevelt, who just as easily accepted them.[13]

An executive agreement formalizing the understanding was drawn up between Roosevelt and Litvinov, with the president spelling out claims to religious rights in very specific terms. Litvinov replied with a recitation of Soviet law, which in no way limited or accounted for earlier anti-religious decrees that were the cause of concern among groups in the United States. He even cited, as evidence that freedom of religion was already respected in the Soviet Union, the very decrees found so offensive by church leaders. Nonetheless, the letter was proclaimed to be the sought-after warranty of religious liberty.[14] Roosevelt later described to his cabinet, knowing his remarks would be leaked to the press, how he supposedly had masterfully cajoled Litvinov into this concession on religious freedom:

[I said:] "You know Max... your good old father and mother, pious jewish people, always said their prayers. I know they must have taught you to say your prayers"... By this time Max was as red as a beet and I said to him, "Now you may think you're an atheist... but I tell you, Max, when you come to die ... you're going to be thinking about what your father and mother taught you"... Max blustered and puffed and said all kinds of things, laughed and was very embarrassed, but I had him. I was sure from the expression on his face and his actions that he knew what I meant and that he knew I was right.[15]

On both a personal and political level, Roosevelt enjoyed retelling this anecdote and made a special point of it when visited by a delegation of catholic clergy.[16] Its real significance seems to have been largely lost on him, however. It revealed above all not Litvinov's susceptibility to Roosevelt's charm—the commissar was as hard a realist as his master in Moscow—but Roosevelt's own capacity for wishful dependence on, and overconfidence in, the virtues of personal diplomacy.

Similar executive arrangements were made regarding U.S. concerns over COMINTERN propaganda and subversion, and legal protections for Americans in Russia.[17] A fourth agreement concerned outstanding debts from the tsarist and Kerensky years that the Soviet government refused to honor. That resolution of the quarrel was imperative could be seen in the Johnson Debt Default Act (1934), then wending its way through Congress. The Act prohibited loans to countries in default on their indebtedness to the United States. William C. Bullitt used mention of the Act to effect in his talks with Litvinov, and appeared to be making progress in forcing concessions. But once again Roosevelt personally intervened, this time to greatly deleterious effect. Instead of allowing the State Department to work out precise arrangements, he spontaneously "made a 'gentleman's agreement'" with Litvinov in which the exact amount owed was left open and the meaning of the term "loan" he scribbled into the text was left unclear.[18] Whereas Americans later interpreted "loan" to mean credit tied to U.S. purchases, Litvinov and the Soviets chose to read it more broadly as an untied grant expected from the United States as a precondition of debt payment.[19] Left effectively unresolved, the debt question would bedevil further moves toward a *rapprochement* throughout the 1930s, through its ability to capture public sympathy, including for holders of tsarist bonds and American investors who took a financial loss after 1917.[20]

The psychological impact in the United States of the "Roosevelt-Litvinov" assignment on religious liberty was entirely astonishing, and utterly disproportionate to what had been achieved. Roosevelt never sought and did not obtain from the Soviet Union any assurance against mistreatment of that country's tens of millions of believers, whose fate most concerned religious communities in the United States. All he received was a paper guarantee of the right of a handful of Americans in Moscow to hold religious services. Yet church opinion, along with the country as a whole, gave this aspect of the opening to Russia a standing ovation.[21] Nor was such artless misreading of the religious understanding limited to church opinion. Even that otherwise suspicious and isolationist Chairman of the Senate Committee on Foreign Relations, Nevada Senator Key Pittman, thought recognition was "the greatest diplomatic victory in my memory." He assured Roosevelt that what some might view as a poor compromise on outstanding debt was nothing compared to the "fundamental agreements that you have obtained looking to the establishment in Russia of certain great principles of independence founded upon our conception of religion."[22] As late as 1947, the naive moralism of Cordell Hull was still apparent when he wrote he had not abandoned his belief "that Russia and the United States, especially after the agreements reached at the time of recognition, had no conflicting national aims."[23]

The United States had the opportunity in 1933 to extract from the Soviets firm and clear understandings on pre-existing controversies such as those concerning mistreatment of American citizens and repayment of national debts: principle and interest for once harmonized. Moscow was very concerned about the Japanese threat and eager to draw Roosevelt into cooperative security arrangements in Asia. Clearly, Roosevelt should have allowed the State Department more time to prepare the agreements, and not personally intervened in the negotiations as he did. Out of eagerness to score a quick personal triumph on the domestic scene, however, he failed to achieve a clear understanding with the Soviets.[24] An even less flattering judge of this maneuver is George F. Kennan, who argues that in attaching spurious conditions to recognition, as he puts it, Roosevelt was concerned merely with the "outward aspects of carefully worked-out technical-legal documents. . . . He was interested only in their momentary psychological effect on the American public, not on [sic] their effectiveness in practice."[25] That judgment is substantially correct, but also only half the tale. Once the Japanese threat faded in 1934, the opportunity to extract concessions from Moscow no longer existed, and American-Soviet relations began to drift back onto the rocks of earlier disputes over citizens' rights, debts, and the COMINTERN. Clearer agreements would not have prevented that development, as demonstrated by the continuing high levels of anti-Soviet domestic opinion and Moscow's violations of even the clear agreements signed in 1933. On the other hand, legal clarity at least might have brought home—not least importantly to Roosevelt himself—that dealings with the Soviet Union were best undertaken on a basis of tough realism, not cozy personal contacts and informal understandings.

DRIFT

It quickly became apparent that the administration had overestimated potential benefits and underestimated the difficulties of post-recognition dealings with the Soviet Union. Indeed, there were soon unfulfilled expectations on both sides, as Moscow slowly realized that Roosevelt had little idea about his policy beyond recognition, and no intention of moving into collective security arrangements ahead of an isolationist public opinion.[26] With no further incentives forthcoming from Washington, and with the threat of war between Japan and Russia abating during 1934, the major reason for Stalin to make good on the concessions made to the United States was removed. Soviet purchases of American goods never rose to expected levels, despite agreement in 1935 on the first American-Russian commercial treaty since abrogation by Congress in 1912 of the old commercial treaty, because of Russian discrimination against American jews.[27] Prior to 1939, American-Soviet trade actually failed to match prerecognition levels.[28]

More damaging still to relations was that the Soviets continued to promote COMINTERN activities, including permitting American communists to participate in a 1935 meeting in Moscow. That violation of one of the Roosevelt-Litvinov agreements led to a stiff U.S. warning that support for subversion and propaganda would "preclude the further development of friendly relations."[29] Protests were lodged as well over repeated violation of the agreement on rights of American citizens, signaling revival of a very old irritant in relations.[30]

Concerning debt negotiations, despite Roosevelt's larger interest in easing the Soviets into the camp of the western democracies, his administration rather stiffly insisted on its interpretation of the recognition agreement.[31] Similarly, Soviet negotiators appear never to have understood the real domestic constraints limiting Roosevelt's ability to compromise. He needed a concession on the debt question in order to placate domestic opponents of a closer relationship with Moscow, so that he could claim sufficient progress to permit moves on the larger issues of peace and security. The Soviets, particularly Stalin, never understood how the U.S. political system limited executive authority, and certainly had little conception of the extent to which their own interests were tied to the perceptions of the American public through the isolationists in Congress.[32] Thus, as the bond of interest *vis-à-vis* Japan weakened, within two years negotiations on the debt ground to a halt.[33] With no breakthrough to demonstrate that the opening to the Soviet Union had brought real benefits, Roosevelt was held back by his fear of isolationist opinion from all but rhetorical efforts to bring the Soviets together with the British and French in support of the peace in Europe, or to underwrite security in Asia. Talk was cheap; but without the nation behind a commitment to collective security, talk was all Roosevelt had.

Nor did the situation improve in 1935, after the Geneva Disarmament Conference failed with a dramatic withdrawal by Hitler. The United States declined a Soviet invitation to join a permanent peace conference. Roosevelt knew the initiative was intended to draw him into European peace and security affairs *contra* Germany, and that domestic opinion would reject any such connection.[34] On that score, the recognition agreements were proving something of a liability. Settlement of the debt question, an end to COMINTERN activity in the United States, and the other agreements had been held up as important symbols of Soviet sincerity. Without follow-up adherence, those who opposed recognition in the first place were convinced they had been right, and blocked additional moves toward a full *rapprochement*.[35] Roosevelt had relied overmuch on symbolic gestures as a substitute for policy, only to find his policy subsequently tripped up by those symbols. Even so, the major fault was not his. By 1935 Stalin, who had far greater room to maneuver in negotiations on issues such as the debt but failed to do so, demonstrated that he understood the importance of symbolism no better. The Soviet Union was more realistic than the United States about collective security measures necessary to preserve the peace in the 1930s, largely because the threat loomed on its borders. Yet it too proved incapable of moving past stumbling blocks that would prove trivial when compared to the cost of the cataclysm to come. Neither nation was able to overcome its isolationism in time, or in sufficient measure, to effectively act against the fascist powers that threatened both.

Despite anger and disappointment over the Soviet response to debt negotiations and revival of the COMINTERN, Roosevelt still strove to make minor improvements in relations as part of his larger strategy of encouraging a Soviet alignment with Britain and France. In 1935, he signed a trade agreement granting the Soviet Union most-favored-nation status.[36] But such minor adjustments were no longer enough. As Edward Bennett puts it in his fine study of Soviet-American relations in the 1930s, "when President Roosevelt and Secretary Hull gave evidence that internal politics were influencing their conduct of foreign policies, the Russians demonstrated that they were no longer interested in games of pretense without definite collaborative objectives."[37] In fact, the assessment was being made in Moscow that while it was preferable to form a collective front to avoid war, if war came it was desirable to have it fought by others.[38] Many Americans came to the latter conclusion as well. The passage of the first Neutrality Act in 1935 signaled that the United States was determined not to become involved to even a minimum level in establishing collective security arrangements, a position its leaders at all levels repeatedly affirmed. As Americans retreated into a "plague on all their houses" isolationism, Moscow saw decreasing need to appease U.S. public opinion as a prelude to foreign policy cooperation. Besides, Washington was no longer central to the question of whether there was to be war or peace. Control of that outcome henceforth hovered between London and Berlin.

Behind the public diplomacy of the 1930s a dynamic was developing in U.S. foreign policy with great long-term effects: Roosevelt and top career officers in the State Department were moving apart in their assessment of the character and ambitions of the Soviet Union. The president's personal self-confidence and suspicion of "conservatism" in the State Department led him to ignore severely critical reports and warnings about the savage nature of Stalin's regime, emanating from the American embassy in Moscow.[39] For example, while negotiating a few symbolic and legal freedoms for American citizens, little account was made of the forced collectivizations in the Ukraine and elsewhere that led to enormous suffering, artificial famine, and millions of deaths.[40] Among the few who did notice, isolationism competed with opposition to the Soviet Union. Such was the case of Republican Representative Hamilton Fish, son of the former Secretary of State, who introduced a resolution of sympathy and condemnation in the House in 1934 but refused to go beyond rhetoric, and was a leading opponent of military preparedness legislation.[41] Thus, rather than a repeat of the generous response to a Russian famine such as occurred in the 1920s, virtually nothing was done. Bullitt, appointed as the first U.S. Ambassador, reported joining with Stalin, who proposed "a toast 'To President Roosevelt, who in spite of the mute growls of the Fishes, dared to recognize the Soviet Union.' His reference to Hamilton Fish created considerable laughter."[42] Bullitt later changed his mind about the Soviet system after seeing firsthand its oppressive police state apparatus at work, especially in the purge trials that began in 1934 and lasted through the middle years of the decade.[43]

It is not clear that Roosevelt totally gave up his own vague, essentially optimistic views about Russia. In fact, he downplayed reports about the significance of the great purges embarked upon by Stalin.[44] He generally showed little interest in Soviet internal developments, content to rely on the rosy assessments made by Joseph E. Davies, who replaced Bullitt as ambassador in 1936. So utterly gullible was Davies that he once reported about a purge trial he witnessed, "on the face of the proceedings so far ... the government has overwhelmingly established its case." He qualified that judgment only with the remarkably obtuse observation that "motives for sincerity of confession" by the defendants remained a "matter of conjecture."[45]

In contrast, talented career officers stationed in Moscow, such as George Kennan, Charles Bohlen, and Loy Henderson, were deeply affected by the purges and utterly dismayed at the appointment and reactions of the new ambassador. The embassy staff actually met the night of Davies' arrival to consider a mass resignation in protest of the appointment.[46] Kennan later wrote that the effect of his residence in Moscow during the purge years "was never to leave me. Its imprint on my political judgment was one that would place me at odds with official thinking in Washington for at least a decade thereafter."[47] Embassy dispatches portrayed the Soviet system as morally irredeemable and its leaders as undependable. They thereby helped to reinforce the conviction of other career officers in Washington that close cooperation with Moscow was neither possible nor desirable over the long term, and that trouble lay ahead for Soviet-American relations.[48]

Informed Americans could see little difference between Stalin's savagely efficient eliminations and Hitler's 1934 purge of Ernst Roehm and the SA stormtroopers (*Sturmabteilungen*). Specifically, the special antipathy of catholics for the Soviet Union had not abated since the executions of priests in Russia and anti-communist papal encyclicals of the 1920s. Matters were complicated after 1936 by Soviet support for what many catholics viewed as the anti-clerical Republican cause in the Spanish Civil War.[49] Understandably, the general public also did not see major differences between the domestic practices of the Soviet Union and that of the fascist countries.[50] However, as the likelihood of war grew, crucially important differences in foreign policy between the Soviet Union and other totalitarian countries were widely recognized. In 1937, a majority of Americans ranked the Soviet Union along with Japan, Germany, and Italy as the nations they most disliked, yet only 9 percent of those polled held the Soviets responsible for the international arms race, by then well underway. In contrast, 38 percent considered Germany responsible for the arms race, while 32 percent blamed Italy.[51] That represented an important nuance in attitudes toward the Soviet Union, and permitted Roosevelt a shift from neutrality toward more open opposition to the Axis, with a corresponding move toward a renewed security understanding with Moscow.

Roosevelt first needed to clear the way for a fresh initiative toward Soviet Russia within his own administration. He ordered the Russian Section broken up in order to minimize what he saw as its obstruction of his Soviet policy, and he characteristically looked outside the State Department for "special envoys" such as Bullitt and Davies to carry his personal diplomacy directly to Stalin.[52] Roosevelt signaled the shift in his famous "Quarantine speech" of October 1937.[53] Thereafter, he pushed for a minimum of defense preparedness, especially concerning the Navy. The isolationists in Congress and the nation were still a dominant force, however. Their obstruction of even basic preparedness measures compelled Roosevelt to still rely primarily on a diplomacy of rhetoric. Thus, despite the new sense of urgency he felt as the old order contracted under fascist pressure, he was thrown back onto the feeble 1933 policy of seeking to use the Soviets to stiffen the spines of the western democracies. Once again, because he could not convince the American people and Congress to do the job themselves, or loosen strict neutrality enough for him to aid others, he was left with nothing of real value to offer Stalin.

Roosevelt did authorize a visit to Vladivostok by a U.S. naval squadron in 1937, but whatever deterrent effect that might have had was undermined by the obvious isolationism of the United States as a whole. He was talking a better show, but as yet could offer no substantial aid to those whom he asked to stand up to the Axis nations. Moreover, he felt compelled for domestic political reasons to repeatedly declare that America would fight only if attacked.[54] Nor did the Soviets make any effort to remove symbolic irritants in relations that might have improved Roosevelt's chances with Congress and public opinion. Instead, they continued unnecessarily damaging and petty policies such as harassment of U.S. citizens and embassy officials, and obstinate refusal to permit departure of Soviet women married to Americans.[55]

In 1938 one real measure of support for Stalin that Roosevelt felt able to extend—agreement to build a battleship for the Soviet navy—fell victim to obstruction from within his own administration. Similarly, his effort to establish a secret channel to Moscow to share information on military and naval technology was blocked by isolationists and anti-communists in the Navy and War Departments.[56] Betrayal of Czechoslovakia at Munich by Britain and France in March of that year confirmed his belief that the Soviet Union was the only other armed nation available to stiffen the resolve of the democracies to stand against Germany. However, Stalin reacted to Munich by reassessing his basic options, as collective security had been abandoned by the other major powers in favor of appeasement. The Soviets therefore sought to isolate themselves from the coming conflict while simultaneously making moves—such as sacking Litvinov, openly identified with the old collective security policy—that might still shock the West into real cooperation against Nazi Germany.[57]

Relations with the United States accordingly assumed a low priority for Moscow, but embassy staff misread the change, suggesting the time was ripe to press settlement of the debt question.[58] By the spring of 1939, such preoccupation with posturing was in direct conflict with a real principled diplomacy of defense of the balance of power, and thereby of democracy, in Europe. Roosevelt understood that, but was still unwilling to lead beyond where he thought public opinion might follow. Americans and Soviets thus missed each other's moment. Each nation had groped toward the other over the course of the 1930s in hope of finding a modicum of security; then feeling rebuffed, each had retreated into its own wounded isolationism.

DISILLUSIONMENT

By mid–1939 Nazi Germany had already swallowed its two small, independent neighbors, Austria and Czechoslovakia. There could be no question that the main threat to U.S. interests and to American values and principles was headquartered in Berlin, not Moscow. Yet in the face of these developments, and partly because of them, Roosevelt was unable to win repeal of the several Neutrality Acts,[59] or to respond positively when Stalin made one final effort to construct an anti-fascist coalition over the course of that fateful summer.[60] American officials now began to worry that a separate Soviet deal to deflect Hitler might be in the works.[61] They were right. The announcement came on August 22nd that a Nazi-Soviet Non-Aggression Pact had been signed that freed both nations from fear of a two-front war.

Of course, almost immediately the Non-Aggression Pact cleared the path for Hitler's drive east toward Warsaw, which came within two weeks.[62] The subsequent outbreak of war between Germany, France, and Britain was followed by Soviet tanks moving west into Poland to an occupation line agreed in advance with the Germans. That broke the last, thin reed of perceived difference between the Soviet Union and Nazi Germany in the eyes of the American public.[63] Millions of Polish-Americans reflected bitterly on the fourth partition of their ancestral homeland, supported in their fierce opposition to the Soviet Union by other catholics concerned for the welfare of Polish co-religionists.[64] They were joined in this sense of revulsion by millions of other Americans, stunned at what they regarded as the naked cynicism of Stalin's deal with Hitler. In January 1939, 83 percent of Americans polled had expressed a preference for a Russian over a German victory if those countries should go to war. After the Nazi-Soviet Pact that general preference remained, but overall favorable perceptions of Russia plummeted.[65]

More than the assault on Poland, the Soviet Union's winter war against democratic Finland in late 1939 embittered relations with the United States. Roosevelt was in a quandary. He had not invoked the Neutrality Acts to cover Russia's participation in the partition of Poland, fearing that would only drive Stalin deeper into Hitler's embrace. He similarly was reluctant to do anything over the invasion of Finland that might push Russia closer to Nazi Germany. On the other hand, he was moved by the plight of the Finns and personally angered by Stalin's apparent naked opportunism. He decided to ban sales to the Soviet Union of certain strategic metals, appealed to Stalin not to bomb Finnish cities, revived his earlier call for a "moral embargo" on sales of aircraft to aggressor countries (which proved just as ineffective in war as it had in peace), and opened fresh lines of credit to enable Finland to purchase munitions.[66] Roosevelt decided against breaking diplomatic relations with Moscow, although the House of Representatives nearly took the matter out of his hands when it came within three votes of denying appropriations for the

Moscow embassy. Lastly, he endorsed the expulsion of the Soviet Union by the League of Nations, a futile moral gesture made at the final meeting of that tragically hapless organization.[67]

Roosevelt's desire to assist the Finns, however minimally, was at odds with America's prevailing mood of isolationism. Congress thus resisted the effort to aid Finland, supported in its obstruction by a general public that disapproved of Soviet actions and admired Finland, but remained nervous about any measure that might involve America in the war in Europe.[68] In December 1939, one poll showed 88 percent of Americans with extensive sympathy for Finland. Yet a poll taken two months later revealed that 77 percent opposed entry into the wider European war even if it seemed likely that Nazi Germany would defeat Britain and France. Senate isolationists thus opposed aid to Finland out of fear that the United States thereby might be dragged into the war through a side door.[69] That took the sting out of a spontaneous public outcry that otherwise had begun to catch Stalin's attention.[70]

Roosevelt's anger at the Soviet action and frustration over Senate myopia on national security policy came together momentarily in February 1940. Deliberately selecting a mainly pro-Soviet youth organization as his audience, he declared that he had changed his mind about Russia. He said that, like his listeners, he too had once hoped that:

Russia would work out its own problems, and that its government would eventually become a peaceloving, popular government with a free ballot, which would not interfere with the integrity of its neighbors. That hope is today either shattered or put away in storage against some better day. The Soviet Union, as everybody who has the courage to face the facts knows, is run by a dictatorship as absolute as any other dictatorship in the world.[71]

A profound ambivalence thus ran through Roosevelt's thinking: deep anger toward and moral alienation from the Soviet Union, coupled with a recognition that ultimately he would have to work with Stalin if the nazi threat was to be countered.

That basic, strategic conclusion was not altered even by the events of midsummer 1940. Rather, the conviction was deepened that Germany was a fundamental threat far outweighing the distant distaste most Americans felt for the Soviet Union. France fell under the German jackboot in a mere six weeks in May and June, following the even more rapid conquest of Norway and Denmark, and the Low countries. Stalin took advantage of the cover and the opportunity of war in the west to occupy all three Baltic countries ceded in a secret protocol to the Nazi-Soviet Pact, and in a follow-up frontier treaty in which he had traded rights to the Polish provinces of Lublin and Warsaw to Hitler in exchange for Lithuania.[72] He also forced Rumania to give up its provinces of Bessarabia and Bukovina. Despite anger in Washington over these moves, strategic considerations quite properly outweighed the temptation to indulge in futile moral gestures such as breaking diplomatic relations. As ruthlessly opportunist as Stalin appeared, Roosevelt and even the public realized Hitler's appetite for conquest was more immediate and probably more insatiable.[73] That was indeed the case, as the Axis states expanded further over Europe, Africa, and Asia during 1940 and the early months of 1941. The administration at this point began to consider ways to assist the Soviets resist the onslaught that it believed was coming, sooner or later.[74]

The soundness of Roosevelt's reading of events—if not of his policy reaction to them—was confirmed, this time beyond any doubt, by the nazi invasion of the Soviet Union on June 22, 1941. That event of course proved a major turning point in American-Soviet relations. With Churchill's enthusiastic agreement, Roosevelt immediately decided to give all possible assistance to the Soviets, including extending Lend-Lease aid.[75] His public education efforts over the previous months and years—in which he had played to anti-Soviet sentiments when necessary, but overall had sought to convince Americans that the main threat came from the Axis—was beginning to pay off, greatly aided by the force of events. Reflecting the impact of the Nazi-Soviet Pact, the attacks on Poland and Finland, and the annexations of 1940, after Hitler's invasion of Russia some 35 percent of Americans polled in October 1941 still believed the Soviet Union and Nazi Germany were equally detestable. Another 32 percent thought there was little to choose between the totalitarian states internally, but considered that Russia was just slightly better than Germany. The key result came in answer to the question about which side Americans wanted to win the war. Despite their low opinion of Russia, most still preferred a Soviet victory.[76]

However, there was one large block of anti-Soviet opinion that neither Roosevelt nor Hitler could so easily dissolve. American catholics continued to cling to such fierce anti-communist convictions that they posed a significant obstacle to getting approval of Lend-Lease for the Soviet Union through the Congress. Once again, Roosevelt was somewhat hoisted on his own petard: he had repeatedly upheld in his foreign policy statements the idea that religious belief was a major source of "democracy and international good faith."[77] He even counted freedom of religion as one of the "Four Freedoms" upon which he wanted to see the postwar order reconstructed, in an expedient oversimplification that was both comforting and domestically politically effective.[78] Hence, it would be disastrous for him to have to admit that antagonism to organized religion informed Soviet domestic law and practice. In September 1941, he thus expressed convenient optimism about the future of religious liberty in the Soviet Union, in a letter sent to Pope Pius XII in order to solicit the Pontiff's acquiescence in Lend-Lease to Stalin:

> I believe there is a real possibility that Russia may as a result of the present conflict recognize freedom of religion. . . . I believe that the survival of Russia is less dangerous to religion, to the church as such, and to humanity in general than would be the survival of the German form of dictatorship. Furthermore, it is my belief that the leaders of all churches in the United States should recognize these facts clearly and should not close their eyes to these basic questions and by their present attitude on this question directly [*sic*] assist Germany in her present objectives.[79]

In this correspondence Roosevelt used his personal representative to the Vatican, Myron C. Taylor, appointed in December 1939 in anticipation of just such domestic difficulties with catholics. Pope Pius—who knew better than Roosevelt the real conditions under which believers labored in the Soviet Union—replied with polite generalities, avoiding any mention of conditions in Russia. Yet the key from Roosevelt's point of view was that Pius drew a distinction between assistance to the Soviets and support for communism, which left a moral opening for catholics in the United States to support Lend-Lease.[80]

Instead of pressing that point home, Roosevelt adopted another tactic: he would try to persuade catholics that things were getting better in Russia on the religious front. A strange pattern thus began to develop in Roosevelt's policy approach to the Soviet Union, one of leadership at home through dissembling and even outright deceit where the possibilities of straight talk had not been exhausted. In late September 1941, he suggested during a press conference that reporters acquaint themselves with the freedom of religion clause of the Soviet constitution (Article #124), which also declared the right of the state "equally to use propaganda against religion." He next described this limitation as "essentially what is the rule in this country, only we don't put it quite the same way." He concluded: "Since the Soviet constitution declares that freedom of religion is granted, it is hoped ... an entering wedge for the practice of complete freedom of religion is definitely on its way."[81] Yet just six months earlier his own administration had protested desecration of the catholic church in Moscow that serviced American embassy officials and citizens, in accordance with terms of the 1933 recognition agreements.[82] When an outcry arose in catholic (and other) circles over the inaccuracy of Roosevelt's characterization of Soviet domestic practice, the State Department tried to soothe the ruffled feathers of church leaders with a release attesting that freedom of worship was denied equally by communists and nazis. Even faced with a practical problem of overcoming catholic opposition to his Lend-Lease proposal, Roosevelt could not resist appending to the Department's draft the accurate but also somewhat morally mischievous conclusion that: "Hitler's armies are today the chief dangers of [sic] the Americas."[83]

There is no question that the clear intention behind Roosevelt's optimistic depiction of the state of religious affairs in the Soviet Union was an effort to forestall church opposition to his proposal to extend Lend-Lease to Stalin. He told Soviet Ambassador Constantine Oumansky: "If Moscow could get some publicity back to this country regarding the freedom of religion [in Russia] it might have a very fine educational effect before the next Lend-Lease bill comes up in Congress."[84] Embassy staff were requested to obtain formal assurances that the Soviet Union would respect freedom of religion in the future. They did so easily enough, given the degree of Soviet need for U.S. Lend-Lease supplies. In transmitting the Soviet reply, the embassy accurately warned that "the Soviet Government will give lip service and make a few gestures to meet the President's wishes but is not yet prepared to give freedom of religion in the sense that we understand it." That was not a caution the Roosevelt administration cared to hear, however, or at least not one it was willing to discuss with the public. House Majority Leader John McCormack subsequently advised the White House that a great advantage could be had "from a psychological angle" among American catholics if the United States intervened on behalf of a number of Polish priests held in Soviet concentration camps. Assistant Secretary of State Adolf Berle agreed to press for release because it "would mean definite assistance in allaying some of the catholic opposition to aid to Russia."[85] The Soviets were told that freedom for the Polish clerics (seized during the 1939 invasion of eastern Poland) was sought "not with the intention to interfere in Soviet internal affairs [sic]," but in the hope that Moscow could facilitate Roosevelt's effort to extend it the maximum of assistance.[86]

The most practiced student of catholics and American foreign policy, George Q. Flynn, argues that Roosevelt's efforts were only superficially cynical, that "the president seriously hoped to promote religious freedom in Russia."[87] While that was probably true on one level, there is little doubt that on another he was deliberately misleading. After all, in 1942 he once bluntly admitted to Morgenthau: "I am perfectly willing to mislead and tell untruths... if it will help win the war."[88] Yet there was even more to it than that, as Robert Dallek succinctly points out:

Roosevelt knew full well that there was no freedom of religion in the Soviet Union. Nor was he blind to the fact that he could extend Lend-Lease help to Russia without demonstrating her devotion to religious freedom. But . . . convinced that only a stark contrast between freedom and totalitarianism would provide the emotional wherewithal for Americans to fight, Roosevelt wished to identify the Russians, regardless of Soviet realities, with Anglo-American ideals as fully as he could. The effort to depict the Soviet Union as reformed, or reforming, on the issue of religious freedom was chiefly an expression of this concern.[89]

The criticism here is not that Roosevelt and others lied: with stakes so high, lying was perhaps a defensible tactic in the service of national survival and defeat of fascism. The problem was that he may have lied *unnecessarily*, before he really tried an all-out campaign of using the presidential bully-pulpit to convince catholics and other anti-Soviet and isolationist Americans that massive material aid to Russia was in the interest of the United States—which of course it clearly was. Instead, as the war progressed, additional deceits built upon the first, until real damage was done to the long-term interest of having a willing, newly enlightened public behind the great efforts of war and peacemaking that lay ahead.

MOLDING PUBLIC OPINION

After the nazi invasion of Soviet Russia and Imperial Japan's surprise attack on Pearl Harbor five months later, the American public began to revise its low opinion of the Soviet Union.[90] As had happened in 1917, Americans evinced a need to regard their new Russian ally as moved by democratic ideals similar to their own.

Many, though by no means all, downplayed or forgot about Stalin's purges, the persecution of religious and other minorities since the revolution, and Soviet attacks upon or annexations of territories from Poland, Finland, the Baltic States, and Rumania. By 1943 that shift in opinion was complete, with solid majorities of Americans of nearly all backgrounds reporting favorable views of the Soviet Union and belief in the possibilities for postwar cooperation.[91] What brought about this sea-change in public opinion? Kennan argues insightfully that the main cause was naiveté and ignorance, asserting that most Americans did not realize that:

Russia's involvement in the war was neither the doing nor the preference of her own rulers; that, on the contrary, they had made desperate efforts to remain aloof from it, and would, had this been possible, have witnessed without a quiver of regret further Western reverses in the war, provided only that the contest was sufficiently bloody and prolonged to exhaust Germany's warmaking potential along with that of its Western opponents.[92]

Another major cause of the shift in opinion surely was a natural sense of shared burden and common purpose with the Soviet people. Whatever the character of the Soviet government, many Americans—including catholics who otherwise remained deeply suspicious of Moscow—now looked directly to the undoubted heroism, suffering, and sacrifice of millions of ordinary Soviets.[93] Yet that still does not explain how the Soviet Union, over time, came to be seen by a majority of Americans not just as an ally in a defensive war against fascism, but as a partner in reconstruction of the postwar order along democratic lines.

The leading cause of this crucial change in opinion was that the president himself set out to cultivate a false impression that Stalin endorsed Anglo-American ideals such as those laid out in the Atlantic Charter of August 1941. Signed by Roosevelt and Churchill at their meeting in Newfoundland, the Atlantic Charter laid out the common principles and aspirations of the United States and Britain, including reference to a postwar world in which "all the men in all the lands may live out their lives in freedom from fear and want."[94] Americans were also told the Soviets accepted that peace would be reconstructed according to Roosevelt's vaunted though vague "Four Freedoms": of speech and religion, and from want and fear (of aggression).[95] Just as he had earlier sought to mollify catholics by claiming that freedom of religion was coming in Russia, Roosevelt now played to the tendency of the general public to oversimplify by

Americanizing the objectives and interests of wartime allies, regardless of reality. He was not alone: other administration officials and prominent men associated with the president's policies likewise set out to mold and distort perceptions. In *Mission to Moscow*, a huge bestseller published in 1941 and later turned into a Hollywood film, Joseph C. Davies wrote:

The Russia of Lenin and Trotsky—the Russia of the Bolshevik Revolution—no longer exists.... [The] Russian people, the Soviet government, and the Soviet leaders are moved, basically, by altruistic concepts. It is their purpose to promote the brotherhood of man and to improve the lot of the common people. They wish to create a society in which men may live as equals, governed by ethical ideals. They are devoted to peace. They have made great sacrifices attempting to achieve those spiritual aspirations.[96]

Davies elsewhere proclaimed that Soviet communism was established "after all, on the same principle of the 'brotherhood of man' which Jesus preached." Far from disagreeing about the internal nature of Soviet society and the putative altruistic and spiritual motivations of Stalin, the president endorsed Davies' views privately as well as publicly.[97]

Roosevelt also fed a personal disposition in that direction with denial of negative assessments and advice coming from experts in the State Department, which he further circumvented by appointing several "special envoys"—including Joseph Davies once—to carry his views and policies directly to and from Stalin. Similarly, Roosevelt placed enormous stock in the importance of meeting personally with Stalin and Churchill to discuss the largest issues of conduct of the war and disposition of the victory and postwar settlement. He pressed for such meetings from the earliest days of U.S. involvement, believing them critical in spite of the fact that for the first two years he met stiff resistance, masquerading as preoccupation if not indifference, on the part of Stalin.[98] Bullitt, that gifted but most fickle amateur diplomatist (he resigned in disgust from both the Wilson and Roosevelt administrations), recalled that Roosevelt sought out such meetings and dismissed warnings about the character and ambitions of Stalin because, he reportedly said: "'I just have a hunch that Stalin is not that kind of man.... I think that if I give him everything I possibly can and ask nothing from him in return, *noblesse oblige*, he won't try to annex anything and will work with me for a world of democracy and peace.... It's my responsibility... and I'm going to play my hunch.'" That phrasing probably caricatures Roosevelt's statements. Nonetheless, there is truth in Bullitt's portrait of Roosevelt as overly confident of the role of personal diplomacy and vague statements of principle, and too optimistic that Stalin could be coaxed into postwar cooperation on a grand scale.[99]

Nor was the administration alone in its belief in the expediency of misinforming Americans about the Soviet Union's internal affairs. Other important political figures cooperated in the effort. After two days in Moscow in 1942, defeated Republican presidential nominee Wendel Wilkie told his Soviet hosts that the visit made him realize how unfairly their system had been represented to the American people. Ambassador William H. Standley reported back to Washington that Wilkie said to the Soviets:

> Enemies of the Soviet Union caused many Americans to believe that the Soviet Government did not permit freedom of religion . . . and was persecuting those who practiced religion. He now knew that the stories of religious persecution . . . were false. . . . It was now his understanding that the Soviet Government was opposed to priest craft [sic] as distinct from religion. He personally also had little respect for priest craft and . . . hoped that the American people could be brought to understand what the real situation was in the U.S.S.R.

Wilkie boasted that millions of Americans had confidence in him as "they knew that he was a man who frankly told the truth and the whole truth and that he could be trusted." Without blushing, he next stated that "if he saw something which he did not like or which [if] made known in the United States might create an unfavorable impression, he would remain silent to it."[100] He published *One World*, an account of his whirlwind global tour, the following year; it sold several million copies. In a chapter on his brief sojourn in Moscow he delivered a paean of praise for Stalin, whom he described as "a simple man, with no affectations or poses," adding, "Russia is an effective society. It works."[101] America's top political leadership thus presented to the public a vision of easy cooperation with a rapidly liberalizing Soviet ally, under the stern but wise leadership of "Uncle Joe" Stalin. There would be hell to pay when the truth came out about what Uncle was up to at home and in eastern Europe.

NOTES

1. See Joan Hoff-Wilson, *Ideology and Economics* (University of Missouri Press, 1974); and Thomas R. Maddux, *Years of Estrangement* (Florida State University Press, 1980): pp. 1–26 *passim*.

2. Robert Browder, *Origins of American-Soviet Diplomacy* (Princeton Uni-

versity Press, 1953): pp. 25–48; James K. Libbey, *American-Russian Economic Relations 1790s to 1990s* (Regina, 1989): pp. 47–69.

3. Browder, *Origins of American-Soviet Diplomacy*: pp. 69–70; and Henry L. Stimson (with McGeorge Bundy), *On Active Service in Peace and War* (Harper, 1947): p. 199. Stimson was not without his own predilection to moralism on the issue. See *FRUS, The Soviet Union, 1933–1939*: pp. 1–2.

4. Robert Kelly, head of the Russian Section, is criticized severely in John Richman, *The United States and the Soviet Union* (Camberleigh & Hall, 1980): pp. 31–41. Kelly's memorandum on the preconditions of recognition, which is more balanced than his image in the secondary literature might suggest, is in *FRUS, The Soviet Union*, 1933–1939: pp. 6–11; other State Department views also in *ibid.*, pp. 14–24.

5. Robert E. Herzstein, *Roosevelt and Hitler* (Paragon House, 1989): pp. 78–83.

6. Peter Filene, *Americans and the Soviet Experiment 1917–1933* (Harvard University Press): pp. 82–88; and George Q. Flynn, *American Catholics and the Roosevelt Presidency, 1932–36* (University of Kentucky Press, 1968): pp. 122–49.

7. Cordell Hull, *Memoirs of Cordell Hull*, Vol. II (Macmillan, 1948): p. 294.

8. Edward M. Bennett, *Recognition of Russia* (Blaisdell, 1970): pp. 93–94; and see *idem, Franklin Roosevelt and the Search for Security* (Scholarly Resources, 1985): pp. 11–12. It is unclear who first suggested making religious freedom a prerequisite of recognition. Hull claimed credit for himself in his *Memoirs*, Vol. II: p. 294; while Browder credits the President, *Origins of Soviet-American Diplomacy*: pp. 113–14.

9. On U.S. assessments of Soviet interest in recognition see *FRUS, The Soviet Union*, 1933–1939: pp. 12–13; also Edward M. Bennett, *Franklin Roosevelt and the Search for Security*: p. 16–17. On the negotiations *per se* see Donald G. Bishop, *The Roosevelt-Litvinov Agreements* (Syracuse University Press, 1965); and Richman, *The United States and the Soviet Union*: pp. 133–72.

10. Hull, *Memoirs*, Vol. II: p. 300.

11. Morgenthau's private notes on the meeting are cited in Edward M. Bennett, *Recognition of Russia* (Blaisdell, 1970): p. 116. Also, see *FRUS*, 1933, Vol. II: pp. 807 ff.

12. Hull, *Memoirs*, Vol. II: p. 301.

13. *FRUS*, 1933, Vol. II: pp. 807 ff.

14. *FRUS, The Soviet Union*, 1933–1939: pp. 25–37.

15. Quoted in Robert Dallek, *Roosevelt and American Foreign Policy, 1932–1945* (Oxford University Press, 1979): p. 81.

16. A slightly different version than the one given here is quoted in Frank Freidel, *Franklin D. Roosevelt* (Little, Brown, 1990): p. 175.

17. *FRUS, The Soviet Union*, 1933–1939: pp. 25–37.

18. *Ibid.*, pp. 25–29.

19. Bennett, *Search for Security*: pp. 18–20; Freidel, *Roosevelt*: p. 175.

20. The debt issue was capable of arousing private passions as much as fifty years later. See Letters section, *NYT*, November 15, 1990. It also gave rise to Supreme Court decisions that proved greatly important during the Bricker amendment controversy of the 1950s, discussed below; *United States v. Belmont*, 301 U.S. 324 (1937); and *United States v. Pink*, 315 U.S. 203 (1942).

21. Filene, *Americans and the Soviet Experiment*: pp. 271–76; and Maddux, *Years of Estrangement*: pp. 24–25.

22. Quoted in Bennett, *Recognition of Russia*: p. 127.

23. Hull, *Memoirs,* Vol II: p. 306; and see Richard Burns, "Cordell Hull and American Interwar Internationalism," in Norman Graebner, ed., *American Diplomacy, 1865–1945* (UPA, 1985): pp. 137–59.

24. Freidel, *Roosevelt*: pp. 172–73.

25. George F. Kennan, *Russia and the West Under Lenin and Stalin* (Little, Brown, 1961): p. 299.

26. The theme is handled with subtlety and sophistication in Bennett, *Search for Security*: pp. 25–68, *passim*; also Maddux, *Years of Estrangement*: pp. 27–43.

27. Libbey, *Economic Relations*: pp. 52–60; and *DRAR*: pp. 70–83. On the 1912 abrogation question see Cohen, "Abrogation of the Russo-American Treaty," pp. 3–41; Gary Dean Best, *To Free a People* (Greenwood, 1982): *op. cit.*; and the author's "The United States and Tsarist Anti-Semitism," *op. cit.*

28. Bullitt warned that trade would be erratic and politicized, via the clever device of editing a 100-year-old dispatch from the embassy illustrating the historic roots of Russian fear of foreign contacts and influence. *FRUS, The Soviet Union, 1933–1939*: pp. 291–96. Also see Browder, *Origins of Soviet-American Diplomacy*: pp. 176–96; and Vera Dean, "The Outlook for Soviet-American Trade," *Foreign Policy Reports* (August 1934): pp. 134–44.

29. *FRUS, The Soviet Union, 1933–1939*: pp. 242–43, 249–51; Department of State, *Press Releases* (July–December, 1935): pp. 147–52; and "Soviet Reply to the American Protest," *SDFP*, Vol. III: pp. 138–39.

30. *FRUS, The Soviet Union, 1933–39*: pp. 491–503, 535–36.

31. *Ibid.,* pp. 170–71.

32. See Bennett, *Search for Security*: pp. 25–45.

33. "Press Statement by Litvinov on the Breakdown of the Soviet-American Debt Negotiations," *SDFP*, Vol. III: pp. 117–18.

34. *FRUS, The Soviet Union, 1933–1939*: p. 155; Bennett, *Search for Security*: pp. 47–54.

35. See the summary of press coverage in *ibid.,* pp. 65–67. On the general subject of isolationism in this period, see Manfred Jonas, *Isolationism in America, 1935–1941* (Cornell University Press, 1966): *op. cit.*

36. *FRUS, The Soviet Union, 1933–1939*: pp. 193–223, *passim.*

37. Bennett, *Search for Security*: p. 72.

38. *Ibid.,* pp. 69–71; and Adam B. Ulam, *Expansion and Coexistence,* 2nd ed. (Holt, Rinehart and Winston, 1974): pp. 209–79.

39. An incisive discussion of the general effect of Roosevelt's personality on his foreign policy is Dallek, *Roosevelt*: pp. 3–20.

40. On the Ukrainian famine see Robert Conquest, *Harvest of Sorrow* (University of Alberta Press, 1986); especially pp. 308–21 for the weak western response.

41. *Congressional Record,* 73rd Cong., 2nd Sess., House Res. #39a.

42. *FRUS, The Soviet Union, 1933–1939*: p. 59.

43. Bullitt's sharp change of opinion during his time as ambassador is recounted in Beatrice Farnsworth, *William C. Bullitt and the Soviet Union* (University of Indiana Press, 1967): pp. 116–78.

44. Estimates vary of the number of Stalin's purge victims, but many millions probably died and certainly millions more were condemned to internal exile. The outstanding account, containing the latest Soviet figures, is Robert Conquest, *The Great Terror: A Reassessment* (Oxford University Press, 1990): pp. 484–89; also see Roy A. Medvedev, *Let History Judge* (Knopf, 1971); (Macmillan, 1968); and Aleksandr Solzhenitsyn, *The Gulag Archipeligo, 1918–1956* (Harper & Row, 1974–1978).

45. Quoted in Maddux, *Years of Estrangement*: p. 63. Joseph E. Davies' recollection of the purges and related matters is in his *Mission to Moscow* (Simon & Schuster, 1941): pp. 155–280.

46. Freidel, *Roosevelt*: p. 177. And see Richard Ullman, "The Davies Mission and United States-Soviet Relations, 1937–41," *World Politics* (January 1957): pp. 221–37; George F. Kennan, *Memoirs, 1925–1950* (Little, Brown, 1967): pp. 82–84; and Charles E. Bohlen, *Witness to History, 1929—969* (Norton, 1973): pp. 44-56.

47. Kennan, *Memoirs: 1925–1950*: p. 70.

48. For sharply critical appraisal of the so-called "Riga Axioms" (or the dominant State Department view of Russia formed prior to recognition), see Daniel Yergin, *Shattered Peace* (Houghton Mifflin, 1977): pp. 17–41.

49. Thomas A. Bailey, *America Faces Russia* (Cornell University Press, 1950): pp. 278–79; Wilson Miscamble, "Catholics and American Foreign Policy From McKinley to McCarthy," *Diplomatic History* (Summer 1980): pp. 234–36; and George Q. Flynn, *Roosevelt and Romanism* (Greenwood, 1976): pp. 29–62.

50. Les Adler and Thomas G. Paterson survey prewar opinion about Russia and Germany in "Red Fascism: The American Image of Totalitarianism," *American Historical Review* (April 1970): pp. 1048–49. Cf. the moderate rebuttal by Daniel M. Smith, "Authoritarianism and American Policy-Makers in Two World Wars," *Pacific Historical Review* (August 1974): pp. 303–23.

51. George Gallup, "American Institute of Public Opinion, Surveys, 1935–38," *Public Opinion Quarterly* (July 1938): p. 387.

52. An excellent discussion of this break with the State Department is Bennett, *Search for Security*: pp. 95–113.

53. Department of State, *Press Releases*, October 9, 1937: pp. 276–79. On the significance of the speech see Robert A. Divine, *Reluctant Belligerent*, 2nd ed. (John Wiley, 1979): pp. 47–53; and more generally, *idem, Illusion of Neutrality* (University of Chicago Press, 1962): pp. 200–228. Its reception by the Soviets is discussed in Bennett, *Search for Security*: pp. 96–101.

54. See Divine, *Reluctant Belligerent*: pp. 14–41; *idem, Illusion of Neutrality*: pp. 229–313; and the highly critical essay by Norman Graebner in his *America as a World Power* (Scholarly Resources, 1984): pp. 31–63.

55. Cases of arrest, denial of visas, obstruction of departure, and other such violations are reported in *FRUS, The Soviet Union, 1933–39*: pp. 708–27, 845–919; and *ibid.*, 1939, Vol. I: pp. 629–37.

56. Maddux, *Years of Estrangement*: pp. 85–89; Bennett, *Search for Security*: pp. 120–41.

57. A subtle treatment of this theme is Ulam, *Expansion and Coexistence*: pp. 257–73; also see Marcia L. Toepfer, "The Soviet Role in the Munich Crisis," *Diplomatic History* (Fall 1977): pp. 341–58.

58. *SDFP,* Vol. III: p. 290; and *FRUS, The Soviet Union,* 1933–1939: pp. 593–94.

59. Divine, *Illusion of Neutrality:* pp. 229–85.

60. *FRUS, The Soviet Union,* 1933–1939: pp. 731–37; and Bennett, *Search for Security:* pp. 165–73.

61. *FRUS, The Soviet Union,* 1933–1939: pp. 744–57.

62. Text in *SDFP,* Vol. III: pp. 356–61. On talks leading to the pact see Department of State, *Nazi-Soviet Relations, 1939–1941: Documents from the Archives of the German Foreign Office,* Raymond Sontag and James Beddie, eds. (GPO, 1948): pp. 1–91. Also see the previously unavailable Soviet documents published as "Around the Non-Aggression Pact," *International Affairs* (October 1989): pp. 81–116.

63. See Adler and Paterson, "Red Fascism," pp. 1050–51.

64. Flynn, *Roosevelt and Romanism:* pp. 141–42.

65. "American Institute of Public Opinion—Surveys, 1938–1939," *Public Opinion Quarterly* (October 1939): p. 596.

66. *Public Papers and Addresses of Franklin D. Roosevelt,* Samuel I. Rosenman, ed. (Macmillan, 1941), Vol. VIII: pp. 586–94; and Robert Sobel, *Origins of Interventionism* (Bookman Associates, 1960): pp. 91–94.

67. Alexander DeConde, *History of American Foreign Policy,* 3rd. ed., Vol. II (Scribner's, 1978): p. 584.

68. "Gallup and Fortune Polls," *Public Opinion Quarterly* (March and June, 1940): p. 102.

69. For a summary of press and other reactions to the attack on Finland see Maddux, *Years of Estrangement:* pp. 114–27; more generally see John C. Donovan, "Congressional Isolationists and the Roosevelt Foreign Policy," *World Politics* (April 1951): pp. 299–316.

70. Ulam suggests the public reaction in the United States so impressed Stalin it may have favorably affected the postwar settlement of Finland's special status. *Expansion and Coexistence:* pp. 290–91.

71. "Address to the American Youth Congress," February 10, 1940, *Roosevelt: Public Papers,* Vol. IX: p. 93; and see Dallek, *Roosevelt:* pp. 208–13, where this anecdote is placed in the broad context of Roosevelt's struggle with Congress and public opinion.

72. "Soviet-German Friendship and Frontier Treaty," September 28, 1939, *SDFP,* Vol. III: pp. 377–79. The Baltic States were formally annexed in August 1940. For newly released documents from the Soviet archives see "The Baltic Countries Join the Soviet Union," *International Affairs* (March 1990): pp. 134–42; and (April 1990): pp. 97–124.

73. Ralph B. Levering, *American Opinion and the Russian Alliance, 1939–1945* (University of North Carolina Press, 1976): pp. 15–38; and Maddux, *Years of Estrangement:* pp. 128–46.

74. Among numerous studies of this question see George Herring, *Aid to Russia, 1941–46* (Columbia University Press, 1974); Raymond Dawson, *Decision to Aid Russia, 1941* (University of North Carolina Press, 1959); and Robert Jones, *Roads To Russia* (Oklahoma State University Press, 1969).

75. Maddux, *Years of Estrangement:* p. 147; and see the superb study by Waldo

Heinrichs, *Threshold Of War* (Oxford University Press, 1988), especially pp. 92–117. Text of the Lend-Lease agreement in *DRAR*: pp. 86–88.

76. "Gallup and Fortune Polls," *Public Opinion Quarterly* (Spring 1942): pp. 152ff. A concise study of State Department attitudes is Maddux, *Years of Estrangement*: pp. 147–62.

77. "Annual Message to Congress," January 3, 1940, *Roosevelt: Public Papers*, Vol. VIII: p. 1.

78. Freidel, *Roosevelt*: pp. 360–62.

79. "Letter from President Roosevelt to His Holiness," September 3, 1941, *Wartime Correspondence Between President Roosevelt and Pope Pius XII*, Myron C. Taylor, ed. (Macmillan, 1947): pp. 61–62.

80. "Reply of His Holiness to President Roosevelt," September 20, 1941, *ibid.*; and Freidel, *Roosevelt*: p. 376. Also see George Q. Flynn, "Franklin Roosevelt and the Vatican," *Catholic Historical Review* (July 1972): pp. 171–94; and *idem, Roosevelt and Romanism*: pp. 165–69.

81. Press conference, September 30, 1941, *Roosevelt: Public Papers*, Vol. X: pp. 401–2. See Article 134 of the 1936 Soviet Constitution, in Ian Brownlie, *Basic Documents of Human Rights* (Clarendon, 1971): p. 27 [hereafter cited as *BDHR*].

82. *FRUS*, 1941, Vol. I: pp. 998–1000.

83. "Aid to Russia," October 13, 1941, *Roosevelt: Public Papers*, Vol. X: p. 418. On the protest against desecration of churches see *FRUS*, 1941, Vol. I: pp. 998–1000; and Flynn, *Roosevelt And Romanism*: pp. 159–60 for an account of catholic and editorial reaction.

84. *FRUS*, 1941, Vol. I: p. 832.

85. *Ibid.*, pp. 997–1005.

86. *Ibid.*, p. 1004. The *sic* refers to the fact that the United States refused to recognize Soviet annexation of eastern Poland, making the assertion that arrest and detention of Polish citizens was an "internal" Soviet affair odd in the extreme.

87. Flynn, *Roosevelt And Romanism*: p. 158.

88. Quoted in Dallek, *Roosevelt*: p. 336.

89. *Ibid.*, p. 298.

90. Levering, *American Opinion and the Russian Alliance*: pp. 39–62.

91. *Ibid.*, pp. 97–145; and see Warren B. Walsh's compilation of wartime polls, "What the American People Think of Russia," *Public Opinion Quarterly* (Winter 1944–1945): pp. 513–22.

92. George F. Kennan, "The U.S. and the Soviet Union," p. 678. Lending credence to this charge, in November 1939 Stalin blamed the war on Britain and France, claiming they had attacked Germany first after they "rudely rejected... Germany's peace proposals." "Statement on Allied Responsibility for the War," November 29, 1939, *SDFP*, Vol. III: p. 406.

93. On the brief wartime lull in catholic antipathy for the Soviet Union see Miscamble, "Catholics and American Foreign Policy," p. 236.

94. Draft and final versions, along with a firsthand account of the Charter's composition, in Winston Churchill, *The Grand Alliance*, Vol. III of his *The Second World War* (Bantam, 1962): pp. 366–80. Also, see the emphasis on freedom of religion in the 1940 Democratic platform, and explicitly on the Four Freedoms and Atlantic Charter in the 1944 platform, in *NPP*: pp. 388, 402–4.

95. "Four Freedoms Speech," January 6, 1941, *DAH*, Vol. I: p. 449; and see

Cathal Nolan's "Road to the Charter: America, Liberty and the Founding of the United Nations," *Paradigms* (Autumn 1989): pp. 26–29.

96. Davies, *Mission to Moscow*: p. 511. An unusually positive view of Davies' role is Elizabeth Maclean, "Joseph E. Davies and Soviet-American Relations, 1941–43," *Diplomatic History* (Winter 1980): pp. 73–93.

97. John L. Gaddis, *The United States and the Origins of the Cold War, 1941–1947* (Columbia University Press, 1972): pp. 35–36; quoted at p. 36.

98. See the extensive correspondence between FDR and Stalin touching on this issue, reproduced in *DRAR*: pp. 96–127.

99. William C. Bullitt, "How We Won the War and Lost the Peace," *Life Magazine*, August 30, 1948: p. 94; and see Edward Bennett, *Franklin D. Roosevelt and the Search for Victory* (Scholarly Resources, 1990): *passim*.

100. *FRUS*, 1942, Vol. III: pp. 645–46.

101. Wendel Wilkie, *One World* (Simon & Schuster, 1943): pp. 53, 83; also see his "We Must Work with Russia," *NYT Magazine*, January 17, 1943.

3 THE GREAT DIVIDE

Americans were quite unprepared for the steady turn for the worse Soviet-American relations began to take in 1944, as serious disputes hidden by the threat of nazism began to bubble to the surface with the approach of victory.[1] The necessity of cooperation with the Soviets in defeating the Axis did not erase vast differences in social systems, or preclude divisions over postwar territorial annexations or application of the principle of self-determination. These differences became pronounced in Allied counsels by mid–1943, when the tide of battle so turned that serious consideration could be given to shaping the postwar world. Wartime pressure to agree upon the peace raised a basic dilemma for the United States: how to satisfy the Soviet Union's postwar demands on eastern Europe given that country's huge contribution to the battle against Germany, without stirring up a domestic reaction through reversion to notions such as the balance of power and spheres of influence, publicly discredited by Roosevelt? The answer, or so it was thought in the White House, was to keep wartime commitments vague and at the level of general principle, deferring conflict over real solutions until after victory over the Axis.[2] Just as with the recognition agreements of 1933, Roosevelt resorted to declarations of the great principles of U.S. foreign policy—self-determination, peace without annexations, free trade, and respect for human rights. He did so primarily to cover the fact that he was unable to bridge differences with Stalin on crucial details of how those principles were to be applied in light of postwar Soviet power, interests, and ambitions. And he did so in the face of the fact that during the war shrewdly critical assessments of Soviet internal policy and predictions of its foreign policy objectives were made by the Moscow embassy staff and experienced State Department officers in Washington.[3]

MAINTAINING THE ALLIANCE

Right from the start of the Soviet-American alliance of World War II, Roosevelt was faced with tough decisions concerning defense of the principles enshrined in the Atlantic Charter from expansionist Soviet claims. The territories of most concern were the Baltic States and eastern Poland annexed under terms of the secret protocol to the Nazi-Soviet Pact, still neither acknowledged nor renounced by Moscow. As early as February 1942, the United States had to decide whether to continue recognition only of the Soviet Union's pre-Nazi-Soviet Pact, 1939 borders, or recognize its expanded 1941 borders. Secretary Hull took the lead on the issue, insisting on rejection of Stalin's proposal for a new secret protocol among the Allies; that was the signal awaited by some officials in the State Department to seek repatriation and better treatment for some 10,000 Latvians believed to have been deported to the Siberian gulag.[4]

The British, more mindful of their desperate needs of the moment, went ahead with a separate agreement recognizing an expanded Soviet Union. Sumner Welles bitterly opposed the treaty as encouraging more territorial demands. He then sought to ameliorate its more baneful consequences by obtaining a subagreement permitting free emigration for the Baltic populations, to avoid later accusations of the West "having negotiated a Baltic 'Munich'." However, the British balked at further territorial concessions regarding the more important Polish border, and the Soviets rejected the American proposal on free emigration.[5] Welles stated, with foresight, "We are getting ourselves into a dangerous position, both morally and realistically, and, I may add, in terms of American politics."[6]

The turning point in the wartime alliance diplomacy came in 1943, when the Allies began to anticipate victory and therefore to consider the shape of the peace to come. The change was both signaled and represented by the split that developed between the Soviet Union and the West over Soviet complicity in the massacre of thousands of Polish army officers found buried in the forests of Katyn. A subject of much controversy, Soviet responsibility for the Katyn massacre was finally established beyond doubt in 1989 and 1990.[7] At the time, however, Stalin and Foreign Affairs Commissar Vyacheslav Molotov used accusations of Soviet responsibility as a pretext to label the Polish government-in-exile in London as fascist, sever relations with it, and transfer recognition to Polish communists formed into a National Committee entirely beholden to Moscow for legitimacy, and awaiting only the advance of the Red Army to take power in Poland. This development and not the massacre *per se*, which Roosevelt and Churchill were prepared to play down, was the wedge Stalin drove between the Allies.

Roosevelt was greatly displeased with the turn of events, but without any effective leverage, he sought muted public criticism of the Soviets from the London Poles. He thought that if he could meet with Stalin face-to-face he could impress upon him the need for compromise, not least to placate the U.S. public, then being told the war would end in a peace based on Atlantic Charter principles such as self-determination.[8] He might have listened more closely to the report of a May 1943 conversation Welles had with Litvinov. Believing he might be purged, Litvinov spoke candidly about the failure of Stalin to understand the importance of U.S. public opinion. When Welles reiterated that the peace was to be built on the Four Freedoms in any case, Litvinov warned that Stalin would never accept such a view.[9]

The question of Polish self-determination continued to divide the Allies for the rest of the war, and beyond. The dispute worsened with the foreign ministers' conference held in Moscow in late summer 1943, where Hull insisted that free elections would have to be held in Poland and the Baltic States after the war's end, while offering territorial concessions, and Stalin stuck to the position that the London Poles were fascist dupes who could not be permitted to take power.[10] Roosevelt finally got his wish for a face-to-face meeting with Stalin at Teheran in November 1943. Yet instead of addressing the problem of Poland directly, he told Stalin that with millions of Polish voters in the United States, he was not prepared to discuss the Polish question in detail until after the 1944 elections.[11]

But Poland would not wait. The question flared openly as the Red Army halted just shy of Warsaw, while for 62 days in August and September 1944, the *Wehrmacht* and *Waffen SS* savagely crushed an uprising of the Polish resistance. Pleas to Stalin for relief to the antinazi forces in Warsaw were ignored; even a request for landing rights in Soviet-held territory so that Allied air forces might supply the Poles was denied.[12] Churchill asked Roosevelt to join him in a protest to Stalin, but Roosevelt declined.[13] The episode raised grave doubts among key advisors about the postwar wisdom and possibility, though not of course the wartime utility, of a policy of conciliation of Soviet demands.[14] The Roosevelt administration was from that point badly divided over what was to be done about Russia. More important, the Allies were already beginning to quarrel over the postwar settlement, with Hitler not yet dead. Papered over during wartime out of expedience and necessity, a crevasse of conflicting principles and interests had appeared that would eventually widen into the chasm of the Cold War. One last, great attempt had to be made to close the fissure, at Yalta.

Edward Bennett provides a succinct summary of the essential problem facing the U.S. delegation at Yalta: "Americans knew what Russia demanded [in eastern Europe], knew that the United States could not effectively resist Soviet objectives without war, and still insisted that the Russians surrender their claims." As for tactics: "Roosevelt decided that at Yalta he would have to persuade Stalin that the United Nations could replace spheres of influence in guaranteeing Soviet security."[15] Put another way, should the West, as Kennan suggested, have written off the Baltic States and Poland in order to avoid an unwinnable contest for control of those territories?[16] Perhaps, from a *realpolitik* point of view. But that proposition went too far in conceding Soviet claims—there was, after all, a major difference between accepting a legitimate Soviet sphere of influence in bordering states and acceding to a sphere of domination and even occupation.

Furthermore, it was only superficially realistic, for it failed to consider the very real factor of U.S. (and western) public opinion. If faced with yet another postwar repudiation of the principles for which the public thought the war was being fought, the risk would have been run of a return to isolationism deeply threatening to U.S. and western interests over the long term.[17] Lastly, writing off eastern Europe underestimated the possibilities of economic diplomacy, given the Soviet need for reconstruction assistance. A tougher line might thus have been taken earlier, as Ambassador to Moscow W. Averell Harriman suggested, to bring home the point that Soviet security could not be had at the expense of the security of others, or security through the UN. However, the real problem was that although Roosevelt would not concede his principles, he also chose not to support them with stronger measures. He kept instead to his old habit of making vague commitments, such as in the Declaration on Liberated Europe, leaving details to later and to others.[18] That device served him as a substitute for facing tough decisions about the conflicts of interests then emerging, and about realistic limits to American power and influence in the Soviet neighborhood. Key issues thus were solved on the ground, over the next few months and years.

AFTER YALTA

There is not room here to review the origins of later Cold War disputes about the Yalta conference.[19] Suffice it to say that within weeks of the meeting in the Crimea, it became apparent that the Soviets upheld a much different interpretation of the main Yalta agreements from that of the western Allies.[20] By March 1945, it was clear that a Soviet takeover of Rumania was well underway, and that Stalin had no intention of permitting the Polish government-in-exile in London to displace a pro-Soviet regime established at Lublin in 1944.[21] The dispute intensified following the defeat of Germany in May 1945. The western Allies, drawing on what they thought were the central lessons of the collapse of the Versailles peace settlement, supported self-determination for eastern Europe and limits on reparations from Germany. The Soviets, however, considered the establishment of "friendly states" along their borders as essential to their national security, and reparations from Germany as required for reconstruction of their war-ravaged economy. As John L. Gaddis frames the problem:

The Russians did not immediately impose communist regimes on all the countries they occupied after the war.... But the Soviet leader failed to make the limited nature of his objectives clear. Having just defeated one dictator thought to have had unlimited ambitions, Americans could not regard the emergence of another without the strongest feelings of apprehension and anger.[22]

Similarly, Adam Ulam writes of Stalin: "The man in the Kremlin was not a Hitler, but was, at least insofar as foreign policy was concerned, a prudent statesman, carefully calculating the pros and cons of every Soviet venture."[23] Nonetheless, Churchill broached to the U.S. public in his famous "iron curtain" speech given at Fulton, Missouri in March 1946 a hardening western attitude toward compromise with Stalin's Russia.[24] Afterwards, events moved very quickly, as the decision was taken rapidly to rehabilitate the defeated Axis powers in order to preserve them from falling into the Soviet orbit.

After the war, Europe was economically prostrate. In consequence, even though the Soviet Union may have had no interest in military expansion, it appeared to a number of key officials that the stage was set for a Soviet takeover of vital western European countries by proxy communist parties.[25] Nor did the Soviets discourage the use of force by Greek communists, or abjure from threats against Iran and Turkey. The balance of power, only recently restored at great cost in lives and matériel, hence seemed poised to shift once again into hands hostile to America's interests.

The crisis came to a head in February 1947, when Britain indicated that it no longer could offer protection to the eastern Mediterranean, traditionally considered within its sphere of influence. President Harry S Truman therefore announced that the United States was assuming Britain's responsibility for the defense of Greece and Turkey. In the process he elevated ideological conflict to the central place in American-Soviet relations, and made a sweeping commitment to help "free peoples to maintain their free institutions and their national integrity against aggressive movements that seek to impose on them totalitarian regimes."[26] In July 1947, *Foreign Affairs* magazine published Kennan's famous "X" article, identifying the Soviet Union as the central challenge to global security and proposing a strategy of flexible containment to forestall a shift in the balance of power out of America's favor.[27] The installation of a communist government in Czechoslovakia in February 1948, and the Berlin blockade that same year, seriously aggravated the conflict.[28]

With *de facto* division of Germany and the creation of NATO in 1949, equilibrium returned to Europe. However, this new balance was understood not in limited classical terms, but as a global ideological and geopolitical contest. Consequently, American strategists soon perceived peripheral interests as vital, which helped lead to application of great means (notably in Korea and Indochina) to counter minor, not mortal, perils.

Still, initial hardening of the Truman administration's attitude toward Stalin's Russia principally resulted from *realpolitik* considerations. Simply, it was prudent to be fearful of the possible domination of the continent by the Soviet Union, the only surviving great power capable of establishing hegemony over Europe. But there was an important, supporting reason why that worm in the mind burrowed deep during the Cold War: the response was also conditioned by the old notion that lasting peace must ultimately be built on a foundation of liberty and free trade. Melvyn Leffler nicely sums up this aspect of U.S. policy:

At the end of World War II, the United States possessed incomparably more power than any other nation. Aware of this, U.S. officials hoped to sustain the wartime alliance, transform vanquished enemies into democratic and capitalist friends, and persuade imperial allies ... to pursue orderly de-colonization policies on the periphery. If friends as well as foes could be convinced of the beneficent character of a liberal capitalist multilateral order, U.S. officials believed the world could enter a new era of peace and harmony.[29]

There was a darker side to this notion and national ambition, however: policymakers might be tempted to create a manichean image of both the contest and the enemy for the sake of arousing an otherwise naturally isolationist public to acceptance of great sacrifice and the struggle that lay ahead.

For instance, in a memorandum to Truman from Henry L. Stimson (written at Potsdam in July 1945) the president was advised that "no permanently safe international relations can be established between two such fundamentally different national systems." Stimson held out hope that the Soviets might be persuaded to liberalize their domestic regime in the near future, if encouraged by the prospect of a share in America's nuclear secret. He assured Truman: "That something can be accomplished is not an idle dream. STALIN [sic] has shown an indication of his appreciation of our system of freedom by his proposal of a free constitution to be established among the Soviets."[30] Privately, Stimson conjectured that the problem "boiled down to the possibility of getting the Russians to see that the real basis of the evil was the absence of freedom of speech in [sic] their regime and the iron-bound rule of the OGPU."[31] At first Truman agreed with Stimson's assessment that freedom and peacetime cooperation might be prised out of Russia, though he later would come to see the Soviets as in part acting out age-old tsarist ambitions of conquest and expansion.[32] After all the "blood, sweat, and tears" of World War II, hope died as hard among top officials in the United States as among democratic populations at large, that reasonable men in Moscow and the West might together construct a just, democratic, and lasting peace.[33]

Others who played important roles in shaping postwar policy, such as Ambassador Harriman, Assistant Secretary of War John J. McCloy, and career officers in the embassy in Moscow, were profoundly pessimistic about the usefulness or success of Stimson's idea of somehow enticing Stalin into domestic liberalization.[34] They helped move Truman from the qualified optimism of Stimson's memorandum to more dire conclusions about the Soviet Union. These advisors recognized that Stalin was moving past creation of an open sphere of influence acceptable to the West, to imposition of an exclusive sphere of domination inherently threatening to American interests, as well as a repudiation of great power cooperation on peace and security.[35] Yet as shown below, even such hard-headed men as Harriman, McCloy, Bohlen, and Kennan made the reassessment partly out of a reawakened repugnance for Soviet internal practices. Furthermore, that adverse reaction to mistreatment of individuals clearly was incurred by Soviet behavior, perhaps more so than by the murky motivations surrounding expansion into eastern Europe. In short, despite protestations of realism at the highest levels of policy-making, human rights concerns were edging their way into calculations of policy toward the Soviet Union, via a perceived connection between internal repression and the likelihood of external aggression.

Particularly important in eroding American goodwill was Moscow's unbending disregard for the rights and welfare of American citizens trapped by the war in Soviet-controlled territory. This longstanding controversy over mistreatment of Americans in Russia erupted again just as the war in Europe drew to a close. This time, it had a three-part focus: repatriation of American and other Allied POWs; reunification of Soviet wives with their American husbands; and Soviet refusal to permit some 2,000 U.S. citizens to depart Russia, and condemnation of several hundred to forced labor camps in the gulag. Such disputes were of course in themselves marginal to the dominant conflicts of the Cold War. Yet they were influential in confirming the predilection of policy-makers and the general public to regard the Soviet Union as akin to Nazi Germany, both in terms of its internal character and its approach to foreign policy. In this way, the potential for Soviet aggression came to be seen as deriving in part from the absence of majority, democratic restraints on the will to power of the ruling minority in Moscow. In other words, through expansive internationalism America's own security came to be seen as ultimately indivisible from the cause of liberty in the lands dominated by Moscow. This idea would powerfully grip the public, which never conceived the notion in such articulate terms but nonetheless clung to a perception that democracy pacified; that plain folks everywhere always opposed war, which was the folly of the wicked and the few. That image helped sustain support for the Cold War consensus for two decades, reinforcing foreign policy fears of another Munich potentially lurking behind each proposed compromise.[36]

REPATRIATION

After mid-1944, advancing Soviet armies began to overrun camps crowded with Allied POWs abandoned by the retreating Germans. Similarly, American and Allied armies on the western front liberated hundreds of thousands of Soviet prisoners. The senior U.S. military officer in Russia, Major General John R. Deane, estimated the total of Russian POWs in German hands at three to five million, and the total of American POWs at about 75,000.[37] At the end of August, Harriman proposed to the Soviets that the Allies agree on mechanisms for repatriation of liberated prisoners. No reply was received until November, when Molotov accepted "in principle" the U.S. proposal. But just one month later Molotov shifted abruptly, refusing access to Allied POWs and accusing the United States of mistreating Soviet prisoners.[38] A lengthy, detailed, and conciliatory reply was sent to Molotov by Acting Secretary of State Joseph Grew. It had no effect.[39] Harriman concluded that this refusal to cooperate in repatriation, although vastly greater numbers of Soviet POWs were involved, sprang from a desire to keep western observers out of Poland (where most liberated POW camps were located) until the pro-Soviet Lublin regime was firmly established. Deane shared this view that Soviet leaders were more concerned with their position in Poland than good relations with the West, and cared least of all about the millions of Soviet POWs suffering from delayed repatriation.[40]

One scholar suggests that in addition to protecting interests in Poland, the Soviets may have been humiliated over the presence among their POWs liberated in the West of tens of thousands captured wearing German uniforms, most of whom expressed great fear at the prospect of being repatriated.[41] Most of these soldiers belonged to the "Armed Forces of the Committee for the Liberation of the Peoples of Russia," an anti-Soviet Russian army sponsored and equipped by the Germans and led by a former Soviet Lt. General, Andrey A. Vlasov (himself taken prisoner by Germany in 1942).[42] Numerous ordinary Soviet POWs also were fearful about returning, and with good reason. Mark Elliot has pointed out that under Soviet law, "the penalty for premeditated surrender into captivity not necessitated by combat conditions is death by shooting," while Decree #270 (1942) declared "a prisoner captured alive by the enemy is *ipso facto* a traitor."[43] Even so, the first concern of western governments was to facilitate the return home of their own nationals. Hence it was agreed at Yalta to facilitate repatriation of all POWs and displaced persons.[44]

However, the Soviets remained intent on installing a friendly (communist) regime in Poland. They had in fact for months before Yalta conducted mass transfers of Polish and German civilian populations out of territories east of the Oder-Neisse line that they intended to annex, whatever the West said. That had been done without the agreement of Roosevelt or Churchill.[45] It is therefore not surprising that despite the agreement on POWs, Stalin adamantly refused permission to U.S. contact teams to visit camps on Polish territory, and also refused Roosevelt's request for landing rights to facilitate air evacuation of liberated POWs. Only after repeated, insistent protests by Harriman and Deane did Moscow finally allow a single U.S. officer and one doctor into Poland, and then rendered their mercy mission useless by ordering them not to leave the city of Lublin.[46]

Throughout the closing months of the war, U.S. public opinion continued to be favorable toward the Soviet Union.[47] But for many Americans, in particular catholics, the treatment accorded Poland and the Baltic States was a test case of the promises made in the Atlantic Charter, and of Roosevelt's whole approach to the Soviet Union.[48] The delay in repatriation of U.S. POWs several months after the Red Army had liberated them and Poland thus led to growing public concern. Also, Harriman appealed to Roosevelt to intervene personally, as he and Deane had gotten nowhere on the issue. On March 4th, Roosevelt complied, sending an urgent personal appeal to Stalin requesting that a relief airlift be allowed to operate out of Poland. He wrote: "I regard this request to be of the greatest importance not only for humanitarian reasons but also by reason of the intense interest of the American public in the welfare of our ex-prisoners of war and stranded aircraft crews." Stalin replied that all that was necessary was being done for Allied POWs, and declined permission for an airlift on the grounds that "on the territory of Poland and in other places liberated by the Red Army, there are no groups of American prisoners of war, as all of them, except the single sick persons who are in the hospitals, have been sent to the gathering point in Odessa."[49]

Harriman had personal knowledge of the real situation because three American officers had somehow managed to make it to the embassy in Moscow, to report that hundreds of U.S. POWs had indeed been left behind in Poland, and were receiving little to no help from the Red Army (the figure included at least thirty Americans hospitalized in the town of Wegheim). He cabled Roosevelt on March 8th that "there appear to be hundreds of our prisoners wandering about Poland trying to locate American contact officers for protection."[50] When he learned of Stalin's earlier reply to the President he was enraged, identifying the statement that all American POWs were safely in Odessa as a lie. He expressed satisfaction with arrangements for those few who had made it on their own to Odessa, but added:

I am outraged ... that the Soviet Government has declined to carry out the agreement signed at Yalta in its other aspects, namely, that our contact officers be permitted to go immediately to points where our prisoners are first collected, to evacuate our prisoners, particularly the sick, in our own airplanes, or to send our supplies to points other than Odessa, which is 1,000 miles from [the] point of liberation.[51]

Roosevelt made another direct appeal to Stalin, this one more blunt, on March 17th. It was met with a second refusal of access, in the course of which the Marshal made the breathtakingly brazen claim that, "if it concerned me personally I would be ready to give way even to the detriment of my own interests," but his commanders did "not want to have around odd officers [sic] who ... need looking after" and who might distract from the important business of war. Adding insult to injury, he repeated Molotov's accusation that Soviet POWs were being abused in camps in the United States.[52]

On March 24th, Harriman—even more infuriated than before, if that was possible—cabled Washington:

Stalin's statement that our liberated prisoners are in Soviet camps under good conditions is far from the truth.... Hardships undergone have been inexcusable. No effort whatsoever has been made by the Red Army to do anything until our men drifted into camps... some hundreds of miles from points of liberation and our men would have starved if it had not been for the generosity and hospitality of the Polish people.[53]

He also now informed Roosevelt of what he believed was the real reason for Soviet delaying tactics: Molotov expected U.S. recognition of the Lublin government as a *quid pro quo* for access to POWs. He advanced the judgment that, "the Soviet Government is trying to use our liberated prisoners of war as a club to induce us to give increased prestige to the Provisional Polish Government by dealing with it in this connection as the Soviets are doing in other cases." He later told Roosevelt, with some acuity, "when the story of the treatment accorded our liberated prisoners by the Russians leaks out I cannot help but feel that there will be great and lasting resentment on the part of the American people."[54] Interestingly, this baleful experience was a central factor in hardening Harriman's view of how to deal with the Soviet Union.[55] Similarly, General Deane reported in his memoirs, "If, in my sketchy account of the prisoner-of-war episode, I have given the impression that I plumbed the depths of despair, I can only say that that impression is correct."[56] Through a blind rigidity at the top, the Soviets were rapidly throwing away the goodwill earned in the West by their enormous war effort.

On the Soviet side, a complaint of some merit was that the United States did not immediately repatriate all those claimed by Moscow as its POWs. On May 3rd, Joseph Grew explained to the Soviet *chargé* in Washington why the U.S. military had not repatriated those Soviets captured in German uniform:

All persons who claim Soviet nationality captured by the American armed forces while serving as members of the German armed forces in German uniforms are transferred to the Soviet authorities for repatriation to the Soviet Union. However, this Government must reserve the right to retain in a prisoner of war status those persons who themselves of their own accord insist upon being treated as German prisoners of war thereby bringing themselves within the scope of the Geneva Prisoners of War Convention.

In fact, Grew's main concern was not fastidious respect for the law of war. He admitted that the real reason for refusing to force Soviets captured in German uniform to return to Russia was fear for the safety of American POWs—the nazis had warned they would retaliate against American prisoners still in their hands.[57] However, Germany signed an unconditional surrender, on all fronts, on May 7th, 1945; hostilities formally ended at midnight on May 8th.[58] Thus, within a week of Grew's note, German surrender eliminated fear of retaliation by the nazis. Exchanges of POWs and other displaced persons of all nationalities speeded up immediately, directly through Germany. This quickened the pace of repatriation and soon dissipated concerns about access to POW camps in Soviet-held areas. But it left the Americans in a quandary about what to do with Soviet POWs who did not want to go home.

Now it was the Soviets who demanded strict adherence to the Yalta

Agreement on repatriation, a changed situation that presented the western Allies with something of a moral dilemma: namely, were those POWs who did not wish to return to the Soviet Union to be forced to do so? The sharpness of the question was not so clear to contemporaries as it might appear in hindsight. After all, the Soviets were allies in the savage war with Germany that had just ended, and they were to join in the war against Japan (as agreed at Yalta) within months. Furthermore, some of those captured in German uniform actually had inflicted U.S. casualties, and others had voluntarily collaborated with the nazis. The initial response was therefore unambiguous. Five days after the German surrender, Grew wrote Secretary of the Navy James Forrestal that, as Germany no longer could take retaliatory action against American POWs, it was advisable to hand all Soviet POWs over to Moscow's control. Within a month, Grew dropped all reference to the notion that Soviet POWs captured in enemy uniform should be treated strictly according to the Geneva Conventions, describing such persons instead as "traitors to one of our allies" who "should be turned over to the appropriate Soviet authorities."[59]

In the meantime, the State-War-Navy Coordinating Committee had made an *ad hoc* decision to forcibly repatriate a small group of Soviet nationals who claimed to be German POWs, and therefore to enjoy the protections of the Geneva Convention.[60] That decision was a violation of Article 3 of the 1929 Convention, which defined POWs as, "Members of armed forces of the Parties to the conflict, including members of militias *and voluntary corps* which are regularly constituted"; and Article 11, which stipulated that "prisoners of war cannot be transferred by the Detaining Power to any Power not party to the Convention." Vlasov's army certainly had been a regularly constituted enemy unit, and despite American efforts in 1941, the Soviet Union had refused to become party to the 1929 Convention, partly owing to the refusal of the Swiss government to extend diplomatic recognition.[61] Moral unease may have been reflected in the Committee deferring a decision on a proposal by the Secretary of State to approve forced repatriation in all cases. Nevertheless, it appears that its *ad hoc* decision was read as a precedent for a general policy of involuntary repatriation.[62]

Events moved even faster in the field. Representatives from the Supreme Headquarters, Allied Expeditionary Force (SHAEF) and the Supreme Command of the Red Army met on May 23rd, at Halle, Germany, to arrange repatriation of all Allied nationals. They gave the problem a high priority in allocation of transport, and a plan was agreed to whereby some 30,000 Soviet citizens per day were delivered to the Russian occupation zone in Germany. General Dwight Eisenhower, then Supreme Commander of SHAEF, reported (conservatively) to Washington that at least one million displaced Soviets awaited repatriation in the western zones of Germany.[63]

Three weeks later, Harriman dispatched a grim cable from Moscow. He reminded Secretary of State James F. Byrnes that the Soviet Union was not a signatory of the Geneva Convention, and that Soviet authorities had "never been at pains to disguise their scornful attitude toward Soviet troops taken prisoner" by Germany. He added:

> It is known that repatriates are met at ports of entry by police guard and marched off with little ceremony to unknown destinations. Trainloads of repatriates are passing through Moscow and continuing east.... Given [the] Soviet attitude towards surrender, it is probable that prisoners are assumed guilty of desertion unless they can produce convincing evidence of mitigating circumstances. Those found serving in German uniform will probably be charged with anti-state activity. It is quite possible that persons considered guilty of deliberate desertion or anti-state activity are being shot.... [The great] bulk of repatriates . . . are probably being placed in forced labor battalions.[64]

Meanwhile, in Europe and the United States, the new policy of forced repatriation led hundreds of Soviet POWs to commit suicide, singly or *en masse*. In one camp in Austria, 134 Soviets committed suicide over two days in June, after which the British compelled the remaining 30,000 to entrain for Moscow. At Fort Dix, New Jersey, an attempted mass suicide by 154 Soviet POWs was interrupted only by Military Police tear-gassing the camp; three prisoners hanged themselves, the remainder then were handed over to Soviet authorities.[65] By July, the State Department firmly decided that all members of Vlasov's army be returned to the Soviet Union. The Combined Chiefs of Staff arrived at an independent decision to repatriate some fifty thousand Cossacks, who also had fought with Germany. Ironically, the level of violence required of the Allies to force tough veterans of the eastern front to entrain for Russia, in compliance with Soviet wishes, formed the basis of Moscow's propaganda charges that the United States was mistreating Soviet POWs and frustrating their desire to return home.[66]

Notwithstanding Harriman's warning about the probable fate of repatriates, and in spite of the unpleasant events at Fort Dix and elsewhere, it is difficult to see how the United States (or Britain) could have done other in mid–1945 than continue to ship Soviet POWs to Russia, when necessary, involuntarily.[67] Added to the consideration that those captured in German uniform might rightly be regarded as quislings, the need to bring Russia into the war against Japan, with the expected consequent reduction in American casualties, was overwhelming.

On somewhat more shaky moral ground was a secondary consideration that repatriation usefully demonstrated a continuing willingness to cooperate with Stalin.[68] The Yalta Agreement pertaining to repatriation of all Allied nationals was thus upheld at the Potsdam conference (July 17th–August 2nd), and involuntary POW repatriations continued during the summer of 1945.[69] The United States accepted an obligation to repatriate *all* displaced Soviets, not just POWs. However, profound moral as well as legal disagreement with Moscow existed over whether the term "Soviet citizen" encompassed refugees from the Baltic States and eastern Poland. Moscow claimed former residents of those territories as Soviet citizens. But the United States did not recognize Soviet claims to the annexed areas, and upheld a policy (decided by the Joint Chiefs of Staff) whereby those who had lived outside the 1939 borders "cannot be repatriated to the Soviet Union unless they affirmatively claim Soviet citizenship."[70] All other Soviet citizens, defined as those who had been domiciled within the Union's pre-annexation 1939 frontiers, were to be repatriated, using force when necessary.[71] What had begun as an understandable decision to forcibly return POWs who had fought with the Germans was extended to include ordinary POWs and even innocent civilians. Moral distinctions were becoming blurred by an expediency born of wartime ambiguities, as well as postwar hopes for continuing great power cooperation.

While the policy of involuntary repatriation was understood as a political, and perhaps even military, necessity by senior officials in Washington and London, it was not in fact a legal obligation. Harriman wrote after the war that the possibility that hundreds of thousands of Soviets would refuse to return home never occurred at the time to those who negotiated the Yalta Agreement on repatriation. He added:

Not a word in the agreement required the American and British commanders to forcibly repatriate Soviet citizens against their will. But the Russians insisted upon that cruel interpretation and the Western Allies went along... shipping trainload after trainload of former prisoners and slave laborers, including women and children, back to Russia.[72]

This policy quickly incurred intense moral anxiety among those on the ground charged with implementation. In August 1945, Alexander C. Kirk, Political Advisor to SHAEF, wrote to Byrnes to ask for guidance. He explained that petitions were arriving from Soviet POWs facing repatriation (another had been sent to the Red Cross) in which they claimed the status of "political refugees" and begged in the "name of humanity" not to be returned to Russia. Byrnes simply instructed Kirk to screen them to ensure none were Poles or from the Baltic States, and then to repatriate them.[73]

Walter Bedell Smith, later Ambassador to the Soviet Union but in 1945 working in Germany, was less than candid in his memoirs when he wrote that on "one occasion" an overzealous unit had exceeded its mandate by forcibly entraining Soviet POWs. And it was sheer dishonesty when he wrote: "We immediately issued instructions that we would not forcibly repatriate anybody except actual war criminals, since it was entirely contrary to our principles to force the return to the Soviet Union of any of these people."[74] In fact, this *was* U.S. policy. Referring to the same incident as Smith, Robert Murphy, the Political Advisor for Germany, wrote Byrnes that:

In applying the policy of forcible repatriation there has been a number of unpleasant incidents involving violence such as the forcible seizure by our troops of 100 Russians at a church service resulting in serious injuries on both sides. A considerable number of suicides by Russians... are also taking place. Please clarify my understanding of our policy. Did we at Yalta assume the specific obligation to return these Russians by force if necessary?

Byrnes reiterated to Murphy that where necessary, forced repatriation was official policy, cabling: "For your confidential information, [the State] Department has been anxious in handling these cases to avoid giving Soviet authorities any pretext for delaying return of American POWs of Japanese now in Soviet occupied zones, particularly in Manchuria."[75] Questions arose about this issue in 1953 during hearings on the nomination of Charles Bohlen as Ambassador to the Soviet Union. Bohlen was asked by Senator Homer Ferguson: "How do you account for the fact that we did not sense what was going on and refuse to carry out an agreement that not only enslaved these people but took their lives?" Bohlen answered: "There were 60,000

American prisoners... under the control of the Red Army, and the purpose was to get those prisoners back."[76] Harriman too, regretfully confirmed that the decision to use force was taken out of fear of retaliation against American POWs liberated by the Red Army.[77] In the confused circumstances of 1945, moral obligations did not extend much past one's own people or immediate purposes, at the highest policy-levels.

However, Allied soldiers began to object to the policy. Letters home and visits to the front by congressmen, eager to see what their wartime voting records had done to Germany, led to a groundswell of opposition. Eisenhower, responding to concerns from within the ranks, requested a reconsideration of policy from the State Department.[78] In late September, Acting Secretary of State Dean Acheson advised Byrnes that the United States was required only to facilitate, not compel, repatriation; and that public opposition was growing and threatening other, more important Yalta agreements. The State-War-Navy Committee deliberated for several months, while the repatriations continued to clear up messy facts on the ground. In December, it too concluded that the United States was not bound to repatriate involuntarily any ordinary Soviet citizens, but said that the use of force should continue with regard to POWs captured in German uniform or who had deserted from the Red Army.[79] This policy was phrased succinctly, if somewhat crudely, by Elbridge Durbrow, Chief of the East European Affairs Division in the State Department. He wrote: "The United States Government... does not consider that Soviet citizens who are not traitors, deserters, renegades or quislings should be forced to return to the Soviet Union against their will."[80] It was only in mid-1947 that Secretary of State George C. Marshall decided that not even those who collaborated with Nazi Germany should be repatriated to Soviet bloc countries against their will. Forced repatriation went against the U.S. tradition of granting political asylum, he belatedly declared, and the practice finally was brought to an end.[81]

SOVIET WIVES

A second case of disrespect for human rights that adversely influenced western perceptions of the Soviet Union was the refusal to grant exit visas to Soviet wives of foreign citizens. The Soviets had long refused to grant exit visas to women married to foreigners, a practice that had at times seriously troubled relations with Washington before World War II.[82] During the war the matter was of course handled very quietly, in accordance with Roosevelt's overall effort to soften the American public's image of repression in Russia. Nevertheless, the plight of women separated from their American husbands and families remained an irritant even during the wartime alliance. In particular, it reinforced the already strong distaste for the Soviet Union's internal system extant among officers at the Moscow embassy and within the State Department.[83]

After the fall of Germany, public pressure built behind a demand for reunification of American husbands—many of whom had served on convoys delivering supplies essential to the Soviet war effort, through Archangel and Murmansk—with their Soviet wives and children. The State Department received multiple requests from members of Congress for intercession on behalf of these divided families; powerful administration figures such as Secretary of the Navy James Forrestal also pressed for action.[84] Repeated appeals to the Soviets produced no positive results. Public puzzlement, then frustration and anger, mounted at the delay in family reunification. Byrnes therefore personally emphasized to Molotov the need for a resolution when the two met at the Moscow Conference of Foreign Ministers in December 1945. But not even that direct, high-level appeal effected a favorable settlement, and the dispute dragged on through 1946.[85]

In fact, just over a year after Byrnes' meeting with Molotov, matters grew much worse. In February 1947, the Soviet Union decreed it a crime for a citizen to marry a foreigner. Furthermore, Stalin told the British Foreign Secretary, Ernest Bevin, that none of the hundreds of Soviet women married to foreigners prior to promulgation of the new decree would be permitted to leave. U.S. Ambassador Walter Bedell Smith asked Andrey Vyshinsky, Soviet Assistant Commissar for Foreign Affairs, for an explanation of those remarks. Smith then reported to Washington that Vyshinsky said: "[the] Soviet Government considers that every Soviet citizen has an obligation to discharge to the state and that no citizen would be permitted to shirk that obligation by extirpating himself [herself?] and going abroad."[86]

The hardened Soviet position was not adopted without adverse effect on important American opinion. Smith attached an angry commentary to his report, arguing that prohibition of marriage to foreigners sharply illuminated Soviet totalitarianism and revealed an attitude on the part of the Russian state toward its citizens "reminiscent of [the] relation between feudal lord and serfs."[87] Embassy and State Department officials made repeated remonstrances on individual cases, each utterly rebuffed. Then, convinced that quiet diplomacy no longer offered any chance of a successful resolution to the dispute over exit visas, in December 1948, the United States placed the question of separated spouses before the U.N. General Assembly. That body adopted a resolution calling upon the Soviets to withdraw measures taken against the wives of foreign citizens.[88] Far from aiding a solution, such public diplomacy may have further entrenched Soviet unwillingness to facilitate reunification of families.

The Moscow embassy staff urged that future diplomacy on the issue remain private. They advised Washington, "vigorous Soviet reaction to the airing of the question of the Soviet wives... underlines the characteristic unwillingness of the Soviet Government to admit an error or retract a policy once such decision or policy has become the subject of public controversy."[89] These punitive measures against the Soviet wives of foreigners lasted until Stalin's death in 1953, causing one leading student of Soviet foreign policy to remark, "the inhumanity of [the practice] is less striking than its incredible pettiness."[90] Yet pettiness too can impress, especially when it is so cruel and capricious. And during critical years of the early Cold War, leading policy-makers were impressed by the foolish intransigence, as much as the cruelty, of refusing to allow the wives of some 350 Americans to leave Russia.[91]

AMERICANS IN THE GULAG

Even more damaging to American-Soviet relations was severe mistreatment of U.S. citizens, including imprisonment of several hundred under conditions of forced labor. The problem of ensuring respect for the rights of Americans in Russia, especially those of dual nationality, was one of long standing. It had been thought solved with the 1933 recognition agreement guaranteeing legal rights and protections to U.S. citizens. However, that agreement had proved of little value when Stalin moved against foreigners during the purges of the late 1930s in a bid to insulate the Soviet population from outside contacts and influences. So serious and extensive was the problem, the "foreign cell" in a prison in Minsk was sometimes called the *Amerikanka*.[92] Numerous protests were lodged over Soviet mistreatment of naturalized Americans, ranging from refusal of embassy access, to imprisonment, to forced labor and possible execution.[93] Of course, given the overriding importance of the war effort, neither before nor after Pearl Harbor were U.S. protests linked to other aspects of the relationship, such as Lend-Lease.

The main case prior to formation of the Grand Alliance involved some 500 American dual citizens present in eastern Poland when that territory was occupied by the Red Army in 1939. The Soviets consistently blocked efforts by the Polish-Americans to communicate with U.S. authorities and stopped them from traveling to Moscow to confirm their citizenship claims. (In contrast, the nazis permitted Americans to leave occupied western Poland.) Washington told Moscow it considered the matter "analogous to detention" and that it was of "grave concern" to the United States.[94] By January 1941, the embassy had lodged more than 80 notes of appeal or protest, without satisfactory result.[95] The dispute stemmed in part from the fact that historically Russia never recognized the American doctrine that individuals had a right of expatriation (or naturalization), and hence refused to acknowledge that anyone born in the Soviet Union, or of Soviet parents, could become a U.S. citizen or cease to be a Soviet.[96] Yet as Vyshinsky admitted in a rare candid moment, it also represented the entrenched power of the Soviet secret police, who were utterly immune to appeals on humanitarian grounds, and even to the foreign policy arguments of Soviet diplomats.[97]

If remonstrances and protests over the rights and treatment of Americans in Russia could continue even during the most desperate days of 1941 and 1942, it should not be surprising that the question reemerged forcefully as World War II drew to a close. The problem was magnified and complicated because when the Red Army pushed the nazis out of the territories claimed by the Soviet Union in 1939 and 1940, an additional 2,000 persons who asserted that they were U.S. citizens came under Soviet control. Through painstaking effort, the State Department was able to confirm that 600 of the 2,000 were in fact American citizens, with 100 claims considered to be invalid. The great majority of the remainder were believed to have a valid claim, but were unconfirmable owing to interception of their communications with the embassy.[98] The United States tacitly accepted that little could be done to stop eastern Poland, the Baltic States, and bits of Rumania and Finland from disappearing into the Soviet Union, in a replay of the annexations of 1939–1940. But it did not accept that when Soviet citizenship subsequently was imposed by decree on the inhabitants of the annexed areas, no exception was made for naturalized (and in some cases even native-born) Americans, who found themselves lucklessly trapped behind the Soviet Union's unilaterally extended frontiers.

Americans from the Baltic States or eastern Poland newly claimed by the Soviet Union as its own citizens faced enormous difficulties. Not only was their foreign status denied, any display of a desire to renounce Soviet citizenship (such as asserting foreign citizenship) was treated as little short of treasonable. Moreover, throughout 1945 and 1946 all attempts by U.S. dual citizens to leave Soviet territory were blocked, their letters were intercepted, and persons visiting the embassy in Moscow were harassed, questioned at length, and sometimes arrested. At worst, persistence in asserting U.S. citizenship led to loss of one's livelihood, which served as a pretext for charges of "parasitism," and upon conviction, deportation to a forced labor camp in the gulag. The State Department calculated in 1947 that of 220 persons claiming U.S. citizenship who had been sentenced to forced labor, two-thirds actually were Americans.[99] Of course, the United States vehemently protested such mistreatment of its citizens. The Soviets, however, proved unmovable, at times even refusing to permit native-born Americans to leave Russia. For example, when yet another in a series of high-level appeals for relief was made in 1947, Vyshinsky responded that individuals whom the United States claimed were its native-born citizens could not "be divested of Soviet citizenship merely by force of the fact of their birth on American territory."[100]

In many cases Soviet authorities unilaterally declared that the persons in question were Soviet citizens, and therefore that American officials had no business even asking after them, and certainly would not be permitted access to them. More simply, sometimes it was denied that persons named in a given petition were in the country. In that way the Soviets prevented from leaving a number of those whose status as Americans was verified and documented by the embassy or the State Department in Washington, who were not dual citizens, and over whom the Soviet Union therefore had no defensible legal claim.[101] Why was this extraordinary position adopted? Moscow embassy staff believed that Soviet intransigence derived from four causes. First, a need to avoid the propaganda disaster of people fleeing socialism to find sanctuary in the capitalist West. Second, a sense of security risk, since most of the people concerned came from areas of the Soviet Union closed to foreign travel. Third, an interest in demonstrating that the annexed areas of Poland and the Baltic

States, where most of the dual-citizenship Americans resided, were now Soviet. And lastly, a supposition that the United States was in any case powerless to remedy the situation.[102]

In 1948, the embassy staff gave up hope of persuading the Soviets to permit Americans to leave. Ambassador Smith cabled Washington that "further representations here . . . appear useless and even embarrassing." He urged instead a new *quid pro quo*. He suggested that, if consistent with American law and principles, Soviets convicted of criminal offenses and imprisoned in the U.S. zone in Germany might be traded for Americans in the gulag.[103] Serious consideration was given to the proposal. However, Marshall had just cancelled forced repatriations and decided that not even the chance to free Americans justified a reversal of that decision. On the other hand, an exchange involving prisoners in Germany willing to return to the Soviet Union was approved (there were about thirty Soviets in jail in the American zone).[104] Smith subsequently contacted General Lucius D. Clay, U.S. Military Governor for Germany. Clay's deputy, Major General George Hays, informed the Soviet Military Administration in Germany that he would not proceed further with the return of Soviet prisoners until Moscow resumed "negotiations concerning the repatriation of American citizens under detention in the Soviet Union." But this tough line worked no better. Soviet Lieutenant General Mikhail Dratvin shot back that all persons whom the United States said were Americans either were not or had left the Soviet Union, and demanded the unconditional release of all Soviet prisoners in Germany.[105]

Quiet diplomacy failed to gain release of the Americans; public diplomacy proved counterproductive on other such issues; even the suggestion of prisoner swapping had failed. In a long and embittered report in January 1949, *chargé* Foy Kohler summarized the conclusions drawn by the embassy staff from that series of setbacks. He advised that the Soviet Union was utterly determined "to prevent the departure of American citizens on any available grounds," adding:

With the exception of the period preceding the War of 1812, perhaps never have so many American citizens been subjected to comparable discriminations, threats, police interrogations, and administrative punishments, all for no greater offence than that of attempting to assert their American citizenship and depart from a country whose regime they abhor.

Kohler explained that the embassy had taken the extraordinary step of counseling "in instances where the citizen involved is threatened with arrest and deportation to Siberia or other punitive action, not to persist in asserting his or her claim to American citizenship." All that could be done now was to warn the world of the threat Soviet Russia posed to international security, as revealed by its heartless record on human rights. He advised that every effort should be made to communicate internationally:

The basic truth that the Soviet dictatorship is as ruthlessly destructive of personal liberties as any known to history and that its repeated protestations concerning the resolution of all conflicting interests between the individual and the state in the U.S.S.R. is as overweening a "big lie" as ever emanated from Adolf Hitler's Third Reich.[106]

Perceptions had come full circle: the Soviet Union was again viewed as it had been before the war, as akin to Nazi Germany at home and, by analogy, in its likely foreign policy behavior. In good measure, that image—which made it difficult for western publics and statesmen to consider compromise with the Soviets—was a result of repression large and small, intransigently pursued by Stalin.

The Soviet Union's disregard for the welfare of Americans trapped in the East by the war was a contributory cause to the breakdown in trust that began just after signature of the Yalta agreements. Among the first Soviet violations of the Yalta understandings, as perceived by Washington, was delay in repatriation of POWs from Poland. Stalin's duplicity encouraged the suspicion that he could not be trusted to adhere to other, more fundamental agreements on the dispensation of the postwar order in Europe. The United States also momentarily violated the agreement on repatriation, by declining to return those captured in German uniform until it was clear no reprisals could be taken against Americans in German hands. Unlike the Soviets, however, who showed an utter lack of consideration for the welfare of their POWs and sought only to ensure that none escaped punishment through a failure to return, Washington's violation arose out of humanitarian concern for the safe passage home of its captive soldiers. The United States then violated the 1929 Geneva Convention by forcing Soviet nationals taken prisoner while wearing German uniform to return to Russia. It did so principally to ensure early repatriation of American POWs liberated by the Red Army in Manchuria, but another consideration was to encourage continued cooperation from Moscow. Top officials still believed that postwar cooperation remained a real possibility, and was the greater good even when measured against the known, dire fate of repatriates. And yet, that experience also reawakened moral repugnance for Stalin's Russia. It thus helped remind Americans that they were attempting to construct a liberal postwar order in cooperation with a most illiberal partner.

Even had the events of the Cold War not unfolded as they did, it is possible that relations would have deteriorated significantly after 1945 over the question of Moscow's abusive treatment of American citizens. In any case, heavy-handedness toward Americans within Soviet jurisdiction made it additionally difficult for officials in Washington to avoid seeing a parallel between the Soviet Union and Nazi Germany. Once such an analogy was drawn, it would prove next to impossible for the United States to view cooperation with the Soviets as viable. Americans believed that stable, pacific relations between nations required respect for individual liberty within nations. With Stalin's regime seen as irredeemably illiberal, a classical distinction between a state's internal character and its external behavior had little appeal to U.S. policy-makers, or the public. Yet it needs to be stressed that the parallel to Nazi Germany was drawn in light of the harsh reality of Moscow's disrespect for the rights and welfare of individuals. And Soviet contempt for liberty was nowhere made so clear to the United States as in the utterly uncompromising and arbitrary treatment meted out to innocent Americans trapped behind the iron borders of the Soviet Union.[107]

NOTES

1. See the results in *Public Opinion Quarterly* (Spring 1945): p. 103.
2. That thesis is nicely elaborated in Edward Bennett's fine study of wartime relations, *Franklin D. Roosevelt and the Search for Victory* (Scholarly Resources, 1990); a different emphasis is Whittle Johnston, "Franklin D. Roosevelt and the Wartime Strategy for Peace," in Norman Graebner, ed., *American Diplomacy, 1865–1945* (UPA, 1985): pp. 161–98.
3. Typical examples are *FRUS*, 1944, Vol. IV: pp. 1214–23, and 1945, Vol. V: pp. 1122–23. A more critical assessment of the conclusions of the State Department is Daniel Yergin, *Shattered Peace* (Houghton Mifflin, 1978): pp. 17–68.
4. *FRUS*, 1942, *Soviet Union*, Vol. III: p. 408.
5. *Ibid.*, pp. 539–41; Bennett, *Search for Victory*: pp. 44–52; Robert Vitas, *The United States and Lithuania* (Praeger, 1990): pp. 56–62.
6. *FRUS*, 1942, Vol. III: p. 540.
7. Early studies include Louis FitzGibbon, *Unpitied and Unknown* (Bachman and Turner, 1975); and Henri de Montfort, *Le Massacre de Katyn* (Presses de la Cité, 1969). And see the long-repressed evidence published by Poland in 1989, in *NYT*, February 17 and 19, 1989; and the Soviet admission of guilt in *NYT*, April 13 and 14, 1990. Documents released under *glasnost* are in Natalia Lebedeva, "The Katyn Tragedy," *International Affairs* (June 1990): pp. 98–115.

8. Roosevelt-Stalin correspondence in *DRAR*: pp. 112–13.

9. *FRUS, British Commonwealth*, 1943: pp. 522–24; and see the discussion of this episode in Bennett, *Search for Victory*: pp. 80–82.

10. Roosevelt-Stalin exchanges on Poland, *DRAR*: pp. 132–37, 142–44; and see Cordell Hull, *Memoirs of Cordell Hull*, Vol. II (Macmillan, 1948): pp. 1263–66.

11. *FRUS, Conferences at Cairo and Teheran*, 1943: pp. 513–75; and see Charles E. Bohlen, *Witness to History 1929–1969* (Norton, 1973): p. 151.

12. Roosevelt-Stalin correspondence on the Warsaw uprising in *DRAR*: pp. 151–54.

13. Winston Churchill, *Triumph and Tragedy* (Bantam, 1962): pp. 118–22.

14. On the reaction to the Warsaw uprising see W. Averill Harriman (with Elie Abel), *Special Envoy to Churchill and Stalin, 1941–1946* (Random House, 1975): pp. 335–65; Robert Dallek, *Roosevelt and American Foreign Policy, 1932–1945* (Oxford University Press, 1979): pp. 463–66; and Churchill, *Triumph and Tragedy*: pp. 110–24.

15. Bennett, *Search for Victory*: p. 147.

16. Kennan quoted in *ibid.*, p. 148.

17. On this fear as a motivation in Roosevelt's approach to Yalta, see John L. Gaddis, *The United States and the Origins of the Cold War* (Columbia University Press, 1972): pp. 133–65.

18. Text in *FRUS, Conferences at Malta and Yalta*, 1945: pp. 971–72.

19. *Inter alia* see Churchill, *Triumph and Tragedy*: pp. 313–45; Arthur Schlesinger Jr., "Origins of the Cold War," *Foreign Affairs* (October 1967): pp. 22–52; Adam B. Ulam, *Expansion and Coexistence*, 2nd ed. (Holt, Rinehart and Winston, 1974): pp. 367–77; Yergin, *Shattered Peace*: pp. 42–68; Edward R. Stettinius, *Roosevelt and the Russians: The Yalta Conference*, Walter Johnson, ed. (Doubleday, 1949); and Vojtech Mastny, *Russia's Road to the Cold War* (Columbia University Press, 1979). See also the fine review essay by John Gaddis, "The Emerging Post-Revisionist Synthesis on the Origins of the Cold War," *Diplomatic History* (Summer 1983): pp. 171–204.

20. For just-released Soviet archival evidence that suggests Stalin had quite aggressive postwar plans in Europe see R. C. Raack, "Clearing up the History of WWII," *SHAFR Newsletter* (March 1992): pp. 27–40. Also see John Gaddis *et al.*, "The Soviet Side of the Cold War," *Diplomatic History* (Fall 1991): pp. 523–63; and Kenneth Jensen, ed., *Origins of the Cold War* (United States Institute of Peace, 1991); both of which reprint the "Novikov Telegram." Cf. William Taubman, *Stalin's American Policy* (Norton, 1982).

21. New evidence that strongly confirms Stalin's determination to settle the Polish question in advance of Yalta is in R.C. Raack, "Stalin Fixes the Oder-Neisse Line," *Journal of Contemporary History* (October 1990): pp. 467–88.

22. Gaddis, *Origins of the Cold War*: p. 355.

23. Adam B. Ulam, "Forty Years of Troubled Coexistence," *Foreign Affairs* (Fall 1985): p. 17.

24. Text in *Vital Speeches*, March 15, 1946: pp. 329–32; cf. Martin Gilbert, *Churchill: A Life* (Henry Holt & Co., 1991): pp. 863–69.

25. Gaddis, *Origins of the Cold War*: pp. 296–304; *FRUS,* 1945, Vol. V: pp. 817–20; 866–67. Kennan's famous "long telegram" is in *ibid.*, 1946, Vol. VI: pp. 696–709.

26. Text of the "Truman Doctrine," in Henry S. Commager, ed., *DAH*, 7th ed. (Meredith, 1963) Vol. II: pp. 524–26. Also see Dean Acheson, *Present at the Cre-*

ation (Norton, 1969): pp. 217–25; and Walter Isaacson and Evan Thomas, *The Wise Men* (Simon & Schuster, 1986): pp. 393–402.

27. "X" (George Kennan), "The Sources of Soviet Conduct," *Foreign Affairs* (July 1947): pp. 566–82; *idem*, "Containment Then and Now," *ibid.* (Spring 1987): pp. 885–90; and Walter Lippmann, "The Cold War," *ibid.*, pp. 869–84.

28. Those events were crucial in ending western hesitation about forming a transatlantic military alliance. See *Memoirs of Harry S Truman 1946–52*, Vol. II (Da Capo Press, 1956): pp. 130, 240–43. A moderate, post-revisionist study of the complex of factors that went into Truman's decision to "get tough with the Russians" is Gaddis, *Origins of the Cold War*: pp. 282–361; cf. Melvyn P. Leffler, *A Preponderance of Power* (Stanford University Press, 1992): pp. 100–219.

29. Leffler, *A Preponderance of Power*: p. 496. Also see the essays on the division of Germany by Jean Smith, and on the Marshall Plan by Hodge and Nolan, in *idem*, eds. *Shepherd Of Democracy? op. cit.*

30. *FRUS, Conference of Berlin (Potsdam)*, 1945, Vol. II: pp. 1155–57.

31. Stimson's diary entry, July 19, 1945, quoted in *ibid.*, p. 1155n. The OGPU, (later the NKVD, and later still the KGB) oversaw the purges and forced collectivizations of the 1930s.

32. *Ibid.*, pp. 1155–57; and see J. Garry Clifford, "President Truman and Peter the Great's Will," *Diplomatic History* (Fall 1980): pp. 371–86, especially p. 381n38.

33. Polls cited in Walsh, "What the American People Think of Russia," pp. 513–22, and *idem*, "American Attitudes Toward Russia," *Antioch Review* (June 1947): pp. 183–90.

34. See Isaacson and Thomas, *The Wise Men*: pp. 295–305.

35. Eduard Mark, "Charles E. Bohlen and the Acceptable Limits of Soviet Hegemony in Eastern Europe," *Diplomatic History* (Spring 1979): pp. 201–13; and see the December 1945 discussion paper reproduced as "The Bohlen-Robinson Report," in *ibid.* (Fall 1977): pp. 389–99.

36. An exploration of this theme that roots the impulse in "American exceptionalism" and national mission is the author's "La liberté est-elle divisible?" *Études Internationales* (September 1991): pp. 509–31.

37. John R. Deane, *The Strange Alliance* (Viking Press, 1947): pp. 182–83.

38. *Ibid.*, p. 188; and Russell Buhite, "Soviet-American Relations and the Repatriation of Prisoners of War, 1945," *Historian* (May 1973): pp. 385–86.

39. *FRUS*, 1945, Vol. V: pp. 1067–72.

40. Deane, *Strange Alliance*: pp. 183, 190. Ulam attributes the delay simply to "the unavoidable red tape and confusion always present in wartime." He concedes, however, that concern over "any stories the ex-prisoners might carry west concerning the behavior of the Red Army in Poland" was a contributing factor. *Expansion and Coexistence*: p. 380.

41. Buhite, "Repatriation," pp. 385–86.

42. *FRUS*, 1945, Vol. V: p. 1099n.

43. Mark Elliot, "The U.S. and Forced Repatriation of Soviet Citizens, 1944–1947," *Political Science Quarterly* (June 1973): p. 259. And see Article 133 of the 1936 Soviet Constitution, in *BDHR*: p. 28.

44. "Agreement Between the United States and the Soviet Union Concerning Liberated Prisoners of War and Civilians," *FRUS, Conferences at Malta and Yalta*, 1945: pp. 985–97. On negotiations leading to the agreement see *ibid.*, pp. 413–55,

687–97, 751–57, 863–66. Negotiated prior to Yalta, it was signed at the conference by Deane, not Roosevelt. Harriman, S*pecial Envoy*: pp. 416–17.

45. Raack, "Stalin Fixes the Oder-Neisse Line, " pp. 474–78.
46. Deane, *Strange Alliance*: pp. 190–201; Harriman, *Special Envoy*: p. 421; and Stettinius, *Roosevelt and the Russians*: p. 310.
47. When asked, "Do you think Russia can be trusted to co-operate with us after the war?" 55 percent responded "yes, " while 31 percent said "no." Although 60 percent recognized that the Soviet Union would want more territory after the war, 51 percent said it should not receive any (32 percent thought it should). *Public Opinion Quarterly* (Spring 1945): pp. 102–3.
48. George Q. Flynn, *Roosevelt and Romanism* (Greenwood, 1976): pp. 219–24.
49. *FRUS*, 1945, Vol. V: pp. 1072–83; and *DRAR*: p. 158.
50. Harriman, *Special Envoy*: pp. 420–21.
51. *FRUS*, 1945, Vol. V: pp. 1072–83. Harriman was referring to Articles 2, 3, and 4 of the Yalta "Agreement Concerning Liberated Prisoners of War and Civilians, " cited in Note #44, *supra*.
52. *Ibid*., pp. 1082–83; and *DRAR*: p. 159. On May 3rd, the State Department responded to public unrest with a press statement rebutting allegations of American mistreatment of Soviet POWs. Department of State, *Bulletin*, May 6, 1945: p. 864.
53. *Ibid*., pp. 1085.
54. *Ibid*., pp. 1085–86.
55. Harriman, *Special Envoy*: p. 422; and see Herbert Feis, *Churchill, Roosevelt, Stalin* (Princeton University Press, 1957): pp. 596–98n; and Buhite, "Repatriation," p. 396.
56. Deane, *Strange Alliance*: p. 202.
57. *FRUS,* 1945, Vol. V: pp. 1093–94.
58. On suspicions surrounding the "Bern talks" on German surrender, see Harriman, *Special Envoy*: pp. 432–35; Roosevelt-Stalin correspondence in *DRAR*: pp. 161–66; and Bennett, *Search for Victory*: pp. 177–81.
59. *FRUS*, 1945, Vol. V: pp. 1095–99.
60. *Ibid*., pp. 1095n, 1099.
61. *Draft Revised Conventions for the Protection of War Victims* (Red Cross, 1948). Emphasis added. On the 1941 U.S. effort to gain Soviet adherence see *FRUS*, 1941, Vol. I: pp. 1005–24.
62. For example, see Grew's July 11th citation of the Committee's decision in *FRUS*, 1945, Vol. V: pp. 1098–99.
63. *Ibid*., p. 1095.
64. *Ibid*., pp. 1097–98.
65. Elliot, "Forced Repatriation," p. 253.
66. *FRUS*, 1945, Vol. V: pp. 1098–1102.
67. See the sensitive introduction by Hugh Trevor-Roper, in Nicholas Bethell, *The Last Secret* (Andre Deutsch, 1974): pp. ix–xiv.
68. A bitter critique of British policy on this score, which suggests a continuing conspiracy to keep wartime records secret, is Nikolai Tolstoy, *Victims Of Yalta* (Hodder & Stoughton, 1977): p. 430; also, *idem, The Minister and the Massacres* (Century Hutchinson, 1986). More balanced is Bethell, *The Last Secret: passim*. Also conspiratorially minded, but about U.S. policy, is Julius Epstein, "American

Forced Repatriation," *Ukrainian Quarterly* (Autumn 1954): pp. 354–65; and *idem, Operation Keelhaul* (Devin-Adair, 1973): pp. 23–72.

69. *FRUS, The Conference of Berlin*, 1945, Vol. I: pp. 794–801; Vol. II: pp. 367–74, 497–574, 1162–66.

70. *Ibid.*, 1945, Vol. V: p. 1076.

71. *Ibid.*, pp. 1103–5. On repatriation of civilians see E.F. Penrose, "Negotiating on Refugees and Displaced Persons, 1946," in *Negotiating With the Russians*, R. Dennett and J. Johnson, eds. (World Peace Foundation, 1951): pp. 139–68.

72. Harriman, *Special Envoy*: p. 416.

73. *FRUS*, 1945, Vol. V: pp. 1103–4.

74. Walter Bedell Smith, *My Three Years in Moscow* (J.B. Lippincott, 1950): pp. 25–26.

75. *FRUS*, 1945, Vol. V: pp. 1104–5.

76. *Congressional Record*, Senate, Committee on Foreign Relations, *Nomination of Charles Bohlen*, Hearings, 83rd Cong., 1st Sess., p. 57. Also quoted in Elliot, "Forced Repatriation," p. 266.

77. Harriman, *Special Envoy*: p. 416.

78. *FRUS*, 1945, Vol. V: p. 1106n. Eisenhower maintained he had been but dimly aware of the practice of forced repatriation. Given the scope of his duties, that may well have been true. See his cursory treatment of the subject in *Crusade in Europe* (Doubleday, 1948): p. 439. A bizarre book claiming Eisenhower approved the massacre of one million German POWs is James Bacque, *Other Losses* (Stoddart, 1989); cf. the devastatingly critical review by Stephen Ambrose, and report on a conference of Eisenhower scholars, in *NYT Book Review*, February 24, 1991.

79. *FRUS*, 1945, Vol. V: pp. 1106–9.

80. *Ibid.*, p. 1110.

81. "Policy on Repatriation of Displaced Persons," Department of State, *Bulletin*, June 1, 1947.

82. See *FRUS, The Soviet Union*, 1933–1939: pp. 534–35, 844–45; and for representative prewar cases, *ibid.*, 1941, Vol. I: pp. 936–51.

83. *Ibid.*, 1944, Vol. IV: pp. 877–81.

84. *Ibid.*, 1945, Vol. V: pp. 1148–61.

85. *Ibid.*

86. *Ibid.*, 1947, Vol. IV: p. 722.

87. *Ibid.*

88. *UNGA*, Doc. A: p. 842.

89. *FRUS*, 1948, Vol. IV: pp. 923–25.

90. Ulam, *Expansion and Coexistence*: p. 402. The right of women freely to change their nationality was proclaimed in Article 5 of the Declaration of Elimination of Discrimination Against Women (1967). Text in *BDHR*: pp. 183–87.

91. Figure cited is from *FRUS*, 1949, Vol. V: p. 619; and see Smith, *My Three Years in Moscow*: p. 26.

92. Text of agreement in *FRUS, The Soviet Union*, 1933–1939: pp. 33–34. Examples of prewar arrest and detention of U.S. citizens during 1937, 1938, and 1939 in *ibid.*, pp. 491–503, 708–25, 904–18.

93. Intense and bitter exchanges took place in the months immediately after Pearl Harbor; at least one case involved an American citizen held under a death sentence. *Ibid.*, 1941, Vol. I: pp. 943–51.

94. *Ibid.*, 1939, Vol. I: pp. 628–37; and 1940, Vol. II: p. 165.

95. *Ibid.*, 1941, Vol. I: pp. 928–29.

96. On antecedents of this problem see Chapter One, Note #3, *supra*.

97. *FRUS*, 1941, Vol. I: p. 936.

98. *Ibid.*, 1949, Vol. V: pp. 618–19.

99. *Ibid.*, 1947, Vol. IV: p. 720. A personal recollection of mistreatment is Alexander Dolgun (with Patrick Watson), *Alexander Dolgun's Story* (Alfred A. Knopf, 1975).

100. *FRUS*, 1947, Vol. IV: pp. 728–30.

101. *Ibid.*, pp. 735–41.

102. *Ibid.*, 1949, Vol. V: pp. 549–56.

103. *Ibid.*, 1948, Vol. IV: pp. 902–3.

104. *Ibid.*, pp. 906–7, 943n.

105. *Ibid.*, pp. 942–43; and 1949, Vol. V: pp. 574–75, 664–66.

106. *Ibid.*, pp. 549–56. With nothing more to lose, the United States went public, asking the U.N. to equate forced labor in the Soviet Union to the use of slave labor by the nazis. Department of State, *Bulletin*, February 27, 1949: pp. 248–49.

107. In midsummer 1992, Russian president Boris Yeltsin wrote to the Select Committee on POW-MIA Affairs to confirm for the first time from an official Russian source that on several occasions the Soviet Union detained U.S. citizens and servicemen, including 716 during WWII, several of whom died in captivity. The letter was sent in response to a peculiar outburst of interest stimulated by remarks Yeltsin made during a trip to the United States, when he indicated that American POWs might be still alive in Russia. *President Boris Yeltsin to the Select Committee on POW-MIA Affairs, Senator John F. Kerry, Chairman* (n.d.), author's copy. And see "Yeltsin Confirms Soviet Involvement with American POWs," *Select Committee on POW-MIA Affairs,* press release, June 12, 1992.

4 RHETORIC AND REALISM

Following World War II, the United States had sought the creation of a stable and cooperative international system. It wanted to continue the experience of wartime great power cooperation by rooting it in a network of multilateral economic and security institutions, framed at Bretton Woods, and at Dumbarton Oaks and San Francisco. Through these institutions—underwritten by U.S. power now dedicated to active internationalism—the free movement of goods and ideas, and the promise of collective security, could sustain national economic and security interests. Beyond that, it was hoped and believed that they would also help provide for a genuinely free, and mutually beneficial, liberal-capitalist world order. Out of this vision of enlightened self-interest, of the United States as a shepherd of democracy and prosperity, Americans would regain some of the security they had lost, while preserving and expanding the economic prosperity they enjoyed.[1] But what of Russia? The Soviets may not have been in a position to threaten directly western Europe or the Far East militarily, but Germany and Japan were dangerously weak and open to Soviet political influence. If those two great centers of industrial capacity—as Kennan pointed out in his "X" article and more importantly, his "long telegram"—drifted into the Soviet orbit, then there would be a real threat to U.S. economic and security interests in an open trading system and favorable balance of power.[2]

THE MORALITY OF CONFRONTATION

At first, the main U.S. response was political and economic, as fit the nature of the perceived threat. The Marshall Plan, bilateral aid, discreet (that is, covert) support to democratic political parties, and launching of the Bretton Woods institutions were all used to shore up western Europe and Japan, and to integrate them into an American-led system of political and economic cooperation. The initial response of policy-makers to the breakdown of postwar cooperation with Russia thus was largely prudent and guided by enlightened self-interest.[3]

Two salient events in 1949, the communist victory in China's civil war and detonation by the Soviet Union of an atomic bomb, inflamed the right wing in the United States, alarmed senior officials in the Truman administration, and changed the nature and the course of the Cold War. Those events, coming on the heels of the coup in Czechoslovakia and the Berlin Blockade, combined with a sense that however far-fetched the notion of a Soviet military strike against western Europe, it was still necessary to re-arm against it, to stiffen conventional and nuclear deterrence. The perception of a shift in the balance of power in Moscow's favor also induced Truman to direct the State and Defense Departments to undertake jointly a basic review of strategic policy. What resulted in April 1950 was the single most influential National Security Council document in U.S. foreign policy since the end of World War II: NSC-68.[4]

Paul Nitze, the principal drafter of NSC-68, gave the report a dramatic, even sinister, language not usually encountered in internal memoranda. It described the postwar world as torn by "a basic conflict between the idea of freedom under a government of laws, and the idea of slavery under the grim oligarchy of the Kremlin." It then defined U.S. purposes as strictly limited and liberal, as seeking to ensure "the integrity and vitality of our free society, which is founded upon the dignity and worth of the individual." This was juxtaposed against the Soviet leadership's "fundamental design ... to retain and solidify their absolute power" not only at home, but abroad as well. Human rights perceptions thus were helping to define the Cold War, as they reinforced an older American belief that only liberal democracies were inherently pacific. For example, NSC-68 concluded that to sustain the Soviet system domestically, Moscow required "dynamic expansion of [its] authority and the ultimate elimination of any effective opposition."[5] The analogy to Nazi Germany therefore was complete, and the policy implications seemed clear: the West must never make the mistake of appeasing Soviet aggression; it must oppose all such attempts wherever they were seen to occur; and at the very least, it must heavily re-arm in order to better deter aggression in the first place.

Containment, already the wise watchword of Washington's political and economic policy, was given a dangerously exaggerated global military twist as well. Moreover, respect for human rights—understood primarily in terms of traditional western notions of civil and political, but also economic liberties—came to be seen as one of the distinguishing characteristics of the conflict with Soviet Russia.[6] It is most ironic, therefore, that NSC-68—a document that was itself imbued with moral distinctions—should go on to sanction virtually any means to defend the interests of the democracies in ultimately triumphing over the Soviet and totalitarian idea. In the manichean struggle that it depicted, bad means would have to be used to attain good ends. As a result of this consensus on the moral character of the struggle among the foreign policy elite (those who could not agree, such as Kennan, were shunted aside), American policy would henceforth often avoid explicit considerations of principle and morality. Instead, it would subsume such questions under the all-justifying doctrine of containing the expansion of what was seen, and described, as an unalterably evil power that itself observed no principled or ethical restraints on the conduct of its diplomacy, open or secret.[7] As a result, in the great and historic contest that followed, support for the rights of some persons and nations would occasionally be sacrificed by the United States not just in the age-old interest of *realpolitik*, but in the name of preserving those rights over the long term. Ultimately, that paradox would help undo the consensus that underlay America's Soviet policy. But for the next twenty years, NSC-68 helped infuse official perceptions of the Cold War with a tone of moral, as well as geopolitical confrontation.

And yet, though more harshly stated, the analysis of NSC-68 was little different in substance from the characterization of the sources of Soviet conduct made by Kennan and others several years earlier. The significant departures came in its tone, the scale of the threat it described, and its contention that, "the assault on freedom is worldwide now, and ... a defeat of free institutions anywhere is a defeat everywhere."[8] The perception that U.S. security was indivisible from the independence of all noncommunist nations and that the threat from Soviet power was global, led inexorably to the conclusion that the United States would have to assume unprecedented peacetime military commitments to reinforce its diplomatic and political prestige, as well as to forestall erosion of its influence in Europe and Asia.

That the Truman administration was prepared to exaggerate the Soviet threat to the public in order to overcome entrenched isolationism in Congress has been well established; that it was preparing to do so again with NSC-68 seems likely.[9] But in a coincidence of great consequence, North Korea attacked South Korea just months after Truman approved NSC-68, appearing to confirm the administration's most dire predictions about Soviet expansionism. It was quickly and widely assumed that the order had come directly from Moscow (as it may well have done), and that if aggression was to be stopped before it could really get started, the Korean peninsula was the place where a stand would have to be made.[10] The comparison between the Soviet Union and Nazi Germany now became nearly irresistible, as the Truman administration quickly determined that the United States would not again stand idly by while a brutal dictatorship moved against a small, independent nation.[11] More negatively, those who saw communist states as motivated primarily by ideology rather than traditional nationalisms or state interests claimed that Korea proved them right. That assertion and perception would have baleful consequences for long-term U.S. policy, particularly in guiding the United States into direct confrontation with local Asian communisms.

Truman sent troops to Korea for the limited purpose of preserving South Korean independence and the general purpose of signaling that aggression would be opposed by force.[12] General Douglas MacArthur's tactically decisive landing at Inchon and the subsequent rout of North Korean forces ensured that the limited goal of American intervention was met, and might have accomplished the more general purpose as well. However, the General and the administration succumbed to the temptation to take advantage of the North's defeat, and crossed the 38th parallel in an attempt to reunite the peninsula under a western-oriented government. Insufficient account had been taken of the interest of China in North Korea's survival, and in keeping U.S. troops distant from its borders. Massive Chinese intervention on November 26, 1950 nearly overwhelmed the U.N. forces and, in MacArthur's words, led to "an entirely new war." The Korean Conflict subsequently developed into a grinding war of attrition that wore down U.S. military reserves, leading to a significant expansion of the defense budget, and eroded domestic support for an activist foreign policy.[13] It also took a steady toll on Democratic party hopes of retaining the presidency. Although conservative-isolationists avoided that discredited label, in both parties, and in Congress, they soon were in open revolt against the liberal and internationalist direction taken in postwar foreign policy by the Truman administration.

What to do about Korea was the central issue of the 1952 presidential election. Polls taken during the campaign indicated that the electorate was confused and divided over how to resolve the problem. The public generally opposed the war, but also did not want either to withdraw or escalate in the hope of victory.[14] The campaign was the most vituperative in memory, with voters eventually settling on the Republican nominee, Dwight D. Eisenhower, principally because he promised to "go to Korea" and end the war (which he did within six months of taking office). Yet even while opposing the Korean conflict, for reasons of political advantage the Republicans had also promised during the campaign and in their platform to pursue "liberation" of the "captive peoples" of eastern Europe. Under the crushing pressures of the Cold War, "liberation" was the hardened form that human rights questions concerning the Soviet Union took for the next two decades. Yet the promise of liberation, if seriously pursued, would mean even worse tensions with Soviet Russia, and possibly war on a scale to dwarf the stalemated and increasingly futile conflict in Asia. How had the shrewd and careful hero of World War II, and former NATO commander, gotten into that quandary, and could he extract himself?

LIBERATION: RHETORIC AND REALITY

The concept of liberation was first outlined by John Foster Dulles in May 1952.[15] Republicans quickly warmed to the considerable domestic political advantages of the slogan. They made a platform promise to end "the negative, futile, and immoral policy of 'containment' which abandons countless human beings to a despotism and Godless terrorism, which in turn enables the rulers [of the Soviet Union] to forge the captives into a weapon of our destruction."[16] The Democrats were stunned by the charge, but soon fired back in kind. Sensing building public pressures in support of a more activist rhetoric, in their platform the Democrats also promised: "We will not abandon the once-free peoples of Central and Eastern Europe who suffer now under the Kremlin's tyranny in violation of the Soviet Union's most solemn pledges at Tehran, Yalta, and Potsdam."[17] Truman then warned that to "try to liberate these enslaved peoples at this time might well mean turning these lands into atomic battlefields."

Faced with such a strong counterattack, the Republicans retreated from more extreme rhetoric. Eisenhower made public assurances that he intended "to aid by every peaceful means, but only by peaceful means, the right to live in freedom." Privately, he berated Dulles for forgetting to stress in campaign statements that only peaceful means were under consideration. As historian Robert A. Divine points out, the Republican promise to aid liberation of eastern Europe therefore principally served to paper over differences between the isolationist wing of the Republican party, led by Senator Robert A. Taft, and its internationalist wing, which clearly embraced Eisenhower in order to deny Taft the nomination.[18] The need to internationalize the Republican party was also Eisenhower's main reason for deflecting Democratic feelers and accepting the Republican nomination.[19]

After the election the split in Republican ranks remained, and as described in Chapter 8, grew even wider with the fight over the "Bricker Amendment." Meanwhile, leading Democrats moved to back Eisenhower's continuation of Truman's basic policy of containment and activist internationalism. Lyndon Johnson once put it this way: "We cannot allow the Republicans to jump off the cliff, because they will carry the nation with them."[20] Eisenhower thus embraced bipartisanship in foreign policy both because he had little choice, with even senior Republicans opposing his appointments and policies, and more importantly to repair the Cold War consensus damaged by the 1952 election fight. In that effort, he and Dulles found the rhetoric of conservative internationalism domestically useful, as well as personally satisfying.[21] In practice, however, their "liberation" policy was highly restrained, amounting to upholding of the United States as a moral and political example to the world,[22] alongside a strategic sense that the Soviet bloc might best be dismantled not by attempts at conciliation such as marked the Truman years, but by application of relentless pressure.[23] At the same time, pressure from the right meant that Eisenhower was not as free as he might have liked to take diplomatic advantage of Stalin's death, and the consequent thaw in both Soviet internal repression and foreign policy rigidity.[24] An opportunity to significantly ease tensions thus was missed.

Still, Eisenhower responded carefully to the suppression by the Soviets of an uprising in the German Democratic Republic (GDR) in July 1953.[25] Similarly, during a crisis in Poland and the rebellion in Hungary in 1956 (which followed publication of Nikita Khrushchev's "secret speech" denouncing Stalin), Eisenhower was careful to surround expressions of hope for liberty for the people of those nations with assurances that the United States had no intention of intervening. Preoccupied with the building Suez crisis, he also refused to permit covert aid to the rebels.[26] During the Polish crisis, Dulles too clarified the limits to liberation. He told one interviewer: "Our job is only as exponents of freedom, to keep alive the concept of freedom, because that is a contagious thing, and if anybody is going to catch it, it's going to be the Poles."[27] Regarding the revolt in Hungary, he declared that intervention "would be madness," and chided those who called for action that the "only way we can save Hungary at this time would be through all-out nuclear war."[28] The administration thus refused to unleash the émigré guerrillas that the CIA had trained for possible use in eastern Europe.[29]

In an address in November 1956, Eisenhower faced the question of how the United States had upheld its principles during these crises. He came to the politically lame, yet statesmanlike and prudent conclusion that it had done so by denouncing the crushing of eastern European freedoms, while abstaining from the use of force.[30] Vice President Richard Nixon also came to that strategic conclusion, which helped restrain his policy as President over a decade later.[31]

Congress, rather than the administration, still used bellicose language about events behind the "Iron Curtain" long after the bloody suppression of the Hungarian uprising demonstrated the limits of U.S. influence in eastern Europe and the dangers of raising unrealistic hopes of outside assistance.[32] In fact, it was Soviet anger over a 1959 congressional resolution proclaiming "Captive Nations Week" that caused Khrushchev to verbally assail Nixon, whose firm response led to their famous "kitchen debate."[33] For his part, Eisenhower explicitly disavowed forceful liberation in a 1958 letter to Nikolai Bulganin, Chairman of the Soviet Council of Ministers.[34] He thus strictly limited efforts to fulfill the campaign promise to actively assist liberation of eastern Europe.

Despite rhetorical distancing from Truman and containment, Eisenhower's policy toward the Soviet Union sprang from similar geopolitical assumptions and moral presumptions. It differed mainly in the force posture on which it relied.[35] In fact, to a much greater extent than either his predecessor or successor in the White House, Eisenhower sought to lessen Cold War tensions and slow down the arms race.[36] He and Dulles recognized that national security was best served by acquiescence in the *status quo* of Soviet domination in eastern Europe.[37] Because they believed (correctly as matters turned out) in the ultimate futility of Soviet efforts to suppress nationalism in that region, they were quite prudent about avoiding direct entanglements. Their rhetoric, as unfortunate as it sometimes was— and it was far less so than comparable Soviet rhetoric—aimed primarily at placating the right wing of the Republican Party, as well as the Congress. That is how guileful suggestions that Soviet hegemony might be overturned by U.S. power and influence, in favor of democracy and respect for human rights, should be seen.

INTERVENING FOR DIVERSITY?

President John F. Kennedy strode into office determined, as he put it in his Inaugural Address, that the United States would "pay any price, bear any burden, meet any hardship, support any friend, oppose any foe to assure the survival and the success of liberty."[38] As Eisenhower had feared, he was a young president too much in a hurry, and too unaware of his own insufficiencies—a trait shared by several of his top advisors. Stephen Ambrose aptly puts the difference this way:

Republican rhetoric had consisted of unrestrained hostility to the Soviet Union and emphasized permanent war with communism.... Republican action, however, was restrained and cautious. The Democratic rhetoric under Kennedy favored coexistence.... [but] actions revealed a dynamic militancy, which traditional Cold Warriors like Acheson and Truman could and did applaud.[39]

Kennedy thus overtly and aggressively promoted democratic values in relations with other countries, especially those in the Third World, that he saw as the key to breaking the Cold War stalemate. He sought to impress democratic goals on Latin America, for instance, through the Alliance for Progress. He also dealt more positively than had the previous administration with democracies such as India, which had not always adhered to the U.S. line on Cold War issues. On the other hand, he seemed obsessed with Third World communisms, such as that of Fidel Castro and the Cuban Revolution, beyond the bounds of reasonable national interest.[40]

It was in part under the mantle of such ambitious internationalism, even moral chauvinism, that Kennedy led the country deeper into the morass of conflict in Indochina. And it was at this larger, abstract level, that human rights and liberties fit into his strategic vision, and his "quest for victory" in the Cold War.[41] During a later period, when human rights were high on the public foreign policy agenda, Arthur Schlesinger Jr. (one of Kennedy's staunchest academic defenders) wrote, "[Vietnam] interrupted Washington's movement towards human rights as a major theme of foreign policy."[42] But that was part of an effort by Schlesinger and former Kennedy aides to try to exonerate their old boss for decisions that had helped immerse the country in a wrenching war. There is not room here to assess the full debate over Kennedy's share of responsibility for the stumble into Vietnam, toward which several key steps were taken on his watch. Yet surely Schlesinger's is too easy a view of Kennedy's role, and of the relationship of human rights to national security during this troubled period. He was perhaps closer to the mark in 1971, a period when the foreign policy audience was more open to arguments derived from *realpolitik* reasoning, when he wrote:

The primary motive [for intervention] . . . had little to do with national interest at all. It was, rather, a precise consequence of the belief that moral principles should govern decisions of foreign policy. It was the insistence on seeing... Vietnam as above all a moral issue that led us to construe political questions in ethical terms, local questions in global terms, and relative questions in absolute terms.[43]

In short, as even his most admiring aides and friendly historians later implicitly recognized, Kennedy's rhetoric about bearing the burdens of the whole world, along with the excessive military commitments of the Truman Doctrine and NSC-68, came home to roost in Indochina.

Cold War tensions were near their worst during the first two years of Kennedy's term as president, but not just because he was a less prudent statesman than Eisenhower. A main cause of the deterioration in relations was the exceptionally belligerent, high-risk foreign policy conducted by Khrushchev (symbolized for many by his boorish display of shoe-pounding in the United Nations in the fall of 1960). Within months of Kennedy's inauguration, Khrushchev reaffirmed Soviet support for wars of "national liberation," trumpeted a major increase in his country's announced defense budget, and raised new fears about European stability by approving construction of the Berlin Wall.[44] One specialist on the Soviet Union, Dimitri Simes, describes Khrushchev's approach to foreign policy as regularly threatening other Soviet leaders "with excessive rapprochement with the West or with excessive confrontation with it." He adds that "risky and sometimes embarrassing games in the world arena were among the reasons the Soviet ruling strata finally had enough of Khrushchev."[45]

Kennedy also resorted to high-risk strategies, such as authorizing the "Bay of Pigs" invasion of Cuba and, when that failed, asking the CIA to assassinate Castro.[46] Moreover, he indulged in rhetoric more hostile and uncompromising than almost any used throughout the Cold War. For instance, he declared the contest "a struggle for supremacy" with a "ruthless, godless tyranny," and stated that the world since 1945 had been engaged in "a global civil war." He also persisted in identifying ideological differences as the main reason why Soviet Russia was a threat to western security. Rather than basing policy on the need to resist forcible changes in the balance of power, he continued to mislead the U.S. public that "the enemy is the Communist system itself—implacable, insatiable, unceasing in its drive for world communism."[47]

An atmosphere of near-constant crisis developed as Khrushchev repeatedly probed American resolve. Matters came to a head during the confrontation over Soviet placement of ballistic missiles in Cuba in October 1962.[48] Following successful resolution of that tense and extremely dangerous crisis, a brief thaw in relations developed. During 1963 an important treaty banning atmospheric tests of nuclear weapons was signed; the "hot line" was established between the White House and the Kremlin; talks began on a possible ban on weapons in space; and a significant sale of surplus U.S. grain was made to the Soviet Union.[49] Tensions abated after the Cuban crisis partially because both sides had been frightened into greater restraint in bilateral relations. The several agreements signed in 1963 between the United States and the Soviet Union also were made possible by the fact that Khrushchev's strategic bluff had been called. The Soviet leader had played that game since the "missile gap" controversy of 1960, which Kennedy himself had knowingly capitalized on to push for an expanded U.S. nuclear program.

The more lasting Kennedy legacy was a swollen defense budget (even before expenditures on Vietnam are calculated), and five times as many ICBMs as Eisenhower had thought sufficient to U.S. security. His rearmament program encouraged the Soviets to undertake a matching nuclear build-up.[50] Not until achieving strategic parity later in the decade would Soviet leaders again risk a major confrontation; but neither would they consider arms control negotiations that promised to lock them into a position of permanent strategic inferiority. In all this crisis and confusion, what had happened to American principles and the defense of human rights?

The Kennedy administration's foreign policy appears to have been driven by an understanding of the problem of Soviet power (and Third World revolution) that reflected a deep-seated, Wilsonian view of international relations; but one that lacked Wilson's respect for the limits of intervention, and for self-determination as a cardinal principle of successful U.S. diplomacy. The old theme of American exceptionalism, with its implied national obligation to promote liberty abroad, was laid out in a seminal internal policy paper drafted by Walt Rostow, then chairman of the State Department's Policy Planning Council. Rostow began by noting in passing that "it was not necessary that all societies at all times accept democratic values." Yet virtually in the same breath he argued that it was "in the American interest that the societies of Eurasia, Africa, and Latin America develop along lines broadly consistent with our own concepts of individual liberty and government based on consent."[51] This important paper encapsulated a fundamental confusion in the administration's diplomacy.

Kennedy and his top advisors, both publicly and privately, said their intention was to balance power internationally to preserve a pluralistic world; that is, one where no great power, and especially not the Soviet Union, was completely dominant. But they often acted in contradiction of that aim by attempting to apply U.S. power unilaterally to create and secure a world of pluralists—at times, in areas of the Third World, it appeared they thought it was possible to do so *ex nihilo*. Their model of success, as befitted a generation both scarred by World War II and tempered by the postwar successes of U.S. policy, was the democratization and reconstruction of Germany and Japan, and some of the minor Axis nations (Austria and Italy). Those great accomplishments had of course come about largely through the extension of economic assistance and U.S. security guarantees, which aided in the integration of much of Europe and Asia into an American-led economic and security system. Kennedy thus sought a balance of power *vis-a-vis* the Soviet Union and China, while also trying to recreate underdeveloped national societies on democratic lines and integrate them into the western economic system. Hence, the strategic accommodation with Moscow during 1963 occurred simultaneously with expanded involvement in resistance to local communisms in the Third World. Nowhere was this basic confusion between balancing power and commitments and exporting democracy greater, and nowhere did it have more tragic consequences, than over the growing conflict in Vietnam, as is evident from a store of recently released documents.[52]

John L. Gaddis maintains that Kennedy and his advisors believed "the American national interest was not to remake the world, but to balance power within it," and that intervention "might be necessary . . . but it would be intervention on behalf of diversity, not in opposition to it." He reads Rostow's paper as a call for *realpolitik* tolerance for a diversity of nations, including communist countries, rather than as favoring support to nations that respect individual diversity. In consequence, he suggests that Kennedy "did not take seriously the rhetoric of his inaugural address," and explains the overextension of security commitments to nonvital areas of the Third World, such as South Vietnam, as arriving "at universalism by the back door: the United States really would need a world resembling it in order to be secure."[53] But there is an alternative explanation. It is also possible to accept that Kennedy and Rostow meant what they said and wrote; that the administration walked through the front door to universalism, out of a rooted belief that U.S. institutions ultimately could survive only if the world was made safe by the universal triumph of democratic principles. This interpretation is easier to reconcile with the central theme of many of Kennedy's foreign policy statements and actions. While he may have had private doubts, he more frequently spoke and acted as though he truly believed in an American mission to promote liberal values abroad, to enhance national security by seeing democratic institutions established in other countries.[54]

It is worthwhile here to note Kennedy's effort to link the democratization of foreign societies to his Soviet policy as it pertained to eastern Europe. That was an area where he hoped and believed he could make greater headway than had Eisenhower and Dulles. At the time, Senator Kennedy had supported the "liberation" policy of the Eisenhower administration, and its efforts to drive economic and nationalist wedges into the cracks that appeared in the Soviet bloc following Stalin's death. As one student of Kennedy puts it:

[He] had been particularly enthusiastic about the [Eisenhower] administration's effort to sustain Yugoslavia.... Here was a chance, in the

Senator's mind, to encourage nationalism in other eastern European countries, thereby disrupting the Soviet bloc.... Kennedy had collaborated with the administration to protect these and other initiatives against those in Congress who continued to think in terms of a monolithic communism and thus were critical of Eisenhower's policies.[55]

In a rare moderation of rhetoric, but in keeping with his preferred image of movement from the Eisenhower period, after the 1960 election President Kennedy publicly distanced himself from the "liberation" talk of the previous administration. He declared his intention to develop special links in trade, aid and cultural policies—human exchanges and so forth—with the eastern bloc, which he privately hoped would slowly prise eastern European countries from Soviet control (the Soviet Union itself he appeared to regard as impenetrable by such devices).[56] But this too was not really a departure: Eisenhower and even Truman had tried to use economic levers to accomplish much the same goals in the region.

However, Congress under Kennedy again began to obstruct rather than assist executive efforts to more flexibly approach relations with communist countries. Kennedy had partly himself to blame for that. His self-serving rhetoric inflamed public opinion, and dampened wider awareness of what he and others had known for years: that the Soviet bloc was *not* monolithic, and in fact suffered from enormous internal stresses, national conflicts, and economic weakness. Then his series of confrontations with the Soviets in other regions undermined any chances a policy of enticement might have had to widen the cracks evident in Moscow's control of the region, not least owing to the hardening effect those crises had on congressional and public opinion.[57]

Rather than expanding trade and contacts with the minor nations in the Soviet bloc, Congress after the Bay of Pigs suspended the issuing of export licenses to Yugoslavia and Poland. Following the 1961 Berlin crisis, Congress again moved to block expanded economic diplomacy toward eastern Europe; during 1962, it moved to prohibit aid to any communist country, even Yugoslavia.[58] Congress thus tied the hands of the executive, refusing to allow effective differentiation between communist societies, and declining to take advantage of breaks in the facade of monolithic Soviet power. It did so partly as a result of the administration's ill-considered rhetoric, but also out of its own myopia and inertia about adjusting to shifts in the Cold War. Therefore, Kennedy too had to settle for a policy—if it can be called that—of mostly verbal support for liberty for the "captive peoples" of the Soviet Union and bloc.

FROM CONFRONTATION TO DÉTENTE

Lyndon Johnson exhibited a confusion in his strategic thinking and Soviet policy similar to that which had characterized Kennedy's approach, an outcome largely explainable by the fact that he retained most of Kennedy's key advisors. Johnson was sincerely interested in moving toward *détente* with the Soviet Union, but like his predecessor, he was primarily concerned with the deterrent effect of America's reputation for resolve, which he came to believe hinged on "staying the course" in Indochina.[59] Unlike Kennedy, however, he sought to match words and deeds more closely in bilateral relations with the Soviets. Johnson thus refrained from provocative rhetoric. More importantly, even while escalating a war against a Soviet ally in southeast Asia, he helped create new hope for arms control by resolving long-standing disputes with Moscow over a series of lesser issues. In other words, he acted to remove minor irritants in the relationship that had long hindered negotiations on more substantial matters.

As a result, more agreements were signed with the Soviet Union between 1963 and 1968 than in the entire preceding thirty years. These included a consular convention that increased official contacts and reinforced the shaky standing of the Roosevelt-Litvinov assignments on religious and civil protections for American citizens in the Soviet Union; an extension of existing arrangements for cultural exchanges; resolution of a bitter dispute over fisheries; the first civil aviation agreement between the two countries; mutual reduction of production of fissionable materials; the Outer Space Treaty, which prohibited stationing of nuclear weapons on the moon, planets, or in space; and most important, the Treaty on Nonproliferation of Nuclear Weapons.[60] Of course, blocking further progress along this road on the American side was Johnson's insistence on a deepened political, and eventually direct U.S. military commitment, to the battle against local communists in Indochina.

Despite the steady immersion of the United States in the war in Vietnam, Johnson declared that the progress made across that range of bilateral issues meant "the Cold War glacier seemed to be melting." He determined to warm the climate of relations further not by winding down the war, but by negotiating a major arms control treaty before he left office.[61] Johnson seemed blithely unaware of any conflict between his view of the war as crucial to deterring the Soviets elsewhere and his belief that he could deal with Soviet-American bilateral relations as a distinct realm of policy-making. At least in the attempt, his task was eased by the fact that during the 1960s deteriorating Soviet relations with China made relaxation of tensions with the United States a compelling interest for Moscow.[62] Furthermore, the Soviet strategic build-up, stimulated by humiliation over the crisis in Cuba and Kennedy's nuclear program, was beginning to undercut the U.S. strategic advantage.[63]

As rough parity was reached, serious arms control for the first time was in the interest of both parties. The Soviet Union no longer needed to fear that an agreement would freeze the *status quo*, leaving it strategically inferior. Simultaneously, it was no longer as relevant to the United States that arms control might help the Soviets close the strategic gap (as Japan had done under the terms of the Washington and London Naval Treaties of 1921–22 and 1930, respectively). Considerable progress then was made toward an agreement to limit both strategic delivery and defense systems. Johnson thereby laid the groundwork for what later became the Strategic Arms Limitation Talks (SALT), with its Anti-Ballistic Missile (ABM) rider. In sum, by mid–1968 something of an informal *détente* in American-Soviet relations was evolving, to a limited degree insulated from the conflict in Indochina.

Soon, however, another crisis that centered on Moscow's domination of an eastern European nation and its willingness to use force to maintain the outer colonies of its empire erupted, this time in Czechoslovakia. The so-called "Prague Spring" of liberal reform undertaken by Alexander Dubcek's regime in 1968 was a fundamental challenge to Soviet control of the whole of eastern Europe—a precursor of what was to come a generation later, in 1989. And as those later events clearly demonstrated, a loosening of control over the satellite countries threatened communist party control and the domestic stability of the Soviet Union itself. These connections must have been clear to the neo-Stalinist old guard that had succeeded Khrushchev, for by June it was apparent even to outsiders that unless the Soviets intervened, they stood to lose control of much more than just Czechoslovakia: they stood to lose eastern Europe, and with it, to suffer a fatal setback in the Cold War.[64]

Yet one thing the building Czech crisis did *not* threaten to upset was the *détente* then being worked out between Moscow and Washington. In light of past responses against forcible suppression of national revolts in East Germany, Poland, and Hungary, the Soviets had to believe they were chancing only a temporary derailment of relations with Washington and the West. They could put an end to Czechoslovakia's experiment in "socialism with a human face" and the Americans would surely bark about self-determination and human rights; but bogged down and overcommitted as the United States then was in Vietnam, it was not likely to bite. Still, Soviet leaders could not have expected what they actually got: Washington, and almost all other western capitals, said little or nothing about the budding crisis over liberalization and reform within the eastern bloc.

While pressures for intervention in Czechoslovakia built within the Soviet bloc, as far as can be told with the main archives still closed, the Johnson administration made little effort to dissuade Moscow from using force to resolve the crisis—it certainly did not do so publicly. Nor did it offer much public moral support to Dubcek's plans for liberalization and reform. One prominent expert on Czech affairs, H. Gordon Skilling, writes:

Washington "loudly stood aside," giving every possible signal of her noninvolvement.... No public statements were made that would have warned the Soviet Union of the harmful effects on her own interests of a resort to force. President Johnson ... indicated that the USA was giving highest priority to *détente* and made no references whatever to the gathering crisis.[65]

Indeed, Secretary of State Dean Rusk made a point of signaling that intervention would not derail the improvement in U.S.-Soviet relations. He repudiated earlier warnings by some lower ranking State Department officials that the use of force against Dubcek would make cooperation with Moscow on other matters difficult, and declared that Washington was "not involved ... in any way in the situation" unfolding in Prague.[66] George Ball, then U.S. Ambassador to the United Nations, recalled Johnson's mood on being told of the invasion as one of "sardonic detachment." Ball was asked to take over the issue by talking up a good show in the Security Council. He did so, recalling in his memoirs that "the diplomats on the spot indulged in rhetoric and playacting for the consumption of their governments and hometown newspapers." Even the Soviet Ambassador, Yakov Malik, played along. As Ball remembered it: "Once the television cameras had been turned off . . . at three in the morning, he came around the table, pounded me on the back, and said, 'Well, I certainly kept you up late, didn't I?'"[67]

It is therefore difficult to accept Johnson's later depiction of his policy as relying on public criticism and private persuasion to deter the use of force. He wrote shortly before his death: "We hoped . . . increasing world criticism, combined with the confidence a great power like the Soviet Union should have, would convince Moscow not to crush the modest liberalism among the Czechs."[68] Perhaps that was how he wished it had been. But in fact, when the Soviets subsequently rolled into Prague with more than half a million Warsaw Pact troops, the administration was reduced to making futile pleas for "moderation" by Moscow. Only after it appeared a move might also be made against Rumania and Yugoslavia were strong warnings sent to the Kremlin about the consequences for U.S.-Soviet bilateral relations of the use of massive force in the heart of Europe.[69] Even then, Adam Ulam suggests the main deterrent to additional Warsaw Pact action against Rumania and Yugoslavia was the warning given Moscow by those countries that they would resist invasion.[70] Czechoslovakia no longer was, in Neville Chamberlain's infamous phrase, "a far-away country of which we know little." But it remained a nation to which the West could provide no practical assistance, and for which it was not prepared to take even declaratory risks. The Czechs would remember that caution in 1968 as something akin to another betrayal. Never again fully trusting the West, they would be among the last of the eastern European states to chance breaking free of Soviet control during the heady, reformist days of 1989 and 1990.

Johnson's critical response to Soviet suppression of reform and liberalization in Czechoslovakia, heavily muted as it was, also was short-lived. He later wrote that he simply "waited for withdrawal of Warsaw Pact forces from Czechoslovakia and a quieting of the atmosphere in Central Europe" before resuming talks about a summit meeting where he hoped to achieve a longed-for breakthrough on arms control.[71] As Skilling notes, nothing in Johnson's post-invasion rhetoric or behavior "suggested that the desire to maintain good relations with the U.S.S.R. and to continue the pursuit of *détente* had in any way been abandoned, or that the hope of eventual success had been seriously shaken."[72] In a less than surprising but still disturbing measure of the growing isolationist temper in the wake of Vietnam, Senator Eugene McCarthy, who wounded Johnson with his challenge for the Democratic nomination, criticized the President for even calling a meeting of the NSC on the night of the invasion. McCarthy made the bizarre argument that Johnson had thereby given undue attention to the events in Czechoslovakia.[73] The Senator need not have worried. After Ball played out his weak hand of protest in the Security Council, Johnson publicly affirmed on September 10th, just three weeks after the invasion, that efforts to improve relations with Moscow would continue. He said: "We hope—and we shall strive—to make this setback a very temporary one."[74] A war against peasant communist guerrillas and infiltrators in a distant and peripheral Asian country was considered a vital national interest, requiring the direct intervention of half a million U.S. troops. Meanwhile massive use of Soviet force in central Europe to reverse modest liberalizations was dismissed as a "setback" to improved bilateral relations. Never was the disjunction greater between real national interests and a misplaced national commitment and crusading zeal.

In fact, it was the Soviets who dashed Johnson's hopes for a summit to discuss various nuclear issues, which they had calculatingly agreed to the night before their tanks entered Prague.[75] The sole sanction imposed by the United States for this latest example of a massive armed incursion by the Soviets into a neighboring country, to suppress national self-determination and crush liberal reform, was a six-month delay in ratification of the Nonproliferation Treaty. The Cold War consensus among the foreign policy elite in the United States had clearly cracked already, over Vietnam. The effects of that division were being felt in the streets of American cities, but more importantly in a disproportionately weak response to Soviet military action, and the threat of further action, in the heart of Europe—the centerpiece and major prize of the Cold War.

While the national agony over Vietnam still had several years to run, the Czech crisis demonstrated that the United States no longer indiscriminately identified its national security with the success of liberty in *all* foreign lands. A measured withdrawal from strategic overcommitments and a more nearly classical, balance of power approach to the conduct of U.S. foreign relations appeared to be a real possibility for the first time since the onset of the Cold War. In November, President-elect Richard Nixon warned that he was going to make such major changes in foreign policy after his inauguration. To prepare the way, Nixon privately torpedoed Johnson's effort to salvage a last personal success from a summit, by telling the Soviets he would not be bound by understandings reached with the outgoing administration made after the election.[76]

NOTES

1. John L. Gaddis, *The United States and the Origins of the Cold War 1941–1947* (Columbia University Press, 1972): pp. 1–31; Melvyn P. Leffler, *A Preponderance of Power* (Stanford University Press, 1992): *passim*, and pp. 496–99; and see Chapters 7 and 8, on the United Nations.

2. The Long Telegram and "X" article cited in Notes #25 and #27, in the preceding chapter. Also see David Mayers, "Containment and the Primacy of Diplomacy: George Kennan's Views, 1947–48," *International Security* (Summer 1986): pp. 124–62; and *idem*, *George Kennan and the Dilemmas of U.S. Foreign Policy* (Oxford University Press, 1988): pp. 105–60.

3. See John L. Gaddis, *The United States and the End of the Cold War* (Oxford University Press, 1992): pp. 48–50; Michael Hogan, *The Marshall Plan* (Cambridge University Press, 1987); and Hodge and Nolan, "'As Powerful As We Are': From the Morgenthau Plan to Marshall Aid," in *Shepherd of Democracy?, op. cit.*, pp. 55–72.

4. Paul Nitze revisited those events in "America: An Honest Broker," *Foreign Affairs* (Fall 1990): pp. 1–7. For his view of the Soviets and foreign policy decision-making see his memoir, *From Hiroshima to Glasnost* (Grove Weidenfeld, 1989).

5. *FRUS*, 1950, Vol. I: pp. 234–92. Also reproduced in Steven Rearden, *The Evolution of American Strategic Doctrine*, SAIS Papers In International Affairs (Westview, 1984): pp. 89–131.

6. For example, see Truman's Inaugural Address in 1949, *DRAR*: p. 182.

7. See Gaddis, *End of the Cold War*: pp. 53–55. Cf. Richard Melanson, "The Foundations of Eisenhower's Foreign Policy, " in *idem* and David Mayers, ed., *Reevaluating Eisenhower* (University of Illinois Press, 1989): pp. 31–39.

8. *FRUS*, 1950, Vol. I: pp. 234–92; and Nitze, "Honest Broker," pp. 4–5.

9. Concerning the administration's exaggeration of the Soviet threat to Greece and Turkey in support of the Truman Doctrine, see Howard Jones, *A New Kind of War* (Oxford University Press, 1989); and see Truman's assertions that the Soviets actually planned conquest of the United States itself. *DRAR*: pp. 185, 191. But cf. Vojtech Mastny's account of Soviet policy, the best to date. He argues that the failure of the West to set limits to Stalin's ambitions, because he was incapable of limiting himself, set off the Cold War. *Russia's Road to the Cold War* (Columbia University Press, 1979); Taubman essentially agrees with that thesis, in *Stalin's American Policy*: pp. 8–129.

10. On Stalin's role in North Korea's aggression see Adam B. Ulam, *Expansion and Coexistence*, 2nd ed. (Holt, Rhinehart and Winston, 1974): pp. 517–21; and Alexander George and Richard Smoke, *Deterrence in American Foreign Policy* (Columbia University Press, 1974): pp. 157–59.

11. See Truman's pronouncements in *DRAR*: pp. 183–92. Ernest R. May notes that "Truman was comparatively slow to make the equation between Stalin and Hitler. Only after the North Korean attack on South Korea did he become a

complete believer." See his "The Cold War," in Joseph Nye, ed., *The Making of America's Soviet Policy* (Yale University Press, 1984): p. 227.

12. Still useful early accounts are Arthur Grey, "The Thirty-Eighth Parallel," *Foreign Affairs* (April 1951): pp. 482–87; and Alexander George, "American Policy-making and the North Korean Aggression," *World Politics* (January 1955): pp. 209–32.

13. A concise summary is Stephen Ambrose, *Rise to Globalism*, 6th ed. (Penguin, 1991): pp. 116–31.

14. Poll cited in Norman Graebner, *The Age of Global Power* (John Wiley, 1979): p. 107.

15. John Foster Dulles, "A Policy of Boldness," *Life*, May 19, 1952; and Robert Divine, *Foreign Policy and U.S. Presidential Elections, 1952–1960* (New Viewpoints, 1974): pp. 25–27.

16. *NPP*: p. 499.

17. *Ibid.*, p. 476. On the question of Soviet and U.S. violations of wartime agreements see Melvyn P. Leffler, "Adherence to Agreements," *International Security* (Summer 1986): pp. 88–123.

18. Quoted in Divine, *Presidential Elections*: pp. 25–26, 53–54.

19. Stephen Ambrose, *Eisenhower,* Vol. I, *General of the Army, President Elect* (Simon & Schuster, 1983): pp. 500–49.

20. Quoted in Robert Dallek, *Lone Star Rising* (Oxford University Press, 1991): p. 433.

21. An insightful analysis of Eisenhower's public philosophy, which led him to view the Cold War in modified moral terms, is Melanson, "Foundations of Eisenhower's Foreign Policy," pp. 41–50.

22. See *NPP*: p. 499; and John Foster Dulles' remarks on American exceptionalism in *Vital Speeches*, February 1, 1954: p. 234. More generally, see Bennett Kovrig, *The Myth of Liberation* (Johns Hopkins University Press, 1973).

23. John L. Gaddis, *The Long Peace* (Oxford University Press, 1987): pp. 174–94; and Michael Guhin, *John Foster Dulles* (Columbia University Press, 1972): pp. 129–58.

24. See Eisenhower's address to the American Society of Newspaper Editors, in *DRAR*: pp. 262–63; his 1956 letter to Nikolai Bulganin, in *ibid.,* pp. 294–95; and the administration's temperate report on Soviet forced labor, in Secretary of State, *American Foreign Policy: Current Documents* [hereafter *AFPCD*], 1956: Docs. G: p. 40–41.

25. *DRAR*: pp. 289–90.

26. Entry for November 8, 1956, in *The Eisenhower Diaries*, Robert H. Ferrell, ed. (Norton, 1981): pp. 333–34; Gaddis, *The Long Peace*: pp. 189–90; and Chester Pach and Elmo Richardson, *The Presidency of Dwight D. Eisenhower* (University of Kansas Press, 1991): pp. 131–32.

27. "Face the Nation, October 21, 1956," transcript in *The Eisenhower Administration: A Documentary History*, R. Branyan and L. Larsen, eds. (Random House, 1971), Vol. I: p. 666.

28. Quoted in Divine, *Presidential Elections*: p. 174.

29. John Ranelagh, *The Agency* (Simon & Schuster, 1987): pp. 302–9; and Gaddis, *The Long Peace*: pp. 189–90.

30. *DRAR*: p. 268.

31. Richard M. Nixon, *RN: Memoirs* (Grosset & Dunlap, 1978): pp. 181–84.

32. See House concurrent resolutions #204, of August 6, 1957; and #343, of June 24, 1958, in *DRAR*: pp. 260–61. Nixon believed Radio Liberty and Voice of America broadcasts helped stir unrest. *RN*: p.183. But that may not have been true. See Ranelagh, *The Agency*: pp. 308–9.

33. Divine, *Presidential Elections*: p. 194. That resolution also moved George Kennan to pen lines of bitter frustration with diplomacy in the unruly republic. See his *Memoirs: 1950–1963* (Little, Brown, 1972): pp. 97–100.

34. *DRAR*: p. 302. For Eisenhower's anguish and frustration over his inability to provide assistance to the Hungarian rebels, see his *Waging Peace, 1956–1961* (Doubleday, 1965): pp. 62–70, 86–87, 95. Also see Ambrose, *Eisenhower*, Vol. II, *The President*: pp. 347–75.

35. John Gaddis, *Strategies of Containment* (Oxford University Press, 1982): pp. 127–97.

36. See Robert Divine's short but important book, *Eisenhower and the Cold War* (Oxford University Press, 1981): pp. 105–55; Ambrose, *Eisenhower*, Vol. II, *The President*: pp. 131–35, 520–31; and Thomas Soapes, "A Cold Warrior Seeks Peace," *Diplomatic History* (Winter 1980): pp. 57–72.

37. A collection that goes some distance toward revising Dulles' historical reputation is Richard H. Immerman, ed., *John Foster Dulles and the Diplomacy of the Cold War* (Princeton University Press, 1990); see especially the essays by John Gaddis and Ronald W. Pruessen.

38. Department of State, *Bulletin*, February 6, 1961: pp. 175–76; and see Thomas G. Paterson, *Meeting the Communist Threat* (Oxford University Press, 1988): pp. 191–205.

39. Ambrose, *Rise to Globalism*: p. 182.

40. See Thomas G. Paterson, "Fixation with Cuba," in *idem*, ed., *Kennedy's Quest for Victory* (Oxford University Press, 1989): pp. 123–55.

41. See the other essays in *ibid*.; and see *idem*, *Meeting the Communist Threat*: pp. 191–210.

42. Arthur Schlesinger, Jr., "Human Rights and the American Tradition," *Foreign Affairs* (1978): p. 511.

43. *Idem*, "The Necessary Amorality of Foreign Affairs," *Harper's Magazine* (August 1971): p. 76.

44. On Khruschev's resort to "dazzling improvisations" in foreign policy see Ulam, *Expansion and Coexistence*: pp. 572–694. Also see Georgi Arbatov's characterization of Khruschev as simple and impulsive, relying on bluff and bluster to make the United States overestimate Soviet power. Report on a conference held at the Institute of the United States and Canada, Moscow, in *NYT*, December 27, 1990.

45. Dimitri Simes, "Soviet Policy Toward the United States," in Nye, ed., *America's Soviet Policy*: pp. 297–98.

46. On the Kennedys, the CIA, and Cuba, see Thomas Powers' study of Richard Helms, *The Man Who Kept the Secrets* (Knopf, 1987): pp. 139–43.

47. "Campaign Address," September 23, 1960; and "State of the Union Message," January 11, 1962," in *Memorable Quotations of John F. Kennedy*, Maxwell Meyersohn, ed. (Crowell, 1965): pp. 6–8, 17.

48. Studies that incorporate new Soviet and U.S. documentation on that crisis

include James G. Hershberg, "Before 'The Missiles of October,'" Bernd Greiner, "The Soviet View: An Interview with Sergo Mikoyan," and commentaries, all in *Diplomatic History* (Spring 1990): pp. 163–98, 205–56; James Blight and David Welsh, eds., *On the Brink* (Hill & Wang, 1989); *idem*, and Bruce Allyn, "Essence of Revision," *International Security* (Winter 1989–1990): pp. 136–72. Among older works see Nikita Khrushchev, *Khrushchev Remembers* (Andre Deutsch, 1974): pp. 509–14; Robert Kennedy, *The Thirteen Days* (Norton, 1969); and Graham Allison, *Essence of Decision* (Little, Brown, 1971).

49. Bernard Firestone, *The Quest for Nuclear Stability* (Greenwood, 1982): pp. 38–44.

50. Ambrose, *Rise to Globalism*: p. 186.

51. "Basic National Security Policy," March 1962, draft quoted in Gaddis, *Strategies of Containment*: p. 203.

52. Some 1,500 pages of documentation on his crucial final months in office make it clear that Kennedy's Vietnam policy was both maladroit and adrift, and that he had no definite or discernible plans to pull out. See *FRUS*, 1961–1963, Vol. III, *Vietnam; January–August, 1963*; and Vol. IV, *Vietnam, August–December, 1963*, released in late 1991.

53. Gaddis, *Strategies Of Containment*: pp. 201–9.

54. See "Campaign Address," September 17, 1960, and "Address at Frankfurt, West Germany," June 25, 1963, in Meyersohn, *Memorable Quotations*: pp. 9, 20. Paterson also takes the words of the Inaugural Address more seriously than does Gaddis, in *Meeting the Communist Threat*: pp. 202–3.

55. A. Paul Kubricht, "Politics and Foreign Policy: A Brief Look at the Kennedy Administration's Eastern European Diplomacy," *Diplomatic History* (Winter 1987): pp. 55–65; quoted at p. 56. Also see George Ball, *The Past Has Another Pattern: Memoirs* (Norton, 1982): pp. 165–68.

56. *Ibid.*

57. Kovrig, *Myth of Liberation*: pp. 327–28.

58. Kubricht, "Politics and Foreign Policy," pp. 59–62.

59. That is Johnson's recollection, in *The Vantage Point* (Holt, Rinehart and Winston, 1971): pp. 23–24. The impression of Johnson as a most reluctant interventionist comes through strongly in a collection of hitherto unpublished documents, just released by the Office of the Historian of the Department of State: *Vietnam: 1964* (GPO, 1992).

60. Johnson, *The Vantage Point*: pp. 474–86.

61. *Ibid.*

62. A masterful discussion of the effect of U.S. involvement in the Vietnam war on mitigating the Sino-Soviet split is Ulam's *Expansion and Coexistence*: pp. 695–725.

63. Mikoyan confirms that view in Greiner, "The Soviet View," p. 221.

64. Ulam, *Expansion and Coexistence*: pp. 738–46; and see H. Gordon Skilling, *Czechoslovakia's Interrupted Revolution* (Princeton University Press, 1976): pp. 617–758.

65. *Ibid.*, pp. 731–32.

66. Quoted in S.W. Barton and Lawrence Martin, "Public Diplomacy and the Soviet Invasion of Czechoslovakia," in *Public Diplomacy and Political Change*, Gregory Henderson *et al.*, eds. (Praeger, 1973): pp. 262–63.

67. Ball, *The Past Has Another Pattern*: pp. 440–43.
68. Johnson, *The Vantage Point*: pp. 486–87.
69. Barton and Martin, "Soviet Invasion of Czechoslovakia," pp. 265–68.
70. Ulam, *Expansion and Coexistence*: p. 745.
71. Johnson, *The Vantage Point*: p. 489.
72. Skilling, *Czechoslovakia's Interrupted Revolution*: p. 755.
73. Harry Schwartz, *Prague's 200 Days* (Praeger, 1969): p. 223.
74. Quoted in Henry Kissinger, *White House Years* (Little, Brown, 1979): p. 132.
75. Johnson, *The Vantage Point*: pp. 487–90; Ball, *The Past Has Another Pattern*: pp. 440.
76. Nixon, *RN*: pp. 345–46.

5 HUMAN RIGHTS AND DÉTENTE

Nixon and his *éminence rouge*, National Security Advisor and later Secretary of State, Henry Kissinger, wanted to limit security commitments through overt attention to principles of *realpolitik*. They sought to disengage from the military commitment to South Vietnam in order to return containment policy to its original, primary reliance on political and economic means. That policy would also free the resources necessary to sustain NATO, and allow the United States to focus on core areas of strategic concern in industrialized Europe and Asia. With all that accomplished, they hoped, perhaps it would be possible to repair the foreign policy consensus broken by Vietnam.[1] Therefore, they needed to better manage the adversarial relationship with the Soviet Union.

Nixon and Kissinger sought to institute a shift to a clear balance of power approach to the problem of Soviet power, and had a sophisticated conception of how relations with Moscow ought to be conducted.[2] They realized it was not communism *per se* that threatened western security, but the combination of great national power and entrenched hostility evident from Moscow: they thought only the Soviets had capabilities sufficient to challenge the balance of power, matched with an impulse to expansion and pronounced antagonism toward the West. Nixon hence felt free to make an overture to China, which although also fiercely hostile, feared more the possible applications and consequences of Soviet than American power. After two years of secret negotiations, he made his dramatic and historic visit to China in 1972.[3]

BREAKING NEW GROUND

China feared the Soviets with good reason: their troops clashed bloodily along their common border early in the 1960s, and again in 1969 along the Ussuri River. At one point Moscow quietly queried Nixon as to the probable U.S. response to a Soviet pre-emptive strike against China's nuclear facilities. Nixon sternly warned the Kremlin against using nuclear weapons against Beijing.[4] That incident helped bring about the *rapprochement* with China, which was the most significant outcome, and Nixon's trip to Beijing the most striking symbol, of the new realism in U.S. foreign policy. As Nixon told an affirmatively nodding Chairman Mao Tse-Tung in 1972: "What brings us together is a recognition of a new situation in the world [the Sino-Soviet split] and a recognition on our part that what is important is not a nation's internal political philosophy. What is important is its policy toward the rest of the world and toward us."[5] In turn, as better relations with China brought enough pressure to bear on Hanoi, Nixon slowly disengaged the United States from direct participation in the struggle in Indochina. Kissinger later explained this change succinctly. "The China initiative," he said, "restored perspective to our national policy. It reduced Indochina to its proper scale—a small peninsula on a major continent."[6] Reductions in the direct commitment to Vietnam were later generalized into the "Nixon Doctrine," which Kissinger once summed up as: "America cannot—and will not—conceive *all* the plans, execute *all* the decisions and undertake *all* the defense of the free nations of the world."[7]

Once relations with Moscow were decoupled from the idea of a monolithic communist threat, the administration's Soviet policy distilled into three operational principles: "concreteness," or dealing with specific causes of tension rather than seeking to alter the general temper of the relationship; "restraint," or an expectation that the Soviets would desist from unilateral action to exploit international crises; and "linkage" between the strategic and political environments, which essentially meant tying arms control and trade to Soviet cooperation on regional and political problems.[8] The principle of linkage proved the most difficult to implement. But after two years of persistence against a background of open hostility between China and Soviet Russia, and Nixon's astute playing of "the China card," the Soviets accepted the notion of linkage. Breakthroughs then were made across a range of issues. High-level visits became commonplace, and bilateral agreements were signed on over a dozen different subjects. Among these were settlement of most questions surrounding the status of Berlin; an end to disagreement over Russia's outstanding Lend-Lease debts; the first SALT agreement; and the ABM treaty. Moreover, Moscow appeared to be demonstrating restraint in conflicts involving client states in the Middle East and in Indochina. Linkage thus seemed to be working, and by the end of 1972 bilateral relations between the United States and the Soviet Union were at their best in many years.

Despite the success of the new approach at the level of grand strategy, Nixon and Kissinger were accused of amoralism, or even of immorality, for their putative abandonment of traditional notions about American exceptionalism and national mission.[9] Schlesinger, among others, makes the common charge that Nixon "embraced without visible disgust governments both of the authoritarian right ... and of the totalitarian left."[10] It was up to Congress, such critics argued then and since, to reassert the dedication to foreign policy morality they liked to believe had traditionally imbued American statecraft.[11] But how? The device that presented itself was to bind presidential strength and independence with a host of human rights restrictions applying to aid and trade relations. Specifically, Congress moved to restrict military and economic aid to countries that engaged "in a consistent pattern of gross violations of internationally recognized human rights."[12] That assuaged moral concerns about the conduct of the Vietnam war, and promised to limit new strategic commitments and make it difficult to keep unpopular ones.

It was no accident that one of the first bilateral initiatives aimed at cutting off funds to South Vietnam.[13] That was done ostensibly to put a stop to mistreatment of POWs, but really to quicken the pace of "Vietnamization" and force U.S. disengagement. After years of blocking human rights in the United Nations (see below) and ignoring them in bilateral policy, Congress pitched its challenge to the "imperial presidency" in terms of the cardinal American principle of defending individual liberties, largely to retrench from commitments first made to South Vietnam in the name of defending its national liberty. Battle thus was joined over whether Congress or the president would control the "moral high ground" of foreign policy, and thereby set the broad parameters for U.S. engagement in world affairs.

Seeking to secure respect for rights in other countries in the daily intercourse of state-to-state relations has an internal logic all its own. The concept of active promotion of individual rights and liberties expressed the universalist side of the coin of American exceptionalism, which if made the core of U.S. foreign policy as some in Congress professed to wish, stood to simultaneously weaken existing security ties and require the United States to act as policeman to the world. It was precisely that outcome that Nixon and Kissinger resisted as contrary to the pursuit of more limited and crucial national interests in maintaining a global balance of power, and in managing the Cold War relationship with the Soviets and Chinese. But the administration was not blameless either. Its rhetoric about *détente* encouraged excessive optimism about the degree of cooperation to be expected from Moscow, and caused some neo-isolationists (on the left, this time) to believe the United States might even safely disengage from its policy of containment.[14]

Meanwhile, the administration's devotion to precepts of *realpolitik* seemed to define national interests in overly narrow, even exclusive terms of geopolitical and military security. The result was a great clash between the executive and Congress, in which Nixon may have dragged out disengagement from the war, but Congress too hastily moved to drop security commitments to unpleasant regimes without full regard for the consequences. In its eagerness to wrap up the American stage of the war, a growing reaction within Congress threatened to replace the amorality (or more properly, moral relativism) of Cold War *realpolitik* with an alternative that might end up in empty posturing. The real test, of course, would come in policy toward the Soviet Union.

JACKSON-VANIK

In April 1973, Nixon proposed a comprehensive Trade Act that included extension of Most-Favored-Nation (MFN) status to the Soviet Union, as part of the policy of linkage of trade benefits to Soviet foreign policy restraint.[15] In Congress, an unusual coalition quickly formed around an amendment proposed by influential Senator Henry "Scoop" Jackson (D–Wash.) and Representative Charles Vanik (R–Ohio), precluding MFN as long as the Soviets restricted jewish emigration. Jackson led an influential group of Senate Democrats who, along with conservative Republicans, were hostile in principle to *détente*, as they did not trust in any cooperative dealings with the Soviets. It seems clear that this group saw the amendment as a way to undermine *détente* by encumbering the trade bill with a provision the Soviets might not be able to accept. Not a few liberals joined in supporting Jackson-Vanik, some for reasons of genuine principle, others because they saw it as containing the presidency—the real target of much so-called "foreign policy" legislation on human rights in the mid-1970s. Most business groups opposed Jackson-Vanik, but powerful union interests supported it out of opposition to the Trade Act's overall assault on protectionism. Organized labor hoped to force Nixon to veto the act rather than see his larger purposes in proposing it hijacked by Congress. Lastly, prominent jewish leaders supported the amendment because they hoped sanctions would advance the goal of free emigration more effectively than had quiet diplomacy; and that attracted wide Democratic support in Congress, for electoral reasons.[16] In the hands of that powerful coalition, linkage lost its original meaning—where the administration sought to relate concessions on trade, credits, and access to high technology to Soviet foreign policy, Jackson-Vanik linked trade to altered internal behavior.

Nixon and Kissinger did not want to link Soviet emigration policy or treatment of dissidents to trade, but they had not entirely ignored those issues either. In 1969, Kissinger informed Ambassador Anatoly Dobrynin that the United States would look favorably on Soviet regard for western concerns about free emigration, and requested action on cases involving special hardship.[17] On several occasions Nixon, too, raised the issue of jewish emigration with Soviet leaders, including General Secretary Leonid Brezhnev.[18] Although the Soviets refused to recognize emigration as a right, some hardship cases were resolved, and overall levels rose from a low of 400 in 1968 to some 35,000 in 1973.[19] It is unclear whether the increase reflected western coaxing, or mainly internal considerations. Russian anti-semitism may have come into play, as well as an interest in getting rid of malcontents without having to reopen the Stalinist gulag.[20]

For whatever reasons, the high jewish emigration levels were unprecedented in the postwar period, and indeed in Soviet history. Moreover, the Soviets appeared to be quietly linking, in a positive sense, emigration levels to tangible benefits and improved relations: on the same day a Soviet grain purchase was announced in Washington, higher levels of jewish emigration were announced in Moscow.[21] In one sense at least, therefore, Jackson-Vanik aimed at solving a problem already beginning to ease. Kissinger thus was not entirely unjustified in his later complaint that he and Nixon were "being pushed to do what we already largely had accomplished: to spur Soviet emigration."[22]

During the first half of 1973, the administration underestimated the threat Jackson-Vanick posed to its grand strategy for U.S. foreign policy. At first, with Nixon fresh from his landslide victory over George McGovern and as yet untarnished by the Watergate scandal, the chances of MFN being withheld appeared fairly small. Kissinger later admitted that he and Nixon both realized too late that Jackson-Vanik posed "a fundamental challenge to one of the pillars of our foreign policy." Without publicity, they continued to broach the issue of jewish emigration and the plight of dissidents. Moscow responded by easing an exit or "education" tax on jews that had antagonized a broad spectrum of American public opinion. Thinking matters settled, Kissinger informed Dobrynin that no outstanding issues stood in the way of implementing the Trade Act.[23] He was mistaken.

Watergate soon corroded Nixon's ability to influence Congress on foreign policy, where his pre-eminence had previously been unquestioned. In addition, the attention paid Jackson-Vanik by the national media made it politically risky to oppose a measure ostensibly aimed at increasing jewish emigration and improving human rights conditions. Moreover, each time the Soviets made a concession, Jackson set more ambitious preconditions for MFN. That tactic, employed by a seasoned senator, raised suspicions that Jackson was not really interested in securing higher levels of jewish emigration so much as in killing *détente*, while also improving his chances for the 1976 Democratic nomination among jewish voters.[24] In any case, the controversy increasingly intruded into the calculations and conduct of U.S.-Soviet relations.

Support for Jackson-Vanik soared in September 1973, when Soviet dissident Andrei Sakharov wrote an "Open Letter" to Congress urging adoption of the amendment, and asking that it be extended to include "Germans, Russians, Ukrainians, Lithuanians, Armenians, Estonians, Latvians, Turks, and members of other ethnic groups."[25] Nixon then tried to have MFN removed from the Trade Act, but the House voted in favor of the amendment in December. That shifted the battle into the Senate, Jackson's home turf. Nixon expressed to Dobrynin his "profound contempt for the alliance that had combined to defeat MFN," adding, "We must not let temporary setbacks ... interfere with or poison the relations between the two superpowers."[26] But he was by then too weakened by Watergate to withstand the coalition supporting Jackson-Vanik, on one hand out of opposition to *détente*, and on the other, in hopes of solidifying jewish electoral support while simultaneously weakening the "imperial presidency."

Early in 1974 Jackson added a new demand, passed to the Soviets through Kissinger: must give a written guarantee that jewish emigration would never fall below specified levels. Moscow balked at providing formal assurance on what it regarded as a domestic matter, though it tacitly agreed that on a *per annum* basis exit visas would not be issued at less than 1973 levels. Jackson then revised the number upward, to 60,000 visas per year. The Soviets countered with an offer to permit 45,000 jews to emigrate, a figure well beyond anything hoped for five or even two years earlier. Yet Jackson upped the ante once again, insisting that no fewer than 100,000 visas would suffice.[27] Nixon pleaded with Brezhnev, when they met in June in Moscow, "to make some sort of a gesture on jewish emigration, if only to pull the rug out from under Jackson and some of the media critics."[28] The Soviets declined, no doubt sensing that Nixon's domestic problems might mean he could not deliver the trade package, or carry through on other aspects of *détente*.

The Watergate crisis climaxed during the summer of 1974, thrusting aside issues of trade and jewish emigration until after Nixon's resignation in August. The only major development was a successful June effort, led by Senator Adlai Stevenson (D–Ill.), to attach to renewal of the Export-Import Bank Bill an amendment placing sharp limits on credits available to the Soviet Union.[29] Nixon's successor, Gerald R. Ford, was a man whose prior experience as Minority House Leader made him sympathetic to increased congressional influence over the conduct of foreign policy. Also, while retaining Kissinger, Ford shared neither his Secretary of State's *realpolitik* convictions nor his penchant for secret, "back-channel" diplomacy. Just five days after his inauguration, Ford told Dobrynin that Moscow would have to accept Jackson-Vanik in some form or there could be no MFN. He then passed on yet another fresh demand from Jackson: linkage must go beyond jews, to embrace emigration rights for Baltic peoples, Baptists, and others.[30] Thus began a turn away from Nixon and Kissinger's foreign policy, even while Kissinger remained in office. With no political base in the Republican Party, and having alienated his potential institutional base in the State Department, Kissinger could do nothing to stop the drift away from geopolitical linkage and restraint, toward congressional intervention and renewed confrontation with the Soviet Union. He could not even prevent the humiliation of Ford's order that the word *détente* be struck from the administration's lexicon.[31]

Some senators were prepared to accept Soviet assurances of 55,000 visas for jews per year, but not Jackson. Moscow ruminated on his ultimatum on the higher figure until October. Brezhnev then angrily warned against interference in Soviet internal affairs.[32] Undaunted, and perhaps delighted, Jackson publicly crowed—on the lawn of the White House, with national network news cameras running—that he had forced Moscow to bend, and could do so again. That performance, and the release of Dobrynin's "off-the-record" assurances to Kissinger on emigration levels, reportedly infuriated Brezhnev.[33]

Jackson went even further. On the day of the vote in December, he got Senator Robert Byrd (D–VA) to sponsor an amendment even more restrictive of credits to the Soviets than the Stevenson Amendment. The Senate passed the amended Trade Act by a vote of 77 to 4. Ford signed it three weeks later. As passed, the economic package gutted benefits to the Soviets by limiting their credits to $300 million, and nullifying a $7 billion deal with an American consortium to exploit Siberian gas fields and permit exports to the United States and Japan.[34] Ten days later the Soviets repudiated the entire agreement. Thereafter, they recalled Dobrynin for consultations, drastically cut the number of exit visas granted to jews, and launched a stepped-up repression of political dissidents.[35]

Jackson-Vanik proved counterproductive in almost all regards and from the point of view of nearly all its major backers. The satisfaction conservatives felt at the blow struck against *détente* was countered by the strength of a post-Vietnam, neo-isolationist mood in Congress. For instance, within a year the Clark Amendment to the Foreign Assistance Bill and the Tunney Amendment to the Defense Appropriations Bill prevented Ford from sending even indirect aid to groups fighting against Soviet-Cuban intervention in Angola; those amendments would not be repealed until 1985.[36] Business groups also lost market share, to European and Japanese competitors. Organized labor, which thought it gained from Soviet renunciation of the Trade Act, lost because it had helped to set a precedent of trade sanctions as a popular and easy "solution" to complex diplomatic problems; and of course labor also lost jobs when American export companies failed to penetrate Soviet markets.[37] The U.S. taxpayer also lost, as a Lend-Lease settlement providing for almost $1 billion in repayment of Soviet debts tied into the Trade Act fell by the wayside.[38] The American jewish community became ambivalent, even divided, over Jackson-Vanik. Many welcomed its symbolic support, while others came to see the practical failure of trying to coerce internal changes in a proud and powerful state such as the Soviet Union.[39]

The success of Jackson-Vanik's challenge to executive prerogative in foreign affairs both sprang from and reinforced a congressional reaction against the presidency stemming from Vietnam and Watergate. While many liberal-internationalists at first saw that as positive, they did not appear to recognize that human rights linkage in Soviet policy had opened the floodgates to a full-scale conservative assault on *détente*. Jackson subsequently led a bipartisan attack on efforts to draft a SALT II agreement, while other conservatives courted Soviet dissidents such as Sakharov and Aleksandr Solzhenitsyn, and highlighted Soviet internal practices in their effort to influence public opinion into rejecting *détente*.

Meanwhile, well-intentioned but nearsighted congressional liberals excessively attacked U.S. security and political commitments to Third World states. That added arrows to the conservative quiver once the Soviets began to exploit the contraction of U.S. commitments in Africa and the Gulf. Hence, also losing from adoption of Jackson-Vanik were those northern Democrats and liberal-internationalists in Congress who had supported it at the rate of 130 in favor to 16 votes against in the House. They had done so, as I. M. Destler puts it, because "its morality and its politics appealed to them. They too supported human rights. They too had jewish (and labor) constituents. U.S. diplomatic credibility or economic ties with Moscow were not of comparable importance."[40]

But perhaps the most important consequence of Jackson-Vanik was that the United States lost flexibility over use of the economic instrument as a key tool in relations with the Soviet bloc. Because the 1974 Trade Act was an omnibus bill, and the amendment applied to *all* communist countries, presidents were subsequently unable to take advantage of eastern social and economic weaknesses to widen differences between the Soviet bloc states, by drawing some into a closer relationship with the western economic and trading system. Just as Congress had done under Kennedy, it refused to permit the executive branch to make real and useful distinctions on a country-by-country basis in policy toward eastern Europe. It thereby forced successive presidents and the State Department, which needed to undertake a more flexible economic diplomacy despite congressional obduracy, into making hypocritical waivers on human rights conditionality when applying for MFN for, say, Yugoslavia or Rumania. And it raised the quotient of hypocrisy over China too, where geopolitical and trade considerations required making specious human rights distinctions even when the real situation might have been worse than that in the Soviet Union. Lastly, Jackson-Vanik split U.S. economic policy away from that of its allies, who moved to fill in the gap in credits and sales to the Soviet Union. Within months of the Act's passage, Moscow signed credit agreements with the British, Germans, and others valued at $10 billion.[41]

While liberals whittled away at the stick of defense spending and security commitments needed to restrain the Soviet Union, conservatives had moved to deny the carrot of trade and credit needed to entice Moscow into more restrained foreign policy. The first impulse would not survive the Soviet invasion of Afghanistan and the defense build-up of the Reagan years. But Jackson-Vanik would remain on the books into the 1990s, prohibiting presidents from offering MFN to the Soviets without first obtaining formal assurances, which Moscow refused to grant, on free emigration for jews and others. It thus did much more than block Nixon's linkage conception and policy; it encroached on the ability of all subsequent presidents to conduct a balanced, purposive policy toward Moscow.

Congress seized control of policy toward the Soviet Union, without much concern for the reality that in doing so it contributed to the collapse of *détente*; influenced Soviet emigration policy for the worse; blocked trade as an inducement to Soviet restraint; and stymied efforts to drive an economic wedge between the Soviet Union and eastern Europe. For the next several years Congress actually seemed less interested in Soviet foreign policy and more in marginal, Soviet domestic affairs. That meant Moscow was able to use emigration to influence U.S. policy at least as much as the reverse was true: it could turn the spigot on and off, in line with the ebb and flow of *détente*, and in much the same way that it used ethnic German emmigration after 1972 to try to influence Bonn.[42]

What was the administration responsibility for this disaster? Clearly, Nixon's mistakes over the Watergate scandal played directly into the hands of those who wished to undermine the new directions in which he was taking the country's foreign policy. Additionally, there was the secrecy with which Nixon and Kissinger conducted their most important foreign policy negotiations, and their deliberate exclusion of the State Department in favor of a tight circle of trusted aides. That tactic became habitual and even deteriorated into paranoia toward the end. It had served them well over the China breakthrough, but in the longer term it undercut their key policies by causing resistance in the bureaucracy, and filling a reservoir of suspicion both among the press and in Congress that attached to everything they later attempted.[43]

In this they failed what Kissinger himself called the "acid test" of statecraft: creating and sustaining public support for policies, so they may survive the political vicissitudes of the moment.[44] Robert Beisner frames that dilemma well in an incisive recent essay, wherein he argues: "Kissinger's rejection of ideology in foreign affairs helps account for the thinness of his public support.... [He] confused a fear of ideology's excesses with its condemnation."[45] After Nixon's resignation, Kissinger set out to garner support in a type of domestic "shuttle diplomacy," in which he criss-crossed the country speaking to dozens of by now highly skeptical constituencies.[46] It was, of course, much too late. Senate barons such as Jackson opposed the content of his policies, while important domestic groups were alienated by his language and style. Initiatives once widely viewed as brilliantly agile and innovative now were seen as cynical, and possibly immoral.

MULTILATERAL DIPLOMACY

After decades of Cold War in which both sides had concentrated more on consolidating their own spheres of influence than challenging that of the other side, a *détente* had developed by the early 1970s in which rhetoric was tempered but more real efforts were made to undermine the legitimacy and power position of one's opponent.[47] That was one aspect of the Helsinki Final Act, signed in 1975 in conclusion of the first set of meetings of the Conference on Security and Cooperation in Europe (CSCE), a multilateral breakthrough stimulated more by the emergence of an independent West German *ostpolitik* than by U.S. interest or initiative.[48]

The West obtained a great deal from the CSCE. Moscow acknowledged that the U.S. role in European security was legitimate, and perhaps even came to see it as conducive to Soviet security (as a constraint on Germany and a barrier to Anglo-French nuclear cooperation). Tension over Berlin and the disputed status of the Germanies also was eased, and agreement was achieved on a series of confidence-building measures (CBMs) designed to support *détente*. What did the West give up? Despite a great deal of hyperbole on the right over the "surrender" of eastern Europe, the Final Act did not grant Moscow the full *de jure* recognition of the postwar situation that it craved.[49] Helsinki did require West Germany to postpone reunification, and tacitly accepted a Soviet sphere of influence and special interest in eastern Europe (spelled out informally in the so-called "Sonnenfeldt Doctrine," which called for an "organic" relationship to be cultivated between the Soviet Union and eastern European states).[50] Yet, that was little more than a recognition of reality, in any case.

In a sophisticated new understanding of security, at the CSCE it was appreciated by the West, and particularly Europeans, that while NATO was required to deny the Soviet Union opportunities for aggression, "to limit the motives for aggressive action was also important."[51] Among the most lasting achievements at Helsinki, as matters have turned out, was legal recognition of the liberal-internationalist thesis that lasting and real security in Europe must be based on the free flow of persons and ideas—on respect for human rights and the dignity of individuals. That notion was a fundamental threat to the *status quo* within the Soviet bloc, and a more effective diplomatic thrust than all the earlier talk of "liberation." Through formal introduction of this idea into an accord the Soviets badly wanted for other reasons, the western powers at the CSCE successfully turned the focus to internal preconditions for security, and thereby pointed to Soviet and eastern bloc repression as a source of general concern. The Soviets, preoccupied with territorial questions, "misjudged the real thrust of Helsinki: the destabilizing potential of Basket III [the human rights and contacts provisions] for domestic politics."[52] It is especially ironic, therefore, that the reaction to the Final Act in the United States ranged from lukewarm, to indifferent, to distantly hostile. For instance, candidates Ronald Reagan and Henry Jackson both opposed the Final Act, and there was widespread editorial criticism of Ford's decision to travel to Helsinki to sign the document.[53]

It was at this point that Congress somewhat redeemed itself. It reinvigorated U.S. policy concern with human rights in the Soviet bloc by setting up the Commission on the CSCE, a Helsinki watchdog body that included members of the House, Senate, and executive. At first, the Ford administration resisted the idea of such a body, with reports circulating that Kissinger actually colluded with Dobrynin to prevent Commission members from obtaining visas to enter Soviet bloc countries.[54] But when faced with a threat by key Republican members to withhold support for Ford's re-election campaign, the administration reluctantly joined the Commission.[55] Since then, the Commission has contributed greatly to development of congressional oversight expertise and awareness of the CSCE process, and institutionalized concern with human rights in the eastern bloc in a way Jackson-Vanik did not.[56] It also kept executive attention on Basket III provisions of the Final Act, and prepared the way for congressional acceptance and oversight of CSCE follow-up conferences (at Belgrade in 1977; Madrid in 1980; and Ottawa in 1985). This has turned out to be even more important than it seemed at the time, as the CSCE has so far survived the end of the Cold War and breakup of the Soviet Union and empire, and may yet offer itself as a principal vehicle for reconstructing European security, partly on a basis of respect for human rights and representative government.

THE NEW MORALISM

Despite progress on the multilateral and institutional fronts, domestic politics more than any other factor still drove human rights policy toward the Soviet Union. Left or right, in the approach to the 1976 elections it was politically advantageous to assert a high moral content for one's proposals for foreign policy, and for good measure, to contrast them directly to those of Nixon and Kissinger. Candidates Ronald Reagan and Jimmy Carter, in particular, did this (albeit with different emphases). Thus, the conservative, or Reagan, wing of the Republican Party drove through a platform statement on "morality in foreign policy," that aimed at associating Ford with the detested amoralism of Nixon's and Kissinger's *realpolitik*.[57] Conservatives had neither forgotten nor forgiven Ford's earlier refusal to meet with Aleksandr Solzhenitsyn, which they read as a sign of moral decay at the center of *détente*.

The same mood of longing to return to traditional American idealism infected liberals. The actual genesis of candidate Carter's human rights advocacy is traceable to a simple bargain struck by the national platform drafting committee of the Democratic Party. The party's liberal, or McGovern, wing wanted a plank calling for an end to aid to military dictatorships, such as that which took power in Chile in 1973. Its conservatives wanted an anti-Soviet, anti-communist human rights plank. Senator Daniel Moynihan of New York suggested the deal: "Why not oppose any form of aid? 'We'll be against the dictators you don't like the most,' I said across the table . . . 'if you'll be against the dictators we don't like the most.' The result was the strongest platform commitment to human rights in our history." Yet Carter did not pick up the issue for some time. Moynihan reports that as late as the Democratic convention, "Carter representatives were at best neutral."[58]

Carter seems to have realized the electoral potential of the human rights issue only after Ford blundered in answering a question on Soviet suppression of eastern European liberties. During the second presidential debate, Ford emphatically declared: "There is no Soviet domination of eastern Europe and there never will be under a Ford administration."[59] Carter pounced on the answer and the issue. From then on, human rights were a major theme in his campaign. One advisor later admitted: "There was no specific planning for a particular human rights campaign or program. . . . Fate intervened—happenchance things, letters—that blew the issue up unexpectedly." It was pursued as it "drew such enormous attention and acclaim—especially from the right . . . [it] gave the President maneuvering room."[60] That admission is in line with George Ball's recollection of a meeting where Carter was to consult him on foreign policy. Ball remembers that while Carter was "voluble about his campaign plans . . . [he] scarcely mentioned policies or what he hoped to do when he became President."[61]

These electoral origins lent their erratic character to later policy, especially as by Carter's own admission he "did not fully grasp all the ramifications of our new policy," including that it "was to cut across our relations with the Soviet Union."[62] Also, some senior Carter appointees to human rights positions in the State Department and United Nations had no foreign policy experience or expertise, instead earning their *bona fides* in the domestic civil rights movement. Carter thus took office without a real understanding of what his promises might entail, and not fully aware of the limits other important national interests would place on the expression of liberal principle.

It quickly became common for Carter and other administration spokesmen to uphold the new emphasis on human rights as having ended the moral turpitude that supposedly had previously characterized U.S. foreign policy.[63] Four months after his inauguration, Carter told a commencement audience at the University of Notre Dame that he had "reaffirmed America's commitment to human rights as a fundamental tenet of our foreign policy."[64] Some officials took this theme so far that they claimed to have introduced a wholly novel concept to U.S. foreign policy.[65] Inverting the thesis that involvement in Vietnam arose from an excessive, not diminished, sense of mission, National Security Advisor Zbigniew Brzezinski doggedly maintained in his memoirs: "It was Carter's major accomplishment that . . . America was seen again, after the years of Watergate and the Vietnam War, as standing for its traditional value of freedom."[66] Carter himself declared at Notre Dame that America at last was "free of that inordinate fear of communism" that he believed "once led us to embrace any dictator who joined us in that fear." He continued: "Through failure, we have now found our way back to our own principles and values. . . . We can no longer separate the traditional issues of war and peace from the new global questions of justice, equity, and human rights."[67] That was the key to what was coming: without planning it, the administration's rhetoric was leading it toward linkage of human rights with *détente*, arms control, and other critical security interests.

Carter did not want confrontation with Moscow. He thought that "he could maintain good relations with the Soviet Union, and enlist it in deeper arms reduction, even while launching his crusade against human rights violations and for democratic values."[68] The Soviets, on the other hand, saw the human rights thrust for what it could become: a challenge to the legitimacy of their political and social system. It did not help matters that, coincidentally, they had just decided that a crackdown was necessary to silence dissidents emboldened by *détente* and the CSCE.[69]

In the first weeks of the new administration, a flurry of initiatives were undertaken toward the Soviet bloc. Statements were issued supporting the Helsinki watch group, Charter '77 in Czechoslovakia, and well-known Soviet dissidents Andrei Sakharov and Aleksandr Ginsburg. Dobrynin protested, which surprised Carter and caused him to give a public assurance that he did not wish to aggravate relations.[70] He told Dobrynin in private that the United States would "not interfere in the internal affairs of the Soviet Union," but added that he expected "all existing agreements to be carried out, including those relating to human rights," such as the Universal Declaration and Helsinki Accords. In mid-February, still blithely immune to the thought that the Soviets might link human rights to other matters even if he did not, Carter wrote to Sakharov, giving his "personal pledge to promote human rights in the Soviet Union."[71] In response, Brezhnev rebuked Carter, saying he would not "allow interference in our internal affairs, whatever pseudo-humanitarian slogans are used to present it."[72] Andrei Gromyko reinforced that message ten days later.[73]

The sharpness of the Soviet response again surprised Carter.[74] Yet he did not desist from making moral gestures. After hesitation, he entertained at the White House another well-known dissident, Vladimir Bukhovsky.[75] The Soviets thereupon arrested a number of dissidents and jewish activists, such as Anatoly Scharansky and Yuri Orlov. Secretary of State Cyrus Vance met Andrei Gromyko in Moscow, in late March. At that meeting the Soviet Foreign Minister rejected Carter's proposals on SALT, and broadly hinted that his government might link progress in arms control to noninterference in Soviet internal affairs. Vance later recalled:

I do not believe our human rights policy was the cause of the failure of the Moscow negotiation, although it did affect the general atmosphere in which our talks took place. Our position on human rights matters had undoubtedly irritated the Soviets, but it did not cause them to reject our proposals. The Soviets were much too pragmatic to let their deeper security interests be jeopardized by matters that were only an irritant.[76]

Carter later wrote that pursuing human rights "did create tension between us [and the Soviets] and prevented a more harmonious resolution of some of our other differences."[77] In fact, he was caught on the horns of a dilemma of his own fashioning. The Soviets were hinting that negotiation of SALT II depended on the United States downplaying human rights. Yet any suggestion that the administration might be willing to soft-pedal its human rights policy would tend to undercut support for SALT II among conservatives.

This *naïveté* about the implicit linkage between human rights and other strategic goals *vis-a-vis* the Soviets was evident throughout the administration, at least at first. Kenneth W. Thompson reports that at a conference held at the University of Virginia in June 1977, "Almost without exception, administration spokesmen, then in their first six months in office, saw no contradiction or even any tension between a strong human rights campaign and the pursuit of other objectives in foreign policy. It was argued that strategies to advance SALT II and nuclear nonproliferation would not be influenced by the crusade for human rights."[78] In a press interview given in June 1977, Carter made the frank admission that he had not anticipated the Soviet response. "There has been a surprising, adverse reaction," he said, "to our stand on human rights. . . . That's provided a greater obstacle to other friendly pursuits of common goals, like in SALT, than I had anticipated."[79] Because Carter had used human rights effectively as a catch-all slogan during the campaign, he thought he could use the issue to garner conservative and liberal support for his Soviet policies.[80] Yet there was more in play than Carter's entering office without a clear policy, or his foreign policy *naïveté*. Another problem was that Carter's key foreign policy appointees were following conflicting, and ultimately irreconcilable, approaches to the Soviet Union, and that Carter was unwilling or unable to decide between them.

TOWARD CONFRONTATION

Vance and Brzezinski never agreed on a coherent strategic policy toward the Soviet Union. Presidential Directive (PD) 18, the main document of the administration's national security strategy, was not signed until August 24, 1977. And PD-18 did not clarify policy so much as highlight sharp divisions within the administration concerning the projection of Soviet power into regional conflicts in Africa, Southeast Asia, and the Caribbean.[81] Nor did Vance and Brzezinski agree on the proper place of human rights in policy toward the Soviet Union. Vance preferred broad accommodation with the Soviets, stressing mutual interests in arms control and in limiting regional conflicts. He was resolved to reduce the centrality in U.S. diplomacy of the strategic competition with the Soviet Union, and gave the highest priority to completing negotiations on SALT II, which had been stalled during much of the Ford administration. He therefore preferred to see human rights dealt with, at least concerning the Soviet Union and other eastern bloc countries, by means of quiet diplomacy.[82] But Vance left himself open to criticism by being apparently far less reluctant to criticize, cut aid to, or otherwise sanction smaller powers. Some of his appointees at the State Department have even been described by Carter's respected Undersecretary of State, David Newsom, as "People at the Bureau of Human Rights who, I don't think it is putting it too strongly, came into the Department dedicated to the idea of seeing the overthrow of rightist dictators in such countries as Indonesia, Nicaragua, Iran and the Philippines."[83]

Vance made his limited interest in human rights issues clear during talks with Brezhnev in April 1977. Despite the high profile being given the issue by Carter, Vance declined to meet with Soviet dissidents while in Moscow.[84] He wrote later that when Brezhnev "launched into a diatribe in which he catalogued alleged human rights abuses in the United States, I responded sharply to his charges and stressed the importance of making progress in our talks. We needed concrete progress, not polemics."[85] On another occasion, Vance instructed the U.S. Ambassador to the U.N. Human Rights Commission in Geneva that he should not even mention the arrest of Yuri Orlov.[86]

But some of Vance's subordinates were less chary about offending the Soviets. During preliminary meetings in the lead-up to the Belgrade conference on the CSCE, it became evident that the U.S. delegation was planning an offensive against Soviet bloc abuses. At the meeting itself, which opened in October, the United States followed through with severely critical reports on Soviet practice, especially as it pertained to suppression of the Helsinki watch groups that had sprung up in eastern Europe and the Soviet Union after signature of the Final Act.[87] That satisfied the administration's interest in a high profile for its human rights rhetoric, but also contributed to a substantive stalemate at the meeting and unease among European allies about U.S. appreciation of the larger purposes of the CSCE.[88]

The most important opposition to Vance's preference for a quiet human rights diplomacy came from Brzezinski. He both lobbied for a more aggressive approach to Moscow, and ran major initiatives behind Vance's back. When George Ball discovered the extent and character of this infighting at the highest levels of the administration, he told Vance it was "shockingly unhealthy."[89] However, Brzezinski was on a crusade of his own:

I felt strongly that we were making a fundamental mistake in concentrating so heavily on SALT, without engaging the Soviets in a broader strategic dialogue. In effect, I had profound reservations about both the tactics and the substance of Vance's, and to some extent also the President's, approach to the Soviets. They hoped to use SALT as an opening wedge for developing a broader relationship; I felt that Soviet actions around the world required a firmer response and a more direct and sustained dialogue on what was and was not acceptable. Otherwise I feared we would end up with neither *détente* nor SALT.[90]

Where did human rights fit in? As the "best way to answer the Soviets' ideological challenge." Brzezinski saw in human rights "an opportunity to put the Soviet Union ideologically on the defensive." He hoped thereby to "mobilize far greater global support and focus global attention on the glaring internal weaknesses of the Soviet system."[91]

Vance and Brzezinski attempted in their memoirs to play down the personal animus that grew between them; neither quite succeeded.[92] The struggle went on for over two years, with neither able to persuade Carter to take the plunge entirely in his direction. The president's ambivalence and confusion was evident in a major address he gave in June 1978 to his old school, the Naval Academy. He began by calling for renewed *détente* and mutual restraint, but then spoke harshly of Soviet disrespect for the Helsinki Accords, and even raised the old shibboleth of support for liberation of eastern Europe from Soviet domination. The most shocking line, to those who remembered him chiding the American people for once having had an "inordinate fear of communism," came when he accused the Soviets of trying "to export a totalitarian and repressive form of government."[93] The speech was, in the words of one critic, "so disjunctive in its combined reaffirmation of *détente* and articulation of a confrontational strategy that the general reaction was perplexity."[94]

Personally and politically, Carter could not let go the moralistic *and essentially offensive* claims of human rights. Indeed, he now began—as Brzezinski had urged—to press the issue as a prerequisite for the success of *détente*, just as some congressional proponents of an aggressive human rights policy began to reconsider. Charles Vanik and Adlai Stevenson both backed away from their earlier amendments, and in 1979 came out in favor of MFN for the Soviets, under less stringent conditions. (Scoop Jackson on the other hand, denounced SALT II and accused Nixon, Ford and Carter of attempted appeasement).[95] That might have given Carter the opening he needed to advance the express goal of PD-18 to exploit differences between communist societies, but he had lost control of his own Soviet policy and was unable to seize the opportunity.

While internal divisions pulled the administration in opposite directions, the Soviets showed great insensitivity to Carter's stake in the human rights issue. For instance, within a few weeks of his Annapolis speech Moscow put on trial two prominent dissidents, Scharansky and Ginzburg, a fact that greatly aroused the American jewish community in particular. After a fierce debate, the administration responded with sanctions against the export to the eastern bloc of computers, and oil and gas production technology. However, it soon undercut its own policy by permitting an American company to build an oil drill-bit factory in the Soviet Union. Carter himself described the episode as one of the most inept of his administration.[96] Yet he still vacillated between meeting the public's demand for cooperation with the Soviets on arms control, and its continuing anti-communism, suspicion of Soviet intentions, and support for containment.[97] Also by this time, his broad human rights policy was under heavy fire at home and abroad for its strategic insensitivity and frequent incoherence. For example, he placed a severe strain on relations with South Korea over human rights violations, and his on-again-off-again announcements about withdrawing American ground forces.[98]

Carter rather belatedly rediscovered the virtues of containment, just as his successor would be forced after an initial rejection of compromise to reconsider the merits of *détente*.[99] The two factors that finally forced Carter to choose Brzezinski's position over that of Vance were apparent Soviet geopolitical advances, and a hardening and rightward shift in domestic public opinion. The anti-American turn taken by revolutions in Iran, Nicaragua, and Afghanistan forced Carter to reconsider and then back away from a policy that conservative critics said, not without justification, often reduced to cutting ties with weak, non-communist countries. Brzezinski played this note well, arguing to Carter from 1978 on that in its application to the Third World, the administration's human rights policy was in danger of becoming "one-sidedly anti-rightest."[100]

Second, and partly growing out of a perception of Soviet advances in Africa and the Gulf, there was underway by the middle of 1978 a tidal shift in U.S. public and congressional opinion, carrying in renewed hostility toward the Soviet Union and a willingness to reinforce containment—as reflected in congressional votes to begin the increases in defense spending that carried over into the Reagan presidency. Carter's problem was that by the time he too began to shift, major policy initiatives such as SALT II were fatally undermined by disillusionment with exaggerated images of the benefits of *détente*, and by the entrenched perception that he was a weak and inept president.[101]

The conflict that did irreparable damage in both Washington and Moscow to Carter's hope for a new SALT agreement occurred in the fall of 1979, and was almost entirely of his own making. This incident was the administration's "discovery" of a Soviet combat brigade in Cuba, which Vance and Carter declared "unacceptable."[102] After weeks of crisis-like posturing, and growing disenchantment within Congress and the country, Carter accepted the presence of the brigade (which had been in Cuba for years).[103] Once again, he looked weak and indecisive, with no real foreign policy, and unable to deal firmly or effectively with the Soviets. In Brzezinski's words, the pseudo-controversy over Soviet troops in Cuba "shook public confidence in the Administration and . . . heightened public hostility toward the Soviet Union. It also deprived us of momentum in the SALT ratification process."[104]

Years later, Carter still did not appreciate the damage that had been done. He wrote: "After some difficult weeks, we weathered the storm over the troops in Cuba . . . [and] began to pick up votes [on SALT] as the Senate prepared to set aside the first months of 1980 for the ratification debate."[105] But the final turning point in his administration had been reached. It only added to his difficulties that the recession continued, and anti-American revolutions in Iran and Nicaragua shortly thereafter peaked, reinforcing the public's perception that he was incapable in foreign affairs and that U.S. interests were not well protected as a result.[106]

The *coup de grace* to Carter's policy of cooperation mixed with competition with the Soviets, to the whole effort at *détente* from Nixon to Carter, came in December 1979 with the Soviet invasion of Afghanistan. In a nationally televised interview, he made the remarkable admission: "The action of the Soviets has made a more dramatic change in my opinion of what the Soviets' ultimate goals are than anything they've done in the previous time I've been in office."[107] Bowing to political necessity, on January 4th, 1980, he announced he was withdrawing SALT II from consideration by the Senate. He also imposed an embargo on grain sales to the Soviets that would hurt him badly among farm voters; an unpopular boycott of the Moscow Olympics; as well as a number of other, minor sanctions. Any chance he had to recover from these mistakes before the 1980 election was buried under his extraordinary preoccupation with the hostage crisis in Iran that only ended with his departure from office.[108]

During 1980 opposition to the grain embargo and other sanctions mounted, and was used to great advantage by Ronald Reagan in his campaign. The revolution in Nicaragua soured, from the American perspective; the Soviet build-up in Afghanistan continued; and the revolution in Iran became ever more radical and anti-American. In April Vance resigned, ostensibly over the failed "Desert One" rescue mission to Iran—another humiliation for the whole administration— but more likely because three times subsequent to the invasion of Afghanistan Carter rebuffed his efforts to reopen a dialogue with Moscow.[109] With Carter personally obsessed with events in Iran and under serious challenge from Edward Kennedy in the Democratic primaries, and with Vance gone from the State Department, Brzezinski at last had control of policy toward the Soviet Union. But there was little room in which he could maneuver, and only six months left before the election of Ronald Reagan confirmed that American-Soviet relations had returned to the deepest antagonisms of the Cold War. Like Nixon and Kissinger, Carter too had failed to meet the "acid test" of democratic statesmanship: his uncertain human rights emphasis did not provide the basis for a sustainable foreign policy consensus toward the Soviet Union.

NOTES

1. William Schneider, "Conservatism, Not Interventionism: Trends in Foreign Policy Opinion, 1974–1982," in Kenneth Oye, ed., *Eagle Defiant* (Little, Brown, 1983): pp. 33–64.

2. The best account of Henry Kissinger's views still is his own, in *White House Years* (Little, Brown, 1979): pp. 114–30.

3. Richard M. Nixon, *RN: Memoirs* (Grosset & Dunlap, 1978): pp. 544–80; and see his earlier article, "Asia After Vietnam," *Foreign Affairs* (October 1967): pp. 111–25.

4. John L. Gaddis, *Strategies of Containment* (Oxford University Press, 1982): pp. 183–191; William Safire, *Before the Fall* (Doubleday, 1975): p. 370; and William G. Hylund, *Mortal Rivals* (Random House, 1987): p. 26.

5. Nixon, *RN*: p. 562.

6. Kissinger, *White House Years*: p. 1049.

7. Original emphasis. Quoted in Gaddis, *Strategies of Containment*: p. 298. A solid study is Robert Littwak, *Détente and the Nixon Doctrine* (Cambridge University Press, 1984).

8. Kissinger, *White House Years*: pp. 128–29.

9. Roger Morris sustains a tone of personal moral outrage over the length of *Uncertain Greatness* (Harper & Row, 1977). Seymour Hersh is hypercritical and often shrill, to the point of trivializing the discussion, in *The Price of Power* (Summit Books, 1983).

10. Arthur Schlesinger Jr., "Human Rights and U.S. Foreign Policy" *Foreign Affairs* (1978): pp. 511–12. A more subtle treatment is William P. Bundy, "Dictatorships and American Foreign Policy," *Foreign Affairs* (October 1975): p. 57.

11. *Inter alia*, see David Heaps, *Human Rights and U.S. Foreign Policy* (AAICJ, 1984): pp. 9–14; John Salzberg, "A View from the Hill," in *The Diplomacy of Human Rights*, David Newsom, ed. (UPA, 1986): pp. 13–20; and David Forsythe, "Congress and Human Rights in U.S. Foreign Policy," *Human Rights Quarterly* (August 1987): p. 439. Cf. Kissinger's argument that *realpolitik* emphasizes prudence as the cardinal moral virtue, in Department of State, *Bulletin*, August 5, 1975; and November 15, 1976. And see the concise study by Michael Smith, "Henry Kissinger and the Values of American Realism," in Kenneth W. Thompson, ed., *American Diplomacy* (UPA, 1984): pp. 59–84.

12. Schlesinger, "Human Rights," pp. 511–12.
13. Salzberg, "View from the Hill," p. 13.
14. On the neo-isolationism at work behind much of the human rights legislation in this period see Samuel Huntington, "Human Rights and American Power," *Commentary* (September 1981): pp. 42–43.
15. The Trade Act of 1974, 402-19, U.S.C. 2432.
16. The key study on Jackson-Vanik is Paula Stern's *Water's Edge* (Greenwood, 1979). Also see Peter Ognibene, *Scoop* (Stein and Day, 1975): pp. 182–98; Charles Horner, "Human Rights and the Jackson Amendment," in Dorothy Fosdick, ed., *Staying the Course* (Washington University Press, 1987): pp. 111–28; and Strobe Talbot, "Social Issues," in Joseph Nye, ed., *The Making of America's Soviet Policy* (Yale University Press, 1984): p. 199.
17. Henry Kissinger, *Years of Upheaval* (Little, Brown, 1982): pp. 249–50.
18. Quoted in Nixon, *RN*: p. 1034.
19. Neither Nixon nor Kissinger expected the Soviets to be so forthcoming on emigration. *Ibid*., p. 876; and Kissinger, *Years of Upheaval*: pp. 249–50. Emigration figures in Salo W. Baron, *The Russian Jew Under Tsars and Soviets*, 2nd ed. (Schocken Books, 1987): pp. 318–19.
20. See Maurice Friedberg, "Cultural and Intellectual Life," in *After Brezhnev*, Robert Byrnes, ed. (Indiana University Press, 1983): pp. 261–64; and Adam Ulam, *Dangerous Relations* (Oxford University Press, 1983): pp. 81, 120–24.
21. *NYT*, June 11, 1971. Also see Stephen Ambrose, *Nixon*, Vol. II: *Triumph of a Politician* (Simon & Schuster, 1989): pp. 478–79.
22. Kissinger, *Years of Upheaval*: p. 252.
23. *Ibid*., pp. 253–54.
24. Stern, *Water's Edge*: pp. 19–21; Ognibene, *Scoop*: pp. 182–98; and Raymond Garthoff, *Détente And Confrontation* (Brookings Institute, 1985): p. 356. Horner, a former staffer, defends Jackson as a pioneer of human rights legislation in "Human Rights and the Jackson Amendment," pp. 111–28.
25. Quoted in Baron, *The Russian Jew*: p. 321.
26. Nixon, *RN*: p. 876. Dobrynin was reprimanded for not estimating congressional support for Jackson-Vanik. Stern, *Water's Edge*: p. 103.
27. Kissinger, *Years of Upheaval*: pp. 991–96; Stern, *Water's Edge*: pp. 148–56.
28. Nixon, *RN*: p. 1031.
29. Richard S. Frank, "Trade Report Credits to Soviet Threatened by Eximbank Bill Amendments," *National Journal* (May 11, 1974): p. 684; and Stern, *Water's Edge*: pp. 115–18.
30. *Ibid*., pp. 146–47.
31. Ambrose, *Nixon*, Vol. II: p. 655.
32. Stern, *Water's Edge*: pp. 146–65.
33. Gerald Ford, *A Time to Heal* (Harper & Row, 1979): pp. 138–39, 183; and Garthoff, *Détente and Confrontation*: pp. 456–57.
34. James K. Libbey, *American-Russian Economic Relations: 1790s to 1990s* (Regina, 1989): pp. 112–13.
35. On the Soviet reaction see Ulam, *Dangerous Relations*: pp. 79–82, 120–24; and Robert Huber, *Soviet Perceptions of the U.S. Congress* (Westview, 1989): pp. 19–20, 68–70.

36. Thomas G. Paterson, *Meeting the Communist Threat* (Oxford University Press, 1988): pp. 247–50. Angola also led the Ford administration to reassert Jackson-Vanik. See Kissinger's statement in Department of State, *Bulletin*, February 16, 1976.

37. Libbey, *Economic Relations*: pp. 108–14.

38. Adlai Stevenson and Alton Frye, "Trading with the Communists," *Foreign Affairs* (Spring 1989): p. 55.

39. Stern, *Water's Edge*: pp. 210–11.

40. I.M. Destler, "Congress," in Nye, ed., *America's Soviet Policy, op. cit.* pp. 50–54. Cf. James Sundquist, *The Decline and Resurgence of Congress* (Brookings Institute, 1981); Thomas Mann and Norman Ornstein, eds., *The New Congress* (AEI, 1981); and David P. Forsythe, *Human Rights and U.S. Foreign Policy: Congress Reconsidered* (Florida University Press, 1988).

41. Garthoff, *Détente and Confrontation*: p. 462.

42. Ulam, *Dangerous Relations*: p. 122.

43. Robert Beisner, "History and Henry Kissinger," *Diplomatic History* (Fall 1990): pp. 520–21; and Gaddis, *Strategies of Containment*: p. 275.

44. Henry Kissinger, *A World Restored* (Houghton Mifflin, 1957): pp. 325–26; and see Beisner, "History and Kissinger," pp. 517–19.

45. *Ibid.*, p. 525.

46. A number of these addresses are reprinted in Henry Kissinger, *American Foreign Policy*, 3rd ed. (Norton, 1977).

47. A sophisticated treatment is Pierre Hassner, "Europe: Old Conflicts, New Fears," *Orbis* (Fall 1973): pp. 895–911.

48. Wolfram Hanrieder, "Maturing of a Relationship," in Carl Hodge and Cathal Nolan, eds., *Shepherd of Democracy?* (Greenwood, 1992): pp. 105–122; Mike Bowker and Phil Williams, "Helsinki and West European Security," *International Affairs* (Autumn 1985): pp. 608–13; Michael J. Sodaro, *Moscow, Germany and the West* (Cornell University Press, 1990): pp. 142–54; and John J. Maresca, *To Helsinki: The CSCE 1973–1975* (Duke University Press, 1985); text of the Final Act reproduced at pp. 226–83.

49. Bowker and Williams, "Helsinki and European Security," pp. 608–15.

50. Helmut Sonnenfeldt, a counselor to the State Department, made his controversial remarks to European Ambassadors. They were reported in *NYT*, April 6, 1976; reprinted as Doc. #21 in Vojtech Mastny, ed., *Helsinki, Human Rights, and European Security* (Duke University Press, 1986): pp. 94–98.

51. Bowker and Williams, "Helsinki and European Security," p. 609.

52. Mastny, "Introduction," *Helsinki*: p. 10. And see A.H. Robertson, "The Helsinki Agreement and Human Rights," in Donald Kommers and Gilbert Loescher, eds., *Human Rights and American Foreign Policy* (University of Notre Dame Press, 1979): pp. 130–44.

53. Ford, *A Time to Heal*: pp. 300–302; Garthoff, *Détente and Confrontation*: pp. 478–79.

54. Mastny, ed., *Helsinki*: Docs. #26–29.

55. *Idem*, "Introduction," *Helsinki*: pp. 11–12.

56. For more on this see Margaret E. Galey, "Congress, Foreign Policy and Human Rights Ten Years After Helsinki," *Human Rights Quarterly* (August 1985): pp. 334–72.

57. Ford, *A Time to Heal*: p. 398.
58. Daniel P. Moynihan, "The Politics of Human Rights," *Commentary* (August 1977): p. 22; and see *NPP*: p. 937.
59. Sidney Kraus, ed., *The Great Debates* (University of Indiana Press, 1979): pp. 476–97. On the consequences of this gaffe see Leo P. Ribuffo, "Is Poland a Soviet Satellite?" *Diplomatic History* (Summer 1990): pp. 385–403.
60. Quoted in Elizabeth Drew, "Reporter At Large: Human Rights," *The New Yorker*, July 18, 1977: p. 41; cf. Joshua Muravchik, *The Uncertain Crusade* (Hamilton, 1986): p. 2.
61. George Ball, *The Past Has Another Pattern: Memoirs* (Norton, 1982): pp. 451–52.
62. James Earl Carter, *Keeping Faith* (Bantam, 1982): p. 144.
63. Beisner aptly calls this "the cannot-tell-a-lie righteousness of the Carter administration." See his "History and Kissinger," p. 519.
64. President, *Weekly Compilation of Presidential Documents,* May 30, 1977 [hereafter cited as *Presidential Documents*].
65. See the statements by Patricia Derian and Mark Schneider, quoted in Heaps, *Human Rights*: pp. 23–24.
66. Zbigniew Brzezinski, *Power and Principle* (Farrar, Straus & Giroux, 1985): p. 515.
67. *Presidential Documents,* May 30, 1977.
68. Garthoff, *Détente and Confrontation*: pp. 567–68.
69. *Ibid.*
70. Report of Vance's news conference of January 31, Department of State, *Bulletin*, February 21, 1977; Muravchik, *Uncertain Crusade*: pp. 23–24; and *NYT*, January 28–31, 1977.
71. *NYT*, February 18, 1977; and Carter, *Keeping Faith*: p. 146.
72. *NYT*, March 21, 1977; Brzezinski, *Power and Principle*: pp. 154–55.
73. *NYT*, April 1, 1977.
74. See Carter, *Keeping Faith*: p. 146. Brzezinski recalled that the letter jolted the president, in *Power and Principle*: p. 155.
75. Cyrus Vance interview on *Face the Nation*, Department of State, *Bulletin,* March 21, 1977.
76. Cyrus Vance, *Hard Choices* (Simon & Schuster, 1983): pp. 54–55.
77. Original emphasis. Carter, *Keeping Faith*: p. 149. Cf. Mary Hawkesworth, "Ideological Immunity," *Universal Human Rights* (January 1980): pp. 67–84; and Karl Helicher, "The Response of the Soviet Government and Press to Carter's Human Rights Policies," *Presidential Studies Quarterly* (Spring 1983): pp. 296–304.
78. Kenneth W. Thompson, "Human Rights and Soviet-American Relations," Richard Melanson, ed., *Neither Cold War Nor Détente?* (University of Virginia Press, 1982): pp. 145–46. And see Department of State, *American Foreign Policy Basic Documents,* 1977–1980: Docs. #159–61 [hereafter cited as *AFPBD*].
79. *Presidential Documents*: July 4, 1977.
80. On that point, see Gaddis, *Strategies of Containment*: pp. 347–48.
81. Brzezinski, *Power and Principle*: pp. 177–78, 296–97; Carter, *Keeping Faith*: p. 146. Department of State, *Bulletin*, February 21, 1977; Muravchik, *Uncertain Crusade*: pp. 23–24; Vance, *Hard Choices*: pp. 45–63; Gaddis Smith, *Morality, Reason, and Power* (Hill & Wang, 1986): pp. 65–84; and Raymond Garthoff,

"Eastern Europe in the Context of U.S.-Soviet Relations," in Sarah M. Terry, ed., *Soviet Policy in Eastern Europe* (Yale University Press, 1984): pp. 320–32.

82. Vance, *Hard Choices*: pp. 26–29, 46–47, 100–103.

83. Newsom interviewed in Muravchik, *Uncertain Crusade*: p. 12. Also see Brzezinski, *Power and Principle*: p. 144, where he asserts the human rights policy reduced too often to an assault on "weak or small, non-Communist states that were unable to resist our leverage."

84. Department of State, *Bulletin*, April 25, 1977.

85. Vance, *Hard Choices*: p. 53.

86. Jeane Kirkpatrick, "Establishing a Viable Human Rights Policy," in Howard Wiarda, ed., *Human Rights and U.S. Human Rights Policy* (AEI, 1982): p. 86. This paper originally published in *World Affairs* (Spring 1981): pp. 323–34.

87. See *AFPBD*, 1977–80: Doc. #173. Also, Albert Sherer, "Goldberg Variation," *Foreign Policy* (Summer 1980): pp. 154–59; Dante Fascell, "Did Human Rights Survive Belgrade?" *Foreign Policy* (Summer 1978): pp. 104–18; and *Congressional Record*, House, *Report of the Commission on the CSCE*, 95th Cong., 2nd Sess.

88. Helmut Schmidt and Valéry Giscard d'Estaing expressed concern over the human rights campaign. See Friedbert Pflüger, "Human Rights Unbound," *Presidential Studies Quarterly* (Fall 1989): p. 708; and Helmut Schmidt, *Men and Powers* (Random House, 1989): *passim*.

89. Ball, *The Past Has Another Pattern*: pp. 461–62.

90. Brzezinski, *Power and Principle*: p. 317.

91. *Ibid.*, pp. 124–29, 147–50.

92. Vance, *Hard Choices*: pp. 35–36, 84; and Brzezinski, *Power and Principle*: pp. 36–44.

93. *Presidential Documents*, June 12, 1978; and see Brzezinski, *Power and Principle*: pp. 319–25.

94. Garthoff, *Détente and Confrontation*: pp. 601–6.

95. *Ibid.*, pp. 730–31. Years later, Stevenson denounced Jackson-Vanik as utterly misguided. Stevenson and Frye, "Trading with the Communists," pp. 53–71.

96. Brzezinski, *Power and Principle*: pp. 322–24; and Samuel Huntington, "Renewed Hostility," in Nye, ed., *America's Soviet Policy*: pp. 280–81.

97. On that split in public attitudes see the excellent review by Ralph Levering, "Public Opinion, Foreign Policy, and American Politics Since the 1960s," *Diplomatic History* (Summer 1989): pp. 388–89.

98. Robert Holbroke, Carter's Assistant Secretary for East Asian and Pacific Affairs, later described the decision to withdraw troops in savagely critical terms. See "The Role of South Korea," *Firing Line* Transcript #731, March 25, 1987: p. 10.

99. Beisner, "History and Kissinger," p. 519.

100. Brzezinski, *Power and Principle*: p. 128.

101. See "Opinion Roundup," *Public Opinion* (July–August, 1978); and *ibid.*, (December–January, 1980).

102. Vance maintains that his remarks were misinterpreted by the press and in Congress. See his *Hard Choices*: pp. 358–64; and Department of State, *Bulletin*, October 1979: pp. 63–64.

103. The most complete study is David Newsom, *The Soviet Brigade in Cuba*

(University of Indiana Press, 1987); but also see Garthoff, *Détente And Confrontation*: pp. 828–48.
    104. Brzezinski, *Power and Principle*: pp. 346–53.
    105. Carter, *Keeping Faith*: p. 264.
    106. January 1980, Gallup poll, in Austin Ranney, ed., *The American Elections of 1980* (AEI, 1981): p. 35.
    107. Interview with ABC, cited in Smith, *Morality*: pp. 223–24.
    108. Carter, *Keeping Faith*: p. 594.
    109. Vance, *Hard Choices*: pp. 394–95.

6 BEYOND CONTAINMENT

Ronald Reagan won the presidency at a time when congressional and public opinion strongly favored a tougher policy toward the Soviet Union, including a significant arms build-up. For instance, in March 1981, 81 percent of those polled agreed: "All the tough talk to the Russians will not be effective unless we back it up with a stronger military."[1] A wide, bipartisan consensus also existed within Congress to markedly increase defense spending. In fact, Congress had taken the lead on an arms build-up during the last two years of the Carter administration, and in his final year Carter himself took "a generally harder line toward the Soviets than any president since Eisenhower."[2] Other of the more controversial aspects of the Reagan years had antecedents in Carter's last year, such as the lifting of restrictions on the CIA and the renewed declaration of a willingness to use force to secure U.S. interests (for example, in the "Carter Doctrine" on intervention in the Persian Gulf, and development of a "Rapid-Deployment-Force").

Even so, Reagan took advantage of disgruntlement by charging that *détente*, from Nixon through Carter, had permitted the Soviets to gain strategic superiority and make geopolitical advances in the Third World. He therefore promised to scrap SALT II, pending renegotiation; oppose what he saw as Soviet-inspired revolutions and client states in the Third World; and end human rights sanctions as applied to allies in the Cold War, for which he blamed the fall of the Shah in Iran and the success of the Sandinistas in Nicaragua. He would find less than majority support for intervention and the use of force against supposed Soviet proxies, especially in Central America.[3] But he would enjoy a high degree of consensus on much of his Soviet policy, both in its confrontational and then more accommodating phases. One of the ways he achieved this was, after first seeming to reject Carter's emphasis on human rights, to elevate such concerns to the first rank in American diplomacy by giving them an offensive twist.

ASSERTIVE EXCEPTIONALISM

In his foreign policy rhetoric, Reagan expressed the nation's mood of frustration and assertiveness, and its longing to return to a more innocent image of "American exceptionalism." From his earliest statements he depicted the United States in the classic language of its exceptionalist tradition, as a "shining citty upon a hill," a new Jerusalem.[4] This vision of the nation as having a special virtue and mission, born of liberal values, facilitated a converse view of the Soviet Union—one that revived the Cold War analogy of Soviet Russia to Nazi Germany, where both were seen as evil empires bent on expansion. Among Reagan's more notable remarks on this score was his depiction of Soviet leaders as reserving "unto themselves the right to commit any crime, to lie, to cheat," and his calling Moscow "the focus of evil in the modern world."[5] Such language discomfited specialists, as it seemed unnecessarily confrontational and even bellicose, and was reminiscent of the manichean categories of NSC-68. However, it found a ready audience among the public. In 1984, 56 percent of those polled agreed that "the Soviet Union is like Hitler's Germany—an evil empire trying to rule the world."[6] This sympathetic response occurred not least because, like Carter, Reagan promised to bring diplomacy into line with American ideals and principles, especially support for liberty abroad; and because the simplified, puritan vision of world affairs he offered was deeply rooted in the national self-image.

Open rejection of *realpolitik* in favor of the older view of American mission meant a rededication of U.S. power to the promotion of liberty—and therefore of human rights—as one of the central goals of foreign policy. That fundamental similarity to Carter was not well understood at first, obscured by a bitter fight in the Senate over the nomination of Ernest Lefever as Assistant Secretary of State for Human Rights. Lefever was rejected for having made controversial statements on South Africa and other human rights questions, but also for his argument that: "We have no moral mandate to remake the world in our own image."[7] Replacing him was Elliot Abrams, who argued that human rights should be placed "in the absolute center of our foreign policy."[8]

Others used similar messianic language. U.N. Ambassador Jeane Kirkpatrick floated an "authoritarian" *vs*. "totalitarian" distinction used to justify a reversal of sanctions on non-communist, Third World allies.[9] But she also explicitly stated: "The idea of 'American exceptionalism'... is linked to the concept of human rights which is central to our sense of nationhood. It is an objective we endorse and promote."[10] Kirkpatrick and Abrams were almost certainly sincere; they were also strikingly nontraditional, indeed extremist, in maintaining that "defending... rights or extending them to other peoples is the *only* legitimate purpose of American foreign policy."[11] That Reagan targeted a different group of states than had Carter, who for other reasons was also selective in applying sanctions, should not obscure the fact that thereby Reagan too overtly linked human rights to key national interests, such as arms control. He thus continued and deepened rejection of the *realpolitik* of Nixon and Kissinger.

The main difference from what Carter had attempted came in how the Reagan administration related human rights to containment, for its attitude to the absence of liberty within the Soviet bloc informed its whole strategic approach to the problem of Soviet power. Secretary of State Alexander Haig expressed this concept in March 1981. Borrowing from Kirkpatrick's lexicon, he spoke of how the central threat to human rights lay in the survival and expansion of Soviet totalitarianism. The United States, he argued, as leader of the free world might on occasion have to sacrifice pressure for human rights in some minor allied country to the cause of long-term victory over totalitarianism, which if it succeeded would wipe out human rights everywhere.[12] In short, *containment itself was to be understood as the administration's main human rights policy*.

That was not entirely unusual: Truman, Eisenhower, and Kennedy all understood containment partly in similar terms. Opposing the expansion of Soviet power and influence always had housed an idealistic, human rights component, albeit submerged beneath geopolitical expediency. Nor was a willingness to look away, in the name of a greater cause, when allies violated the rights of their citizens new. What was genuinely different was the *offensive* turn given to the issue by Reagan, and his depiction of American national interests as coterminous with the defense of human rights. In his view, virtually anything undertaken in the name of opposing geopolitical advances by the Soviet Union or that advanced U.S. interests was *ipso facto* supportive of human rights. That neo-conservative stance was given intellectual cover, and in fact heralded as the only "true" human rights policy by, among others, the many Scoop Jackson Democrats who embraced the Reagan crusade against the Soviet Union.[13] Such oversimplification of moral ambiguities in fighting the Cold War led some observers to conclude Reagan had "co-opted" human rights to ulterior, geostrategic purposes.[14] While not without merit, that view underestimates the extremist sincerity with which some Reagan officials believed containment was the human rights policy *par excellence*.[15]

The administration immediately went on the offensive at the CSCE review conference already underway in Madrid.[16] But it made its view of the link between rights and security most explicit in the controversial "Reagan Doctrine," used to justify military aid programs to anti-communist guerrillas in Afghanistan, Angola, and Nicaragua.[17] One analyst aptly suggests the Reagan Doctrine amounted to a democratic variant of the Soviet doctrine of national liberation, for it went far beyond traditional justifications for military intervention.[18] It aimed first at forestalling victories by local communists, but also at increasing the costs to Moscow of what was perceived—not always correctly—as revolutionary turmoil stirred up by Soviet adventurism in the Third World.

Direct intervention, too, found support in the elevated place given human rights by Reagan. Explaining the intervention in Grenada, Abrams said: "To put it simply, we believe that American power is a force for good in the world. We also think that there is a necessary connection between the defense of our national interest and the defense of human rights."[19] Under conditions of anonymity, a senior official explained in 1985: "We debated whether we had the right to dictate the form of another country's government. The bottom line was yes, that some rights are more fundamental than the right of nations to non-intervention, like the rights of individual people."[20] This was not Wilsonianism. It was a radical, unilateral crusade. As in other crusades, the pressure of competing interests and ambition would bend and twist into moral compromises the country could not accept—notably concerning the growing obsession with Nicaragua and involvement in the civil war in El Salvador.

IDEALISM VS. PRAGMATISM

The basic thrust of Reagan's Soviet policy in his first term was to rebuild military strength unilaterally, so as to force upon the Soviets the restraint and reciprocity perceived to have been absent from "one-sided" *détente*. Once that had been achieved, Reagan intended to negotiate new arms control and other agreements from a position of strength.[21] That effort was pursued by Haig and, with more emphasis on limited agreements along the way, his successor, George Shultz.[22] The more careful approach was codified in December 1982, in a National Security Decision Directive that linked containment and liberalization of the Soviet system, and accepted the need for some negotiated agreements.[23] While Haig and Shultz were tough but pragmatic, others were more ideological. Reacting to the Polish crisis of 1980–1981, some saw a chance to accelerate the collapse of the Soviet system. Secretary of Defense Caspar Weinberger, and a number of lesser officials in the NSC and at Defense, appeared determined to speed the already advanced process of Soviet economic and social decline.[24] Kirkpatrick said openly in December 1981:

A new foreign policy must begin from the... irreducible fact that the Soviet empire is decaying at its center, challenged above all by Poland's insistent demands for greater freedom and autonomy, and from the fact of the exhaustion of Marxism as an ideology capable of motivating men and women.[25]

The more cautious Haig later wrote: "It was clear, in the very first discussions of the Polish situation that some of my colleagues in the NSC were prepared to look beyond Poland, as if it were not in itself an issue of war and peace, and regard it as an opportunity to inflict *mortal* political, economic, and propaganda damage on the U.S.S.R."[26]

Reagan's severe anti-Soviet rhetoric, and the huge arms build-up overseen by Weinberger, outweighed an occasional caveat delivered by the Secretary of State. It seemed the administration was seeking to overturn strategic parity between the superpowers in favor of outright superiority. Weinberger denied this. However, there were hints at a different agenda.[27] Confusion deepened in 1983, following Reagan's surprising announcement of the Strategic Defense Initiative (SDI).[28] Was SDI intended, as Reagan said and apparently believed, to replace the "balance of terror" of the Cold War? Or was it, as the Soviets thought, an effort to cripple their economy further with an unaffordable arms race in space weaponry, and an attempt to achieve a first-strike capability by acquiring a second-strike defense?[29]

Reagan also sought to increase Soviet costs with support for Afghan guerrillas, other covert operations, and a ban on the sale of high-technology goods to the eastern bloc. All that was designed to force Soviet leaders to pay greater attention to their worsening domestic woes rather than foreign affairs. Yet Reagan's lifting of the embargo on grain sales, defended on economic grounds, did not help him convince western Europe to place, for geopolitical reasons, sanctions on the sale of natural gas pipeline equipment to the Soviet Union.[30] That effort failed badly, and alienated European opinion even while a major NATO crisis was underway over the deployment of U.S. cruise missiles to offset earlier deployment of some 350 Soviet SS-20 intermediate missiles.[31]

During its first five years, the Reagan administration attacked the Soviet human rights record at every available opportunity, and in nearly every forum. It pushed hard at the CSCE follow-up conferences, and pressed family reunification, emigration, and treatment of dissidents in bilateral talks.[32] In a reversal of the underlying perception of *détente*, it returned to the argument that the problem was not just Soviet power, but the nature of communism. "Many regimes violate human rights," said Abrams in 1983, "but Communist regimes tend to *export* their human rights violations."[33] Brezhnev's death brought little sign of new policies from either country. While Moscow headed deeper into a succession crisis, Undersecretary Lawrence Eagleburger spoke of two unmet conditions to better relations: a restored military balance and Soviet respect for the Helsinki Accords. Despite talk about the ultimate collapse of the old enemy, there was no sense as yet of what was coming. He added: "The next Russian revolution is not just around the corner.... The economy is not about to collapse."[34] The American build-up and political offensive therefore continued, including its human rights aspects. Pressure was kept up over jewish (and other) emigration, which remained below 1970s rates, and over the plight of "*refuseniks*," now routinely imprisoned or confined to psychiatric hospitals. It was hoped to move beyond protest over individual cases, but given an absence of dialogue with Moscow the United States was confined to gestures over the mistreatment of high-profile individuals, especially Sakharov and

Yelena Bonner, who became ever more celebrated in the West after being banished to the grey, provincial city of Gorky.[35]

On other occasions, pragmatists in the administration were able to restrain policy responses, if not the president's rhetoric. When a Soviet fighter shot down a South Korean airliner in September 1983 (killing 269, including 61 Americans), Reagan pronounced the action a "barbaric act," and Shultz treated it as a human rights violation ("massacre") in talks with Gromyko.[36] This was a low point in public relations between the United States and Soviet Union in the early 1980s, but despite sentiment in Congress for a punitive response, Reagan did not urge any specific action in retaliation.[37] The main features of his policy were in place—the arms build-up, support to anti-communist guerrillas, SDI, and a political, economic, and rhetorical offensive against the moral legitimacy of the Soviet system. He could afford to wait.

The potential for serious confrontation between Washington and Moscow was also tempered during this period by multiple restraints on Soviet behavior, including preoccupation with and an inability to pacify Afghanistan; growing unrest in Poland; and a prolonged leadership struggle. That contest was tied to the crisis of economic and political legitimacy within the Soviet Union, and arose from the fact that three Soviet leaders died in under three years: Brezhnev in November 1982, Yuri Andropov in February 1984, and Konstantin Chernenko in March 1985. In one of the few happy coincidences of the Cold War, when Mikhail Gorbachev took power his call for fundamental reform came just as Reagan concluded the strategic corner had been turned, and prepared to enter into serious arms control and geopolitical talks.

The Reagan administration began to shift during 1984 and 1985 from its strident, public confrontation with the Soviet Union toward renewed arms control negotiation and an understanding of limited, mutual interests. It did so for several reasons: the military program was well underway and Reagan could now move to fulfill his promise to negotiate once he had achieved renewed strength; the U.S. and western economies had recovered from recession in 1982, while the decay and weakness of the Soviet economy was becoming readily apparent; NATO had survived arguably its worst crisis, over the missile deployments of the early 1980s; and public opinion, Congress, and America's allies all were pressing hard for more accommodation. Finally, in Gorbachev the Reagan administration at last had a partner with whom it could negotiate; one who said the Soviet Union would retrench in its foreign policy adventurism in order to concentrate on political and economic reform, on *glasnost* and *perestroika*.

Observing the Soviet *nomenklatura* turn to Gorbachev, the administration concluded its tough stance was vindicated by events. In early 1985 Shultz declared: "In the last four years, the underlying conditions that affect U.S.-Soviet relations have changed dramatically." He went on to describe the Soviets as facing "profound structural economic difficulties and restless allies; their diplomacy and their clients are on the defensive in many parts of the world. We have reason to be confident that the 'correlation of forces' is shifting back in our favor." He concluded with a triumphant endorsement of human rights and the rule of law as possible new "organizing principles of an international order that embraces the great majority of mankind. . . . History is on freedom's side."[38]

TRACKING REFORM

The first cracks in the human rights impasse became apparent in 1985, in tandem with the softening in U.S.-Soviet antagonism attendant on Gorbachev's taking control in Moscow and Reagan's re-election. At their first summit, in Geneva in November 1985, major strides were made in the processes of arms control talks and the establishment of confidence-building measures. In addition, the Soviets accepted human rights as legitimately placed on the agenda of bilateral relations. This breakthrough was a reinforcement of multilateral developments at the CSCE follow-up conferences on CBMs in Stockholm in 1984, and human rights (Basket III) in Ottawa in 1985.[39]

Then, over the objections of Richard Nixon, among others, Reagan went much further than ever before in making respect for human rights a precondition of progress on other important issues.[40] Prior to the summit in Reykjavik in October 1986, he promised to "make it amply clear to Mr. Gorbachev that unless there is real Soviet movement on human rights, we will not have the kind of political atmosphere to make lasting progress on other issues." He added: "True peace requires respect for human rights and freedom as well as arms control."[41] Reykjavik is usually remembered for Reagan's refusal to abandon SDI, but this linkage of human rights and arms control was neither trivial nor momentary. Shultz later provided as a justification, paraphrasing Sakharov, that "arms control agreements with a regime that violates human rights cannot be truly successful in guaranteeing international security." He followed through by stressing human rights at the Vienna CSCE follow-up in November, and in meetings with Soviet Foreign Minister Eduard Shevardnadze.[42]

In 1986 jewish emigration from the Soviet Union reached a 20-year low, Sakharov remained in exile in Gorky, and *refuseniks* were confined in large numbers to camps and psychiatric hospitals. Even as Shultz took "cautious encouragement" from the first, halting steps Gorbachev was then making toward real openness and reform, Assistant Secretary Richard Schifter cautioned: "*glasnost* . . . is not freedom yet, not by a long shot."[43] In early December Reagan dismissed talk about *glasnost* in the human rights field as "gestures that reflect posturing more than flexibility."[44] Even the release of Orlov and Scharansky the previous September was suspect, as it had been connected to a complex spy swap also involving a U.S. journalist, Nicholas Daniloff.[45]

The real break came in mid–December, with a dramatic announcement of the freeing of several notable dissidents, including Sakharov and Yelena Bonner.[46] In January 1987, Moscow released 50 prisoners of conscience, and Gorbachev himself linked internal reform and external Soviet behavior. The State Department country report on the Soviet Union was published a few days later. It remained harshly critical, reflecting internal divisions over how to interpret the sincerity and significance of Gorbachev's reforms.[47] That caution was not unique to the administration, then struggling through Iran-Contra hearings and disquiet over revelations about the amateurish process and startling arms control content of the Reykjavik summit.[48] Yelena Bonner was unsure into 1990 whether Gorbachev was "only trying to struggle for his own power or genuine reform; after five years I still don't know. He may seek unlimited personal power. This is the tradition of our history."[49] This hope mixed with uncertainty was captured by Reagan in a provocative yet masterful gesture, when in June 1987, he challenged in Berlin: "Mr. Gorbachev, tear down this wall!"

By mid–1987, structural criticisms of Soviet society continued to be expressed, but the first glimmerings of solid praise for reform in the human rights area were heard as well. That reflected real change in the Soviet Union. Jewish emigration began to rise, more dissidents and *refuseniks* were released, church and ethnic liberalizations began, and the Soviet press and arts community received their first real taste of free expression. Rather than let up, the Reagan administration continued to insist that further progress in human rights be linked both to general improvement in the relationship and verifiable arms control agreements. Partly due to pressure from allies unsettled by the unilateralism of Reykjavik, the role of the Helsinki process and institutions became increasingly prominent in U.S. policy—Reagan had traveled a long and winding road from his initial opposition to Helsinki in the 1970s.[50] Bilaterally, old issues in Russian-American relations continued to irritate: there was only marginal progress on reunification of American families with husbands or wives who were Soviet citizens, and naturalized Americans continued to have their status challenged and denied.[51]

At the Geneva summit, and again when Shevardnadze visited Washington in October, human rights found the spotlight alongside arms control and the settlement of regional disputes.[52] Solid progress was made on arms control, as represented by the Intermediate Nuclear Force (INF) treaty signed at the Washington summit in December 1987. However, human rights were proving trickier. Gorbachev visibly bristled over U.S. criticism, and the summit final communiqué passed over the topic in the barest terms. Still, while the Soviets did not want to be seen bending to pressure, behind the scenes they acted to remove the issue from the agenda by significantly easing emigration and other restrictions.[53] The Soviet Foreign Ministry in early 1988 invited top State Department officers to engage in "roundtables" to sort out human rights issues; these proved to be the most "friendly and polite" talks ever held on the subject.[54]

By 1988 even the most dogmatic on both sides were finding it difficult to deny that a watershed in postwar history was at hand. Solid progress was being made on Strategic Arms Reduction Talks (START); the Soviets were committed to withdrawal from Afghanistan; and resolution of other regional disputes, including Central America and Africa, looked more hopeful. Within the United States, perceptions of the Soviet Union at both the elite policy and popular levels were warmer than anytime since World War II.[55] Reagan said of the change he saw taking place: "The Soviets may be coming to understand something of the connection, the necessary and inextricable connection, between human rights and economic growth."[56]

In May, he traveled to Moscow for another round of what was becoming almost routine summit diplomacy. With important arms control and geopolitical issues settled or advancing under the careful guidance of lower-level experts, Reagan and Gorbachev engaged in a propaganda *battle royal* over human rights. In the full glare of the international media, itself getting unheard-of access to Soviet sites and citizens, Reagan visited churches and met with groups of Soviet dissidents. He clearly enjoyed the chance to try out his populist politics in the midst of the "evil empire." Gorbachev countered, but somewhat weakly. He met with North American natives, portrayed as political prisoners living in an expropriated, racist country.[57] Nixon and Brezhnev could hardly have imagined such scenes, much less partaken of them. Happily, the formal speeches and statements that emerged from the summit were more moderate and measured on both sides.[58]

The final months of Reagan's presidency were not untroubled by human rights problems in the Soviet Union. The forces of nationalism that soon would rend that empire were already visible, bubbling up and over after decades of repression from the center. First in the Baltic States, but then across several other republics, mass demonstrations and strikes got underway during the summer of 1988. Rather than stir up trouble, as some on the hard right desired, Reagan preferred to go out of office husbanding his triumphs and heralding the longer view. After all, peace seemed to be breaking out all over: Iran gave up the fight against Iraq; Cubans were shipping home from Africa; even in beleaguered Central America, the *contra* war was winding down (under congressional pressure). Most important, the end of the Cold War was in sight, and it was ending on western terms and largely in accordance with American principles.

That was not all or even primarily Reagan's doing, but it was largely America's. From Truman on, a nation said to lack the staying power to lead in world affairs had reconstructed much of Europe and Japan from the destruction of World War II, forged and led a great military alliance, and sustained an even greater political and economic coalition. It was, of course, an extremely expensive victory that also saw excessive militarization of the contest; 100,000 American deaths in Korea and Vietnam; and false moral choices that bewildered and alienated a democratic population. And some costs were unique to Reagan, who faced down the Soviets and reasserted American will, but at the price of trillions in national treasure, mostly borrowed against the future. He thereby left unanswered whether in the final battles of the Cold War the national vault was so emptied that nothing has been left to successors to spend on securing the victory. Moreover, that expenditure applies not only to money, but as importantly to moral energy and political will.[59]

DEMOCRACY OR CHAOS?

During the first year of George Bush's presidency, an unprecedented democratic revolution swept over eastern Europe and the world. In one of the most ironic reversals of the Cold War, it was communist regimes that fell like dominoes, right up to and across the borders of the Soviet Union, when communist government toppled in that giant, multinational empire too. The Bush administration essentially sat and watched, applauding quietly, lest provocation lead to a reversal of the process.[60] Its attention was also drawn to other events, in other parts of the world. One of the few places communism refused to fall, where it was again propped up with tanks and bayonets, was in China. The events in Tiananmen Square in June 1989 and after dominated public and administration attention for much of the summer.[61] In December, Bush would find it necessary to send troops into Panama to secure democratic election results and clean out the mess left from previous collusion with petty dictators during the Cold War. That followed months of insisting the Soviets stay out of the unfolding events in eastern Europe, where from May to November, from Hungary to Poland to Germany, the Iron Curtain was torn down, literally, by thousands of hands. Gorbachev had done nothing to arrest events and even seemed to encourage them at times. Exhibiting reciprocal restraint, at least in superpower relations, Bush refused to gloat in public over the undeniable reality that the Soviet Union was vacating Europe, and therefore that the United States and the West had won the Cold War. Instead, between the fall of the Berlin Wall and the invasion of Panama, he hastily arranged a "mini-summit" at sea off Malta, to show that U.S.-Soviet cooperation was intact.

But with Soviet power withdrawn inside its own borders—or at least committed to doing so, for there was no housing for all the returning troops just yet—was it in the American interest to see the process continue and break up the core of the Soviet empire too? The thunderous "yes!" from the Republican right was loud and clear. Yet Bush thought otherwise.

With communism not the enemy, and with Soviet power whittling down, both of its own accord and in formal arms control treaties, Bush appears to have seen chaos as the main obstacle to peaceful progress in the world.[62] Democracy was fine and welcome, of course; yet freedom without responsibility was not an unqualified good, not if it meant uncaged nationalisms roaming loose over Europe and Central Asia. Already there was unrest and bloodshed in Azerbaijan and Armenia (a portent of worse conflicts to come), where not even a horrendous earthquake interrupted ethnic hatreds and the scramble for territory. The threat thus was chaos and Balkanization on an enormous scale; a vision of the Soviet Union violently breaking apart, leaving a residue of weak, quarrelsome, and *irredentist* states, as did the great empires that expired after World War I. Someone had to try to control the political, economic, and military partitions that were coming. Bush therefore decided to anchor U.S. policy to the survival of a central authority over the lands of the Soviet Union; to Gorbachev, or if not the man, at least his reforms. It was a cautious, prudent, and realistic policy largely dictated by the circumstances; it was also destined to fail more quickly than almost anyone guessed or predicted.

For the first several months Bush and his Secretary of State, James Baker, underplayed the changes in the East while they paused to reconsider overall U.S. policy. They said, "realism requires us to be prudent . . . the Soviet Union remains a very heavily armed superpower," and promised to probe Moscow along an agenda of arms control, human rights, bilateral relations, and regional conflicts.[63] They maintained the traditional U.S. policy of nonrecognition of Stalin's incorporation of the Baltic States into the Soviet Union, resisting popular pressures to drive a diplomatic wedge into Soviet affairs with a more assertive courting of Baltic representatives.[64] They wanted Baltic independence, but they wanted to get there through processes that set a peaceful precedent for other areas yearning to break loose. Reform they also welcomed: "We believe *perestroika* is good for the Soviet Union, and we think it is good for the rest of the world." However, reflecting both their analysis of the situation and the poor state of the coffers of the U.S. Treasury, they warned that success or failure "is really dependent on what the Soviets do and not on what we in the West do."[65] Others in the administration, notably Defense Secretary Richard Cheney, were more mired in the past. He refused to admit the Cold War was ending, and insisted on submitting a defense budget that did not reflect the downgraded Soviet threat, and offered no "peace dividend" to the Congress. That raised an outcry against the administration for itself lacking in "new thinking."[66]

The criticism was premature. On May 12th, Bush delivered a major address outlining results of the internal review. He called for relations to move "beyond containment." America, he declared, "has as its goal more than simply containing Soviet expansionism. We seek the integration of the Soviet Union into the community of nations." He then listed five steps this required: reduction of Soviet forces to equality with the West; acceptance of self-determination for all the nations of eastern and central Europe; resolution of regional disputes in which the Soviets had a hand; creation of political pluralism and respect for human rights in the Soviet Union itself; and greater cooperation on global problems. In return, he promised to match the Soviets on arms reduction; set up a satisfactory verification regime ("Open Skies"); and facilitate a cooperative economic relationship, including a temporary waiver of Jackson-Vanik.[67]

In September, Baker met Shevardnadze in Jackson Hole, Wyoming, where they mapped out a remarkable series of agreements on virtually every point of Bush's five-point agenda, from breaking the deadlock on the relationship between SDI and START, to verification and nuclear testing, to "open skies," Afghanistan and Cambodia. On human rights, the Soviets agreed to codify new laws, and to a range of programs and bilateral exchanges aimed at an improved understanding of "institutions, legislation, and practices which affect human rights and humanitarian issues." That reinforced progress made at a CSCE meeting in Paris earlier in the year, where the United States had accepted a Soviet proposition that democracy could indeed take quite different national forms. At the Malta summit in December, Bush committed to a trade agreement granting MFN to the Soviet Union and seeking a waiver of Jackson-Vanik.[68]

Two crises laden with both national security and human rights implications dominated U.S.-Soviet relations in 1990: ethnic conflict in Azerbaijan and Lithuania's declaration of its independence from the Soviet Union. Bush's prudent reluctance to encourage in any way the forceful destruction of the Soviet Union, while yet supporting peaceful change, was made clear during these crises—even at a cost in public perceptions of his commitment to American principles, both at home and amongst some Soviet human rights activists. When the Red Army went into Baku in January, ostensibly in an effort to separate fighting Azeris and Armenians, it was stated that the United States recognized "the right of any state to ensure the safety of its citizens." When the administration was asked if the United States supported independence for Azerbaijan, it was made clear that with the key exception of the Baltic States, whose incorporation into the Soviet Union in 1940 was not recognized, "since 1933, we have recognized the territorial integrity of the Soviet Union."[69]

Baker continued negotiations with Shevardnadze in Moscow in February, and spoke to the Supreme Soviet about its progress toward democratization. Two weeks later, the Lithuanian National Assembly declared its full independence.[70] That act was greeted in Moscow with an economic blockade and the takeover of government buildings by Soviet "black berets." Bush responded with a campaign to convince Gorbachev and Shevardnadze, when the latter came to Washington in April, that while negotiations on issues of vital American interest would continue, agreements of special interest and benefit to the Soviets in the economic realm might not. Congress too indicated that it would link a waiver of Jackson-Vanik to peaceful resolution of the Baltic crisis. On the other hand, Bush correctly pointed out that territorial questions were not clear (Stalin had added lands to the Lithuanian territory annexed in 1940), and suggested that a cooling-off period and referendum might provide a way out to both sides.[71]

The Lithuanian crisis raised new questions about Gorbachev's long-term survivability; an issue heightened by Defense Secretary Cheney's remark that he did not expect the Soviet President to last. Bush vehemently denied that his policy was based solely on support of Gorbachev, and with justice.[72] At a Washington summit at the end of May, diverse agreements were signed that locked in progress across the board in bilateral relations, whatever happened to Gorbachev. Included were agreements on chemical weapons, nuclear testing, atomic energy, student exchanges, maritime boundaries, ocean studies, maritime transportation, civil aviation, long-term grain sales, and a commercial understanding. Joint statements were also issued on major progress in START, and on the treaty on Conventional Forces in Europe (CFE). Bush then politely quoted Sakharov on the connection between individual liberty and international security; and Gorbachev happily quoted FDR back, on the idea of world peace based on the Four Freedoms.[73] Gorbachev might have fiddled while Moscow burned (for instance, spending inordinate time in the Soviet Parliament discussing possible future names to replace "U.S.S.R."), but Bush did not.

Subsequently, other important matters arose—most spectacularly, the possibility of reunification of Germany and the concomitant question of its position within NATO; also, Soviet desires to join the General Agreement on Tariffs and Trade (GATT) and the Organization of Economic Cooperation and Development (OECD). The Baltic situation remained unresolved until midsummer. Bush withheld the Jackson-Vanik waiver pending passage of an emigration law by the Supreme Soviet, and now also pending a break in the deadlock over Lithuania. In June, the Soviets finally lifted the economic blockade. Gorbachev met with the Baltic presidents to work out a solution, and the crisis eased, though it did not end.[74] Attention then was drawn primarily to the Gulf, where on August 2nd Iraq invaded Kuwait, sending the world down a path that soon led to war.

Yet Europe was far from forgotten. Indeed, some of the most historic events since World War II were taking place, obscured from popular perceptions by events in the Gulf. Baker declared the Cold War ended with the surrender of Four-Power control in Germany (the treaty was signed on September 12, 1990). It was as good a date as any historian might pick. He then predicted that in American-Soviet relations, "cooperation can become the norm, not the exception." He also had a dire (and prescient) warning: "Freedom has unleashed age-old ethnic animosities that often shout down the voices of tolerance.... The danger is that the breakdown of the old Stalinist system will outstrip the development of a new system—one built on universal democratic values and the rule of law." What could the West do? He concluded it might help only at the margins.[75]

Meanwhile, on November 21st, a Charter of Paris signed by 34 nations confirmed the ascendancy of American and western principles as the dominant, governing ideas of post–Cold War international relations. It pledged signatories to: "a steadfast commitment to democracy based on human rights and fundamental freedoms, prosperity through economic liberty, and social justice, and equal security for all countries." For the first time, Bush publicly stated that "the Cold War is over.... We have closed a chapter of history."[76] He then went out on a political limb in December, waiving Jackson-Vanik in advance of a Soviet law on free emigration so that Moscow would have credit for food purchases to get through chronic winter shortages and supply problems.[77] Yet Bush always had to operate in the shadow of the Reagan deficits. For instance, at the State Department, Richard Schifter spoke of how the Soviet Union at last "appears wide open... to institutionalize progress on human rights," but added, "as in so many other settings, the limits of our cooperation are ultimately defined by the availability of funds."[78]

During the Gulf War, the newly cooperative U.S.-Soviet relationship played a key part in getting resolutions through the Security Council and encouraging a great coalition to form around American leadership.[79] In early January 1991, the administration admitted to concern that Moscow's handling of its internal affairs might become a real obstacle to further foreign policy successes. Bush and Baker therefore moved to expand contacts with the republics. Baker met with the heads of the three Baltic States, and more quietly, U.S.

officials met with leaders of Armenia, Kazakhstan, Ukraine, Belorussia, and Russia proper.[80]

However, Gorbachev's use of troops in Lithuania, in the midst of the Gulf crisis, threatened Bush's whole approach. At first, needing the Soviets in the Gulf and fearing that greater unrest might lead to chaos in the Soviet Union, Bush took no action other than to publicly deplore the use of force. Subsequently, he announced that economic sanctions were under consideration. Then the Senate passed, by a vote of 99 to 0, a resolution condemning Soviet actions in the Baltic States, and Bush hinted at delay of a promised summit with Gorbachev. The summit eventually was postponed, although the reason given was preoccupation with the war in the Gulf: the very next day the Soviets pulled some of their troops out of the Baltic.[81] And yet, American conservatives were outraged. William Safire went so far as to charge Baker with agreeing to a "mini-Yalta."[82] In reality, things continued to go the way the United States and the West wanted, not just in the Gulf, but when the Warsaw Pact announced it would dissolve itself on March 31st, just weeks away.[83]

Gorbachev turned toward the "old guard" in the winter of 1990-1991 in an effort to stave off the surging movement toward sovereignty in the Soviet Union's constituent republics. That is where the threat to use force had come from in the Baltic States, and one issue over which Shevardnadze resigned. The outlying republics just might have been repressed by Russian force one more time, but during the spring and summer it became clear that the real problem was not what happened in Armenia or Moldavia, it was the rising demand for independence in the Ukraine and the Russian republic itself, embodied for Gorbachev in his personal *bête noir*, democratically elected and widely popular Boris Yeltsin. Try force to repress demands for sovereignty in Russia or Ukraine and you chanced civil war. To avoid that, Gorbachev swung back to a policy of accommodation, seeking concessions from the republics for a new "Union Treaty" that he hoped to cement with concessions and massive aid from the West. It was all too late. The republics saw the Soviet center and president as irrelevant. The Union Treaty agreed to in April left Gorbachev virtually a figurehead. Moreover, the West had taken every concession (surrender, really) that Gorbachev had offered, but now wisely declined to rush to his personal rescue with an aid package in the absence of real structural reform. The United States and its allies sent him home empty-handed in July from their Group of Seven summit in London. That was public, and humiliating, confirmation of what policy-makers had decided six months earlier: direct cash aid would be wasted on a still-unreformed Soviet economy.[84]

The twin crises in Soviet society of political legitimacy and economic decay could no longer be contained. Shevardnadze had sent a shudder through the West about the former with his dramatic resignation as Soviet foreign minister the previous December, when he warned that dictatorship might return to the Soviet Union and reverse much of the progress that had been made.[85] In May, he arrived in Washington to ask for credit to purchase grain and warn about an impending economic collapse. He told Bush that the possibility of famine was threatening democratization. But the administration appears to have concluded by that point that the main problem was Gorbachev's refusal to institute full market reforms, a failure that cooled any ardor for assisting with massive aid. Besides, the Baltic foreign ministers and other republic officials were giving Bush opposite advice, arguing that aiding the old center was the surest way to stifle freedom in the republics. Bush saw food credits in a different light than cash aid: as a humanitarian need, and even as something of a "thank you" for Gorbachev's concessions on other matters of direct American interest.[86] He had already extended some direct aid to the republics, but while he realistically saw the future there, he hesitated to cross the Rubicon and completely abandon Gorbachev and the Soviet center.[87] Meanwhile, congressional resistance to lifting Jackson-Vanik continued despite record outflows of Soviet jews (300,000 in 1990), until the Supreme Soviet passed a free emigration law. Bush's policy also came under attack from isolationists, liberal and conservative, as demands for a "peace dividend" merged with calls for a turn to "America First," a cry raised again in the 1992 presidential primaries.[88]

The beginning of the end came in a tense and heroic three days in August 1991, with a bungled *coup* attempt by the old guard trying to head off signature of the Union Treaty and maintain itself as a central, Soviet authority. The *coup* led to the unquestionable emergence of Boris Yeltsin as the legitimate voice of Russian nationalism and democratic aspiration, and shattered what little interest the republics had left in maintaining central institutions. That contrasted with a speech Bush made in Kiev, when he spoke against nationalism in the republics. His main concerns, even though for a brief while they left him "behind the curve" on the question of center *vs.* republics in the Soviet Union, were that with the breakup of central authority, gains made in arms control and nonproliferation would be placed in jeopardy, and dangerous old animosities might resurface. After the failed *coup*, he therefore held back from recognition of the republics, which moved quickly to assert full sovereignty. In October, Yeltsin announced a separate economic reform program for Russia that forced the pace of change for all the other republics. By November, there was no longer any doubt that power had irrevocably shifted away from Gorbachev, who looked and was a much diminished, even befuddled figure. Bush remained cautious, but let it be known that recognition of Russia and the other nuclear republics (the re-named Bylarus, Kazahkstan, and Ukraine) hinged on finding mechanisms to carry forward arms control treaties, and on a fair solution to the problem of Soviet national debt.[89]

Still, as late as December Baker spoke publicly of his fears that the breakup of the Soviet center might lead to a huge civil war, to dwarf the one then underway in Yugoslavia. He did so on the very day that the decision was taken by leaders of the republics to dissolve the Soviet Union in favor of a "Commonwealth of Independent States."[90] On Christmas Day, 1991, Gorbachev resigned, and the Soviet Union was consigned to the "dustbin of history." At least for the moment, in its place was erected a loose confederation comprising eleven of the old Soviet republics (Georgia and the Baltic States did not join). The communist flag was lowered from the Kremlin, over Kiev, and the other capitals, replaced by the Russian, Ukrainian, and other republican ensigns; and Gorbachev handed over control of all nuclear weapons and codes to Yeltsin. Bush went on national television to praise both Gorbachev for his actions in the past and Yeltsin for his vision of the future, and immediately acknowledged the new state of affairs by extending recognition within hours of Gorbachev's resignation.[91] The Soviet empire was gone; eastern Europe was free; Germany was united and democratic; and western principles of human rights and economic liberty were ascendant, if not yet triumphant, and written into the very architecture of European and Atlantic security. The world would never be the same, nor America's mission or place in it.

NOTES

1. Poll cited in Daniel Yankelovich and Richard Smoke, "America's 'New Thinking,'" *Foreign Affairs* (Fall 1988): p. 4. Also see Thomas Smith, "The Polls: American Attitudes Toward the Soviet Union and Communism." *Public Opinion Quarterly* (Summer 1983): pp. 278–92.

2. Stephen Ambrose, *Rise to Globalism*, 6th ed. (Penguin, 1991): p. 300.

3. For a leading congressional viewpoint, see Stephen J. Solarz, "When to Intervene," *Foreign Policy* (Summer 1986): pp. 20–39.

4. This aspect of Reagan's worldview is succinctly dealt with in Tami Davis and Sean Lynn-Jones, "Citty Upon a Hill," *Foreign Policy* (Spring 1987): pp. 20–38. Cf. Cyrus Vance, "The Human Rights Imperative," *Foreign Policy* (Summer 1986): pp. 3–19.

5. Quoted in Colleen McGuiness *et al.*, eds., *U.S. Foreign Policy: The Reagan Imprint* (Congressional Quarterly Press, 1986): p. 23. Also in *Presidential Documents*: March 8 and 14, 1983.

6. Poll cited in Yankelovich and Smoke, "America's 'New Thinking,'" p. 4; and see Reagan's explicit comparison in Department of State, *Bulletin*, April 1981.

7. *Congressional Record*, Senate, Committee on Foreign Relations, 97th Cong., 1st Sess., *Nomination of Ernest W. Lefever*; and *Supplement*, Chapter 23, Part A. Also in *AFPCD* (1981): Docs. #126–27. More muted tones were used by other officials. See Department of State, *Current Policy*, Doc. #293: July 14, 1981.

8. Quoted in Friedbert Pflüger, "Human Rights Unbound," *Presidential Studies Quarterly* (Fall 1989): p. 711; also *Congressional Record*, Senate, Committee on Foreign Relations, 97th Cong., 1st Sess., *Nomination of Elliot Abrams*, and *Supplement*, Chapter 23, Part A; and *AFPCD* (1981): Doc. #129.

9. That distinction was well-known in political discourse, but Jeane Kirkpatrick's essay on the subject brought her to Reagan's attention. See her *Dictatorships and Double Standards* (Simon & Schuster, 1982): pp. 23–52; cf. other views in *idem, et al.*, "Symposium on Human Rights and American Foreign Policy," *Commentary* (November 1981): pp. 25–63.

10. Quoted in Heaps, *Human Rights*: p. 43. Also see "Address to the *Centro Studi per la Conciliazione Internazionale, Banco di Roma*," May 28, 1981, in Kirkpatrick, *The Reagan Phenomenon* (AEI, 1983): p. 14.

11. Kirkpatrick, "Symposium," p. 42 (emphasis added). Similarly absolutist statements can be found in *idem, Reagan Phenomenon*: pp. 46–53, 79–105; and *idem*, "Foreword," in Joshua Muravchik, *Uncertain Crusade* (Hamilton, 1986): p. xi.

12. *AFPCD* (1981): Doc. #124; and see Pflüger, "Human Rights Unbound," pp. 710–11.

13. For example, former Jackson and Moynihan aide Joshua Muravchik; see his *Uncertain Crusade*: pp. 221–37.

14. Tamar Jacoby, "The Reagan Turnaround on Human Rights," *Foreign Affairs* (Summer 1986): pp. 1070–71. More general critiques of Reagan's Soviet policy include Seweryn Bialer and Joan Afferica, "Reagan and Russia," *Foreign Affairs* (Winter 1982–1983): pp. 249–71; and Alexander Dallin and Gail Lapidus, "Reagan and the Russians," in Kenneth Oye *et al.*, eds. *Eagle Resurgent?* (Little, Brown, 1987): pp. 193–254.

15. That is *not* to agree with the extreme view of Charles Maechling, who charges that Reagan "actually sought to reward the perpetrators of massacre by direct or indirect supply of more up-to-date weaponry, a policy not unlike furnishing gas chambers to Adolf Hitler." "Human Rights Dehumanized," *Foreign Policy* (Fall 1983): p. 133.

16. *AFPCD* (1981): Docs. #150–51; *ibid.*, (1982): Docs. #157–59; and Vojtech Mastny, ed., *Helsinki, Human Rights, and European Security* (Duke University Press, 1986): Docs. #93–118.

17. State of the Union Address, 1985.

18. Kenneth W. Thompson, "Commentary," in Robert Tucker, *The Reagan Doctrine* (Council on Religion and International Affairs, 1985): p. 29. Cf. Jeane Kirkpatrick, *The Reagan Doctrine and U.S. Foreign Policy* (Heritage Foundation, 1985); Stephen Rosenfeld, "The Guns of July," *Foreign Affairs* (Spring 1986): pp. 698–714; and Coral Bell, *The Reagan Paradox* (Rutgers University Press, 1989): pp. 101–120.

19. Department of State, *Bulletin*, February 1984.

20. *Washington Post*, May 26, 1985.

21. *AFPCD* (1981): Doc. #6. On the willingness to negotiate once new strength was achieved see John L. Gaddis, *The United States and the End of the Cold War* (Oxford University Press, 1992): pp. 62–63. Yelena Bonner, wife of the late Andrei Sakharov and human rights activist in her own right, says that Sakharov took the same line: build and deploy missiles as long as the Soviets were doing so, and as a preliminary to disarmament talks. Author's notes of Yelena Bonner's talk to *Striving for Peace: Nobel Peace Prize Forum*, Augsburg College, Minneapolis, Minnesota, February 17, 1990.

22. Alexander M. Haig, *Caveat* (Macmillan, 1984): pp. 95–116; and George Shultz, "New Realities and New Ways of Thinking," *Foreign Affairs* (Spring 1985): pp. 705–21.

23. Raymond Garthoff, drawing upon his many years of service to gain access to authoritative information, provides this summary of the still classified NSDD-75, in *Détente and Confrontation* (Brookings Institute, 1985): pp. 1010–1012.

24. See Weinberger, "U.S. Defense Strategy," *Foreign Affairs* (Spring 1986): pp. 675–97.

25. Kirkpatrick, "Address to the AEI," December 8, 1981, in *The Reagan Phenomenon*: pp. 35–36.

26. Haig, *Caveat*: pp. 238–59 (emphasis added).

27. See Caspar Weinberger, "Defense Strategy," p. 676.

28. *Presidential Documents*: March 23, 1983.

29. Garthoff, *Détente and Confrontation*: pp. 1026–28; and see Steven Miller and Stephen Van Evera, *Star Wars Controversy* (Princeton University Press, 1986).

30. *AFPCD* (1981): Doc. #152. Haig is sharply critical of the pipeline decision, which was highly divisive within the Atlantic community, in *Caveat*: pp. 238–59.

31. McGuiness et al., *The Reagan Imprint*: pp. 25–29, 160–161. On the Euromissile crisis see Michael J. Sodaro, *Moscow, Germany and the West* (Cornell University Press, 1990): pp. 265–316; and Whittle Johnston, "The Reagan Revolution and German Democracy," in Carl Hodge and Cathal Nolan, eds., *Shepherd of Democracy?* (Greenwood, 1992), pp. 141–160.

32. Department of State, *Current Policy*, #492: June 15, 1983; and *AFPCD* (1983): Doc. #157.

33. *Ibid.*, Doc. #112 (original emphasis).

34. *Ibid.*, Doc. #206.

35. *Ibid.*, Doc. #93.

36. *AFPCD* (1983): Doc. #229.

37. McGuiness et al., *The Reagan Imprint*: pp. 29–33.

38. Shultz, "New Ways of Thinking," pp. 707–9, 719–21.

39. AFPCD (1985): Docs. #78, #115; Reagan's address just prior to the Stockholm conference is reprinted in Strobe Talbott, *The Russians and Reagan* (Vintage

Books, 1984): pp. 129–40; also see Mastny, ed., *Helsinki*: Docs. #119–137.
   40. Richard Nixon, "Superpower Summitry," *Foreign Affairs* (Fall 1985): p. 11.
   41. *NYT*, October 8, 1986.
   42. Department of State, *Bulletin*, December 1986; Michael Mandelbaum and Strobe Talbot, "Reykjavik and Beyond," *Foreign Affairs* (Winter 1986–1987): pp. 215–35; Robert Cullen, "Soviet Jewry," *ibid.*, pp. 252–66; and *AFPCD* (1986): Docs. #114–120, #164.
   43. Department of State, *Bulletin*, December 1986; *ibid.*, April 1987. On Soviet jews see *AFPCD* (1986): Doc. #156.
   44. *Ibid.*, Doc. #90.
   45. *Ibid.*, Doc. #164.
   46. Department of State, *Bulletin*, April 1987. In 1990 Bonner told a U.S. audience: "Gorbachev did not release Sakharov, western public opinion did." Author's notes, *Nobel Peace Prize Forum*.
   47. *NYT*, February 17 and 20, 1987. Also see Schifter's long presentations in Department of State, *Bulletin*, April 1987; and the positive response of other officials in *AFPCD* (1987): Docs. #170–78. Cf. Caspar Weinberger's deeply skeptical view of Gorbachev in "Arms Reduction and Deterrence," *Foreign Affairs* (Spring 1988): pp. 700–19.
   48. James Schlesinger, "Reykjavik and Revelations," *Foreign Affairs* (America and the World, 1986): pp. 426–46.
   49. Author's notes, *Nobel Forum*, Minneapolis, February 17, 1990.
   50. *AFPCD* (1987): Docs. #121–29.
   51. *Ibid.*, Doc. #177.
   52. *Ibid.*, Doc. #178.
   53. Marshall Shulman, "The Superpowers," *Foreign Affairs* (America and the World, 1987–1988): pp. 494–515.
   54. *AFPCD* (1988): Doc. #152.
   55. Polls in Yankelovich and Smoke, "America's New Thinking," pp. 4–6.
   56. *AFPCD* (1988): Doc. #153.
   57. Ambrose, *Rise to Globalism*: p. 360.
   58. *AFPCD* (1988): Docs. #154–57.
   59. Insightful reviews of the Reagan era include Michael Howard, "A European Perspective on the Reagan Years," *Foreign Affairs* (America and the World, 1987–1988): pp. 478–93; and Robert W. Tucker, "Reagan's Foreign Policy," *ibid.* (1988–1989): pp. 1–27.
   60. See *AFPCD* (1989): Docs. #1–4, #77; and Michael Mandelbaum, "The Bush Foreign Policy," *Foreign Affairs* (America and the World, 1990–1991): pp. 1–22.
   61. See *AFPCD* (1989): Doc. #80, for Bush on Tiananmen Square.
   62. See Baker's reported comments in *Time*, October 22, 1990: p. 27.
   63. *AFPCD* (1989): Doc. #169.
   64. *Ibid.*, Doc. #78.
   65. *Ibid.*, Docs. #171, #185–86.
   66. *Ibid.*, Docs. #173–74.
   67. *Ibid.*, Doc. #178. The accusation that Bush had no "vision" for his foreign policy is belied by this and other key speeches. Also see *Ibid.* (1990): Docs. #4–5.
   68. *Ibid.* (1989): Docs. #79, #175–76, #183–89.

69. *Ibid.* (1990): Docs. #200–201. Yelena Bonner argued at the time that "U.S. support for the troops in Baku did not help the process of democratization." Author's notes, *Nobel Forum*, Minneapolis, February 17, 1990.

70. *AFPCD* (1990): Docs. #203–9; and *Presidential Documents*: March 19, 1990.

71. *AFPCD* (1990): Docs. #212–19.

72. *Ibid.*, Doc. #220. After dissolution of the WTO, Cheney still called for large military expenditures. *NYT*, February 8, 1991.

73. *AFPCD* (1990): Docs. #225–26.

74. *Ibid.*, Docs. #228–34.

75. For instance, Bush added the Soviet Union to a list of countries to be aided by the new "Citizens Democracy Corps" a 1990s version of the Peace Corps aimed at eastern Europe. *AFPCD* (1990): Doc. #243; and *NYT*, September 13, 1990.

76. The day before, the WTO and NATO signed a mutual nonaggression treaty. *Ibid.*, November 19–22, 1990.

77. *Executive Order #12740*, December 29, 1990, in *Presidential Documents*: January 7, 1991; and see *AFPCD* (1990): Doc. #245.

78. *Ibid.*, Doc. #98.

79. An early study is Graham Fuller, "Moscow and the Gulf War," *Foreign Affairs* (Summer 1991): pp. 55–76.

80. *NYT*, January 7, 1991.

81. *Ibid.*, January 9–18; 22–23; and 29–30, 1991.

82. *Ibid.*, February 14, 1991. The next week, the European powers offered to release $560 million in aid as an inducement to more liberal treatment of the Baltic States. *Ibid.*, February 20, 1991.

83. *Ibid.*, February 26, 1991.

84. *Ibid.*, December 14 and 19–20, 1990.

85. Full transcript of Shevardnadze's statement and Gorbachev's reply in *ibid.*, December 21, 1990; also see *ibid.*, January 2, 1991.

86. *Ibid.*, March 31; and May 7–9, 1991. More generally, see Eduard Shevardnadze, *The Future Belongs to Freedom* (Free Press, 1991).

87. Bush sent direct medical aid to the Baltics and Ukraine. *NYT*, February 7, 1991.

88. *Washington Post National Weekly*, September 16–22, 1991: p. 23.

89. *The Economist*, December 7, 1991.

90. *Ibid.*, December 14, 1991.

91. *NYT*, December 26, 1991.

Part II
The United Nations

7 ACTIVE AT THE CREATION

Franklin Roosevelt's understanding of international security was basically Wilsonian, as he made clear in his famous "Four Freedoms" speech in 1941. But like Wilson, he too took more account of abiding realities of political power than is sometimes recognized.[1] His idea of the "Four Policemen"—the notion that the United States, the Soviet Union, Britain, and China could police the postwar world—recognized that the great powers had a special role to play. He broached that idea in conversations with Vyacheslav Molotov, Soviet Commissar for Foreign Affairs, in Washington in May and June, 1942.[2] Concern for foreign liberties hence appeared to become more muted as Roosevelt's rhetoric was given substance in post-hostilities planning. Yet while it might seem as though Roosevelt abandoned the Four Freedoms (of speech and religion, from want and fear) in favor of the Four Policemen, such a conclusion would be a misreading of both his intent and understanding.

Practically speaking, it became increasingly clear that immediate national security (freedom from fear) would have to take priority in planning over economic and civil aspirations (freedom from want and worldwide freedom of speech and religion). Yet it remained one of Roosevelt's central aims to build long-term international security on a base in which prosperity and respect for liberty reinforced the balance between the great powers. Social and economic goals therefore were integral to the task of reconstruction of the postwar order, as they were the key to political stability and the expansion of democracy. In short, Roosevelt believed that as an essential component of any permanent peace, there had to be improvements in political, social, and economic justice. As Whittle Johnston shrewdly puts it, freedom from fear was clearly the primary aim in postwar planning, but the three subordinate Freedoms spoke to "longer-term efforts to address the injustices from which the will to use force might derive."[3]

However, the extent to which American public opinion would permit U.S. engagement in international affairs in the postwar period was an unanswered question, despite Roosevelt's personal commitment to an active, internationalist role for the country. The rude awakening of Japan's attack on Pearl Harbor, and a successful publicity campaign by internationalist groups, by mid–1942 turned American opinion three-to-one in favor of joining a postwar collective security organization.[4] On the other hand, as late as January 1945, polls showed that 26 percent of Americans still opposed membership in any world organization.[5] Roosevelt and Secretary of State Cordell Hull therefore believed they had to move cautiously. Their principal worry was latent isolationist sentiment, in the country at large but particularly among key Republicans in the Senate.

Most important was Senator Arthur H. Vandenberg, during the prewar period a central figure of opposition to Roosevelt's internationalist policies. Vandenberg had inherited the mantle of leader of the Senate isolationists upon the death of William Borah in January 1940. Vandenberg had consistently opposed Roosevelt before the war, voting against repeal of Neutrality Legislation, Selective Service, and Lend-Lease. But as the war raged on he moved away from isolationist positions, until by the middle of 1943 he was poised to abandon isolationism for good.[6] He eventually agreed to support membership in a world security organization, but attached a condition to his support. Vandenberg told Roosevelt that he would vote for such a major departure from past practice only if he could be assured the overall peace would accord with principles of democracy and disarmament, the very principles the president had laid out in the Atlantic Charter.[7]

Roosevelt made the necessary assurances and Vandenberg, true to his word, threw his considerable political weight behind an effort to get advance congressional approval of American entry into a new international security organization. His efforts were instrumental in converting many (though not all) former isolationists. The break came in September 1943, when the Fulbright Resolution passed in the House, placing that body on the record as favoring U.S. participation in "appropriate international machinery with adequate power to establish and maintain a just and lasting peace."[8] The Senate did not act on the Fulbright Resolution, possibly owing to bruised institutional pride at the usurpation of its legislative lead on foreign affairs. But the Connally Resolution passed in the Senate five weeks later, on November 5, 1943. It too formally endorsed the abandonment of isolationism, stating that the upper chamber recognized "the necessity of there being established at the earliest practical date a general international organization . . . for the maintenance of international peace and security."[9] Vandenberg next successfully pressed the Republican Party to include a similar call for postwar international engagement in its 1944 platform; the Democrats under Roosevelt of course made a similar platform pledge.[10]

To ensure continued cooperation from Senate Republicans, Roosevelt regularly consulted Vandenberg on major issues of postwar planning. Eventually, he appointed Vandenberg a member of the Commission to attend the San Francisco conference, where the U.N. Charter was finalized and formally launched after the President's death. Although never of one mind on policy, Vandenberg and Roosevelt helped reinforce each other's and the country's dedication to a peace resting ultimately on the liberal principles of the Atlantic Charter and the Four Freedoms.[11] In that way, a consensus was built among American leaders that the new collective security organization, known after its sponsoring alliance as the United Nations, should have as one of its cardinal purposes promotion of individual liberty and economic and social justice.

WARTIME PLANNING

Churchill first formulated British views on the question of a postwar security organization in February 1943 while on a train ride returning from a conference with Turkish officials. A copy of the Prime Minister's sketch, which he titled "Morning Thoughts: Note on Postwar Security," was sent to Roosevelt and Hull.[12] Among the more important preliminary meetings where postwar organization was discussed by the Anglo-American powers was during a visit to Washington by British Foreign Secretary Sir Anthony Eden, in the second half of March 1943.[13] Also important in the lead-up to formal negotiations was a set of meetings between Churchill and Roosevelt that took place at the Third Washington Conference in May and the First Quebec Conference in August 1943.[14] Hull delivered a major radio address on the subject on September 17, 1943, launching a serious effort to prepare the public for U.S. membership.[15] Within a few days of that talk, the Fulbright Resolution passed the House; the Connally Resolution passed the Senate some weeks later. In the interim, Molotov expressed Soviet interest in a postwar security organization during meetings at the Tripartite Conference held in Moscow in October 1943.[16] Formal talks on formation of a general security organization began following the release of the Moscow Four Power Declaration, and direct discussion of the issue among the "Big Three" leaders at the Teheran Conference, at the end of November 1943.[17] Follow-up meetings continued on both multilateral and bilateral levels among representatives of the three major powers, later also including China.

Meanwhile, the State Department had been engaged in postwar planning even before American entry into the war.[18] From the beginning, State was concerned with building provisions for promotion of rights and liberties into consideration of a draft charter of any replacement organization for the old League. It was hoped thereby to give flesh to the skeletal principles of the Atlantic Charter and Roosevelt's Four Freedoms. As the administration considered the problem of international organization, it simply was taken for granted that provision must be made for promotion of individual rights and freedoms; doubts arose only concerning the best means of accomplishing that end. The first inclination of State Department planners was to write an international bill, or rather set of bills, of rights to be attached to the larger charter that was a somewhat crude attempt to simulate in the international sphere the experience with the Bill of Rights attached to the American Constitution. Clearly, many career officials in the State Department shared in the national vision of American exceptionalism. Yet most noteworthy is that these ideas about international promotion of rights and freedoms were put forward as early as March 14, 1942, barely three months after the United States entered the war, and at only the second meeting of the Department's Subcommittee on Political Problems.[19]

The subcommittee's work led to a draft Bill of Rights, produced in December 1942. Article I of the draft read: "Governments exist for the benefit of the people and for the promotion of their common welfare in an interdependent world." Moreover, belying recent charges that the United States was unconcerned with social and economic rights, Article II identified as a basic right "minimum standards of economic, social, and cultural well-being as the resources of the country, effectively used, are capable of sustaining."[20]

The centrality of the connection between security and liberty, as between security and social and economic justice, was noted in a later State Department summary of the operating assumptions of the subcommittee: "The subcommittee assumed that the international recognition and, within each state the guaranty, of basic human rights would be conducive to the development of conditions favorable to the maintenance of international peace.... This should include both traditional [civil and political] rights and certain principles of social and economic justice that were beginning to be regarded as basic."[21] The draft Bill of Rights was then set aside while the subcommittee turned to more pressing matters. It was to have been considered later by the full Political Committee, but actually was not taken up by the parent body prior to being abandoned in mid–1943 as impracticable.[22]

It was next decided to approach the whole question of rights by a different route. A Technical Committee drafting the U.N. constitution was asked to address the question of how individual rights might be brought under the powers of the new organization. The committee suggested including an obligation to promote rights in the Charter preamble, rather than in a separate bill. It also suggested making acceptance of "a common program of human rights" a condition of membership in the organization. Once more, State Department planners thus made explicit in their suggested preamble to the Charter a sense that international security and individual liberty were ultimately indivisible.[23] However, more difficulties arose. The Technical Committee had not described the contents of its recommended "common program," or explained the mechanism to implement such a plan. When agreement on implementation measures could not be reached, the idea of an attached Bill of Rights was revived. A revised draft preamble now listed promotion of "freedom, dignity and welfare" as basic goals of the proposed organization, and bound members to give "legislative effect" to an attached Bill of Rights.[24] In an appended commentary, State Department planners listed "safeguarding of certain basic human rights" as one of seven "minimum functions" of postwar international organization and cooperation.[25]

Given these technical difficulties, proposals on human rights and freedoms appeared and disappeared from drafts throughout the rest of 1943 and into 1944. Slowly and reluctantly, during the course of 1944 the State Department and administration moved away from its early plans for an "International Bill" or "common program" of rights. Reference to rights and liberties was removed from the preamble of a December 1943, draft constitution. It also stayed out of a February 1944, "Topical Outline" of the general character and functions of an international security organization. However, rights reappeared under the powers of the General Assembly in an April 1944, plan.[26] But no matter how State Department officials tried to approach the question, they discovered that "no method of international political or judicial enforcement appeared both acceptable and workable."[27] They therefore settled on the idea that membership in the United Nations should place a basic obligation on member states to protect fundamental rights and liberties, with specific duties to be worked out later. The reluctance and frustration from which planners arrived at that compromise is evident in the documentary record. Hence, the State Department and administration continued to deliberate on how to incorporate individual rights a main purpose of a postwar organization right up to the start of discussions by the Allies at Dumbarton Oaks.[28] The draft of working principles that the U.S. delegation carried into those meetings actually included rights under the powers and responsibilities of the General Assembly. There was strong support among U.S. negotiators for placing a provision on rights in the preamble as well.[29] Those and other questions now would have to be settled in consultation with the three other sponsoring powers.

[handwritten annotation: You have to agree to "common program of human rights" as condition of membership]

DUMBARTON OAKS

At the Dumbarton Oaks conference held in Washington from August through October 1944, the U.S. delegation argued that respect for individual rights should be made a basic obligation of U.N. membership. It was the only one of the "Big Four" sponsoring powers to so address the question of individual rights. The Soviet delegation, for one, wanted to keep the conference and the United Nations itself narrowly focused on matters directly relating to great power management of peace and security, and Soviet officials initially objected to the whole idea of sponsoring the promotion of human rights, and even economic and social cooperation, as an essential element of the main U.N. structure.[30] U.S. Ambassador to the Soviet Union W. Averill Harriman reported that Moscow preferred to relegate such questions, which it saw as non-essential to postwar security cooperation, to specialized agencies along the lines of the International Labor Organization (ILO). That reflected an immediate realism on the part of Moscow, in response to what Soviet specialist Adam Ulam has called "a frantic American preoccupation with procedures" at Dumbarton Oaks.[31] But it also sprang from Moscow's fundamental rejection of the U.S. argument that individual liberty was a necessary underpinning of security.

As for the other powers at the conference, China rather confusedly suggested that equality of races as well as states should be made a constitutive principle of the United Nations, in what amounted to a replay of the failed Japanese initiative at Versailles in 1919.[32] But the vagueness of China's proposal meant its implementation was unclear. Would seating on the Security Council or in the General Assembly have to include representation for different races as well as states? And how would such representation be decided? While there can be little question that the Chinese scheme made the European colonial powers, and the "White Dominions" of the British Commonwealth, nervous and uncomfortable, it was too ill-considered and—given the U.S. efforts on human rights—perhaps even redundant.[33] Only Britain came close to venturing proposals comparable to those made by the United States, and then in language borrowed from Roosevelt's insertions into the Atlantic Charter. The British suggested listing among the objects of the United Nations: "betterment of world-wide economic conditions and the well-being of all men by international agreement so that the fear of want may be removed from the world"; and a state obligation "to guard and enlarge the freedom of man [sic] by institutions for the removal of social wrongs." Yet, when the United States tried to give more precise definition to those ideas, the British opposed the American position.[34]

In contrast, the U.S. delegation argued in favor of empowering the General Assembly to "initiate studies and make recommendations.... [about] the promotion of observance of basic human rights."[35] That suggestion proved unacceptable to the Soviet Union, and in some ways was even more objectionable to Great Britain.[36] Differences between the United States on the one hand, and the Soviets and British on the other, became clear when Undersecretary of State Edward Stettinius suggested that the Joint Steering Committee of the Four Powers consider a new set of American proposals on human rights. Stettinius reported to Hull that Sir Alexander Cadogan, speaking for Britain, had "expressed opposition to the reference to human rights and fundamental freedoms, saying that he thought such a provision would give rise to the possibility that the organization might engage in criticism of the internal organization of member states." Ambassador Andrei Gromyko of the Soviet Union reportedly said "it was his personal opinion that the reference to human rights and basic freedom is not germane to the main tasks of an international security organization." Both men indicated they would have to consult their home governments before taking an official position.[37]

Following Cadogan's consultation with London, the British delegation remained reluctant to accept any reference to rights and freedoms. However, the Soviet delegation indicated it had received instructions to accept such a reference, on the condition that it was "coupled with a provision that Fascist or fascist-type states could not be members of the organization."[38] Faced with British obduracy and Soviet parochialization of the issue, U.S. negotiators reluctantly withdrew the proposed article on rights. Stettinius reported to Hull: "The paragraph . . . relating to human rights and fundamental freedoms has been eliminated. [But] we have requested the Soviets and British to send special messages to their governments expressing our hope that this point can be included briefly somewhere in the document."[39] For the moment it was agreed to drop the provision on rights, but the United States reserved the privilege of considering the issue one of the "unsettled questions" at the end of the conference.[40]

Consequently, in the first Four-Power draft of the U.N. Charter the section describing the mandate and responsibilities of the General Assembly omitted mention of any role concerning rights. Yet the U.S. delegation persisted. When consulted by Stettinius, "the group as a whole urged that some reference to the promotion of human rights and fundamental freedoms be included in the draft proposals. Most members felt that the Russian proposal concerning Fascist or fascist-type states should not be included."[41] Stettinius recorded in his diary the next day that he personally told Roosevelt "how disappointed we were that we had not yet succeeded in getting the human rights and fundamental freedoms statement into the [draft Charter], but that we would continue to press the matter as hard as we know how. I told him we had obtained agreement that Cadogan and Gromyko would raise this as a special matter with their Governments and he was gratified by that."[42]

Six days later the U.S. delegation was surprised by an unexpected turn of events. Responding to Washington's direct request to Moscow and London that individual rights be treated as a "special matter," the Soviets indicated that they had worked out a compromise with the British. Gromyko informed Stettinius that Moscow would accept the U.S. Charter amendments on rights, but only if the reference was made under Chapter IX, which dealt with economic and social arrangements. Moscow still did not want reference made to rights in the preamble, which set out the basic purposes of the organization. Wishing to avoid an open quarrel over what by that point amounted to a simple statement of aspiration, Stalin acceded to Roosevelt's wish to have a reference to rights placed in the Charter. On the other hand, the reference was diluted significantly by the move to the paragraph under economic and social cooperation; and only at that point did Britain follow the Soviet example.[43] Stettinius noted in his diary that the President was "gratified by these developments and felt the inclusion of the human rights sentence was extremely vital. He seems rather surprised that the Soviets had yielded on this point. He apparently felt that its inclusion would aid much in the success and acceptance of the plan [in the U.S.]."[44]

A proclamation of principle was a long way from the State Department's original projection of an International Bill or a common program. Nevertheless, without American tenacity at Dumbarton Oaks the idea of international promotion of fundamental freedoms clearly would not have achieved even the weak approval it did, and might never have been considered by other powers as a subject appropriate for review by the United Nations. Even so, senior officers in the Department's Office of Special Political Affairs remained dissatisfied with the treatment accorded the human rights article at Dumbarton Oaks. During internal preparations leading up to the larger conference to be held at San Francisco in April 1945, they met eighteen times to consider outstanding issues. At those meetings the expert working group gave special attention to the desirability of altering the Dumbarton Oaks decision to place human rights under the Economic and Social Council (ECOSOC). It wanted a return to the original U.S. position of respect for liberty, in particular regarding freedom of information and religion, given prominence as a central purpose of the United Nations and a main support of long-term peace and international security; and it wanted some kind of International Bill of Rights attached to the Charter.[45] It is important to note these facts, because a curious myth has taken hold in the recent secondary literature that the United States played an insignificant, or even obstructionist, role on the question of including human rights in the

U.N. Charter. In this literature the singular American effort at Dumbarton Oaks (indeed, that conference as a whole) is mostly ignored, while U.S. efforts at San Francisco are downplayed, derided, and often misunderstood.[46]

If not from American efforts at Dumbarton Oaks, from where is U.N. concern with human rights supposed to have come? Curiously, a number of recent articles identify small powers and American domestic lobbies at the San Francisco conference as the originators of U.N. involvement with individual rights. One such version is by the first Director of the U.N. Division of Human Rights, John P. Humphrey, whom it must be said was in a position to know better. In his memoirs Humphrey paints a scenario in which U.S. Non-Governmental Organizations (NGOs) and smaller country delegations supposedly played the dominant role in securing recognition for human rights in the Charter. He writes that together these groups "conducted a lobby ... which was largely responsible for the human rights provisions of the Charter." He then adds, somewhat gratuitously, "the United States delegation ... wanted nothing in the Charter which might serve as a pretext for not ratifying it, and therefore resisted the pressure. But in a dramatic, last-minute session, Stettinius, the secretary of state [sic], agreed to support the minimum demands of the lobbyists. The U.S. delegation then persuaded the other great powers to accept the amendments. How this was achieved has never been explained."[47] As shown below, however, that is a rather garbled account that takes too much at face value the moral posturing of smaller countries and NGOs, and greatly underestimates the role of the U.S. delegation in Four-Power discussions.[48]

In reality, when first offered the opportunity by the U.S. to comment on the Dumbarton Oaks proposals, almost no small power raised (let alone exhibited interest in strengthening provisions for) human rights. Canada and Brazil were most concerned with gaining special recognition as "middle powers," and most Latin American states pressed similar prestige points about the desirability of small power consultation and participation in decision-making. Only Belgium objected to the relative absence of a declaration of principles in the proposals; that was clearly not the fault of the U.S. delegation, which had repeatedly sought acceptance of such provisions from the other sponsoring powers. Besides, Brussels cited not individual rights, but a lack of reference to state (or at least group) centered principles such as self-determination.[49] Moreover, even had small powers and private U.S. groups provided the moral leadership claimed for (and sometimes by) them, it required the determined backing of one of the four sponsoring great powers to place and keep the subject on the agenda. As demonstrated at Dumbarton Oaks, only the United States among the Big Four was willing to throw its diplomatic weight into the balance on issues of human rights and fundamental freedoms. Not surprisingly, therefore, that was a role it was prepared to play again at the formal founding conference of the United Nations, held at San Francisco beginning in April 1945.

SAN FRANCISCO

A test of U.S. resolve on questions of rights and liberties came quickly at San Francisco, for the Americans encountered certain uncomfortable facts concerning the diplomatic Pandora's box they helped open with their decisive support at Dumbarton Oaks for concern for individual rights. This occurred even though the delegation had been appointed by Roosevelt before his death, and spanned the domestic political spectrum, including such Republican notables as Vandenberg and Dulles.[50] The delegates had consulted widely with domestic interest groups and lobbies of all types, in an effort to maximize public input and avoid later misunderstandings about U.S. purposes in joining the United Nations. In the process, they became aware of rapidly rising, indeed excessive, expectations among certain groups. It soon was apparent that a number of domestic organizations wanted to push the issue of human rights beyond where either most other states or the majority of the American public seemed likely to follow.

Trying not to unleash that kind of unrestrained idealism had been a major concern of Roosevelt's during his last months. He was convinced the public was developing exaggerated expectations about the potential for U.N. actions to solve global social and political problems, and he remembered well the mood of dashed hopes that had undermined Wilson's effort to gain Senate consent to membership in the League of Nations. Prior to his death, Roosevelt cautioned that extreme idealism might backfire and lead to renewal of isolationist sentiments. He warned that America's security rested foremost on its willingness to remain engaged in world affairs. He told Congress:

Perfectionism, no less than isolationism or imperialism or power politics, may obstruct the paths to international peace. Let us not forget that the retreat to isolationism a quarter of a century ago was started not by a direct attack against international cooperation but against alleged imperfections of the peace. . . . We can fulfill our responsibilities for maintaining the security of our own country only by exercising our power and our influence to achieve the principles in which we believe and for which we have fought.[51]

Roosevelt's caution on that occasion was belied by his earlier flights of rhetoric about a liberal new world order. He had built up public and congressional support for membership in the United Nations largely through appeal to the more liberal principles and aspirations of the country.[52] Now, after his death, both the delegation at San Francisco and his successor in the White House were faced with a surge of rising demands about the liberal character the public believed the United Nations and the postwar world was supposed to take.

More immediately, the United States discovered that its assumption that the Rights of Man were self-evident was both unexamined and difficult to sustain. The Soviet delegation, for its part, arrived at San Francisco under instructions to ensure that as long as promotion of rights was going to be listed as a function or purpose of the United Nations, the operative paragraph should include the phrase, "in particular the right to work and the right to education." The Americans and British united in objecting to specification of some rights but not others, on the grounds that to do so would unfairly elevate listed rights, and thereby unnecessarily denigrate those that remained unspecified. Faced with strong Anglo-American opposition, the Soviets eventually withdrew what was, after all, mostly a contentious propaganda suggestion.[53] Yet later commentators have pointed to this incident as putative evidence that the United States was opposed to precise international elaboration of rights, especially in the economic and social realm.[54] That ignores the fact that the Truman administration only objected to elaboration *in the Charter itself*, and did so because it seemed neither practicable nor possible to gain wide agreement at San Francisco on which rights should be listed.

Just as importantly, the administration was deeply concerned that too many changes to the Four-Power agreements hammered out with difficulty at Dumbarton Oaks might make the Soviet Union skittish about joining the United Nations. And it apparently needs to be reiterated that until very late in the San Francisco conference it was far from certain that the Soviet Union would finally agree to membership in the United Nations. The possibility that Moscow might refuse at the last minute was very real, and threatened the whole project of postwar cooperation through international organization, a scheme behind which the Roosevelt and Truman administrations had placed a great deal of prestige and expended much energy, and on which the country had placed a large share of its hopes for a better world.

Two major questions were outstanding even as Nazi Germany collapsed in early May and the final deadlines for decisions approached in San Francisco: (1) Stalin's demand for a wide interpretation of the veto, and (2) his insistence on separate representation for all fifteen of the Soviet Republics. Negotiations on these issues were tense and often heated. At one point Truman said privately that he had decided the United States would *not* press ahead with plans for the United Nations if Moscow withdrew. Thus, as he put it to Harriman, "without Russia there would be no world organization." Stalin finally agreed to accept a more narrow veto (which pleased small powers as well as the United States), and Truman agreed to permit the Soviets three General Assembly votes (one each for Russia, Belorussia, and the Ukraine).[55]

Furthermore, the Truman administration accepted that detailed elaboration of rights, including economic and social rights, would follow from its proposal to move the rights article back into the preamble, thereby making it a fundamental obligation of membership in the United Nations. Going into the conference it also intended to argue for an International Bill of Rights to be attached to the Charter, a working draft of which State Department legal and political officers had in hand since 1942. The blanket assertion that the United States was at best ambivalent toward enumeration of economic and social rights cannot be reconciled with numerous supportive references in internal State Department draft bills and memoranda.[56] More generally, the charge does not stand up against the record of informal U.S. cooperation with the League; Roosevelt's New Deal legislation; his 1944 proposal to Congress of an "Economic Bill of Rights"; and especially not his call for an International Bill of Economic Rights, made in the 1945 State of the Union address. Also, the charge is contradicted by Truman's later sponsorship of economic and social measures in 1947 proposals for an International Bill of Rights, which went so far as to refer to employment, social security, and even "cultural well-being" as rights.[57]

On specifics, one analyst illustrates his argument that the United States opposed economic and social rights at San Francisco by citing Washington's rejection of a suppositive "right to full employment."[58] In reality, however, that dispute came down to a debate over wording, with the U.S. delegation prepared to accept more realistic language expressing a desire for the "highest possible level of employment."[59] Moreover, in 1944 the United States had made a concerted effort to revive the ILO, and in particular, to overcome historic ILO objections to Soviet trade union membership in that organization. It was hoped in Washington that in the postwar era the world community thereby might be able to address the threat to peace believed to arise from depression and want by setting aside, to the extent possible, ideological differences and cooperating on economic interests on a functional basis.[60] It is also worth noting that Truman personally endorsed the idea of employment and other labor rights to the U.S. delegation at San Francisco.[61] Suggestions that at the founding conferences the United States was uninterested in or actually opposed to international promulgation and promotion of human rights (including social and economic) therefore simply do not accord with the facts.

What the American delegation would not approve was, in Vandenberg's words, an attempt by some small and poor nations to imbed in the Charter "the fantastic objectives which are being written into the Social and Economic Council."[62] There is of course room for legitimate disagreement with the good, and conservative, Senator about whether such objectives were indeed "fantastic." But there is no cause to doubt his personal sincerity, or his deep concern that the United Nations should become involved with the protection of individual rights. Vandenberg also believed ECOSOC and similar bodies were sufficient to the task of economic reconstruction. More to the point, he was worried that further emphasis on international economic and social programs could raise the hackles of his fellow Senate Republicans, many of whom were still learning to live with the New Deal. He wondered aloud to other members of the delegation about the chances that his Senate colleagues might object that a global New Deal was in the works, complete with a worldwide Public Works Administration or War Production Board.[63]

Vandenberg's was an influential opinion, and his sense of the Senate was of great interest to the president. Truman later recalled:

> We knew the Charter of the proposed organization had to be acceptable to the United States Senate. We did not want to run the risk of another League of Nations tragedy, with the United States standing in isolation on the sidelines. I specifically instructed ... Stettinius to consult Senators [Tom] Connally and Vandenberg on every move he made in order to get full agreement. If he could not get these men to go along, he was to call me, and

I would try to resolve the issues by telephoning them personally.... I wanted these two key figures to have access to me at all times.[64]

The U.S. delegation frequently discussed this perceived danger of reviving latent isolationism in the United States by treading on local, state, or congressional prerogatives with what might be seen as excessive international oversight provisions.[65] It was in that context that Dulles predicted (sadly, with considerable accuracy) that segregation in the South could feed into isolationism by causing some southern senators to oppose international human rights programs.[66]

Despite such reservations, the fact is that at San Francisco the United States once again led in seeking great power acceptance of international responsibility to promote individual rights and fundamental freedoms. It was the American delegation that re-opened the question of a preamble reference, among other proposals, and that pressed these initiatives in Four-Power discussions over Soviet and British objections.[67] Vandenberg was personally determined to have the Charter emphasize that peace must be established on a basis of justice and liberty, seeing that as his major task and contribution as a member of the U.S. team.[68] Most other members of the delegation were similarly committed to pressing human rights issues, as was the President.[69] The major constraint on action in the United Nations was *not* indifference to human rights questions among the delegates or within the administration. The dominant concerns restraining American efforts on human rights related to practical requirements of diplomacy.[70] Such considerations were not always appreciated at the time by domestic interest groups, or subsequently.

Perhaps the best measure of U.S. seriousness was that despite the above listed concerns, at San Francisco the Americans renewed their quest to elevate promotion of fundamental rights and freedoms to the status of a basic purpose of the United Nations. The U.S. delegation unanimously agreed that as one of its few, carefully selected suggestions for alteration of the Dumbarton Oaks agreements, it should insist that the obligation to promote rights be returned to the paragraph outlining the basic purposes of the United Nations. It then went further, asking that the General Assembly be empowered to make recommendations on "situations likely to violate the principles enunciated in the Atlantic Charter."[71] When Stettinius communicated that resolve to Truman on April 19th, the President added his personal support to the idea. Then he too went further. He later recalled: "I emphasized to Stettinius the importance of the point dealing with a declaration on human rights. I felt very strongly about the need for a world 'bill of rights,' something on the order of our own."[72] It was only *after* that decision was taken by the delegation, and *after* it was personally affirmed by the president, that Stettinius met with NGO consultants representing American business, labor, church, and civic organizations, and heard their own emphatic desire to secure additional provision for rights in the Charter.

It is true that Stettinius was personally moved by the passion with which consultant NGOs spoke of the need for international action. The minutes of the U.S. delegation meeting for May 2, 1945, record that he "thought it had been an excellent meeting and he had been deeply impressed by the discussion. The consultants had shown themselves especially concerned about the expansion of the reference to human rights and fundamental freedoms."[73] Yet, there is little evidence to suggest that the NGOs did more than reinforce an already existing and strong commitment on the part of the administration to press the human rights issue on the other great powers. Stettinius pointed out to the consultants that "at Dumbarton Oaks he personally had voted for recognition of human rights and fundamental freedoms." He did promise that "he would take up the matter of expanding and defining in greater detail what the functions of the organization might be in this respect," but he had been committed to do that by direction of the president, before the May 2nd NGO meeting. Moreover, as Vandenberg pointed out, a number of the measures the NGOs called for were "already included in the United States proposals." The only concrete suggestion traceable to the consultants was the idea of a High Commission for Human Rights. What is most notable about that initiative is not that the consultant groups proposed it, but that the delegation seized upon the idea, brought it before the Four-Power Consultative Group within twenty-four hours, and pressed forcefully and successfully for its adoption.[74]

In the end, the main difference between the consultants and the delegation and administration came down to political seriousness: the NGO lobbyists proved to be not really serious about trying for practical advances in the international promotion of human rights. Instead, the consultants as a whole revealed themselves to be more interested in the symbolism of human rights than in conducting a pragmatic diplomacy that might actually entrench rights in the structure of international organization. At the very meeting where Humphrey and others assert the NGOs exerted persuasive moral force against supposedly resisting delegation members, the NGOs actually declared themselves unconcerned with the possibility that an effort to expand rights provisions at that point in time might fail; and they took no account of the fact that such a failure could threaten the whole U.N. project, human rights articles and all. They told Stettinius that, as the minutes recorded the exchange, "even if the United States Delegation failed in its attempt, the Delegation could put out a statement that it had tried and this would carry a great weight with American public opinion."[75] Yet might not such a foolhardy gesture have carried the American public in the direction of disillusionment with the United Nations, which would be widely seen and portrayed as having rejected basic liberal and American values? Further, might not such a failure and reaction have fed into demands for a return to isolationism? That Stettinius for a moment flirted with the tactic does not speak well of his judgment that day; that the U.S. delegation resisted the invitation to mere moral posing says the opposite about most of its members.[76]

It remained to convince the other sponsoring great powers, particularly the Soviets, to accept at San Francisco what they had refused to adopt at Dumbarton Oaks—a declaration that promotion of human rights and fundamental freedoms was to be a basic purpose of the United Nations and an explicit obligation of its members. The Soviets were still trying to obtain acceptance of the qualifying phrase "in particular the right to work and the right to education." Leo Pasvolsky, Special Assistant to the Secretary of State and a leading member of the American negotiating team, dismissed the Soviet effort as stemming from a desire "to play up to the small nations." Another delegate said, "when you begin to specify the right to work and the right to education, then freedom of the press and freedom of religion would have to be added." Vandenberg summed up the consensus view when he remarked that the Soviet proposal was "all right with him," but added, "if the right to work and to education were named, then there was a long list that should be added such as freedom of assembly, freedom of religion, etc." Senator Connally agreed, commenting that "freedom to petition should also be added in that case."[77]

Dulles suggested that the whole matter be raised that night at the very highest level with the Soviets, during the first Four-Power talks at San Francisco on Charter revision. At the evening meeting, Molotov at first indicated that the American proposal to move reference to rights to the preamble on purposes might be acceptable, but again tried to have the right to work and to an education specially enumerated. Vandenberg's reply to Molotov and the exchange that followed again demonstrate that U.S. policy on human rights at San Francisco was pragmatic and principled, rather than obstructionist. He told Molotov: "Our difficulty was that when you start to particularize there are so many other fundamental rights not included in the language proposed, for example, the right of freedom of religion, freedom of the press, and similar freedoms." The senator then warned Molotov that the U.S. delegation "felt that it would be necessary to go even further if the rights proposed by the Soviet Delegation were to be enumerated." Molotov replied that if it was desired to add more rights he "would have no objection." Vandenberg reminded Molotov that the U.S. Bill of Rights included "numerous other basic rights," and stated that he "would hesitate to pick out one or two of them for special mention." Senator Connally reiterated that "naming of only one or two rights would mean the exclusion of others, and to name them all would be difficult and undesirable ... because if you start to particularize you will have to have a long list."[78]

Faced with this possibility, Molotov relented; he and his master in Moscow had never been more than rhetorically committed to the notion of individual rights anyway. The Soviet delegation agreed to delete the rights to work and an education, retain a more general obligation to uphold a range of basic rights to be specified later, and finally to move the general reference to the Charter preamble as one of the fundamental purposes of the United Nations, and obligations of membership.[79] Subsequently, the U.S. delegation decided that if the Soviets attempted to move an amendment on the right to work in spite of the agreement reached with Molotov and the other sponsoring powers, they "could then insist upon adding to the list such rights as the free flow of information, freedom of worship, and others." At that same meeting of the delegation, and for the same practical reasons, it was decided to work for a general U.N. Charter reference to the principles of the Atlantic Charter, but one also limited by a disavowal of specific enumeration of those principles.[80] It cannot be credibly maintained that the Truman administration and State Department objected to the principles of the Atlantic Charter. Therefore, the decision to avoid enumeration in the case of Atlantic Charter principles serves to confirm that U.S. negotiators had pragmatic motivations for their decision to oppose specific enumeration of rights in the U.N. Charter.

Put differently, there was an implicit tradeoff on rights between the great powers at San Francisco, an exchange that spoke to their larger interests in keeping ideological differences out of the basic structure of the United Nations. If the Soviets would not press ideological issues that might cause difficulties in the Senate and therefore threaten American membership in the United Nations, the United States would not seek to embarrass the Soviets to the point of withdrawal by pressing for freedom of information and other civil and political liberties.[81] China was too weak to have much of an impact on the major questions at San Francisco, and Britain was content in the end to support a general reference on human rights, as long as it could avoid empowering the General Assembly to look into its imperial relations.

Perhaps those political realities are the source of much of the subsequent lamentation about the supposed failure to advance international promotion of human rights at San Francisco. If so, the main point has been missed. For the United States succeeded in its determination to see individual rights and liberties embedded in the U.N. Charter as a support for permanent peace. After all was said and done, as a result of persistent U.S. efforts at the founding conferences, U.N. member states were bound to promote fundamental rights and freedoms as a basic Charter obligation. Enumeration of specific rights and correlative duties could (and did) come later, in a series of declarations and bills.

In closing remarks to the San Francisco conference, Stettinius (now Secretary of State) called upon the General Assembly to "undertake to prepare an international bill of rights which can be accepted by all the member nations as an integral part of their own systems of law, just as our Bill of Rights has been an integral part of our system of law."[82] In a major speech to the final session of the plenary conference, Truman also compared the Charter to the American Constitution, which he described as an imperfect document "which grew and developed and expanded." Echoing Vandenberg, the president stated that, "the principle of justice is the foundation stone of this Charter." He continued in a moving yet also strikingly innocent summation of what America had sought to accomplish with its insistence on international promotion of human rights and fundamental freedoms:

[The Charter] has set up machinery of international cooperation which men and nations of good will can use to help correct economic and social causes for conflict . . . , for freedom from want is one of the basic Four Freedoms toward which we all strive. . . . Under this document we have good reason to expect the framing of an international bill of rights, acceptable to all the nations involved. That bill of rights will be as much a part of international life as our own Bill of Rights is a part of our Constitution. The Charter is dedicated to the achievement and observance of human rights and fundamental freedoms. Unless we can attain those objectives for all men and women everywhere—without regard to race, language or religion—we cannot have permanent peace and security.

Truman ended with a reiteration of the main assumption that underlay the American approach to foreign policy and international organization: the idea that liberal-democratic ideals and institutions might one day bring an end to conditions in which depression and tyranny act as springboards to war. What America hoped for and had worked for in the Charter, he reminded the Assembly, was "a world of free countries—with decent standards of living—which will work and cooperate in a friendly, civilized community of nations."[83] The United States thus again presented its national experience as an ideal of liberty for the world to emulate. Americans for the most part were as yet unaware of the extent to which, given the immediate realities of world politics, they would have to compromise the ideals written into the Charter.

When Vandenberg and Connally returned to the Senate, entering the chamber arm-in-arm, their colleagues greeted them with a standing ovation for their work on the San Francisco delegation. Vandenberg spoke emphatically in favor of Senate consent, and insisted that the most important feature of the Charter was the fact that it sought "above all else to cure the underlying causes of war" by addressing political, social, and economic injustice. The U.N. Charter, he predicted, "can be a new emancipation proclamation for the world . . . The protections for human rights and fundamental freedoms inherent in the San Francisco Charter will inevitably make a better, a wiser, and a safer job of [the peace]."[84] Public opinion in the United States warmly embraced the Charter and the United Nations, favoring membership by 81 percent according to a poll taken in late April 1945.[85] The Senate assented to the Charter on July 28th, by a vote of 89 yeas to 2 nays. The two votes against were cast by Senators David Walsh of Minnesota and Arthur Capper of Kansas. Both were isolationists, still unreconstructed in the aftermath of Pearl Harbor and the bloodshed of World War II (both men had also voted against the Versailles Treaty, and with it the League of Nations).[86] Now they were isolated. The bipartisan delegation had succeeded spectacularly well.[87] Whatever else happened, the United States would not repeat the mistake of allowing disillusionment with an inevitably imperfect peace to cause it to abjure from membership in a world security organization. How unfortunate then, that the practical compromises made at the Four-Power talks, and generally at San Francisco, soon would be forgotten or misunderstood by cynics and idealists alike.

Despite being wary of utopian thinking, in 1945 Roosevelt had told the American public that an age of liberal international relations was at hand, to be created by an act of goodwill between nations and sustained by the commitment of American power. He informed Congress that the settlement reached at Yalta meant "the end of the system of unilateral action and exclusive alliances and spheres of influence and balances of power and all the other expedients which have been tried for centuries—and have failed." He proposed "to substitute for all these a universal organization which all peace-loving nations will finally have a chance to join."[88] Roosevelt was only partially disingenuous. His hopes for lasting peace and security rested in the short run mostly on great power cooperation in preserving the postwar balance of power; that is, on the Four Policemen. But he also shared in a view of world affairs that historically has permeated American thinking about foreign policy: the idea that differing national interests were capable of being harmonized through ecumenical ordination of the Rights of Man. The general triumph of internationalism over isolationism in the United States during and after World War II undoubtedly proceeded from the need to respond to major threats issuing from events beyond America's control. The unique emphasis given promotion of individual liberties and democratic values in the U.N. Charter, and elsewhere in American foreign policy, had much deeper roots in the country's domestic experience and liberal creed.

Roosevelt's wartime vision of a new world order upheld by the Four Policemen and fundamentally sustained by the Four Freedoms was essentially Wilsonian. It therefore appealed to Americans, building up public enthusiasm for the war effort, and later for membership in the United Nations. His ear for domestic opinion in combination with a personal commitment to an internationalist role for the United States led to an insistent communication to Moscow and London indicating that he wanted to see promotion of liberty become an integral part of postwar security arrangements. In thinking about rebuilding world order, Roosevelt and Truman, and many in the State Department, had returned to the old conclusion that liberty at home was in the final analysis dependent on the triumph of liberty abroad.

They sought symbolic representation of this idea in the United Nations. America's status as the world's leading power helped the other great powers set aside practical or ideological reservations about such a provision in the U.N. Charter, at least formally.

However, the symbolic victory for long-term security and individual liberty Washington thought it had won at Dumbarton Oaks and San Francisco faded even more quickly than anticipated. During the negotiations, it already had been intimated that the American conception of individual rights was neither shared nor welcomed by a majority of states. That should not have been a surprise: a few United Nations member states had a passing acquaintance with liberty, but many had none. More importantly, before long critical domestic voices would be raised, charging that setting up the United Nations as an ostensible interpreter of the ancient Rights of Man ill-served that cause. Provision for rights, placed in the Charter partly in an effort to make the United Nations more palatable to domestic opinion, thus soon would contribute to a sharp deterioration in popular and congressional regard for the organization. Within five years the most liberal components of the Charter—those elements for which the United States was primarily responsible and justly laid proud national claim—were to help feed a conservative-isolationist reaction against the peacetime internationalist course upon which the country had at last embarked.

NOTES

1. "Four Freedoms Speech," *DAH*, Vol. I: p. 449. Also see on the early influence of the Four Freedoms in U.N. planning, Craig Wilson, "Rehearsal for a United Nations: The Hot Springs Conference," *Diplomatic History* (Summer 1980): pp. 263–82; and the author's "Road to the Charter," *Paradigms* (Autumn 1980): pp. 24–37.

2. "Report on Pre-dinner Conversations, Roosevelt and Molotov," May 29 and June 1, *FRUS*, 1942, Vol. III: pp. 568–69, 580–81.

3. Whittle Johnston, "Wartime Strategy," p. 183; *FRUS*, 1944, Vol. I: pp. 642–43; Department of State, *Bulletin*, June 17, 1944: p. 552.

4. John L. Gaddis, *The United States and the Origins of the Cold War 1941–1947* (Columbia University Press, 1972): pp. 25–26.

5. *Public Opinion Quarterly* (Spring 1945): p. 101.

6. *Private Papers of Senator Vandenberg*, Arthur Vandenberg Jr., ed. (Houghton Mifflin, 1952): pp. 132–45.

7. Cordell Hull, *Memoirs of Cordell Hull*, Vol. II (Macmillan, 1948): pp. 1635–38; Robert Divine, *Second Chance* (Atheneum, 1967): pp. 47–74, *passim*; and Gaddis, *Origins of the Cold War*, p. 30.

8. *Congressional Record*, H. Res. #25, Vol. 89, Part 6 (1943): p. 7728.

9. *Congressional Record*, S. Res. #192, Vol. 80, Part 7 (1943): p. 9222.
10. *NPP*: pp. 402–13.
11. See the exchange of letters with Roosevelt prior to the senator's appointment, in Vandenberg, *Private Papers*, pp. 151–56.
12. Hull, *Memoirs*, Vol. II: pp. 1625–55; Winston Churchill, *Hinge of Fate* (Bantam, 1962): pp. 711–12.
13. *FRUS*, 1943, Vol. III: pp. 1–40, *passim*.
14. Churchill, *Hinge of Faith*: pp. 802–7; Hull, *Memoirs*, Vol. II: pp. 1237–42.
15. Department of State, *Bulletin*, September 18, 1943, p. 173.
16. *FRUS*, 1943, Vol. I: p. 669; and Conference Document #5: p. 705.
17. *Ibid*., 1943, *Cairo and Teheran*: pp. 529–33, 594–96.
18. Department of State, *Postwar Foreign Policy Preparation, 1939–1945* (GPO, 1949): pp. 1–68 [hereafter cited as *Postwar Preparation*].
19. *Ibid*., p. 84.
20. "Bill of Rights," *ibid*., pp. 483–85, 98–99.
21. *Ibid*., pp. 115–16.
22. Ruth B. Russell, *A History of the United Nations Charter* (Brookings Institute, 1958): pp. 323–24.
23. "Draft Constitution of IO," *Postwar Preparation*: pp. 472–83.
24. Human rights appeared in a distinct paragraph in the State Department's August 14, 1943, draft Charter; *ibid*., pp. 526–32.
25. "Extract from the Accompanying Commentaries," *ibid*., p. 533.
26. "Memorandum for the President, December 29, 1943," from S/S Hull; "Topical Outline, February 17, 1944"; and "Possible Plan for a General International Organization, April 29, 1944," *ibid*., pp. 576–91.
27. Russell, *U.N. Charter*: pp. 323–28; Louis Sohn and Thomas Buergenthal, *International Protection of Human Rights* (Bobbs-Merril, 1973): p. 508.
28. "Preliminaries to Dumbarton Oaks," *FRUS*, 1944, Vol. I: pp. 614–54.
29. "U.S. Tentative Proposals," *Postwar Preparation*: pp. 595–606.
30. "Stettinius to S/S," *FRUS*, 1944, Vol. I: p. 772.
31. "Harriman to the S/S," July 24, 1944, *ibid*., pp. 694–95; Adam B. Ulam, *Expansion and Coexistence*, 2nd ed. (Holt, Rinehart and Winston, 1974): pp. 371–73.
32. "Tentative Chinese Proposals," *FRUS*, 1944, Vol. I: pp. 718–19.
33. For a different view, see Paul G. Lauren, "First Principles of Racial Equality," *Human Rights Quarterly* (Winter 1983): pp. 1–26; and on the Japanese initiative, idem, "Human Rights in History," *Diplomatic History* (Summer 1978): pp. 257–78.
34. "Tentative UK Proposals," *FRUS*, 1944, Vol. I: p. 670.
35. "Tentative U.S. Proposals," *ibid*., pp. 653–54.
36. "Entry for September 8, 1944," *Diaries of Edward R. Stettinius*, T. Campbell and G. Herring, eds. (New Viewpoints, 1975): p. 132.
37. "Stettinius to S/S," September 9, 1944, *FRUS*, 1944, Vol. I: p. 789.
38. "Stettinius to S/S," September 19, 1944, *ibid*., pp. 824–25.
39. "Stettinius to S/S," September 20, 1944, *ibid*., pp. 828–30.
40. Russell, *U.N. Charter*: pp. 423–24.
41. "Stettinius to S/S," Sept. 20, 1944, *FRUS*, 1944, Vol. I: p. 830.
42. "Stettinius Diary," September 21, 1944, in *ibid*., pp. 831–35.
43. Russell, *U.N. Charter*: pp. 423–24.

44. "Stettinius Diary," Sept. 27, 1944, *FRUS*, 1944, Vol. I: pp. 841–43.
45. *Postwar Preparation*: p. 386.
46. See citations in Notes #47, #48, below.
47. John P. Humphrey, *Human Rights and the United Nations* (Transnational, 1984): p. 13; and conversations with the author, Conference on Human Rights, University of Prince Edward Island, Charlottetown, PEI (1984).
48. Humphrey's rendering has influenced the views of subsequent writers. See Tom Farer, "The United Nations and Human Rights," *Human Rights Quarterly* (November 1987): p. 554n21; and David Forsythe, "Human Rights in U.S. Foreign Policy," *Political Science Quarterly* #105/3 (1990): p. 436n4.
49. "Reaction of Non-Participating Governments to the Dumbarton Oaks Proposals," *FRUS*, 1944, Vol. I: pp. 924–59. On the actually hostile Canadian reaction to U.S. proposals on rights see the author's "Reluctant Liberal: Canada, Human Rights and the United Nations, 1944–1965," *Diplomacy and Statecraft* (November 1991): pp. 281–305. Latin American delegations did tend to be more emphatic than the United States, seeing in an International Bill guarantees not offered by their extant political cultures and systems. They became especially enthusiastic after seeing a U.S. draft proposing an "Economic Charter of the Americas" at a conference in Mexico City in February–March, 1948. See State Department, U.S. Delegation Report, Publication #2497 (1948).
50. Franklin D. Roosevelt, *Public Papers of the Presidents* (1944–1945): pp. 565–69.
51. *Public Papers and Addresses of Franklin D. Roosevelt*, Vol. 13, Samuel Rosenman, ed., (Russell & Russell, 1969): p. 498.
52. On Roosevelt's *realpolitik* see Randall Woods, "FDR and the Triumph of American Nationalism," *Presidential Studies Quarterly* (Summer 1989): pp. 567–81; but cf. Johnston, "Wartime Strategy," *op. cit.*
53. Russell, *U.N. Charter*: pp. 779–88.
54. *Inter alia*, see M. Glenn Johnson, "Contributions of Eleanor and Franklin Roosevelt to the Development of International Protection for Human Rights," *Human Rights Quarterly* (February 1987): pp. 26–27; and A. Glenn Mower, *The United States, the United Nations, and Human Rights* (Greenwood, 1979): pp. 7–8.
55. Quoted in W. Averill Harriman, *Special Envoy to Churchill and Stalin, 1941–1946* (Random House, 1975): p. 448; *FRUS*, 1945, Vol. I: pp. 214–858, *passim*; Harry S Truman, *Memoirs*, Vol. I (Doubleday, 1955): pp. 71–72. Truman once exclaimed in exasperation that the United States would press ahead even without the Soviets. *FRUS*, 1945, Vol. V: pp. 252–55. But that was not his real position. See W. Miscamble, "Anthony Eden and the Truman-Molotov Conversations," *Diplomatic History* (Spring 1978): pp. 167–80.
56. For example, U.S. proposals going into Dumbarton Oaks included detailed provision for international economic and social cooperation, even suggesting a grant of semi-executive powers to ECOSOC. "U.S. Tentative Proposals," *Postwar Preparation*, pp. 595–606.
57. Department of State, *Press Releases*, Vol. XX, February 25, 1939: p. 153; "An Economic Bill of Rights, January 11, 1944," *DAH*, Vol. II: pp. 483–85; Roosevelt, *Public Papers*, Vol. 13: p. 498; and Department of State, *Bulletin*, February 16, 1947: pp. 277–78; *ibid.*, December 7, 1947: p. 1075.
58. Johnson, "Contributions of the Roosevelts," pp. 26–27.

59. The best discussion is Russell, *U.N. Charter*, pp. 781–88.
60. "Interest of U.S. in the ILO," *FRUS*, 1944, Vol. IV: pp. 1007–25. It was the prior experience of the League, supplemented by the U.S. proposals at Dumbarton Oaks (and to some extent by small power and NGO efforts at San Francisco) that laid the foundation for United Nations involvement in economic and social issues. Russell, *U.N. Charter*: pp. 777–807; and Inis Claude, *Swords Into Ploughshares,* 4th ed. (Random House, 1984).
61. "Delegation Minutes," May 2, 1945, *FRUS*, 1945, Vol. I: p. 851.
62. "Diary," June 3, 1945, Vandenberg, *Private Papers*, pp. 202–3.
63. "Delegation Minutes," May 23, 1945, *FRUS*, 1945, Vol. I: pp. 850–51.
64. Truman, *Memoirs*, Vol. I: p. 272.
65. Cf. "Delegation Minutes," *FRUS*, 1945, Vol. I: pp. 330–44, 470–71.
66. "Delegation Minutes," May 23, 1945, *ibid.*, pp. 850–51.
67. "Delegation Minutes," May 2, and "Minutes of the Second Four-Power Meeting," May 3, 1945, *FRUS*, 1945, Vol. I: pp. 532–35, 570.
68. Vandenberg anticipated that pushing the idea of rights and justice would cause the Soviets to "buck from Hell to breakfast." *Private Papers*, p. 154; also see pp. 172–75, 185. Truman later confirmed the importance of Vandenberg's role in his *Memoirs*, Vol. I: p. 272.
69. Note the consensus in "Delegation Minutes," April 18, April 27, and May 2, 1945, *FRUS*, 1945, Vol. I: pp. 330–44, 460–71, 528–48.
70. "Delegation Minutes," April 18, 1945, *ibid.*, pp. 340–43.
71. "Memorandum by the S/S to President Truman," *ibid.*: pp. 353–54.
72. Truman, *Memoirs*, Vol. I: pp. 277–79.
73. "Delegation Minutes," May 2, 1945, *FRUS*, 1945, Vol. I: pp. 532–35.
74. *Ibid.*, and "Minutes of the Four-Power Meeting," May 3, 1945, p. 570.
75. "Delegation Minutes," May 2, 1945, *ibid.*, pp. 532–35.
76. *Ibid.*, p. 533.
77. "Review of Soviet Amendments," May 2, *ibid.*, pp. 546–47.
78. "Minutes of the Four-Power Meeting," May 2, 1945, *ibid.*, pp. 548–52.
79. *Ibid.*
80. "Recommendations on Preamble," Purposes and Principles Committee I/1, U.S. Gen. 110, May 16, 1945, *ibid.*, pp. 750–52.
81. "Delegation Minutes," May 23, *ibid.*, pp. 852–53. In contrast, see the otherwise understandable but also bitter conclusion of the great international legal scholar, H. Lauterpacht, in *International Law and Human Rights* (Praeger, 1950): pp. 301–2.
82. Quoted in Sohn and Buergenthal, *International Protection*, p. 509.
83. Reprinted in Truman, *Memoirs*, Vol. I: pp. 289–93.
84. Vandenberg, *Private Papers*, pp. 217–18.
85. George Gallup, *Gallup Polls, 1939–1948* (Random House, 1972): p. 497. In October 1945, still only 71 percent of Americans polled favored joining the United Nations.
86. *Congressional Record*, Senate, July 28, 1945: pp. 7941–8190.
87. Vandenberg jubilantly wrote his wife: "The things [done] at Frisco to remove potential Senate opposition have paid rich dividends." *Private Papers*, p. 218.
88. *Congressional Record*, House, March 1, 1945: pp. 1618–22.

8   AN END TO LEADERSHIP

Harry Truman was a passionate supporter of U.N. promotion of rights and freedoms.[1] In his second Inaugural Address he emphasized the U.N.'s importance, connecting it to what he saw as a critical moment in history, and for American diplomacy: "It may be our lot to experience, and in large measure to bring about, a major turning point in the long history of the human race. The first half of this century has been marked by unprecedented and brutal attacks on the rights of man, and by the two most frightful wars in history." Truman believed it was America's role to lead the world to security and prosperity, and therefore it was essential to provide "continued support for the United Nations and its related agencies." To that end, he pressed hard to obtain funding to relocate the United Nations from Paris to New York, and endorsed elaboration of the principles outlined in the Charter.[2] It was a difficult fight, for despite discrediting of the term after Pearl Harbor, the extent of lingering isolationism in America in the aftermath of World War II should not be underestimated. During this time the 80th ("do-nothing") Congress was controlled by the Republicans, a number of whom worked to delay enabling legislation permitting relocation of the United Nations to New York, and who also opposed postwar commitments such as the European Recovery Program and NATO. On the other hand, two

Republicans played critical roles in overcoming latent isolationism and antagonism to the United Nations in the late 1940s: Senator Vandenberg and Representative Charles A. Eaton, Chairman of the House Foreign Affairs Committee. Truman later recalled that without assistance from those enlightened Republicans, the internationalist course of his foreign policy might have fallen prey to the same forces that sustained the "Twelve Willful Men" of Wilson's day.[3]

CONSTRUCTIVE ENGAGEMENT

Wary of Congress, Truman nevertheless pushed for the Universal Declaration and International Bill of Rights proposed by the United States at San Francisco. The State Department suggested a two-stage drafting procedure: a declaration of principles would be drafted first, with detailed, binding provisions of a bill worked out later. This two-stage strategy derived from the expectation that it would be easier to obtain both domestic and international agreement to a nonbinding declaration, and after that prepared the way, move to a binding treaty. Mrs. Roosevelt, from her seat as Chairman of the U.N. Human Rights Commission (UNHRC), made it clear that while the United States regarded the Universal Declaration as aspirational in character, it was "only the first step in the elaboration of the human rights program called for by the Charter; it was essential that it should be followed by a covenant on human rights, drafted in the form of a treaty and containing provisions for implementation." The State Department made that clear in public releases and in Commission and Third Committee debates.[4] The United States thus voted at Paris to adopt the Universal Declaration in December 1948 largely out of a disinterested humanitarian impulse that welcomed the idea of setting international standards for government treatment of individuals.

The Truman administration subsequently took not merely an active but a leading role on drafting the International Covenants through the early 1950s. It is true that the United States helped split the original single Bill of Rights into two covenants, one on civil and political, and one on economic, social and cultural rights—in a move for which it has received much criticism. But that policy was arguably both reasonable and defensible given the different nature and implementation of political and economic rights, and in any case represented the consensus opinion in the United Nations at the time (hence its adoption by the Commission). Moreover, whether or not one regards the covenants as equal in moral status, they are not equal in the immediacy of their legal obligation. The Economic Covenant obliges states to take steps only "to the maximum of available resources"; however, no comparable derogation exists in the Civil and Political Covenant.[5] In addition, the State Department made a variety of positive proposals on the substantive content of the two covenants, as well as other international rights conventions. A fair perusal of those proposals ought to lead to the conclusion that the United States was serious about the drafting process.[6] Nonetheless, the leading American role in U.N. human rights activities in the late 1940s often goes unacknowledged in the narrow human rights literature, and sometimes is flatly denied.[7]

The administration paid close attention to questions of rights and freedoms in the United Nations because it believed the effort to extend individual liberty abroad was essential to long-term peace and international security. Truman himself repeatedly affirmed a belief in the connection between fundamental rights and security. On one occasion he remarked that "a requisite for peace among nations is common respect for human rights." Another time he went further, saying that "the attainment of worldwide respect for essential human rights is synonymous with the attainment of world peace."[8] He strongly backed the campaign to gain acceptance of a convention on freedom of information, for as he told the General Assembly in 1946, he thought international understanding was crucial to world peace and security.[9] The State Department echoed that thesis with reference to events in eastern Europe. For example, one 1946 report argued that the nazi threat had stemmed in large part from the Hitler regime's "cutting the Germans off from the outside world."[10] That was a clearly intended analogy to the "iron curtain" then descending along the borders of the Soviet bloc states, cutting off contact with the West. To look back on such developments and complain that international promotion of human rights became caught up in the Cold War is to miss the larger point: issues of human rights and fundamental freedoms were helping to *define* the Cold War.[11]

Rising Cold War tensions were not without direct effect on U.S. policy at the United Nations. For one thing, there was deep dissatisfaction with Moscow's early and frequent use of the veto. By 1948 pressure was building in the Senate for Charter reform, and there was widespread anger in the country at large over what was seen as Soviet obstruction of essential cooperation within international organizations.[12] In that atmosphere human rights questions naturally became increasingly contentious. In 1948 Secretary of State George C. Marshall warned the United Nations that Soviet denial of individual liberties threatened further to unravel the fabric of the postwar settlement. "Systematic and deliberate denials of basic human rights," he said, "lie at the root of most of our troubles and threaten the work of the United Nations."[13] Still, the United States continued to enjoy majority support in the General Assembly on most issues, and hope was held out that lesser bodies (such as ECOSOC, which housed the Human Rights Division) were sufficiently removed from political conflict that they yet might be able to work as planned at San Francisco. Worried, but not wholly disillusioned about prospects for U.N. rights programs, the administration pressed its proposals for an International Bill of Rights. It now had the added incentive of using such issues as part of the war of ideas underway with the Soviet Union.

The onset of fighting in Korea sharply heightened perceptions of the political significance of rights questions raised in the United Nations, just as that conflict increased general tensions. Prior to Korea, the United States emphasized cooperative and expansive development of international human rights law and machinery. But the Korean conflict accelerated a shift toward confrontation across the board in relations with the Soviets, including on ideological issues in the United Nations. In a 1950 report to Congress, Truman argued that with the aggression by North Korea, "the basic contrast between the objectives of the U.S.S.R. and its adherents and the objectives of the free nations became even clearer than previously." The Soviets were described as pressing in the United Nations "for acceptance of the view that the individual exists for the advancement of the interests of the community as represented by the state alone." He characterized the United States as instead having worked for "establishment of international machinery to safeguard the basic rights and freedoms of everyone everywhere." He ended with an admonition about the U.N. human rights program that encapsulated the shift in U.S. policy: "Establishment of international machinery is indispensable to protect the individual against the totalitarian attack led today by the Soviet Union."[14]

Rhetoric aside, under Truman the United States continued to support expanded U.N. involvement with the full range of internationally defined rights and freedoms. For example, in 1951 the administration suggested that the UNHRC collaborate with specialized agencies in drafting articles on social, economic, and cultural rights. Given later controversy about the American stance on economic rights, it should be noted that the United States thereby effectively went beyond the position of countries such as India and Lebanon. During the covenant debate, those developing nations had argued that "the two groups of rights were not of equal importance, the full enjoyment of economic, social and cultural rights being, in their opinion, dependent on the assurance of civil and political rights."[15]

By the early 1950s, then, the political *naïveté* evident in the U.S. position on rights at Dumbarton Oaks and San Francisco at last was disappearing. American officials had recognized the essential political nature of disagreements over international definition of rights and freedoms. The Truman administration, in sum, had finally realized (not without a rather belated shock) what the leadership of the Soviet Union and some other nations appear to have known all along. Subsequently, genuine respect for individual liberties as reflected in actual domestic practice and institutions, not mere rhetorical posing, would be heralded as the critical and unbridgeable divide between the West and the Soviet bloc. Until then, the United States had been broadly conciliatory about international rights initiatives it disagreed with, but after Korea it approached those questions more aggressively and with a keener eye for their political implications.[16] U.N. human rights forums thus were revealed to be (some might prefer to say, reduced to) one more arena of Cold War conflict. That tactical shift would hurt the United States in the decolonizing world, for the administration increasingly placed the contest with the Soviets in the United Nations ahead of the search for acceptable accommodation of developing country concerns. These tended to take the form of demands for immediate recognition of economic and social aspirations as full and fundamental human rights.

The decision to deny that certain economic goals and aspirations were on an imperative par with civil and political liberties was based on a number of quite reasonable philosophical and practical grounds.[17] Politically, however, the decision positioned the United States on the horns of a dilemma. It caused genuine puzzlement and resentment among delegates from some poorer nations, who remembered the U.S. position at San Francisco and who could only watch enviously as Marshall Aid poured in to finance the reconstruction of Europe. It also represented, in Mrs. Eleanor Roosevelt's words, a "first-rate propaganda problem in relation to the Soviet Government and its reckless propaganda campaign." She worried that the plan to separate the covenants would generate "a great deal of ill will [and] lose our position of leadership." On the other hand, she recognized that a single, binding covenant, replete with economic and social entitlements, "can cause us a great deal of trouble both in terms of public opinion and in terms of their actual [constitutional] application. Unless very carefully safeguarded, their inclusion in the Covenant would mean the rejection of the whole Covenant by the Senate." Although a presidential election year was upcoming and the matter was threatening to become a campaign issue, Truman personally told Mrs. Roosevelt to "not hang back in going forward with the Covenant."[18]

After a lengthy policy review, the administration decided that if maintaining American leadership in the United Nations meant accepting a single covenant it would do so, whatever the domestic political consequences. However, it would insist on insertion of a federal state clause in any such arrangement.[19] That might have worked, too: a federal state clause would have permitted the United States to make reservations and derogations on economic and social provisions it disagreed with, or that the Senate or states found unacceptable.[20] But it was too late. Everything was about to change for the worse, as domestic rather than international politics intervened to end America's leadership role and permanently damage its prestige on human rights issues within the United Nations.

THE BRICKER AMENDMENT

On September 14, 1951, Senator John Bricker (R–Ohio) introduced a proposed constitutional amendment aimed at limiting presidential treaty-making power.[21] The resolution underwent numerous metamorphoses over the next several years, but in each of its many guises it threatened presidential authority over foreign policy and America's new involvement in international security. When fully developed, the amendment called for three restrictions: (1) the executive was to be barred from entering into treaties that conflicted with the Constitution; (2) all future treaties would require implementing legislation "which would be valid in the absence of a treaty" (this provision was introduced at the behest of the American Bar Association [ABA] and became known as the "which clause");[22] and (3) future executive agreements were to be overseen, and could be rejected, by the Senate as if they were treaties. Debate over the Bricker Amendment absorbed much of newly elected President Eisenhower's time and energy during his first two years in office.

Furthermore, the fact that its principal support came from the legislative wing of his own party meant that much of his broader legislative agenda fell victim to squabbling within Republican ranks.

Recent work on the Bricker Amendment has criticized earlier accounts that stressed the role of isolationism in the controversy. Newer studies emphasize the pronounced hostility of American conservatives for the social and economic content of the U.N. conventions.[23] The explanation offered here incorporates both emphases, suggesting that conservative objections to U.N. human rights treaties provided a vehicle for a wider isolationist assault on the presidency, and its sponsorship under Roosevelt, Truman, and Eisenhower of an international leadership role for America. It was not possible to launch an isolationist attack head-on in the 1950s. Memories of Pearl Harbor and of nazi aggression were just too fresh to allow for that. Disguised isolationism nonetheless was the mainspring of the movement that attacked presidential control of foreign policy through the back door of opposition to U.N. human rights treaties. In short, only on the surface was the Bricker Amendment the offspring of the states' rights movement and conservative concern for constitutional liberties, however misplaced or narrowly defined. Most fundamentally, those concerns in turn were housed within a historic conservative isolationism, sounding most probably its last, loud hurrah.[24]

Conservative-isolationist sentiment coalesced around the Bricker Amendment almost immediately upon its introduction. The amendment soon picked up a multitude of co-sponsors on both sides of the aisle, and gathered support from the ABA, the Daughters of the American Revolution, and similar groups.[25] The response was quick and widespread because behind the Amendment's provisions concerning the treaty-making power were several long-standing conservative grievances. First, there was the abiding states' rights concern with federal legislative and regulatory encroachment: seldom in American history had advocates of states' rights been placed so much on the defensive as they were by Roosevelt's New Deal legislation at home and his, Truman's, and Eisenhower's expansive internationalism abroad. More narrowly, states' rights supporters were insistent on effective revocation of the Supreme Court's 1920 decision in *Missouri v. Holland*, a case which on the surface concerned migratory birds but which expanded the power of Congress to legislate on domestic matters not previously considered part of the federal constitutional domain, when implementing a duly ratified treaty.[26] Jean

Smith, a noted expert on the Constitution and foreign policy, frames the problem this way: "The Bricker Amendment would have nullified *Missouri v. Holland* by ending the distinction between laws and treaties as domestic legislation. To be effective as domestic law treaties would have to be made pursuant to powers granted to the national government in the Constitution."[27]

Lastly, advocates of states' rights sought to place new limitations on executive agreements. Two cases, *U.S. v. Pink* (1942) and *U.S. v. Belmont* (1937), earlier had raised executive agreements to the effective constitutional level of treaties.[28] States' rights proponents had searched ever since for a means to turn back the legal clock; they thought they had found just such a mechanism in the oversight provision of the Bricker Amendment. It was mostly a bonus, in the eyes of those primarily concerned with states' rights, that Bricker also promised to block possible U.N. and federal intrusion into state and local affairs on human rights lines. Besides, general American dissatisfaction with the United Nations by the end of the 1940s extended beyond the conservatives, as for a variety of reasons it became apparent that the organization could not fulfill its promise to facilitate general prosperity and international security.[29]

Still, debate over a constitutional amendment limiting the scope of presidential authority to conclude international agreements, and domestic application of treaties and executive agreements, did not necessarily have to focus on international human rights treaties. Support for a constitutional restriction on executive agreements had been building since World War II, when opposition was spurred by Roosevelt's skillful (but to some, also excessive) use of executive agreements to avoid congressional oversight of his wartime policies. Of course, among the most important wartime executive agreements to stimulate constitutional and other objections were those drawn up at the Yalta Conference.[30] Senator H. Alexander Smith (R–New Jersey) spoke for many when he explained his support for the Bricker Amendment as stemming from opposition to the "outrageous Yalta accords, entered into by President Roosevelt individually ... without even the knowledge of Secretary of State Stettinius."[31] Bricker himself, along with powerful Senate allies such as Wayne Morse, Henry Cabot Lodge, and Robert Taft, loudly condemned the Yalta accords while arguing for adoption of the amendment.[32] Lastly, as Alan Theoharis illustrates in his useful study of the Yalta Accords in American politics, prominent publications like the *Chicago Tribune* and *Saturday Evening Post* "kept the [Bricker] Amendment before the public by using the still-dominant concern about Yalta.... [It was said] the amendment would prevent [future] Yaltas."[33]

It was in the final analysis, therefore, Senator Bricker and his supporters who directed the controversy down the U.N. human rights path. They did so by arguing that U.N. treaties were unnecessary for a country with its own civil rights tradition, but more importantly by stirring up vague fears that the covenants actually would be harmful to the sovereign, democratic life of the United States.[34] However, the agenda of the "Brickerites" clearly was more ambitious and had deeper roots than simple opposition to international conceptions and treaties dealing with matters of human rights. Their attitudes fell within a broad (though not proud) tradition in which limitations on the treaty power are seen as resistance to novel foreign entanglements. The movement essentially represented a broad nationalist opposition to the whole U.N. system and idea, as well as to the internationalist policies and role of America in the postwar era. It hardly can be discounted that John Bricker was a leading figure in the isolationist wing of the Republican Party. As Governor of Ohio (a key state in that part of the country, the midwest, historically most attached to isolationism), he was known as a protege and close lieutenant of the most influential isolationist in America, Robert Taft. Bricker received Taft's endorsement (as well as that of most other isolationists, declared or otherwise) during his 1944 run as the Republican nominee for vice president.[35] In light of his background and political legacy as a Taft Republican and midwest isolationist, a contemporary historian's assertion that "Bricker was not an isolationist" is puzzling; it is also not the judgment of other, older historians.[36]

Conservative-isolationists in Congress had begun to focus on international rights conventions during the late 1940s. One analyst suggests a reason for growing opposition to U.N. conventions was fear among old opponents of the New Deal that "liberals in the Democratic Party intended to use international treaties guaranteeing human rights to force social change in the United States."[37] There is good evidence to support that thesis. ABA representatives testified to the Senate that international elaboration of rights might be used as "a Trojan horse" by New Dealers who sought to continue a social and economic revolution in the United States by extra-constitutional means; and there was also fear of executive encroachment on the power of Congress. Frank Holman, head of the ABA, was so nearly hysterical in his testimony that he actually cited the treaty-making power as posing a danger of totalitarianism in America, asserting the Constitution could be subverted as easily and dangerously as Hitler had subverted the German constitution during his rise to power in the 1930s.[38]

Other proponents of the amendment marched to the beat of a states' rights drummer. Midwest Republicans were prominent among this group, but other regions were represented as well. Democratic Party supporters of the amendment included southern segregationists, traditionally fierce defenders of the prerogatives of state government. Segregationists were awakened to attention in 1947 when the NAACP presented a petition to the United Nations charging that blacks in America did not enjoy full civil rights.[39] A year later, four Supreme Court Justices cited U.N. Charter provisions in support of invalidation of a California land statute that discriminated against Oriental aliens. More generally, states' rights advocates united around the Bricker Amendment out of opposition to a 1942 Supreme Court ruling which held that "state law must yield when it is inconsistent with or impairs the policy or provisions of a treaty or of an international compact or agreement."[40]

While conservatism *per se* clearly played a role in gathering support for the Bricker Amendment, it should not be exaggerated at the expense of the explanation of isolationism. Nor should it be assumed, as some analysts have, that conservatives *in general* approved of racial segregation, and hence uniformly backed the Bricker Amendment.[41] Into the early 1950s participation in developing an International Bill of Rights still had bipartisan (including conservative) support—as did the United Nations itself. The most influential conservatives were also internationalists who shared the conviction that respect for individual liberties was an essential prerequisite of a lasting peace, and who believed that human rights formed a critical divide in the Cold War. Vandenberg was at the pinnacle of his power in 1950 as the leading Republican in Congress, chairman of the Foreign Relations Committee, and President Protem of the Senate. It counted for much among conservatives when he added his respected voice to the cause of support for the United Nations and American leadership in the human rights area, a cause to which he had shown himself personally dedicated at San Francisco. Although discouraged over Soviet use of the veto, Vandenberg wrote in April 1948: "I continue to believe that the United Nations offers the best nucleus around which to build international peace and security."[42] The Vandenberg Resolution—which paved the way for creation of NATO under Article 51 of the

U.N. Charter—began with this preamble: "Peace with justice and the defense of human rights and fundamental freedoms require international cooperation through more effective use of the United Nations."[43] Vandenberg's death from cancer in April 1951 was therefore as untimely as it was unfortunate. It left the Republican Party and the country bereft of strong conservative-internationalist leadership in the Senate just as the isolationist gale of the Bricker Amendment was beginning to blow.

Dulles, like Vandenberg a former member of the U.S. delegation at San Francisco, also spoke out in favor of U.N. involvement with human rights. After Vandenberg, Dulles was the leading molder of Republican opinion on foreign policy, and he too advised:

We must go on with the drafting of a Covenant which will seek to translate human rights into [international] law. . . . It does not minimize our own Declaration of Independence to recognize that the Constitution and its Bill of Rights were required to establish the body of law necessary to achieve practical results. So with the [Universal] Declaration before the Assembly. It is an important proclamation of principle and should be approved.

Dulles went so far as to argue that "provisions of the Charter dealing with the Rights of Man . . . open up possibilities which are even more fundamental than protection of the rights of nations."[44] Reassured by such bipartisan support, Truman had pressed ahead with drafting the U.N. conventions. When he asked for Senate consent to the Genocide Convention in 1949, he argued that U.S. adherence was "essential to the effective maintenance of our leadership of the free and civilized nations of the world in the present struggle against the forces of aggression and barbarism."[45] Dean Rusk, Deputy Undersecretary of State, affirmed that purpose in his testimony to Congress. It was an "inescapable fact," he told the Senate, that other nations "expect the United States to assert moral leadership in international affairs."[46] But the mood of the Senate had changed, and it went unmoved by those appeals.

Truman's request for consent to the Genocide Convention brought to a boil long-simmering anger in the Senate over its effective exclusion from foreign policy decision-making. Anger focused on the relationship among treaties, executive agreements, and the Constitution, culminating in the rush to support the Bricker Amendment; but it really arose over the general conduct of foreign affairs in the postwar world. As the dispute developed, it became clear that a great deal more was at stake than dislike by some conservatives of the idea that the United Nations might become involved in domestic affairs. Members of the U.S. Mission to the United Nations believed support for the amendment represented an assault on the whole structure and concept of postwar American involvement with international organization. They concluded that there was underway "an attack on U.S. participation in the United Nations" that was merely temporarily "concentrated on the work in the human rights field."[47] The State Department grew so concerned about nationwide anti-U.N. sentiment surrounding the Bricker Amendment, that it considered commissioning positive articles "in legal periodicals and other more public media" such as the *Washington Post*. Senior officers were aware that great anger toward them existed on the Hill, stemming from a perception of their high-handedness in advising presidents to use executive agreements to bypass Senate oversight. Dr. Thorsten Kalijarvi, staff associate on the Senate Foreign Relations Committee, told State's Treaty Affairs and Congressional Relations divisions "that there is a feeling on the Hill that the Department of State has repeatedly shown bad faith, that there is a strong feeling that the Executive agencies determine whether to treat an instrument as an agreement to be approved by Joint Resolution or a treaty to be approved by the Senate according to which procedure will be the easiest to obtain [sic] approval." It was feared at State that institutional pride and anger in the Senate over the use of executive agreements might cause even nonisolationist senators to vote for the Bricker Amendment.[48]

With the International Bill of Rights formally split into two covenants by 1952, and with Brickerite opposition rising in the Senate, the State Department conducted a major review of its U.N. human rights policy. It set out to formulate policies responsive: "(a) to the need of maintaining United States leadership in rallying and strengthening the free peoples of the world; and (b) to domestic criticism of specific action taken or contemplated in the promotion of human rights in the United Nations." The Department concluded that the best way to meet those twin goals was to lower the U.S. profile on human rights in the United Nations, without sacrificing longer-term American interests in participation in the program. The final report noted: "It has proved possible, by and large, to gain acceptance of texts which do conform in essentials to American constitutional principles." It then warned, with foresight, that abdication of leadership would harm both U.S. interests and adversely affect the Covenants: "Should the United States abandon the Covenants, it is certain that before their completion the texts would substantially deteriorate and articles would be included utterly unacceptable to the United States. The Covenants will no doubt serve as accepted standards of conduct after their approval by the U.N., whether the United States does or does not ratify them." It was hoped that inclusion of a federal state clause and other derogations and reservations might satisfy enough domestic critics to undermine Bricker, and leave intact the core U.S. policy of support for a wide range of U.N. human rights activities.[49]

The State Department's proposed compromise would have been a reasonable accommodation to political reality. Unfortunately, the Bricker movement was peaking in 1952 and 1953, and elements among its supporters were in no mood to be reasonable. Bricker himself revealed that under cover of his opposition to U.N. human rights treaties lurked the old distrust of foreign entanglements, only now married to odd and sinister suspicions of internationalists in the State Department. He and many of his supporters openly proclaimed their opposition to what they regarded as dangerous, even traitorous, internationalism on the part of the State Department and Truman administration. It is in this wider, xenophobic context that the opposition to U.N. treaties should be seen. Many supporters of the amendment genuinely believed that a threat to American national, as well as state and local, autonomy emanated from a presumed predilection not only toward "global socialism," but also incipient "world government" on the part of the United Nations. However extreme and exaggerated, there was real fear about the possibility of erosion of national sovereignty, and secondarily, executive and international encroachment on congressional powers and states' rights.[50] That is why Bricker vehemently objected even to the separate U.N. Covenant on Civil and Political Rights, a document literally ringing with the inspired phrases of the American civil rights tradition. His objection and that of most of his close supporters was to the whole U.N. project of international organization and cooperation, not just to instruments that enumerated advanced conceptions of economic, social, or cultural rights.[51]

In fairness to Bricker and his supporters, it should be noted that fears about international instruments and U.N. and executive intentions were aggravated by impolitic statements made by officers of the U.N. Human Rights Division. Special note was taken of comments by the Division's first Director, John Humphrey, who described U.N. efforts as seeking "creation of some kind of supranational supervision of [the] relationship between the state and its citizens."[52] The executive branch as a whole was suspected by the Brickerites of being sympathetic to that (putative) goal. Nor was that merely a partisan position. It was argued that the executive, regardless of the party in power, could not be trusted to uphold constitutional liberties. Suspicions overflowed in early 1952 when Dulles startled an ABA audience by saying, in a speech the ABA and Bricker would long remember and frequently quote:

Treaty law can overrule the Constitution. Treaties... can take powers away from the Congress and give them to the President; they can take powers away from the States and give them to the Federal Government *or to some international body*, and they can cut across the rights given the people by their constitutional Bill of Rights. This extraordinary power seems to have been deliberately intended by our founders in order to give the Federal Government untrammeled authority to deal with international problems [emphasis added].[53]

In the lead-up to his nomination as Secretary of State, Dulles retreated from that position. He told Eisenhower's staff (who pressed him on the point) that although a theoretical scenario could be drawn wherein a treaty was used to undercut Constitutional rights, the Bricker Amendment as written must be opposed as it threatened "the ability of the President to deal with current matters, notably U.S. troops abroad."[54] U.S. courts also rarely held, then or since, that international human rights treaties and conventions are either directly enforceable or self-executing.[55] But the damage had already been done. Besides, given that astonishing—if misleading, because nearly unlimited—interpretation of the treaty power, it might be said that Bricker had *some* grounds for what in hindsight otherwise appears as utterly unreasonable fear about adhering to U.N. human rights conventions.

On the other hand, Bricker's suspicions of the loyalties of key officials in the State Department closely resembled the self-serving paranoia of fellow Senator Joseph McCarthy. Bricker once declared to his colleagues in the Senate: "I would suspect the State Department of almost anything it might be charged with in connection with the ulterior purposes of the U.N. and its representatives to undermine the liberties of the people of America."[56] On another occasion he charged that "one-worlders [are] trying to vest legislative powers in nonelected officials of the U.N. and its satellite bodies with a socialist-communist majority".[57] In formal testimony the fiery Ohioan stated his position unequivocally: "I do not want any of the international groups, and especially the group headed by Mrs. Eleanor Roosevelt, which has drafted the Covenant of Human Rights [sic], to betray the fundamental, inalienable, and God-given rights of American citizens enjoyed under the Constitution."[58] Legislatively, however, Bricker seemed to frame his objections more moderately. He sought to limit the internal effects of treaties by making them conditional on validating legislation passed by Congress, and to constitutionally restrict the power of presidents to enter into executive agreements. While somewhat exaggerated in scope, at first glance that did not seem more than the standard procedure observed by most other federal countries.[59] The problem was, as Louis Henkin points out, that "rendering all treaties non-self-executing, and denying Congress the power to implement certain treaties in domestic law . . . would have effectively prevented the federal government from making them."[60] In other words, if the amendment passed, there would be little point to negotiating treaties for which it would be unlikely or impossible to provide implementing legislation. The Senate thus would exercise an effective veto over presidential conduct of foreign affairs.

Bricker was no more trusting of a Republican than a Democratic executive. In spite of President-elect Eisenhower's personal appeal to delay action, he re-introduced his amendment as soon as the Senate met in January 1953.[61] Upon inauguration, Eisenhower thus was faced with a fundamental assault not just on his authority but against the power of the office of the president itself. That represented a concealed isolationist attack on America's leadership in the United Nations and the Cold War, and Eisenhower knew it.[62] Dulles, in contrast, was for a while ambivalent about the controversy. He wrote to Eisenhower that some similar amendment might be necessary if a different administration was in power, one which did not respect limited use of the treaty power. Eisenhower was unimpressed by the argument, memoing back the sharp comment that if such was the case, "then I am for the Resolution. . . . If we must have some amendment to protect our government and our people from what might happen to them under the treaty-making powers of a stupid President and a partisan Senate, then the mere fact we believe there is no danger during the next four years is *not* a good argument [original emphasis]."[63] He confided to his diary: "By and large I think the logic of the case is all against Senator Bricker, but he has gotten almost psychopathic on the subject, and a great many lawyers have taken his side of the case. This fact does not impress me very much.... In any event, such lawyers as ... Foster Dulles and [Attorney General] Herbert Brownell are of the opinion that the effect of the amendment would be to damage the United States materially in its efforts to lead the world in support of the free way of life."[64]

Eisenhower understood that the Bricker Amendment was largely about isolationism. He wrote in his diary in April 1953, of his frustration with the legislative wing of the Republican Party, deriding it for containing "the most stubborn and essentially small-minded examples of the extreme isolationist group in the party."[65] He later told his Special Assistant, James Hagerty, that the amendment was "stupid, a blind violation of the Constitution by stupid, blind isolationists."[66] Eisenhower appreciated that whatever the surface motives of the Brickerites, the underlying thrust of the amendment was to turn the United States back from its internationalist course. That was also the understanding of his cabinet, and of major agencies of the federal government that touched upon matters of international interest, which he asked to assess the potential impact of the amendment on their respective domains.[67]

Eisenhower was deeply concerned that the amendment would hamstring the country's ability to act coherently in foreign affairs, a view reached after a re-reading of the *Federalist Papers*. Citing Alexander Hamilton, he told Dulles that the Bricker Amendment threatened to force an untenable constitutional situation, comparable to that which existed during the period of the Articles of Confederation.[68] Following that conversation, Dulles came to view the amendment as a major threat to America's foreign policy interests, a position the State Department had consistently maintained.[69] The danger also was appreciated by a minority in the Senate (mostly on the Democratic side), and by Eisenhower's old opponent Adlai Stevenson, who spoke out often and vigorously against the amendment's isolationist consequences, pleading with its supporters: "Let's not 'secede from the world.'"[70]

Eisenhower tried to get Bricker and the ABA to drop the "which clause," the technical crux of the controversy, but they would have none of it, insisting on all or nothing.[71] At a cabinet discussion in late February 1953, Dulles therefore first broached a policy change already worked out by the State Department. He proffered that the administration back away from ratification of the Genocide and other U.N. Conventions, which Vice President Richard Nixon identified from his Senate contacts as one focus of support for the amendment. It was hoped that would turn enough single-issue votes to avert the more fundamental, isolationist threat.[72] Worried about the head of steam the amendment had already picked up, Dulles quickly went before the Senate Judiciary Committee and announced that Eisenhower would not sign any new U.N. treaties or seek consent to existing ones. But he admonished that the Bricker Amendment was unnecessary since the administration "is committed to the exercise of the treaty-making power only within traditional limits." He stated that the United States would continue to "encourage the promotion everywhere of human rights and individual freedoms, but to favor methods of persuasion, education, and example rather than formal undertakings which commit one part of the world to impose its particular social and moral standards upon another part of the world community." Often overlooked is that Dulles told the senators, "we shall not withhold our counsel from those who seek to draft a treaty or covenant on human rights," even as he gave the assurance that "we do not ourselves look upon a treaty as the means which we would now select as the proper and most effective way to spread throughout the world the goals of human liberty to which this nation has been dedicated since its inception." Dulles was questioned at length by Republican senators, who left him with a strong impression of their isolationist sentiments. That night he telephoned to warn Brownell (scheduled to testify the next day) that the senators who supported the amendment appeared most interested in the possibility that NATO might be used to station American troops around the world.[73] The U.S. Mission to the United Nations shortly thereafter formally announced the new policy, to mixed international reviews.[74]

In sum, the administration's shrewd response was to undercut wider isolationist implications of the Bricker Amendment by appeasing more narrow demands for rejection of U.N. human rights treaties. Even so, and this is another point not always appreciated, Eisenhower was displeased at having to renounce the U.N. treaties. He immediately sent a message to the UNHRC expressing his "deep personal interest in its work" and stressed that the United States remained "convinced that freedom is an indispensable condition to the achievement of a stable peace."[75] He was furious at having to defend the constitutional powers of the presidency and his personal freedom of maneuver in foreign policy from his own party, especially at a time of national crisis over the stalemate in Korea. Eisenhower declaimed in private: "I'm so sick of this I could scream. The whole damn thing is senseless and plain damaging to the prestige of the United States. We talk about the French not being able to govern themselves, but we sit here discussing a *Bricker Amendment* [original emphasis]."[76] He remained angry as the Senate Republicans—who enjoyed a majority largely due to the coattails produced by his 1952 landslide—continued to press the Bricker Amendment and otherwise obstruct his appointments and legislation.[77]

At one point Eisenhower grew so exasperated with the amendment issue, and was so angered over Republican opposition to his appointments and general lack of cooperation, that he indulged private musings about forming a third, moderate party dedicated to implementing his legislative program.[78] When calmer, he handled the problem in his usual deliberate way. Having reluctantly, though astutely, conceded a comparatively minor U.S. interest in U.N. human rights agreements, he went on the offensive against the continuing danger the Brickerites posed to broad U.S. engagement in international affairs.

In a letter to Senate Republican Majority Leader William Knowland, Eisenhower went on record as "unalterably opposed to the Bricker Amendment." He argued forcefully that to adopt such emasculating restrictions on presidential authority in foreign policy "would be notice to our friends as well as our enemies abroad that our country intends to withdraw from its leadership in world affairs."[79] He next faced head-on those holdout Republicans who still smoldered with anger over the Yalta agreements. He recalled to them that at the time of Yalta, he had advised Roosevelt against proceeding by executive agreement with matters properly reserved for a peace treaty. Yet, Eisenhower strongly defended the constitutionality of Roosevelt's decision, which he believed had been taken in a presidential capacity as Commander in Chief.[80]

The hard lobbying and the tactic of sacrificing U.N. human rights treaties worked. In June 1953, Brownell told Dulles that Bricker was "about beaten," and that the resolution had been watered down to a harmless level by Eisenhower's (mainly Democratic) supporters in the Senate—though in reprisal, Bricker stirred up opposition to the European Status of Forces Agreement.[81] With more tendentious fears concerning U.N. treaties assuaged, the amendment was defeated in 1954. In its most extreme form it was defeated 42 to 50. Hagerty was privately scornful that the administration made a last-minute attempt to save face for Senate Republicans. He fumed cryptically into his diary: "We've won the Bricker fight . . . now isolationists and weak-kneed GOP leaders, trying to avoid [a second] fight, raising another [amendment] on executive agreements—much harder to win this one—'Yalta' etc. No guts, our guys."[82]

Hagerty was referring to a modified proposal known as the "George Substitute" (after Walter George, senior Democrat on the Senate Foreign Relations Committee), which required that all executive agreements be implemented by congressional legislation prior to taking effect. It went down to defeat by just a single vote: 60 to 31. Only fourteen Republicans voted with Eisenhower, while thirty-two (including Knowland) voted against their party's president. That represented the highwater mark of the Bricker Amendment debate, though the controversy continued to pester Eisenhower during much of his remaining time in office.[83] Three years later the Supreme Court put to rest a central issue in the controversy in *Reid v. Covert*. Mr. Justice Black wrote for the Court: "No agreement with a foreign nation can confer power on the Congress, or on any other branch of Government, which is free from the restraints of the Constitution.... Prohibitions of the Constitution were designed to apply to all branches of the National Government and they cannot be nullified by the Executive or the Executive and the Senate combined."[84] Long moribund, Bricker's controversial amendment at last was buried.

SALVAGING FROM THE WRECKAGE

Eisenhower's narrow victory meant that U.S. foreign policy would not, after all, be reduced to a weak state comparable to its condition under the Articles of Confederation. With the failure of the amendment he was free to extend wide-ranging security commitments abroad. But more narrowly, American interests within a variety of international organizations suffered badly. The policy of abstention from U.N. human rights conventions forced upon the Eisenhower administration also extended to arrangements concerning the ILO, and even had ramifications for relations with the smaller former Axis powers: treaties with the minor allies of Nazi Germany had included articles binding those countries to respect fundamental rights and freedoms, but the United States now ceased to press the point. Not wishing to repeat the mistake he had advised Roosevelt to avoid at Yalta, Eisenhower assured Congress prior to the Geneva Summit he was not planning to agree to binding executive agreements that bypassed the Senate.[85] But of course, the area of interest most badly damaged was in the United Nations, where the United States quickly fell out of its historic leadership role in seeing human rights concepts given liberal definition at the international level. The self-imposed ban on signature and ratification of new covenants effectively meant the United States left the field to a growing majority of states whose conceptions of rights, and political agendas, often ran counter to American and western liberal interests. Additionally, the State Department's prediction about the covenants came true: with the United States no longer pushing for a federal state clause, the Soviets rammed through a prohibition on exemptions for federal states, making it all the more difficult for the United States and other federal states to make derogations or reservations prior to adherence at some later date.[86] Despite the failure of the amendment, Bricker and the ABA succeeded in the limited ambition of restricting U.S. adherence to U.N. conventions.

Eisenhower was intent on salvaging what he could of the wreck of his U.N. human rights policy. He saw to it that U.S. delegates continued whenever possible to participate in U.N. forums and programs. After all, neither the president nor the State Department ever shared Bricker's aversion to internationalizing human rights and liberties. Moreover, opposition to U.S. involvement with multilateral forums involved in promoting rights was by no means unanimous among the public. At most, Americans remained divided concerning the merits, advisability, and utility of international rights agreements and activities.[87] Moreover, Eisenhower personally regarded participation in U.N. human rights forums as part of America's international leadership role, furthering long-term national security, and as a proper and natural extension of his own quiet domestic campaign of building a coalition in support of expanded respect for civil liberties.[88]

Although the administration had been constrained to promise that it would abstain on formal treaties, it was decidedly unwilling to renounce what it saw as the natural role of American leadership in the field of promoting liberty, especially as this remained a defining characteristic of the Cold War. It thus continued to involve the United States in U.N. human rights activities as much as politically possible, up to the limit of the promise not to sign new treaties or seek consent to existing ones. U.S. delegations thus did not drop out of debates over the substantive meaning of draft conventions, nor was the administration reluctant to cite U.N. conventions when it criticized violations in other countries. The Universal Declaration was cited regularly, and in 1959 the State Department cited the Genocide

Convention when criticizing China's policies in Tibet, even though the United States had not ratified that treaty.[89]

Eisenhower also sincerely tried, though without much success, to retain as much as possible of America's position of leadership in U.N. human rights forums. He did so by proposing a package of measures, called an "Action Program," intended to improve implementation of obligations that the United States and all U.N. member countries were bound to under the Charter and Universal Declaration. These proposals included fresh initiatives such as a call for biennial reports on implementation by all member states, special investigation of rights problems with global implications, and cooperative provision of technical and advisory assistance. Most features of the Action Program were adopted by the UNHRC and the General Assembly within a few years.[90] Also, despite vehement objections of former supporters of the Bricker Amendment, under Eisenhower the United States became one of the very first countries to submit a detailed report on its domestic practice to the UNHRC.[91] And he instructed the U.S. Mission to quietly continue to help draft specialized conventions, regardless of the prohibition on signature. Lastly, the United States lent formal support to most new declarations of rights, as declarations were not legally binding treaties requiring Senate consent and presidential ratification.[92]

However, when it came time for signature of full treaties, the administration had to resort to inconsistent and unconvincing (given U.S. participation in the drafting process) expressions of doubt concerning the wisdom or efficacy of international codification of rights. Among agreements that the United States clearly supported and contributed to, but forewent signing, were a Convention on the Political Rights of Women, a Supplementary Convention on the Abolition of Slavery, and a Convention on the Nationality of Married Women.[93] Of course, other agreements were opposed on their merits. U.S. delegates thus rejected attempts to couch language of a proposed convention on freedom of information in ways that might have condoned censorship, and opposed Soviet bloc and non-aligned nations' efforts to redefine the idea of a right to national self-determination so it referred to natural resources rather than to political liberty.[94] In 1956, with Brickerite opposition fading, Dulles and the State Department even considered making an exception to the promised prohibition on signature and adherence of new conventions, in order to support conventions on slavery and forced labor.[95] In short, although it is not Eisenhower's reputation in the narrow human rights literature,[96] he accepted that America had abiding political and security, in addition to humanitarian, interests in the U.N. human rights program, and he tried to maintain as active a role in that program as was politically feasible.

At the United Nations founding conferences, American officials had displayed a degree of *naïveté* concerning the nature of international disagreements over the definition and protection of human rights. By the time of the Korean War, however, they had realized that questions of human rights often were profoundly political, and hence that they had become bound up in Cold War policy. Although some effort was made to continue to work out a consensus on a positive international law of human rights, the United States began to approach most U.N. forums and agencies as additional arenas of ideological and geopolitical contest. It is, therefore, an ironic paradox that a faction of mostly conservative Americans soon succeeded in closing off issues of human rights in the United Nations as a potential domain of international (and Cold War) leadership by the United States. The solution to the paradox is that these were isolationist, not internationalist, conservatives. Eisenhower lucklessly inherited their fierce opposition to executive control of foreign policy.

Presidential power had been expanding for decades at the expense of Congress and the states, out of the exigencies of the national emergencies of Depression and war. The offensive aimed at the presidency in the 1950s came mostly from the isolationist right wing of the Republican Party, in close alliance with Dixiecrats and other traditional proponents of states' rights. It therefore had a particular, even a peculiar, social and economic agenda that led it to a tactical focus on U.N. human rights treaties. Yet at its most fundamental, the offensive spoke to popular reaction against the newly internationalist course taken by the country, a path charted by Roosevelt during World War II, and navigated by Truman and Eisenhower following that conflict. But that course, in turn, reflected fundamental realities of American power and responsibility in the postwar world. Eisenhower simply *had* to fight and defeat the Bricker Amendment any way he could, or else be forced to abdicate America's great power responsibilities and surrender its leadership of the West in international affairs.

Postwar disillusionment about the possibilities of building a liberal peace inexorably led many Americans to rejection of the U.N. system, and a reflexive retreat into the illusory safety of isolation. At its most extreme, that reaction saw the United Nations as an actual threat to traditional constitutional liberties in the United States. Such a response had been seen once before, when a significant minority in the Senate grew disgusted with the shape of the peace which followed the sacrifice of the trenches of World War I, and rejected the Versailles Treaty and collective security through the League of Nations. The reaction after World War II was nowhere near so powerful, but it still managed to force the United States to withdraw from a leading role in the very area where it had most put its particular stamp on the United Nations: concern for international promotion and protection of human rights.

Given the voting strength of Bricker and his followers in Congress, Eisenhower salvaged what he could. He deflected the more important threat to the federal treaty-making power and presidential prerogative in foreign policy by throwing supporters of the amendment the bone of U.N. human rights conventions. Forced surrender on the covenants led to an eclipse of American leadership on such matters within the United Nations, a development especially unfortunate because the singular U.S. insistence on making the "Rights of Man" subject to United Nations definition had set wolves among the sheep. After Dumbarton Oaks and San Francisco, the United States and other democratic countries would be thrown onto the defensive in the United Nations by ideological and statist assaults directed against the very idea of individual rights. That difficulty was only compounded by the parochialism of the Senate, which repeatedly refused to consent even to conventions found acceptable by most other democratic nations (such as the Civil and Political Covenant), and that for the most part genuinely enshrined liberal-democratic ideals and values.

In the end, the controversy's most important and lasting outcome was to cause widespread confusion over America's policy toward human rights, its commitment to constructive international leadership, and even its underlying support of the U.N. system and idea. An anomalous situation was created that remains unresolved: the nation most responsible for placing matters of human rights and liberties on the U.N. agenda foolhardily undercut its own leadership role, just as the integrity of the liberal concept of rights was coming under severe challenge in international forums. Yet there is a second, more encouraging lesson as well. Conservative-isolationists played on distrust of the faintly social-democratic character of U.N. human rights conventions as a way of marshalling broad opposition to America's postwar embrace of multilateral cooperation, on a host of fronts. But they failed, and their failure represented but a weak reminder of an earlier Senate's refusal to consent to membership in a world security organization. So, the main point to be made about the controversy is that it symbolized more the passing than the resurgence of the isolationist reaction in America. Eisenhower understood that, just as he understood that the cost of U.S. leadership on the most fundamental issues of international security in the Cold War—on questions that had much greater significance for the idea and success of liberty—was disavowal of U.N. conventions. He hoped the disavowal would be temporary, and that in time the unfounded fears of the isolationists would subside and the United States might resume its "natural" role as a leader on the issue. Yet he appreciated, as a good statesman must, that sacrificing the covenants was a price well paid if it ensured the wider freedom necessary for America to provide constructive leadership on matters of international security.

NOTES

1. Harry S Truman, *Memoirs*, Vol. I (Doubleday, 1955): pp. 289–93; *Public Papers 1945*: pp. 153–55.

2. "Correspondence, William O'Dwyer and S/S George Marshall," *FRUS Supplement: Letters of the Secretaries of State, 1947–1952* (Microfiche): #223 [hereafter, *Letters*]; Truman, *Memoirs*, Vol. II: pp. 226–27.

3. Susan Hartman, *Truman and the 80th Congress* (University of Missouri Press, 1971): pp. 47–70; Truman, *Memoirs*, Vol. II: p. 172.

4. UNGA Res.217A (III), U.N. Doc.A/810 (1948); UNGA, *Official Records* [hereafter *UNGAOR*] 3(1)C.3 (88th–180th meetings): pp. 26–980. *Yearbook of the United Nations 1948–1949* [hereafter *YUN*]: p. 527. Department of State, *Bulletin*, February 16, 1947: pp. 277–78; December 7, 1947: p. 1075.

5. Art. 2 (1) Economic and Social Covenant. Countries supporting the split included Australia, Belgium, Brazil, Canada, China, Denmark, Greece, India, Liberia, the Netherlands, New Zealand, and Venezuela. *YUN, 1951*: p. 482. On the different status of the Covenants see the concise discussion by one of the world's foremost international legal scholars, Louis Henkin, *The Age of Rights* (Columbia University Press, 1990): pp. 20–21; also, cf. Vratislav Pechota, "Development of the Covenant on Civil and Political Rights," in Louis Henkin, ed., *The International Bill of Rights* (Columbia University Press, 1981): pp. 32–71.

6. For example, Department of State, *Bulletin*, February 16, 1947: pp. 277–78; and December 7, 1947: p. 1075.

7. David Forsythe, "Congress and Human Rights in U.S. Foreign Policy," *Human Rights Quarterly* (August 1987): pp. 436–37. Henkin is an exception who fairly acknowledges the U.S. role in *Age of Rights*, pp. 63–67.

8. Quoted in David Heaps, *Human Rights and U.S. Foreign Policy* (AAICJ,

1984): p. 6; and John L. Gaddis, "Morality and the End of the Cold War," pp. 111–12.

9. U.S. President, *Report on the U.N.* (1947): p. 139.

10. Department of State, *Bulletin*, February 19, 1947.

11. "Total Diplomacy," February 16, 1950, *AFPBD*, 1950–1955: pp. 5–10; and Les Adler and Thomas G. Paterson, "Red Fascism: The American Image of Totalitarianism," *American Historical Review* (April 1970): pp. 1046–64.

12. "Memorandum of Conversation: Vandenberg and Rusk," April 13, 1948, *FRUS Letters*: #486.

13. Department of State, *Bulletin,* October 3, 1948: p. 432.

14. *Report on the U.N.* (1950): p. 183.

15. *YUN 1951*: pp. 477–86.

16. Department of State, *Bulletin*, February 27, 1949: pp. 248–49; October 31, 1949: pp. 643–45; *YUN 1950*: p. 524. That did not mean the United States always got its way, however. For example, self-determination was declared a "fundamental human right" and placed in both Covenants. GA Res. 421 (V), December 4, 1950; GA Res. 545 (VI), February 5, 1952.

17. *YUN 1948–1949*: pp. 527–33; *YUN 1951*: pp. 477–83; and see Louis Henkin, *How Nations Behave* (Columbia University Press, 1979): pp. 228–39.

18. "Memorandum of Conversation," May 29, 1951, *FRUS*, 1951, Vol. II: pp. 740–44. Mrs. Roosevelt's hardheaded attitudes and her tough stance against the Soviets within the UNHRC has not always been appreciated. Detractors on the right have tended to underestimate the firmness with which she withstood totalitarian redefinitions of the Rights of Man (an inclusive term, incidentally, which she was perfectly comfortable using); while admirers on the left have downplayed her support for the basic Cold War policies of Truman and Eisenhower. A balanced study is Mary Atwell, "Eleanor Roosevelt and the Cold War Consensus," *Diplomatic History* (Winter 1979): pp. 99–113. On the comparable hardening of attitudes of other U.S. officials at the United Nations, see George T. Mazuzan, *Warren R. Austin at the UN: 1946–1953* (Kent State University Press, 1977).

19. "Position Paper," June 29; "Correspondence," September–October, 1951; "Delegation Minutes," UNGA, November 12 and 13, 1951; "Correspondence," November 1951–January, 1952; *FRUS*, 1951, Vol. II: pp. 744–71; and *UNGAOR*, 1952: pp. 235–403.

20. A Federal State Clause permits reservations concerning legislative prerogatives of state governments. The United States historically inserts such a clause into bilateral treaties. See Nicholas Mitchell, *State Interests in American Treaties* (Garrett and Massie, 1936): pp. 68–96.

21. *Congressional Record,* Senate JR #102, 82nd Cong. 1st Sess., September 14, 1951.

22. Stephen Garrett, "Foreign Policy and the American Constitution," *International Studies Quarterly* (June 1972): pp. 187–220; Duane Tannanbaum, *The Bricker Amendment Controversy* (Cornell University Press, 1988): pp. 7–15.

23. *Ibid.* and *idem*, "Bricker Amendment Controversy," *Diplomatic History* (Winter 1985): pp. 73–93; also, Natalie Kaufman and David Whiteman, "Opposition to Human Rights Treaties in the United States Senate," *Human Rights Quarterly* (August 1988): pp. 318–29.

24. On isolationism generally see Selig Adler, *The Isolationist Impulse* (Abelard/

Schuman, 1957); and Manfred Jonas, *Isolationism in America, 1935–1941* (Cornell University Press, 1966; Imprint, 1990). On conservative-isolationism, see Justus Doenecke, *Not to the Swift* (Bucknell University Press, 1979); Ronald Radosh, *Prophets on the Right* (Simon and Schuster, 1975); and Youngnok Koo, "Dissenters from American Involvement in World Affairs," (Ph.D. diss., University of Michigan, 1966). Also, see Eisenhower's testimony to a special joint session, *Congressional Record*, 82nd Cong. 1st Sess. pp. 54–61. Dean Acheson linked the Bricker Amendment to a widespread, neo-isolationist "political revolt in Congress" that also attacked the Truman administration's liberal trade and immigration policies, and its efforts to provide security guarantees to the shaky democracies of Western Europe. *Present at the Creation*: pp. 633–37. Cf. Robert Accinelli, "Pro-U.N. Internationalists and the Early Cold War," *Diplomatic History* (Fall 1985): pp. 347–62.

25. *Congressional Record*, 82nd Cong. 2nd Sess., Vol. 98, Pt. I: pp. 907–14. George Reedy, principal aide on Johnson's Senate staff, claimed the Bricker Amendment was the most controversial issue faced in his time in Congress. Oral history in Robert Dallek, *Lone Star Rising* (Oxford University Press, 1991): p. 435.

26. *Missouri v. Holland*, 252 U.S. 416 (1920). A typical conservative view is Forrest Black, "*Missouri v. Holland*—a Judicial Milepost on the Road to Absolutism," *Illinois Law Review*, 25 (1937): pp. 911–28.

27. Jean E. Smith, *The Constitution and American Foreign Policy* (West, 1989): p. 114.

28. *U.S. v. Pink*, 315 U.S. 203, 230–31 (1942); *U.S. v. Belmont*, 301 U.S. 324 (1937). And see Louis Henkin's magnificent and erudite study, *Foreign Affairs and the Constitution* (Norton, 1972): pp. 129–71.

29. On State Department worries over growing and generalized disgruntlement with the United Nations in Congress, see *FRUS, Letters*: #219, #223.

30. Alexander DeConde, *History of American Foreign Policy*, 3rd ed. (Scribner's, 1978), Vol. II: p. 778; William Manchester, *The Glory and the Dream* (Little, Brown, 1974): p. 674. It should be noted that Truman also regularly circumvented congressional oversight through the use of executive agreements. In the military area he signed eighteen such agreements concerning overseas basing. See Loch Johnson and James McCormick, "Foreign Policy by Executive Fiat," *Foreign Policy* (Fall 1977): pp. 117–23. Thomas Paterson underplays congressional opposition in "Presidential Foreign Policy, Public Opinion, and Congress," *Diplomatic History* (Winter 1979): pp. 1–18.

31. Quoted in Tannanbaum, *Bricker Amendment*: pp. 79–80.

32. *Congressional Record*, 82nd Cong. 1st Sess. Senate, Pts. 1, 7, 12: pp. 12, 147, 8449–50; 83rd Cong. 1st Sess. C, Pts. 1 and 2: pp. 484–86, 1062–68, 2121–34; 83rd Cong. 2nd Sess. pp. 2154–58.

33. Athan G. Theoharis, *The Yalta Myths* (University of Missouri Press, 1970): pp. 182–85; also see Amy Gilbert, *Executive Agreements and Treaties* (Thomas-Newell, 1973): pp. 57–77. Gilbert views the controversy as constitutional at heart, set off by opposition to Yalta and other executive agreements.

34. *Congressional Record*, 83rd Cong. 1st Sess. Senate, Committee on the Judiciary, Hearings, Treaties and Executive Agreements, S. Rept. #2-3; Henkin, *Constitution*: pp. 151–52.

35. On Bricker's guarded but implicitly isolationist statements on foreign policy in 1944, see the unstintingly adulatory campaign book by Karl Pauly, *Bricker of Ohio* (Putnam, 1944): pp. 204–15.

36. Tannanbaum, *Bricker Amendment*, p. 23. Also, panel discussion, University of Kansas (Lawrence), October 4–6, 1990. DeConde affirms that Bricker was an isolationist, in *History*, Vol. II: p. 183.

37. M. Glenn Johnson, "Contributions of Eleanor and Franklin Roosevelt to the Development of International Protection for Human Rights," *Human Rights Quarterly* (February, 1987): pp. 41–42.

38. *Congressional Record*, Senate, Subcommittee on the Judiciary, Hearings, S.J. Res. 1; S.J. Res. 43 (1953); Frank Holman, "The Greatest Threat to American Freedom," *Wyoming Law Journal* (Fall 1953): pp. 24–38.

39. On midwest Republicans, see Philip Grant, "The Bricker Amendment Controversy," *Presidential Studies Quarterly* (Summer 1985): pp. 572–82. NAACP petition in Johnson, "Contributions of the Roosevelts," p. 42.

40. *Oyama v. California*, 332 U.S. 633 (1948); *U.S. v. Pink*, 315 U.S. 203, 230-31 (1942).

41. Natalie Hevener Kaufman, *Human Rights Treaties and the Senate* (University of North Carolina Press, 1990): pp. 9–37; *idem* and Whiteman, "Opposition in the Senate," p. 10.

42. Arthur Vandenberg Jr., ed., *Private Papers of Senator Vandenberg* (Houghton-Mifflin, 1952): pp. 402–3.

43. *Congressional Record*, Senate Resolution #239, June 11, 1948, 80th Cong. 2nd Sess. (1948), Vol. 94, Pt. 6: pp. 7808–13, 7828–46. Text and additional commentary in Vandenberg, *Private Papers*: pp. 406–12.

44. John Foster Dulles, "Future of the U.N.," *International Conciliation* (November 1948): p. 585.

45. Department of State, *Bulletin*, September 4, 1950: p. 379. Also, see Truman's address reproduced in *ibid.*, July 24, 1950: pp. 123–24.

46. Quoted in Vernon Van Dyke, *Human Rights: The United States and World Community* (Oxford University Press, 1970): p. 130.

47. "Memorandum," May 15, 1952, *FRUS*, 1952–1954, Vol. III: p. 1537.

48. "Memoranda," March 6–12, 1953, *ibid.*, 1952–1954, Vol. I: pp. 1790–94.

49. "Memorandum," February 9, 1953, *ibid.*, pp. 1542–47.

50. *Congressional Record*, 83rd Cong. 1st Sess. Senate, Committee on the Judiciary, Hearings, S. Rept. #2-3; Pauly, *Bricker of Ohio*; and *FRUS*, 1952–1954, Vol. I: p. 1833.

51. For example, see John Bricker's editorial, "U.N. Blueprint for Tyranny," *Freeman* (January 28, 1952): pp. 265–68.

52. Humphrey insists his remarks were "used out of context." Yet in his memoirs he states: "I have said the same thing countless times, because it is true." Years later, he remained bitter toward the ABA and contemptuous of Eisenhower. See *Great Adventure*: pp. 46, 78–79.

53. Quoted in Henkin, *Constitution*, p. 384 n. 35; also, *FRUS*, 1952–1954, Vol. I: pp. 1809–10.

54. *Ibid.*, p. 1778; and Sherwin Adams, *First Hand Report* (Harper, 1961): p. 105.

55. For example, *Fujii v. State*, 38 Cal.2d 718, 242 P.2d 617 (1952) re. the U.N.

Charter; *Doe v. Plyler*, 628 F.2d 448, 453, 5th Cir. (1980) re. the OAS Charter. Also, see Riesenfeld, "Doctrine of Self-Executing Treaties and *U.S. v. Postal*," #74, *American Journal of International Law* (1980); Hurst Hannum, *Materials on International Human Rights and U.S. Constitutional Law* (International Law Institute, 1985): pp. 3–13.

56. *Congressional Record*, Senate (98) Pt. 2, March 18, 1952: p. 2469. Such extremist suspicions were aggravated by the Alger Hiss case, as Hiss had worked on the U.N. Charter and was State's liaison to the United Nations. Dean Acheson links the Hiss case, McCarthyism in general, and rising neo-isolationism in the Congress and on the Republican right in *Present at the Creation* (Norton, 1969): pp. 250–52, 345, 358–70.

57. Quoted in Kaufman and Whiteman, "Opposition in the Senate," p. 313; and see *FRUS*, 1952–1954, Vol. I: pp. 1808–12.

58. *Congressional Record*, Senate (98) Pt. 1, February 7, 1952: p. 912.

59. For example, the federal government in Canada cannot make the country party to agreements that impinge on provincial jurisdiction without prior consent of the Provinces. *Attorney General of Canada vs. Attorney General of Ontario* (1937), AC 326; AC 355.

60. Henkin, *Constitution*, p. 158.

61. Editorial Note, *FRUS*, 1952–1954, Vol. I: p. 1778; Grant, "The Bricker Amendment Controversy," p. 572; Adams, *Firsthand Report*: p. 105.

62. *FRUS*, 1952–1954, Vol. I: p. 1833.

63. "Draft Statement by S/S," and "Memorandum by the President to the S/S," *ibid.*, pp. 1797–1806.

64. Entry for April 1, 1953, *Eisenhower Diaries*: pp. 233–34.

65. *Ibid.* Several former administration officials have confirmed that opposition to the Bricker Amendment flowed from Eisenhower's ingrained internationalism. Quoted in Kenneth W. Thompson, *Theories and Practice in International Relations* (UPA, 1987): p. 66.

66. *Hagerty Diary*, January 14, 1954, in Stephen Ambrose, *Eisenhower*, Vol. II, *The President* (Simon & Schuster, 1984): pp. 154–55.

67. "Minutes: Cabinet Meeting," February 20, 1953; "Views of U.S. Departments and Agencies," *FRUS*, 1952–1954, Vol. I: pp. 1781–91.

68. R. Gordon Hoxie, "Eisenhower and Presidential Leadership," *Presidential Studies Quarterly* (Fall 1983): pp. 595–96.

69. "S/S to Chairman of the Senate Judiciary Committee," May 19, 1952, *FRUS*, 1952–1954, Vol. I: pp. 1768–77, "Draft Statement by S/S," and "Memorandum by the President to the S/S," *ibid.*, pp. 1797–1806.

70. Complete text in *Papers of Adlai Stevenson*, Vol. IV, Walter Johnson, ed. (Little, Brown, 1974): pp. 317–19.

71. "Memoranda," *FRUS*, 1952–1954, Vol. I: pp. 1812–56. Ambrose, *Eisenhower*, Vol. II, *The President*: pp. 68–70; Tannanbaum, *Bricker Amendment*: pp. 133–56.

72. "Minutes: Cabinet Meeting," February 20, 1953, *FRUS*, 1952–1954, Vol. I: pp. 1781–82; "Memoranda," *ibid.*, 1952–1954, Vol. III: pp. 1542–56.

73. "Memorandum," *ibid.*, 1952–1954, Vol. I: p. 1790; *Congressional Record*, Senate, Com. on the Judiciary, Hearings, 83rd Cong. 1st Sess., pp. 823–30; *Eisenhower Administration: A Documentary History*, Vol. I, R. Branyan and L. Larsen, eds.,

(Random House, 1971): pp. 290–97; and editorial note, *FRUS*, 1952–1954, Vol. I: pp. 1807–8.

74. "Memoranda: S/S and U.N. Mission," March–May, 1953, *ibid.*, 1952–1954, Vol. III: pp. 1565–81; and Department of State, *Bulletin*, April 20, 1953: pp. 215–22.

75. "Eisenhower to UNHRC," April 7, 1953, *FRUS*, 1952–1954, Vol. III: p. 1570.

76. Quoted in Charles Alexander, *Holding the Line* (University of Indiana Press, 1975): p. 72; Ambrose, *Eisenhower, President*, Vol. II, pp. 151–52; and *Hagerty Diary*, excerpted in *FRUS*, 1952–1954, Vol. I: pp. 1845–46.

77. In 1953, one version of the amendment mustered sixty-three co-sponsors. *Congressional Record* (1953), S.J. Res. #1.

78. Entry for April 1, 1953, *Eisenhower Diaries*: pp. 233–34.

79. "Eisenhower to Knowland," January 25, 1954, *DAH*: pp. 608–9; and Grant, "Bricker Amendment Controversy," p. 574.

80. Ambrose, *Eisenhower*, Vol. II, *The President*: p. 155.

81. "Memoranda of Telephone Conversations, S/S–Attorney General," June 11 and 24, 1953, and "S/S to the President," June 14, 1953, *FRUS*, 1952–1954, Vol. I: pp. 1815–19.

82. *Hagerty Diary*, February 1, 1954; *FRUS*, 1952–1954, Vol. I: pp. 1843–44.

83. Entries for February 26, 1954; January 17, 1955; and March 23, 1956, *Eisenhower Diaries*: pp. 276, 292, 322–23.

84. *Reid v. Covert*, 354 U.S. 1, 16-17 (1957).

85. H. Parmet, *Eisenhower and the American Crusades* (Macmillan, 1972): p. 404.

86. Department of State, *Bulletin*, April 30, 1953: pp. 579–82.

87. "U.S. Policy," February 17, 1953, *FRUS*, 1952–1954, Vol. III: p. 1551.

88. Eisenhower's reputation on civil rights, as with so much of his record, has undergone revision. See Mark Stern, "Presidential Strategies and Civil Rights," *Presidential Studies Quarterly* (Fall 1989): pp. 769–95; Chester Pach and Elmo Richardson, *The Presidency of Dwight D. Eisenhower* (University of Kansas Press, 1991): pp. 137–57; and Herbert Brownell, "Eisenhower's Civil Rights Program," *Presidential Studies Quarterly* #21/2 (Spring 1991): pp. 235–42. Similarly, Eisenhower's earlier reputation as a rigid Cold Warrior has been revised to emphasize his flexibility as well as firmness. *Inter alia*, see Ambrose, *Eisenhower*, Vol. II, *The President*; Robert Divine, *Eisenhower and the Cold War* (Oxford University Press, 1981); Melanson and Mayers, eds., *Reevaluating Eisenhower*; and Thomas Soapes, "A Cold Warrior Seeks Peace," *Diplomatic History* (Winter 1980): pp. 57–72.

89. Van Dyke, *World Community*, p. 149; and Department of State, *Bulletin*, September 28, 1959: p. 447.

90. *FRUS*, 1952–1954, Vol. III: pp. 1570–80; *ibid.*, 1955–1957, Vol. XI: p. 71; *YUN 1955*, pp. 161–63; "Report of the 11th Session of the UNHRC," April 5–29, 1955, U.N. Docs. E/2731 Corr.1; and "U.S. Amendments," E/AC.7/L.259. Also, interviews by the author, U.N. Centre for Human Rights, Geneva, June 30–July 3, 1986.

91. *FRUS*, 1952–1954, Vol. III: pp. 19–22, 39–79: 1565; Report on the U.N. (1954): pp. 151–58; Department of State, *Bulletin*, April 20, 1953: pp. 579–82.

92. *Ibid.*, April 20, 1953: pp. 579–82; *Report on the U.N.* (1954): pp. 151–58; and (1959): pp. 158–59; *AFPBD,* 1959: #37, #38; *UNGAOR,* 14th Sess. Sup. #16 (A 4354): pp. 19–20.

93. *Report on the U.N.* (1956): pp. 215–17; Department of State, *Bulletin,* October 8, 1956: pp. 561–62; U.N. Docs. E/2824, and E/CONF/24/23.

94. U.N. Docs. A/C.3/L.706 and A/C.3/L.706/Rev.1; A/C/3/PU.828, 834; A/3868; A/3805; *UNGAOR,* 12th Sess. Sup. #18. *AFPBD,* 1958: pp. 153–57; (1959): pp. 137–38; *Report on the U.N.* (1956): pp. 215–17; (1958): p. 186; (1959): pp. 158–62; and *FRUS*, 1952–1954, Vol. III: pp. 1438–39; 1536–81. The Truman administration had opposed changes to Freedom of Information for similar reasons. *Ibid.,* 1951, Vol. II: pp. 785–92.

95. "Memorandum," May 7, 1956, *FRUS*, 1955–57, Vol. XI: pp. 64–65.

96. Dismissive treatments include L. Weiler and Anne Simons, *The United States and the United Nations* (Manhattan Publishing, 1967): pp. 511–12; William Korey, "Human Rights Treaties: Why is the U.S. Stalling?," *Foreign Affairs* (April 1967); Humphrey, *Great Adventure*: p. 177; Johnson, "Contributions of the Roosevelts," pp. 44–45; and Forsythe, "U.S. Foreign Policy," pp. 435–38. Cf. the positive judgment of Eisenhower's respected biographer Stephen Ambrose, in *Eisenhower*, Vol. II, *The President*: p. 450.

9 CONGRESS vs. THE PRESIDENT

Spokesmen for the administration of John F. Kennedy made capital out of distorting Eisenhower's record on U.N. human rights treaties. Given the sweeping nature of the new president's rhetorical claims to international moral leadership—such as his Inaugural promise to bear the burden of the whole world's struggle for liberty—this was a regrettable but perhaps inescapable tendency. For example, although the United States never ceased participation in drafting conventions, Assistant Secretary Harlan Cleveland announced: "We are abandoning a 10-year-old tradition of aloofness. Americans [now] are participating actively in the drafting of international recommendations and conventions in the field of human rights."[1] Yet Kennedy also acted with a circumspection toward Congress that suggested lingering Brickerism still presented almost as much of an obstacle to him as it had to Eisenhower. The administration stressed that ratification of a convention on marriage "would be regarded as constituting a recognition and not an impairment of the constitutional rights of the respective States of the United States."[2] The purpose of Kennedy's rhetoric then was twofold: first, to assuage the anti–U.N. American right; and second, to denigrate in the eyes of the left Eisenhower's motives and record in order to create an impression of his own supposedly more urgent commitment to human rights. While he had little success with the former, judging by secondary literature he enjoyed great posthumous success on the latter.[3]

Kennedy does deserve some credit for presenting to the Senate at least a few, carefully selected treaties. In 1963 he submitted two conventions for approval, one on political rights for women and the other on abolition of forced labor; he also submitted a Supplementary Convention on Slavery.[4] Yet it should be understood that those agreements were chosen as most likely to avoid the constitutional issues that beset the Eisenhower administration, as Kennedy tacitly admitted in a letter accompanying his request for Senate consent.[5] Deputy Assistant Secretary Richard Gardner repeated that assurance, testifying that, "each of these conventions deals with an important human right already guaranteed by our Federal Constitution and by existing Federal law. Consequently, no change in our domestic legislation would be required."[6]

Eisenhower had backed away from all such agreements in order to avoid a constitutional crisis that threatened to strip the presidency of powers needed to protect more important foreign policy interests. Primarily because that constitutional crisis no longer threatened, Kennedy had moved cautiously to reaffirm the executive's fundamental commitment to the United Nations, and to reclaim America's leading position on international human rights questions. Even so, Kennedy misjudged the extent to which Brickerism survived in the Senate, which refused to approve the conventions on political rights for women and abolition of forced labor, and did not accept the supplementary convention on slavery until 1967, well after the president's untimely death.[7]

More important than tactical differences over a handful of U.N. treaties was a more fundamental continuity in policy from Eisenhower to Kennedy: both administrations shared a conception of a direct relationship between U.S. national security and foreign respect for individual rights and freedoms. While this idea became gravely distorted in Kennedy's approach to the conflict in Indochina, it also caused him to endorse U.N. treaties on human rights.[8] At least in that context of legal and rhetorical abstraction, the administration could proclaim the conviction that, "peace and human rights are not only the related goals of mankind ... peace is the ultimate goal of human rights."[9] Gardner summed up the position in unabashed language that could as easily have been drafted by officials of the Roosevelt, Truman, or Eisenhower administrations: "We have learned from hard experience of the intimate interdependence between human rights and our national security. Nazi Germany should have taught everyone the lesson that internal repression is often the handmaiden of external aggression [and] that the destruction of freedom at home can quickly lead to the destruction of freedom abroad." He went on to the emphatic conclusion: "Worldwide progress in the vindication of human rights and fundamental freedoms will also be progress toward creating a peaceful and stable world order." Kennedy himself once asked rhetorically: "Is not peace basically a matter of human rights?"[10]

Kennedy's style was much different from Eisenhower's. His administration was peopled with "young turks," impatient of change and supremely self-confident about their ability to use U.S. power to manage world problems. Like his predecessor, however, in the U.N. he acted within the postwar tradition of chief executives regarding questions of rights. He too asserted the high interest in participation traditional for presidents, compared with indifference and distrust in Congress. He too saw human rights diplomacy not solely as fostering U.S. interests in the success of multilateral institutions, but also as helping to satisfy long-term requirements of national security through attacking the presumed underlying causes of aggression. And he had similar blind spots. He also could criticize the Soviet Union and its allies for politicization of the U.N. human rights agenda, without always appreciating the degree to which his own country and administration might be seen from a Third World perspective as lacking sensitivity to claims and aspirations in the fields of self-determination and economic development.[11] And lastly and most importantly, he too was a Cold War internationalist, believing in direct American involvement to sustain and encourage the transformation of a pluralistic world of conflicting states and ideologies into a world of liberal states, managed by humane pluralists.[12]

A GREAT SOCIETY

Unexpectedly propelled into the presidency by the Kennedy assassination, Lyndon Johnson lacked an independent electoral mandate. He therefore quickly indicated he would carry out most of the foreign and domestic policies of the late president. That promise included support for a range of U.N. humanitarian activities and proposals. Within weeks of taking the oath of office, Johnson told the General Assembly he supported the United

Nations "as the best instrument yet devised to promote the peace of the world and to promote the well-being of Mankind." He then committed the United States to furthering global social and economic justice, in phrases ringing of the Great Society and in a manner reminiscent of Kennedy's inaugural pledge to promote universal liberty:

> Now, on a world scale, the time has come, as it came to America 30 years ago, for a new era of hope—hope and progress for that one-third of Mankind that is still beset by hunger, poverty and disease.... [Any] man and any nation that seeks peace and hates war, and is willing to fight the good fight against hunger and disease and ignorance and misery, will find the United States of America by their side, willing to walk with them ... every step of the way.[13]

Johnson apparently was unable to see much distinction between his beloved Great Society reforms at home and construction of a new world social and economic order. That point was recognized, though not in the sense given here, in a speech to the General Assembly entitled: "The Goal of the United Nations: A Great Society for All Men," and another by Dean Rusk, self-consciously called: "The Universal Appeal of the Declaration of Independence."[14] Yet another president and administration thus began tenure in office convinced that America's national experience was an entirely fit and proper model for the whole world to emulate.

On the other hand, Johnson was extraordinarily astute about domestic politics. He was thus well aware of the problem of ABA opposition to U.N. treaties on constitutional grounds, and of stodgy, anti-U.N. conservatism in the upper chamber. While a senator, he had publicly supported the Bricker Amendment out of fear of its popularity, while agreeing with Eisenhower on its faulty logic and baleful consequences. He once remarked in private:

> It's the worst bill I can think of. It ties the president's hands and I'm not just talking about Ike. It will be the bane of every president we elect.... We've got to stop the damn thing, and I think we can. We don't want to go putting that idea up on billboards though.[15]

In fact, he had played the pivotal Senate role in seeing the Bricker Amendment defeated, even though he voted for it himself once it became clear there were enough nay votes to ensure it would fail. He had in short successfully used the amendment debate to expose the rift in Republican ranks, while preserving executive prerogatives in foreign affairs; or, as his biographer Robert Dallek has put it, "to serve the country's international needs and score points for the Democrats by hidden, highhanded means."[16] Yet not even such legendary mastery in the legislative game in Congress would be enough in the 1960s to save most of the U.N. human rights initiatives from the narrow constitutional stabbings of the ABA, and the more ideological thrusts of the hard American right.[17]

Spurred by the civil rights movement, in the 1960s the American public once again endorsed the idea of U.N. concern for human rights with an enthusiasm not seen since the 1940s. Johnson led the way with support for a General Assembly resolution proclaiming 1968 "International Human Rights Year." He urged rapid completion of the two major Covenants, for which the United States voted in 1967, and signed the Convention on the Elimination of All Forms of Racial Discrimination.[18] U.S. contributions to the U.N. advisory services program were increased, and Washington proclaimed its support for the concept of a U.N. Human Rights High Commissioner. But when Johnson pressed the Senate for its consent to several conventions already signed by the United States but never ratified, including those put forward unsuccessfully by Kennedy, it was the same old story of fanciful constitutional objections and conservative hostility to the United Nations. Six agreements were submitted during his presidency, but he only managed to obtain Senate approval of two: a Supplementary Convention on Slavery first submitted by Kennedy in 1963 and a Protocol on the Status of Refugees.[19] Still, under Johnson the United States did move to greater engagement in the overall U.N. program, and strongly supported a number of new conventions, such as a draft on Religious Intolerance.[20] It also participated in the U.N. International Conference on Human Rights convened in Teheran in April 1968.[21]

Johnson's deep commitment to domestic civil rights might at a glance appear to also explain his dedication to similar international activity. Adlai Stevenson, then Ambassador to the United Nations, once implied such a connection, citing a primary interest in passage of domestic legislation as decisive in the administration's endorsement of the Convention on Racial Discrimination.[22] More often, however, Johnson spokesmen made it clear that they had long-term foreign policy goals in mind. Like previous administrations, they argued it was important to promote respect for individual liberties abroad because foreign repression ultimately posed a threat to

American security.[23] Gardner presented that thesis most starkly in a 1964 address to the World Jewish Congress. He asserted that American power "derives not just from our position as an arsenal of weapons or as a storehouse of commodities but as a base from which to seek the universal realization of the dignity of Man." He added:

Experience of recent years has demonstrated not only the interdependence of nations in their pursuit of basic values but also the interdependence between human rights and national security. We have seen how the destruction of freedom at home in totalitarian societies of the right and the left can lead to the destruction of freedom abroad. Conversely, we know that worldwide progress in the vindication of human rights . . . will also be progress toward creating a peaceful and stable world order.[24]

It should be acknowledged that connecting human rights to war also served the administration in its anti-Soviet publicity efforts, and against North Vietnam.[25] Yet it is as important to realize that such ideas were not being merely cynically expressed. Whatever the merits of the thesis connecting repression to aggression, it informed the thinking of conservative and liberal internationalists alike about the path to sustained world order, and it had been a central component of human rights diplomacy in the United Nations since the end of World War II. At least that was true on the level of chief executives. The Senate, in contrast, seemed forever mired in an obtuse legalism concerning U.N. covenants, most of which remained hostage to the narrowest constitutional interpretations and prejudices of the American far right.[26]

REALPOLITIK AND THE UNITED NATIONS

With the advent of a Third World majority in the General Assembly by the mid–1960s, issues of human rights took on a new twist. In the words of one authority on the U.N. Charter, "instead of an organization concerned with respect for all human rights everywhere, we [had] one almost wholly preoccupied with the elimination of racial discrimination."[27] The Soviets still argued that individuals could not claim U.N. protection against their own state, holding that "jurisdiction in the sphere of human rights is limited to preventing danger to peace and that this means discrimination against an entire racial group, such as in the instance of South Africa's *apartheid*."[28] By 1968, when Richard Nixon won the presidency, the United Nations was also shifting away from a liberal emphasis on the rights of individuals toward a near exclusive concern with collective economic and social rights.[29] In addition, the major realignment of political forces that took place following Israel's decisive victory in the 1967 war helped seal a voting alliance among the Soviet, Arab, and Afro-Asian blocs. Israel and South Africa (Chile was added to that list after the 1973 *coup*) became targets of special criticism, aimed at by a majority of non-western countries in the General Assembly and UNHRC. Among the more notable initiatives taken by that grouping was passage, over fierce U.S. and western objection, of a 1975 resolution condemning Zionism as a form of racism.[30]

Most western and some neutral countries opposed this slippage away from efforts at universal application to mere political targeting. Although the United States and other western nations sometimes proposed their own preferred "hit list" of violators, on the whole they worked to gain acceptance of international machinery that would monitor and protect *individuals* in every country in an evenhanded fashion. The Nixon administration thus proposed or supported reforms such as direct access to international bodies by individual complainants and reaffirmed U.S. approval of a High Commissioner for Human Rights. It also defended expanded participation by NGOs in U.N. forums and deliberations.[31]

Nixon and Kissinger did not want to make a commitment to abstract principles the touchstone of foreign policy, but they did not set out to abandon basic American principles either. Also, they saw greater U.S. cooperation within the United Nations as aiding that forum in becoming a more useful locale for a hoped-for "transition from an era of confrontation to one of negotiation."[32] Lastly, they were interested in obtaining reciprocal cooperation from other states on such matters as oversight of the Geneva Conventions, as the problem of U.S. POWs in Indochina emerged as both a domestic political issue and an obstacle to a negotiated withdrawal by the United States.[33] Thus, although it is seldom acknowledged in secondary literature, Nixon backed U.N. and other multilateral human rights programs more forcefully and consistently than either house of Congress. Like other presidents, he was held back from doing more primarily because his hands were tied by continuing objections in the Senate to taking on fresh treaty obligations.[34]

In early 1970, well before Congress displayed a major interest in the human rights dimension of foreign policy, Nixon resubmitted the Genocide Convention for consideration.[35] In testimony before the Committee on Foreign Relations, U.N. Ambassador Charles Yost voiced the administration's great concern that failure to ratify such conventions was "almost incomprehensible to other nations." He accurately noted that persistent Senate refusal to accept U.N. treaties gave "ammunition to our detractors and perplexity to our friends." He argued forcefully that "ratification of the Genocide Convention . . . would substantially serve our national interest in two ways: first, by its impact on world opinion and, second, by its impact on world law." Finally, he stated the same lament that previous executive branch supplicants had felt when they came before the Committee or full Senate to ask for consent to U.N. human rights treaties. The administration, Yost said, found it "exceedingly frustrating [that] our country should for so long have stood aloof in the community of nations from this treaty which gives such powerful historic expression to our own feelings and principles."[36] Would the senators not set aside their narrow reservations and accept accession to a treaty of which the United States had been a main draftsman? Six different presidents had found the treaty unobjectionable to American principles and important to the national interest; could not the Senate see its way to the same conclusions?

That and other presentations were of no avail. Nixon discovered that attitudes in the Senate had not changed much in twenty years. Then, as Vice President, he had presided over Bricker's introduction of an antagonistic, controversial, and anti-internationalist amendment only partly aimed at blocking accession to U.N. human rights treaties. He encountered once again in the 1970s all the familiar nativist and veiled isolationist arguments against adhering to U.N. conventions. Opponents made the same two basic points: first, that adherence would seriously impair American sovereignty and domestic (especially state and local) autonomy; and second, that international treaties were both unnecessary and might supersede the Constitution, thereby unfairly enlarging the powers of the federal government against the states.[37] That opinion was clung to by some senators in apparent ignorance of the decision in *Reid v. Covert*, in which the Supreme Court had responded to the Bricker controversy by denying that an expansion of federal powers or diminution of congressional or state powers could result from accession to an international agreement.[38] Even an aging John Bricker fired a parting shot from the sidelines, asserting one last time that the Genocide Convention was a direct and subversive threat to the U.S. Constitution, and the United Nations an agent of foreign influence not to be trusted.[39] Neither the narrow facts of the matter nor its international political implications were of much account in the eyes of those senators who voted against the treaty, in sufficient numbers that the upper chamber once more refused to give its consent.

Given Nixon's early support for a number of U.N. human rights reforms and for multilateral treaties and initiatives, and in light of the Senate refusal to consent to the Genocide Convention, it is not possible to accept as accurate the conventional wisdom that he and Kissinger became concerned with rights solely in response to congressional pressure. Nor is it possible to fully credit claims that Congress was the unqualified champion of human rights in American foreign policy during the early- to mid-1970s.[40] With regard to the United Nations, the most that can be said for the role of Congress after 1973 is that it may have indirectly spurred added administration interest in human rights questions.[41] After all, multilateral forums were a locale where issues of rights not only might be raised by an administration wary of making such linkages in bilateral policy, but could be seen to be raised without too much cost. That feature made the United Nations increasingly attractive to the Nixon administration as a vehicle for appeasing critics who did not understand its quiet humanitarian diplomacy, or understanding it, nonetheless considered it insufficient to meet the moral imperatives of democratic foreign policy.[42] But Congress did not produce interest in the issue within the administration *ex nihilo*. Nor did it always respond positively when the executive branch sought to expand U.S. involvement, or clear up confusion about the fundamental American commitment to liberal-international principles and international law. Indeed, rather than being wholly uninterested in rights, Nixon and Kissinger were aware of the damage being done to larger U.S. interests within the United Nations by a history of Senate parochialism.

The usual blanket charge of a lack of executive branch concern with human rights, often made by members or former employees of the legislative branch, therefore misses an important paradox in U.S. foreign policy during the early 1970s. Nixon and Kissinger opposed making strategic commitments conditional on respect for individual liberties (that is, human rights linkage), but largely in order to preserve the freedom of maneuver necessary, they believed, to defense of America's vital national security interests. Congress, on the other hand, enacted bilateral aid and trade strictures on human rights grounds in order to limit the ability of presidents to make sweeping security commitments, such as characterized the Cold War, to other countries; for such commitments were perceived to have pulled the country into the war in Vietnam.

Paradoxically, however, Nixon supported involvement in multilateral human rights activities while the Senate opposed most formal international undertakings. Yet the reasons were similar on both sides of the question: Nixon and Kissinger wanted accession in order to maintain a position of American leadership in the United Nations, and to help in the defense of important allies such as Israel from General Assembly and UNHRC criticism. That effort ran into familiar conservative and constitutionally-based opposition, but also a rising mood of post-Vietnam, neo-isolationism within Congress and among the general population.[43] Despite failure to consent to U.N. conventions, as part of a campaign against the "imperial presidency" House and Senate leaders, and not a few academics, insisted that Congress had taken over the lead on human rights from the executive.[44]

On the whole, however, Nixon (and later Ford) acted within a postwar tradition of executive branch support for U.N. promotion of rights. In only one area was there a marked difference. No doubt reflecting Kissinger's intellectual training and "realist" predilections, under Nixon and Ford the United States did not vigorously press the liberal-internationalist thesis that a necessary connection existed between internal suppression of individual liberties and external aggression. Nevertheless, the United States strenuously objected when faced with a Soviet resolution in the UNHRC to have a suppositional "right to life and peace" declared *the* primary right. That proposal was a none too subtle cover for an ongoing attempt to smother U.N. concern for human rights under a blanket claim of higher state and international interest. The U.S. delegation led NATO and other western and neutral powers in defense of the idea that respect for individual rights was "a foundation for international peace and security rather than, as the U.S.S.R. would have it, that the right to live in conditions of international peace and security was a necessary precondition to the enjoyment of human rights and fundamental freedoms."[45] A Kantian predicate about universal liberty as a prerequisite of world peace had not found a ready niche in Nixon's or Kissinger's worldview, which emphasized a *realpolitik* diplomacy that discounted the internal behavior of states. All the same, the idea was rooted too deeply in American thinking about peace and security to be wholly expunged from foreign policy.

OLD POLICY, NEW EMPHASIS

With regard to the United Nations, one of the few features unique to President Jimmy Carter's human rights diplomacy was a greater willingness than his predecessors to accept definitions given to economic and social rights by international bodies, rather than the clear preference given civil liberties in the western tradition. Carter insisted that he "accorded economic and social rights parity with political and civil rights," and therefore signed and pressed for Senate acceptance of both the Covenant on Civil and Political Rights and the Covenant on Economic, Social, and Cultural Rights.[46] By signing these Covenants, to his credit he became the first president to break with Eisenhower's promise to supporters of the Bricker Amendment not to sign or promote any new, legally binding human rights treaties. Carter was aware of past difficulties over constitutional and ideological objections to the Covenants, and therefore appended a set of reservations that were certainly politically and probably legally necessary, when he submitted them for Senate consideration.[47] The need for him to make such reservations has not always been appreciated, especially by those who tend to see acceptance and ratification of international human rights agreements primarily as a legal rather than a political problem.[48]

At first it appeared that Carter might make better headway than his forebears in the White House. He was assisted by a major change of attitude within the ABA, which after prolonged re-examination of its policy rejected the idea that the Covenants represented a threat to the Constitution. The ABA now endorsed ratification, though it made its support conditional on certain reservations that Carter sought to meet in his attachments to the request for consent.[49] That is not to deny that real constraints confronted Carter's human rights policy in the United Nations. Some of the constitutional objections raised in the Senate were merely obstructionist and obtusely ideological. But more serious and sympathetic critics, some even within the administration, were also troubled, and saw merit in pointing out complications surrounding constitutional or treaty law peculiar to the United States.[50]

Although the Civil and Political Covenant was largely in tune with U.S. conceptions and interpretations, it too was not without problems. Article 19(3), for instance, on derogations on free speech almost certainly went beyond anything upheld as allowable under Supreme Court doctrine.[51]

Despite the more propitious legal climate, Carter too failed to obtain consent. The Genocide Convention was viewed favorably by the Foreign Relations Committee, but not by the full Senate, and the International Covenants fared no better.[52] This time, the Conventions fell prey not just to indifference and the older arguments. They also became targets of a bipartisan hardening of opposition on the right that aimed at Carter's whole approach to foreign policy, and blamed him for a loss of U.S. initiative in the "battle of ideas" with the Soviet Union. Joshua Muravchik points out in a searing and unbalanced, but often penetrating critique, what conservatives in both major parties found objectionable. Missing from Carter's formulation, he contends, were "precisely those economic freedoms honored in the American human rights tradition: the right to own property, the right to engage in commerce, the right to bargain collectively . . . which happen also to be rights to which the main proponents of 'economic rights' on the international stage are indifferent or hostile."[53] Conservatives with a nativist inclination thus were alienated by the effort to enhance U.S. standing in the United Nations by championing notions perceived as foreign to national traditions. In addition, "neoconservatives" (several who like Jeane Kirkpatrick and Muravchik were hawkish JFK or "Scoop" Jackson Democrats on foreign policy) wanted to force a return to hard line Cold War consensus in which human rights were seen as a key weapon against the Soviets. They therefore opposed most U.N. conventions as an unwelcome dilution of what they saw as a more pure, civil libertarian tradition.

Under mounting pressure from the right, in 1979 Carter backed away a little from international definitions, turning to defense of classical liberal notions of rights. For example, the United States cast the sole negative vote on a resolution proclaiming an international "right to development." Officials explained that the United States stood apart from all other western powers out of principled opposition to the resolution's tendentious language that clouded over questions of personal liberty and well-being.[54] Similarly, the Carter administration began to make strenuous criticisms of the U.N. human rights law-making process, especially related to the drafting of a proliferation of new conventions.[55] The official explanation of this shift cannot be discounted entirely, as under the press of events Carter underwent a serious rethinking of his approach to foreign policy, including the whole gamut of human rights initiatives he had taken.[56] But it was at least as important that he was feeling political and ideological heat from the right as he continued to seek Soviet agreement to major arms control proposals while plummeting in the polls. However, his shift on the emphasis given human rights, and on which rights were given emphasis, won him little applause from conservatives while leading to charges of betrayal of principle from activists, some within his own administration. He also received heavy criticism for his overall foreign policy performance from major allies, notably Helmut Schmidt of West Germany and Valéry Giscard d'Estaing of France.[57] Carter thus left office having raised the global profile of human rights, but without creating a sustainable consensus on the appropriate place of moral concerns in American diplomacy, whether at the United Nations, in tandem with important allies, or in relations with major opponents.

TAKING THE OFFENSIVE

As outlined above, during the mid-to-late 1970s Carter and an "imperial Congress" jointly rejected Nixon's and Kissinger's preference for principles of *realpolitik* as a guide to U.S. foreign policy. One result was that they helped pave the way for a neo-conservative attempt to revive an assertive foreign policy during Ronald Reagan's first term. At the core of his statecraft, Reagan was motivated by an interventionist perception of the requirements of moral exceptionalism, one that claimed containment was a human rights policy *par excellence* because it aimed at the presumed source of most threats to liberty: the Soviet Union.[58] From the same mainspring, his administration launched an offensive both against and within the United Nations that surprised most and alarmed many. Old hands at multilateral diplomacy in other western countries, some accustomed to being on the defensive in the United Nations, were startled by the intensity of the effort. Not all allies were pleased when the United States demanded major administrative and political reforms and promised to withhold its major financial contribution until the demand was met. But even displeased allies and the most bitter academic critics later had to admit the policy got both attention and results.[59] Besides, already during the 1960s and

1970s Congress withheld voluntary contributions to certain U.N. programs.[60] Still, the Reagan offensive went further, tapping into nativist sources that had long fed conservative suspicion of international organization. U.S. criticism also was helped by clumsy Soviet actions and the growing paralysis in Moscow brought about by the leadership crisis of the early 1980s. The West thus regained the initiative on such principles as self-determination, lost since decolonization and the Vietnam War, by forcing U.N. criticism of the Soviet Union's invasion of Afghanistan and Hanoi's continuing occupation of Cambodia.[61]

Specifically concerning human rights matters, during the first term Ambassador Kirkpatrick exhibited a combativeness and conviction of political rectitude not seen for years.[62] While often needlessly abrasive and impatient of diplomatic niceties, her strong criticism of U.N. practices was also undoubtedly meritorious in many respects, and over a number of forums and issues. Resolutions were usually heavily politicized; states voted in ideological or regional blocs rather than on the merits of the issues; and certain countries were singled out for ritualistic denunciation, often by worse violators cocooned from criticism by U.N. bloc politics.

To cite just two examples where the administration's objections were merited, in 1984 the Human Rights Committee declared: "Production, testing, possession, deployment and use of nuclear weapons should be prohibited and recognized as crimes against humanity."[63] How the Committee managed to move from concern with the Civil and Political Covenant to suffocation of nuclear weapons was a question well worth raising. In another instance, the United States flatly rejected the idea of an international "right to development" as implying "a right of developing countries to receive assistance, the duty of developed countries to provide assistance as a form of reparations for colonialism, and the necessity of establishing a new international economic order before all human rights can be realized."[64] Reagan also reversed Carter's policy and returned the United States to its traditional objections to the Economic and Social Covenant, in which a distinction was upheld between civil rights and social and economic aspirations.[65]

On the other hand, the United States had partly itself to blame for a number of these problems of politicization of the international human rights agenda. The Human Rights Committee, for instance, had been set up under an Optional Protocol to the Civil and Political Covenant, neither of which the United States ratified.[66]

The prolonged failure of the Senate to accept international instruments was therefore coming home to roost, as offensive resolutions emerged out of agendas unbalanced in part by the absence of American input. Every chief executive since Roosevelt had warned that would happen, but none was heeded by a legislative branch preoccupied with local concerns and smugly convinced the United States had nothing to learn about, or gain from, international human rights treaties and programs. More narrowly, the Reagan administration severely undercut legitimate criticisms by saying it wanted to see a single international standard of judgement, but itself insisting on a lesser standard for regimes it designated merely "authoritarian," as opposed to those considered "totalitarian."[67] It did not help that Reagan and some of his officials publicly encouraged a low regard for the United Nations, and that at times in bilateral policy he openly discounted international law as an inconvenience and an obstacle to the express higher goods of his crusading diplomacy.[68] In this neo-conservative disdain for and alienation from international human rights programs, he most clearly parted company from the policy of all his predecessors in the White House, and moved closer than any other president had to accepting the parochial view of Congress.

However, like much during the Reagan years, U.N. policy divided over his first and second terms. After several years of harsh rhetoric and confrontation, the administration began to express a more traditional executive support for international organization, and for the goals of the U.N. Charter and Universal Declaration.[69] An agreement reached in 1986 effectively established a U.S. veto over major U.N. spending, and the administration became more satisfied that its objections to over-politicization were being heard. Other conflicts, such as over perceived abuses of free speech and freedom of the press in UNESCO, were not resolved to U.S. satisfaction and led to withdrawal from that specialized agency in 1984.[70] Yet even in that respect there was more continuity between the Carter and Reagan policies than is usually credited: under Carter the United States had withdrawn from the ILO until that body abandoned forays into ideological resolutions and returned to a primary concern with the rights of laborers.[71] Furthermore, if U.S. policy was changing after 1985, so too was U.N. practice. U.S. positions and U.N. procedures certainly did not converge, but at least they no longer always clashed. The administration softened its criticisms and learned a new appreciation for the multilateral dimension of diplomacy, though it still tried to target countries such as Cuba for special attention on human rights.[72] Meanwhile, the United Nations responded to the financial pressure and winds of change blowing from Moscow by trimming its bureaucracy and moving away from its own brand of stridency and selective condemnation, though it too continued to be far more selective than any objective observer would like. For example, in 1987 Arab nations banded together to block ECOSOC recognition of an Arab human rights group whose bid for official U.N. observer status was supported by the West.[73]

Even so, the U.S. began to enjoy success in its efforts to improve the U.N. human rights machinery, and on development of new mechanisms to facilitate redress for individual complainants. Thus, the administration pressed hard proposals for extensive reforms to improve the operations of the UNHRC that it originally made in 1981.[74] As early as 1983 an otherwise highly critical assessment of policy by human rights NGOs conceded (somewhat grudgingly) that under Reagan the United States had "spoken out forcefully and effectively" in favor of action on psychiatric abuse, political prisoners, and religious intolerance. The report went on to praise the administration for its cooperation on the problems of "disappearances," political killings, and all unlawful forms of detention.[75] After concessions were made by the General Assembly, the United States even began to undertake, within the UNHRC, criticism of allies such as Chile.[76]

Softening of the authoritarian-totalitarian distinction, and relaxation of the anti-United Nations hardline of the first Reagan term, were complemented by a newly cooperative attitude on the part of the Soviet Union. Moscow too was at last coming to see U.N. human rights programs as more than a vehicle for advancing the Cold War contest, now fading rapidly in any case. Indeed, in February 1989, the Presidium of the Supreme Soviet adopted a decree permitting binding International Court of Justice jurisdiction on six U.N. conventions.[77] Neither the executive nor Congress would go so far in conceding sovereignal liberties. However, the United States did exhibit greater cooperation on thematic issues such as torture and religious intolerance, and in 1987 issued a statement reaffirming that it considered itself bound by the customary international law of human rights.[78] In general, however, Americans rather feebly looked back to non-binding, aspirational clauses of the Charter and Universal Declaration, rather than forward to new treaties and codification of rights.[79] In this respect the Reagan administration once again parted company with its predecessors by coming closest to adopting a traditional congressional rather than executive attitude toward binding agreements on human rights.

The winding down of the Cold War allowed Reagan to succeed on an issue where seven previous presidents had failed: ratification of the Genocide Convention. In September 1984, during the approach to the presidential election, Reagan announced to a largely jewish audience that he intended to seek consent to ratify the Convention. His Assistant Secretary for Human Rights, Elliot Abrams, then explained that the decision had been taken in order to accrue symbolic benefits for U.S. diplomacy.[80] Despite continuing isolationist and nativist objections, after nearly forty years of refusal, in 1986 the Senate at last consented to ratification, though with several reservations collectively referred to as a "sovereignty package."[81] It was still a tough fight, even for a president with the most maneuvering room among conservatives since World War II. Implementing legislation was held up until 1988. The surface difficulty was an effort by southern Republicans to attach an amendment making genocide a capital crime, thereby making the bill offensive to liberals known to oppose capital punishment. Some senators objected to the treaty on the ground that loose definition "might encourage American Indians to sue the United States government for the suffering of their people in the 19th century." Also at stake were nominations of twenty-nine Republicans whose judgeships were being held up by Senate Democrats hoping to seat members of their own party pending victory in the 1988 race for the White House.[82] Not to be outdone, Reagan signed the implementing legislation in front of an invited audience of jewish leaders in Chicago, just days before the country went to the polls.[83] That was a fittingly unseemly conclusion to a forty-year tale of parochialism and bickering, over a treaty which in the 1950s had triggered (though not caused) forced abdication by the Senate of the country's pre-eminent leadership role on human rights in the United Nations. And it may yet turn into a hollow victory, as already a number of European countries have raised formal objections to the U.S. reservations that would stand as a precedent for all treaty states.[84]

CONTRA ISOLATIONISM

The Bush administration's human rights policy within the United Nations also must be viewed as highly constrained by a context of contemporary Brickerism in the Senate; as limited by that instinctive nativist recoil from the wider world that still grips millions of ordinary Americans and not a few senators (or presidential candidates). That such a tradition remains alive among a segment of the electorate became clear in 1992, when it revealed itself as strongly (though not exclusively) present in the right wing of the Republican Party. That surely is one lesson of the 1992 presidential campaign run by Patrick Buchanan, at the time of this writing, on an "America First" theme. In one form or another, that political problem has troubled the U.N. policy of all chief executives. On the other hand, the American public as a whole is today more supportive of the United Nations than at any time since the 1950s.[85] Bush used that opportune moment to fully re-engage the United States multilaterally because he stood within the internationalist tradition consistently represented by the executive branch. Anchored in this central, liberal-internationalist tradition of U.S. diplomacy, he has been able to imaginatively adjust to the enormous changes that shook the United Nations and world system in 1989 and since. He has thus moved to seize new opportunities to link human rights, the United Nations, and regional security in practical ways, such as in ending the several conflicts in Central America.[86]

Like its predecessors, the Bush administration saw U.N. human rights efforts as supportive of long-term western interests in the survival and success of the U.N. system, and in alleviating underlying causes of conflict and war by addressing conditions of deprivation and repression.[87] And yet, Bush has responded to date with a familiar tandem of cautious treaty selection and politically pragmatic acceptance of derogations. Why? It is true that his administration continued the later Reagan pattern of either abstaining from human rights treaties where Senate consent was considered to be unlikely, or introducing domestic reservations into ratification of international agreements. However, there *has* been an important difference, in motive if not in practice. Bush appeared to accept derogations and reservations as an unfortunate political necessity, not as a good in themselves. He put them forward less out of ideology than pragmatic regard for prejudices in the Senate, *à la* Eisenhower. The administration hence refused to endorse a Convention on the Rights of the Child largely because too many senators objected to that treaty's ban on capital punishment for persons under eighteen, or to its lack of definition and protection for the unborn.[88] The administration did argue for quick acceptance of a Convention Against Torture, though once again with incorporation of reservations necessary to appease Senate opponents.[89] In short, U.S. introduction of derogations that even democratic allies sometimes find objectionable continues to be aimed not necessarily at flaws in any given treaty so much as the persistent problem of conservative-isolationist or Constitutional objections at home.

Under Bush, the United States continued to selectively squeeze those U.N. agencies and programs, such as UNESCO and its "New World Information and Communications Order," deemed overly politicized or inimical to freedom of the press or of speech.[90] Bush also picked up where Reagan left off by endorsing a return to paying in full U.S. assessments (or shares of the U.N. budget), including a plan for steadily erasing all arrearages. In addition, he authorized an increase in U.S. voluntary contributions to U.N. technical assistance programs.[91] This re-embrace of the United Nations was, of course, keyed in 1990 by the need to marshal international support for the effort in the Persian Gulf. Yet to suggest that the needs of the Gulf moment were all that underlay U.S. support for a full gamut of U.N. activities would be to seriously underestimate the degree to which Bush began to shift both rhetoric and policy before Iraq invaded Kuwait.[92] He took office with a vision intact for an emerging world order in which America would remain vitally engaged in close concert with its democratic allies. The United States promised to operate henceforth, as James Baker put it in April 1989, without indulging either "a blind isolationism or a reckless unilateralism."[93] That meant right from the beginning that Bush accepted an enlarged role for the United Nations. Happily, this spirit of cooperation—of a self-conscious return to the first principles of the U.N. Charter—was reciprocated, within limits, in the Security Council and General Assembly. An attitude of pragmatism was making itself felt throughout the U.N. galaxy of organizations, with some notable exceptions, even before the system was further shocked and galvanized by Saddam Hussein's mad plunge into Kuwait.[94] Symbolic of how deep this change in attitude ran was repeal in December 1991 of the "zionism equals racism" resolution of 1975.[95]

Early on, Bush spoke of the United Nations and its related agencies—often with great eloquence—as only Roosevelt and Truman had done before him from the bully-pulpit of the White House, as a key resource in the construction of a prosperous, democratic, and therefore peaceful world order. Once again like FDR and Truman, Bush (or his successor) is at last free to openly recognize and speak of the real possibilities for international human rights programs, should he choose to do so.[96] Most presidents have seen such programs as supportive of the personal liberties necessary to sustain national freedoms and international security. However, none since Eisenhower has been so free to invest presidential prestige and leadership in the struggle with Congress for greater engagement in the U.N. system.

American policy on international human rights, as on the U.N. itself, has come almost (but not quite) full circle. For the first time since the fires of victory in World War II cooled into the ashes of Soviet-American confrontation, there is room for policy maneuver. The world in the first years after the end of the Cold War is full again with hopes for humane government and decent standards of living. True, the United States is more wounded and tired than before, yet it may also be a less brash and more wise nation. As a result of its sustained national effort it counts as allies rather than foes the most stable and prosperous, free and powerful nations in the world. The burden of progress within the United Nations, as within world order as a whole, may now be shared in a genuine partnership of strong, interdependent democracies. It only remains to be seen whether the American public will emerge from its current flirtation with isolationism so that after the 1992 election season the United States may take the lead as *primus inter pares* within the United Nations.

NOTES

1. Department of State, *Bulletin*, February 6, 1961: pp. 175–76; and July 8, 1963: p. 41.

2. President, *Report on the U.N.* (1962): p. 307.

3. See the citations in Chapter Eight, Note 96 *supra*. That technique was used on civil rights as well. See Mark Stern, "John F. Kennedy and Civil Rights," *Presidential Studies Quarterly* (Fall 1990): pp. 797–823; and cf. William Chafe, "Kennedy and the Civil Rights Movement," in J. Richard Snyder, ed., *John F. Kennedy* (Scholarly Resources, 1988).

4. *Convention on Political Rights of Women, Treaties and Other International Acts Series* (U.S.) 8289 [henceforth TIAS], 193 *United Nations Treaty Series* 135 [henceforth UNTS]; *Supplementary Convention on the Abolition of Slavery*, 18 UST 3201, TIAS 6418, 266 UNTS 3.

5. Text in President, *Report on the U.N.* (1963): pp. 241–42.

6. Department of State, *Bulletin*, August 26, 1963: p. 321.

7. *Congressional Record*, Senate, Committee on Foreign Relations, *Hearings*, 90th Cong., 1st Sess., February 23 and March 8, 1967, *Human Rights Conventions*, Parts I and II.

8. See the sharply critical, "revisionist" treatment of Kennedy's foreign policy by Thomas G. Paterson, *Meeting the Communist Threat* (Oxford University Press, 1988): pp. 191–210; and *idem*, ed., *Kennedy's Quest for Victory*: pp. 3–23.

9. Department of State, *Bulletin*, July 8, 1963: pp. 42–43.

10. *Ibid.*, August 26, 1963: p. 321; and cf. Dean Rusk, "A Personal Reflection on International Covenants on Human Rights," *Hofstra Law Review* (Winter 1981): pp. 515–22.

11. See President, *Report on the U.N.* (1962): pp. 299–307. But cf. the articulate defense in *AFPCD* (1961): pp. 162–64; and (1963): pp. 198–202.

12. A provocatively negative appraisal of Kennedy's belief in U.S. exceptionalism and mission is Michael H. Hunt, *Ideology and U.S. Foreign Policy* (Yale University Press, 1987): pp. 165–70. A more balanced study is John L. Gaddis, *Strategies of Containment* (Oxford University Press, 1982): pp. 198–205. On the national Cold War consensus during the Kennedy years see Montague Kern *et al.*, *The Kennedy Crises* (University of North Carolina Press, 1983).

13. *White House Press Release*, December 17, 1963.

14. Department of State, *Bulletin*, October 11, 1965: pp. 578–87; and July 20, 1964: pp. 74–78.

15. Quoted in Robert Dallek, *Lone Star Rising* (Oxford University Press, 1991): p. 435.

16. *Ibid.*, p. 436–37.

17. See "Report of the Standing Committee on Peace and Law," and "Report of the Section on International and Comparative Law," both in *Reports of the American Bar Association* #92 (1967).

18. *AFPCD* (1965): Docs. II/61-68. Reservation was made concerning Art. 4, which posed problems for free speech. Each Covenant required 35 ratifications to come into force, a number achieved in 1976 without the United States. UNGA Res.2200 (XXI), December 16, 1966, 21 *UNGAOR*, Sup. 16, A/6316 (1967): pp. 49–58; and 21st Sess., 1966, Annexes, A/6546. Texts in *BDHR*: pp. 199–252.

19. Texts in *ibid.*: pp. 128–52.

20. *Ibid.*, pp. 191–96; President, *Report on the U.N.* (1963): pp. 241–56; (1968): pp. 122–29; Department of State, *Bulletin*, January 16, 1967: p. 104; June 3, 1968: pp. 720–23; and December 30, 1968: pp. 685–90.

21. U.S. opening statement in Department of State, *Bulletin*, May 20, 1968: pp. 661–63; follow-up report in *ibid.*, September 2, 1968: pp. 255–58; and see "Proclamation of Teheran (1968)," in *BDHR*: pp. 253–56.

22. President, *Report on the U.N.* (1963): p. 249; cf. "Human Rights," *AFPCD* (1964): pp. 196–201.

23. See Dean Rusk's statement in Department of State, *Bulletin*, August 28, 1967: pp. 251–52; and cf. *AFPCD* (1965): Docs. II/61-68.

24. Department of State, *Bulletin*, January 6, 1964: p. 22; and *AFPCD* (1966): Docs. II/38-52, #83.

25. *AFPCD* (1965): Doc. II/68; and (1966): Doc. II/47.

26. For example, see *Congressional Record*, Foreign Relations Committee, *Executive Sessions*, 90th Cong., 1st Sess., April 6 to October 11, 1967; and *Human Rights Conventions*, February 23 and March 8, 1967.

27. Leland Goodrich *et al.*, *Charter of the United Nations*, 3rd ed. (Columbia University Press, 1969): p. 17.

28. Gerhard von Glahn, *Law Among Nations*, 6th ed. (Macmillan, 1992): pp. 241–42.

29. See Jack Donnelly, "Recent Trends in U.N. Human Rights Activity," *International Organization* #35/4 (1981): pp. 633–55; but cf. Philip Alston, "The Alleged Demise of Political Human Rights at the U.N.," *International Organization*, #37/3 (Summer 1983): pp. 537–50.

30. UNGA Res. #3379 (1975). On the strong U.S. response within the UNHRC see Alfred D. Low, *Soviet Jewry and Soviet Policy* (Columbia University Press, 1990): pp. 143–44.

31. President, *Report on the U.N.* (1970): pp. 116–17; (1975): pp. 196–98; Department of State, *Bulletin*, January 12, 1970: pp. 41–44.

32. *USFP* (1971): p. 271; and see Nixon's speech to the UNGA in Department of State, *Bulletin*, October 6, 1969; and Secretary William Roger's address in *ibid.*, August 24, 1970.

33. *Ibid.*, p. 313.

34. Conventional views of the role of Congress, concentrating on bilateral measures, include Schlesinger, "Human Rights," pp. 511–12; David Heaps, *Human Rights and U.S. Foreign Policy* (AAICJ, 1984): pp. 9–14; John Salzberg, "A View from the Hill," in David Newsom, ed., *The Diplomacy Of Human Rights* (UPA, 1986): pp. 13–20; and Forsythe, "Human Rights," p. 439. A succinct, insightful, and contrary view is Louis Henkin, *Age of Rights* (Columbia University Press, 1990): pp. 68–70.

35. *USFP* (1969–1970): p. 238; and see *Congressional Record*, Senate, Committee on Foreign Relations, 92nd Cong., 1st Sess. (1971): *Genocide Convention Hearing*: pp. 12–104. For the text of the treaty see *Convention on the Prevention and Punishment of the Crime of Genocide*, 78 UNTS 277; also in *BDHR*: pp. 116–20.

36. Department of State, *Bulletin*, July 6, 1970: pp. 9–10. Also see *ibid.*, March 30, 1970: p. 432; and September 17, 1973: p. 376.

37. *Ibid.*, September 17, 1973: p. 376; and *Congressional Record*, Senate, Committee on Foreign Relations, Subcommittee Hearings, 91st Cong., 2nd Sess., *Genocide Convention*, April 24 and 27, May 22, 1970.

38. See Chapter Eight, Note #84 and accompanying text, *supra*.

39. *Congressional Record*, Senate, Committee on Foreign Relations, 92nd Cong., 1st Sess., *Genocide Convention Hearings* (1971): pp. 137–39.

40. Among accounts that make such claims see Forsythe, "Congress and Human Rights," pp. 382–404; Vogelgesang, "Domestic Politics," pp. 52–64; and Heaps, *Human Rights*: pp. 5–14.

41. See President, *Report on the U.N.* (1976): pp. 211–12 for Kissinger's uncharacteristic declaration that human rights should not be subordinated to conditions of international peace and security.

42. Kissinger gave human rights a high profile in addresses to the General Assembly. See President, *Report on the U.N.* (1975): p. 194; and Department of State, *Bulletin*, October 25, 1976: p. 509.

43. See Ralph Levering, "Public Opinion, Foreign Policy, and American Politics Since the 1960s," *Diplomatic History* (Summer, 1989): pp. 388–89.

44. Congressional Research Service, *Human Rights in the International Community and in U.S. Foreign Policy, 1945–1976* (July 1977); also Foreign Affairs Committee, Subcommittee on International Organization, *Human Rights in the World Community: A Call for U.S. Leadership* (March 1974).

45. President, *Report on the U.N.* (1975): pp. 194-211; (1976): p. 212.

46. Carter officials often described as important departures what were well-established U.S. policies. This was particularly true in the U.N. arena. For example, see Department of State, *Bulletin,* October 24, 1977: p. 559; and *AFPBD* (1977-1980): Docs. VII/159-172.

47. Department of State, *Message from the President Transmitting Four Treaties Pertaining to Human Rights,* February 23, 1978.

48. A scornful, legalistic account that sets out to "expose" the political character of the reservations is Natalie Hevener Kaufman, *Human Rights Treaties and the Senate* (University of North Carolina Press, 1990): pp. 150-74. Cf. Richard Lillich, *U.S. Ratification of the Human Rights Treaties* (University of Virginia Press, 1981).

49. See the views of the ABA's Standing Committee on World Order, in *International Human Rights Treaties, the Rule of Law, and the United States* (ABA, 1978). On the change, cf. E.P. Deutsch, "International Covenants on Human Rights and our Constitutional Policy," *American Bar Association Journal* (March 1968): pp. 238-45; and Michael Craig, "The International Covenant on Civil and Political Rights and United States Law," *Harvard International Law Journal* (Fall 1978): pp. 845-66.

50. See the statements by Warren Christopher and Patricia Derian before the Senate Committee on Foreign Relations, reproduced in Department of State, *Current Policy,* #112, December 1979. Openly sympathetic to reservations on political grounds is Joshua Muravchik, *The Uncertain Crusade* (Hamilton, 1986): pp. 75-111. Hostile for opposing political reasons, but with arguments couched in terms of legal obligations, is Kaufman, *Human Rights Treaties*: passim.

51. See *Congressional Record*, Senate, 96th Cong., 1st Sess., *International Human Rights Treaties,* Hearings on Exec. C.D.E. and F. (1980).

52. See *Congressional Record*, Senate, 94th Cong., 2nd Sess., *Senate Executive Report* (1976), 94/23; Frederic L. Kirgis, *1981 Supplement to International Organizations in Their Legal Setting* (West, 1981): pp. 160-99; also, Philip Alston, "U.S. Ratification of the Covenant on Economic, Social and Cultural Rights," 84 *AJIL* 365 (1990).

53. Muravchik, *Uncertain Crusade*: p. 90.

54. President, *Report on the U.N.* (1979): p. 157.

55. "Statement by Jerome Shestack, U.S. Delegation," Third Committee of the UNGA, U.N. Doc. A/C.3/35/SR.56 (1980): pp. 12-14.

56. James Earl Carter, *Keeping Faith* (Bantam, 1982): *passim*; and Zbigniew Brzezinski, *Power and Principle* (Farrar, Straus, & Giroux, 1983): pp. 319-25, 403-25.

57. Friedbert Pflüger, "Human Rights Unbound," *Presidential Studies Quarterly* (Fall 1989): p. 708. Helmut Schmidt was the most determined foreign critic of Carter at the time, and has not let up since leaving office. See his *Men and Powers*: *passim.*

58. Note the focus on the Soviets in Department of State, *Country Reports on Human Rights Practices for 1981* (February 1982); also see Coral Bell, *The Reagan Paradox* (Rutgers University Press, 1990); Michael Howard, "European Perspective on the Reagan Years," *Foreign Affairs* (America and the World, 1987/88): pp. 478-93; and Robert W. Tucker, "Reagan's Foreign Policy," *ibid.* (1988/89): pp. 1-27.

59. See David Forsythe's hostile treatment, where it is nontheless grudgingly

conceded that withholding assessments produced "the contemporary push for reform of U.N. administration and finances." Forsythe, *The Politics of International Law* (Lynne Rienner, 1990): pp. 117–40, quoted at p. 133.

60. Programs from which funds were withheld included the U.N. Special Fund (or U.N. Development Program), refugee relief for Palestine, and UNESCO. "U.S. Participation in International Organizations and Programs," House, Committee on Foreign Affairs, *Report*, Staff Study Mission, 96th Cong., 1st Sess., (GPO, 1979).

61. Department of State, *Current Policy* #293, July 1981.

62. *Ibid.*, #353, November 1981; and *AFPCD* (1981): Doc. #130.

63. Quoted in J. Gomez del Prado, "U.N. Conventions on Human Rights," *Human Rights Quarterly* (November 1985): p. 510.

64. President, *Report on the U.N.* (1981): p. 174.

65. Department of State, *Current Policy* #1091, September 1988.

66. Text in *BDHR*: pp. 232–36.

67. See *AFPCD* (1981): Docs. #130–32; and (1982): Doc. #127.

68. *Congressional Record*, House, 98th Cong., 1st Sess., "U.S. Role in the United Nations," (1984): *passim*, but especially Appendix VIII.

69. See *AFPCD* (1984): Doc. #70. An intemperate view is Francis Boyle, "Afterword," in Forsythe, *Politics of International Law*: pp. 117–40.

70. *NYT*, March 13, 1987; and *U.N. Chronicle*, #24/1 (February 1987).

71. *AFPCD* (1981): p. 26.

72. *NYT*, March 13, 1987. Also see the changed tone in *Congressional Record*, House, Subcommittee on Human Rights, 100th Cong., 2nd Sess., *Hearings* (1988): *Recent Developments in the United Nations System*.

73. *NYT*, March 5, 1987.

74. President, *Report on the U.N.* (1981): p. 215.

75. Americas Watch *et al.*, *Failure: The Reagan Administration's Human Rights Policy in 1983* (January, 1984): p. 102.

76. *AFPCD* (1987): Doc. #100. 77. See 83 *AJIL* 457 (1989); Glahn, *Law Among Nations*: p. 240; and *NYT*, March 9, 1989.

77. See 83 *AJIL* 457 (1989); Glahn, *Law Among Nations:* p. 240; and *NYT*, March 9, 1989.

78. *AFPCD* (1988): Docs. #82–85; and Lawrence J. LeBlanc, *The United States and the Genocide Convention* (Duke University Press, 1991): p. 257, Note #11.

79. See *AFPCD* (1987): Doc. #99.

80. *Ibid.* (1984): Docs. #91–92; also *ibid.* (1985): Doc. #76.

81. *Congressional Record*, Senate, Committee on Foreign Relations, 99th Cong., 2nd Sess. (1986): *Genocide Convention*; and see the text of reservations and implementing legislation reproduced as Appendices C and D in LeBlanc, *Genocide Convention*: pp. 253–56.

82. *NYT*, September 27, 1988.

83. *Ibid.*, November 5, 1988.

84. LeBlanc, *Genocide Convention*: pp. 11-12.

85. *Gallup Poll Monthly* (October 1990): pp. 15–19.

86. Bush supported an initiative linking a U.N. human rights observer mission to a negotiated peace in El Salvador. *AFPCD* (1990): Doc. #99.

87. The Bush administration accepts that the United Nations has a "special responsibility" in the human rights area. *Ibid.*, Doc. #77.

88. Department of State, *Current Policy* #1237, December 1989.
89. *AFPCD* (1990): Doc. #95.
90. *Ibid.* (1989): Doc. #66.
91. *Ibid.*, Doc. #64; and *ibid.* (1990): Docs. #71–82.
92. For example, see his first Inaugural Address, but especially his September 1989 speech to the UNGA. *Ibid.* (1989): Docs. #2, #4.
93. *Ibid.*, Doc. #3.
94. Breakthroughs on peacekeeping, preventive diplomacy, and regional cooperation were laid out by the Security Council in early 1992. *NYT*, January 31, 1992. Among exceptions, UNESCO and the FAO remain at this time mired in politics of regional and bloc confrontation.
95. Congress passed a resolution demanding repeal in 1990. S.J. Res. 246, June 29, 1990: 104 Stat. 285. Bush made a public request for repeal in September 1991, and the UNGA cancelled the resolution on December 16th. *Economist*, January 3rd, 1992.
96. *AFPCD* (1989): Doc. #4.

CONCLUSIONS

Two world wars and a long, fitful peace during the Cold War have raised questions about the relationship between liberty and security to a permanent status in the debate over U.S. foreign policy. Underlying much of America's approach to the outside world have been key assumptions about the presumed, inherent differences between democratic and non-democratic regimes. U.S. statesmen have tended to assume that expanding the zone of democracy and liberal-capitalist prosperity is the best way to pacify both traditional, authoritarian regimes and the virulent totalitarianisms of the 20th century, while simultaneously fulfilling national interests in expanding trade and access to strategic materials. In reconstructing international order after 1945, there thus was widespread U.S. acceptance of the need to emphasize human rights and basic freedoms, as well as political participation and economic cooperation in international relations. It was the United States which pushed human rights within the United Nations when other great powers were hostile or indifferent, and most smaller powers were concerned with matters of their own prestige and representation. This accomplishment has been obscured by the unfortunate subsequent reluctance of the United States to accept those same binding standards in law, although its record is better than many in practice. That nativist, isolationist reaction was born as much of the exceptionalist tradition of American nationalism as was the effort to export human rights and democracy, yet it was confined largely to the U.N. sphere. More importantly, the United States underwrote the recovery of Europe and Japan within a framework of liberal-capitalism, and provided security for those key areas in a double containment of the defeated Axis powers and the Soviet Union. That too derived from an enlightened sense of self-interest in seeing hostile centers of foreign power pacified by prosperity and representation, or contained until their internal contradictions forced such reform.

American statesmen were powerfully motivated to act on declared liberal principles in the immediate aftermath of World War II because those principles were manifestly also conducive to advancing other national interests, not least in the economic realm. This is not a trivial or cynical point: liberal principles helped channel American diplomacy into constructive directions in a way that *realpolitik* prescriptions never did, and probably cannot. That is not to deny that United States policy-makers have acted in unprincipled ways on occasion; Americans too, like others before them, have found the burdens of leadership and power in a hostile and competitive world corrosive of cherished moral values. At times, they too have used declared principle as a cover for less noble national purposes. They also have mistaken self-interest for a disinterested principle, or exaggerated principle over interest, most spectacularly in the aftermath of World War I and later, in Vietnam. But after World War II they matched liberal principles with key national security and economic interests in a creative outburst that has seldom, if ever, been equaled. Proselytizing for democracy and economic cooperation among the capitalist states was not solely ideological or self-serving, though it had elements of both those motivations. It grew forcefully out of the experience of the Depression and New Deal, which legitimatized the role of government in capitalist democracies in addressing social and economic injustices; it also arose from the encounter with nazism, read as demonstrating an intimate connection between domestic repression, antagonism to liberal-democracy, and external aggression. The emphasis on individual rights and liberties, both bilaterally and multilaterally, was therefore an integral part of the postwar American definition of international order.

Whether Americans now return to their old pattern of behavior, lurching between passive and active manifestations of a self-appointed liberalizing mission, is a question of cardinal interest for all. The

United States has not always led the democratization of international affairs graciously or well, nor has it always led willingly or wisely. In addition, it sometimes has acted in ways that produced unforeseen or deleterious effects, both for itself and for others. That surely has been the experience of excessive, reflexive interference in hemispheric affairs, and of Cold War blunders of perception in opposing communist insurgencies where the threat was merely local. Those are worrisome examples of the misuse of preponderant power. But far more critically for world order, America has at times abdicated in whole or in part from its otherwise inescapable leadership role. Although dampened by World War I and World War II, that urge to isolationism has never strayed far from the surface of American politics. It reappeared in the 1950s on the right, in the 1970s on the left, and is in the air again across the political spectrum, as the post-Cold War era opens. Can the United States moderate its tradition of swinging back into self-absorption following a sustained involvement in world affairs? Can it learn to behave like a "normal" and not an "exceptional" nation that does not insist its interests, unlike its principles, are universal? The jury remains out at this time.

Already the lessons of the Depression and World War II are fading from living memory, and now rarely can be evoked to touch the popular imagination or motivate public will. The country is jaded from the moral, as much as the economic and political costs, of waging the Cold War. With that contest over, it is not readily apparent to large segments of the public that the United States still has a vital interest in staying engaged in international affairs, and committed to sustaining and reforming world order. Yet if isolationism is one face of the coin of national mission (a "city upon a hill"), its other facet is enlightened engagement. In addition to pointing out the sins of the Cold War, Americans need to be reminded that it was they who succeeded in making over in a democratic image several of the world's most strategic and wealthy countries. Today most of the great powers, including two formerly fascist and aggressive nations, are liberal-capitalist societies allied to the United States. Russia and the former communist republics of the Soviet Union and eastern Europe, to one degree or another, are trying to follow the American and European example of representative government and market economics. A growing community of nations therefore now gives overt emphasis to individual rights in how they seek to organize their national political economies. As a result, they also express these ideals in the conduct of foreign relations, to the point that they have begun to underwrite regional and international security. Although this signal historical development is not solely an American accomplishment, its wide success is nearly unimaginable without America's postwar promotion of economic recovery, commitment to sustaining democracy in western Europe and Japan, and insistence on elevating liberal and humane principles onto the daily agenda of international politics.

The long-term implications for American statesmen of the collapse and disintegration of the Soviet empire and sphere of dominance present a problem and an opportunity nearly as great as that faced in 1945. America and Europe are less than certain or in agreement about how to respond to the continuing disintegration of basic order, and the implosion of the regional economy, in the former Soviet territories. That collapse has already sprung several nuclear powers full-grown from the body of the old Union; seen ethnic violence flare into larger-scale national conflicts; and opened the door to civil and interstate war on the European continent, or at least in its eastern half. The fundamental and as yet unanswerable question for American diplomacy, therefore, is whether over the median and long-term liberty and democracy, or chaos, is dawning in the East? It is worrisome, though not unanticipated, that these events are occurring even as isolationist stirrings are felt once more in the United States. Americans are increasingly preoccupied with budget and tax policy, and with repairing the decayed social and economic infrastructure that is certainly one legacy of the Cold War struggle with the Soviet Union. The reflex into nativism has already begun, and threatens the ability of America to provide the financial and political leadership, in combination with Japan, Germany and the EC, necessary to navigate formerly communist areas to calmer international waters. Panic is not in order, but it is already time to be concerned at the faltering of leadership and public will, for instance over provision of aid and credits to Russia.

The democracies in the post-Cold War world face a crucial debate on the appropriate balance between their long-term interest in the acceptance of pluralism internationally, and their short-term need for security achievable through a balance of power. In the rather shaky "New World Order" that has replaced the Cold War, old questions of how individual and national liberty relates to international security will be more germane, pressing, and opportune than at any time in the past. To what extent should democracies seek to actively export their values and institutions, to make their style of politics universal, so as to protect what has been gained already? What measures are best suited if that goal is settled upon as a central element of American foreign policy? Is the liberal-internationalist impulse, that tendency to see national security as ultimately guaranteed by a remaking of the world into a pluralist confederation of free societies, indulged at the expense of more important and immediate national interests, or does it in fact reinforce them? These are key questions for the 1990s, as they have been for most of this, the bloodiest of centuries. They cannot be answered only in the abstract; they must be debated fully and openly in the public realm.

The insistent demand of the American public that foreign policy reflect liberal values needs to be addressed directly by international relations analysts. That is perhaps especially true for those who, like the author of this study, tend to work out of the realist analytical tradition. "Realists" must appreciate that the idea of promoting liberty and human rights abroad has taken a progressively more important place in the foreign policy of most democracies, and not just the United States. The preponderance of American power has meant that democratic conceptions and assumptions also have been embedded in the structures and processes of international organizations. At the very least, justifications that accompany the conduct of contemporary foreign policy are laced with the language and concepts of liberal-democracy. Analysts must still point out where such ideas are used as cover for more self-interested policies. But to ignore or dismiss as trivial the apparent democratic revolution in world politics, to insist that democratic nations do not approach foreign policy differently from other types of states, simply is not realistic. In what may be an emergent age in which most of the great powers are also democratic, critics should not be content to wag a finger at American and other democratic statesmen and publics for their penchant to tilt at the windmills of foreign suppression of liberty. There are important questions about the proper role of principle in democratic statecraft still without satisfactory answers.

Alexis de Tocqueville observed over one hundred and fifty years ago that in "the control of society's foreign affairs democratic governments do appear decidedly inferior to others. . . . Foreign policy does not require the use of any of the good qualities peculiar to democracy but does demand the cultivation of almost all those which it lacks." In addition, democracies are often repelled by the exigencies required of statecraft by the fact that the world is populated as well by non-democratic states, varying from petty tyrannies, to entrenched feudal systems, to totalitarian great powers. What may be done to ease those dilemmas particular to democratic, and therefore to American, foreign policy? A sound starting point for a diplomacy that seeks a prudent, reasonable match between means and democratic ideals would be recognition that the greatest contribution to be made is preservation of the basic economic and political infrastructures of the community of democratic nations. This theme is already striking a receptive chord in calls for conversion of now-excessive military expenditures to civilian programs, and a restructuring of the West's defense posture so that no one state or people feels unduly burdened.

There is little question that the United States will continue to coordinate defense policy with other, major democratic countries. But that is not enough, and should it come to be seen as enough, it will pose a passive danger to peace and security rather than an answer. The Gulf War clearly demonstrated that in the foreseeable future America still must lead more than it can follow. Because of the successes of its past foreign policy, however, it no longer need do so quite so alone. That war also revealed that how the sharing of burdens is worked out with the other democracies, and non-democracies, is perhaps the single greatest challenge facing American statecraft in years to come. Another is deciding on a basic principle for American diplomacy which can rally a popular majority in the effort to sustain the necessary commitment to international responsibility. The promotion of democracy and human rights may be part of the answer to this second question. During the first decades of the Cold War, that idea provided a consensus for great accomplishments and constructive engagements—that moral underpinning to containment has too often been overlooked—before devolving into rigidity, excess, and ill-considered interventionism. During its latter half, on the other hand, the idea of exporting democracy only spuriously united liberals and conservatives, who read into it quite different agendas and "hit lists" of nations to be sanctioned. Well, times have changed.

The possibility now presents itself to go beyond a conception of a pro-democracy and human rights policy as requiring sanctions. Too often in the past, imposing sanctions alienated more sectors of the public than it pleased, and split conservatives and liberals over the most appropriate target states. Just as importantly, sanctions often asked certain sectors of the population—for instance, farmers or exporters—to carry an unfair share of the burden of national policy, or damaged other important national interests *vis-à-vis* foreign competitors. And sanctions have seldom had any discernible effect on other than the weakest states. Those are among the main lessons of the baleful experience with Jackson-Vanik. Of course, it is still possible to withhold special benefits, particularly in the area of military and non-humanitarian economic assistance now that few Third World states are strategically vital to United States security. Fierce divisions over whom to sanction should not arise so readily now. But in all but egregious cases, trade should not be interfered with through linkage to human rights abuses; that is more likely to raise domestic opposition to policy than it is to affect the target country, or bring about amelioration of suffering. It can even be argued that penetrating closed societies, such as China, economically is the best way to generate pluralist demands and forces—something not tried toward eastern Europe or the Soviet Union, largely owing to congressional myopia and rhetorical overindulgence by several presidents.

In short, a pro-democracy policy that relies solely on sanctions and negative incentives probably is not sustainable over the longer-term. Equally, a policy that reduces to mere rhetorical exhortation about the benefits of freedom is unlikely to be well-received abroad, and might properly be dismissed as hypocritical or even cynical. If defined less aggressively, however, a pro-democracy and human rights policy could capture wide public support, right across the political spectrum. Such a policy would have to accept the necessity of cooperating with other democracies and international organizations in promoting realistic standards of humane state behavior in the political, economic, and social realms. That means a concerted effort, by whomever is elected president in 1992, to use the bully-pulpit of the White House to convince the American public that the United Nations is reforming and now better deserves financial and political support. For instance, it can be explained to the public that as the most likely power to be called upon to send troops into new trouble zones, relatively small outlays in support of U.N. functions in peacekeeping and preventative diplomacy are in the best interest of the United States, not only in terms of less American blood spilled but also financially. Readjustment of burden-sharing here too can help, with the American share falling commensurately with the rise in contributions from those countries now seeking an enhanced role in multilateral institutions and diplomacy.

It should be helpful in recommitting to the United Nations to return to the bipartisan wisdom of FDR and Arthur Vandenberg, who recognized that the U.N.'s special concern for human rights could potentially engage the wide sympathy and support of the American people. The U.N.'s role needs to be better explained, and divorced from the lingering ideological quarrels between liberals and conservatives over how to wage the Cold War. It can also be explained that the absence of American participation over the years contributed to the warping of certain U.N. human rights programs, and that recommittment should begin to correct these abuses. If necessary to carry a majority in the Senate, presidents should accept derogations when seeking to ratify the major Covenants. Some on the left will object to this suggestion as diluting the "purity" of international standards; even more on the right will object to any involvement, representing as they do that tradition in American politics which sees national, let alone international, regulations as intrusive into local affairs. Yet if the price of engagement in international standard-setting in human rights, as a support for a larger foreign policy principle of promoting democracy, is certain derogations to please at least moderate conservatives, then that price should be paid. That is surely one of the main lessons to be gleaned from Eisenhower's subtle handling of the Bricker Amendment.

Other suggestions can be made, but remain to be debated. For instance, how much of the defense cuts should be channeled into programs seeking *positive* reinforcement of reforms and progress toward democracy in other countries, particularly in eastern Europe and the former Soviet lands? This is probably the way policy needs to be packaged to the American people: as conversion of defense spending, rather than new foreign outlays in a time of domestic cutbacks. Less expensive programs are also possible: legal, press, academic, and most importantly business exchanges; the "Democracy Corps"; expansion of the activities of the United States Institute for Peace, and the efforts of the United States Information Agency; IMF conditionality; opening membership in the GATT; and so forth. The window of opportunity to help bring democracy and prosperity to Russia and its immediate neighbors may be fleeting. The Reagan build-up and the Cold War in general drained the national coffers, and have tired and confused many about old ideas of national mission. Yet, conditional upon structural reforms in recipient countries and in coordination with affluent allies large and small, this effort to save the victory of the West in the Cold War must be made. It is crucial to progress toward a more stable world order.

Once again, the role of public education is key, for these efforts simply cannot be sustained to fruition without the informed support of the American people. The president has the key role to play in this regard. He must provide the requisite national vision; he must supply understandable policy principles to lift the nation out of its parochialism and self-absorption in admittedly hard times. He must, in other words, connect his foreign policy to Americans' historic sense of liberal mission, without encouraging either an overzealous crusading spirit or a reactive retreat into the illusory security of semi-isolation. Other leading politicians and pundits should also abjure from the easy temptation to indulge in excessive, and often unfair, criticism of the contributions of major allies. If Americans are to be asked for continued support of international organizations and help to build a more equitable world order, they need to know the facts about the significant financial and other efforts already made by allied nations. Lastly, the public must be educated to the reality that liberal-international principles are not universally accepted; supporters of the liberal-international order are limited in membership and unequal in capabilities; and as a result, clear, democratic choices will not always be available to policy-makers. American foreign policy will therefore still have to operate in that less-than-ideal realm identified by Niebuhr, where ethics and power combine in a vortex of compromise and moral ambiguity.

SELECT BIBLIOGRAPHY

INTERVIEWS

United Nations Center for Human Rights, Geneva.
Human Rights Foundation, UPEI, Charlottetown, Prince Edward Island.

GOVERNMENT PUBLICATIONS

Congress. *Congressional Record*.
Congress. House. Committee on Foreign Affairs. *International Protection of Human Rights* (1973).
Congress. House. Committee on Foreign Affairs. Subcommittee on International Organization. *Human Rights in the World Community: A Call for U.S. Leadership* (March 1974).
Congress. House. Congressional Research Service. *Human Rights in the International Community and U.S. Foreign Policy, 1945–1976* (July 1977).
Congress. Senate. Committee on Foreign Relations. *Relations with Russia*. GPO, 1921.
Department of State. *American Foreign Policy: Basic Documents*.
Department of State. *American Foreign Policy: Current Documents*.
Department of State. *The Brest-Litovsk Peace Conference*. GPO, 1918.
Department of State. *Bulletin*.
Department of State. *Country Reports on Human Rights Practices*.
Department of State. *Current Policy*.
Department of State. *Digest of International Law*.
Department of State. *Letters of the Secretaries of State, 1947–1952*. Microfilm.

Department of State. *Nazi-Soviet Relations: Documents from the Archives of the German Foreign Office*. GPO, 1948.
Department of State. *Notes Exchanged on the Russian-Polish Situation*. International Conciliation Pamphlets #155 (October 1920).
Department of State. *Papers Relating to the Foreign Relations of the United States* (1867+)
Department of State. *Postwar Foreign Policy Preparation, 1939–1945*. GPO, 1948.
Department of State. Foreign Service Institute. *U.S.-Soviet Summitry: Roosevelt through Carter*. GPO, 1987.
National Archives. *Records of the Department of State Relating to Internal Affairs of Russia and the Soviet Union, 1910–1929*, Microfilm Publication #M316.
President. *Public Papers of the Presidents of the United States*.
President. *Report on the United Nations* (1946+).
President. *A Compilation of the Messages and Papers of the Presidents*.
Secretary of State. *Treaties and Other International Acts Series*.
Secretary of State. *United States Foreign Policy: Documents*.
United Nations. *Official Records*.
United Nations. *Treaty Series*.
United Nations. *Yearbook of the United Nations*.

PUBLISHED DOCUMENTS

—American Bar Association. *Reports*.
—Commission on Russian Relief. *The Russian Famines: 1921–1922, 1922–1923*. National Information Bureau, 1923.
—*Draft Revised or New Conventions for the Protection of War Victims*. International Committee of the Red Cross, 1948.
—*Foreign Policy Reports*. Foreign Policy Association (1922+).
—*Gallup Poll Monthly*.
—*Nixon Presidential Press Conferences*. Coleman Enterprises, 1978.
—*Soviet Documents On Foreign Policy, 1917–1941*. 3 Vols., Jane Degras, ed. Oxford University Press, 1951.
—*Stalin's Correspondence with Churchill, Attlee, Roosevelt, and Truman*. Dutton, 1958.
—*Vital Speeches of the Day*. NYC News Publishing, 1934+.
Adler, Cyrus and Aaron Margalith. *With Firmness in the Right*. American Jewish Committee, 1946.
Baker, Ray S., ed. *Woodrow Wilson: Life and Letters* (8 Vols.). Doubleday, 1939.
Bernstein, B.J. and A.J. Matusow, eds. *The Truman Administration: A Documentary History*. Harper and Row, 1966.
Branyan, R. and L. Larsen, eds. *The Eisenhower Administration 1953–1961: A Documentary History*. Random House, 1971.
Brownlie, Ian, ed. *Basic Documents on Human Rights*. Clarendon, 1971.
Chandler, A. and Stephen Ambrose, eds. *Papers of Dwight D. Eisenhower* (Vols. 1–9). Johns Hopkins, 1970–1978.
Commager, Henry Steele, ed. *Documents of American History*. 7th ed. (2 Vols.). Meredith, 1963.
Etzold, Thomas and John L. Gaddis. *Containment: Documents on American Policy and Strategy, 1945–1950*. Columbia University Press, 1978.

Fred, L., ed. *State of the Union Messages, 1790–1966*. Chelsea, 1966.
Gallup, George. *The Gallup Poll, 1935–1971*. Gallup, 1972.
Jados, Stanley, ed. *Documents on Russian-American Relations*. Catholic University Press, 1965.
Johnson, Walter, ed. *Papers of Adlai Stevenson*. Little, Brown, 1974.
Kesaris, Paul, ed. *Confidential U.S. Diplomatic Post Records: Russia and the Soviet Union* (10 reels Microfilm). UPA, 1982.
Link, Arthur S. ed. *The Papers of Woodrow Wilson* (66 Vols.). Princeton University Press 1966–1988.
Mastny, Vojtech, ed. *Helsinki, Human Rights, and European Security* (Duke University Press, 1986): pp. 94–98.
Porter, Kirk and Donald Johnson, eds. *National Party Platforms, 1840–1968*. University of Illinois Press, 1972; 1979.
Rauch, Basil, ed. *Franklin D. Roosevelt: Selected Speeches, Messages, Press Conferences and Letters*. Holt, Rinehart & Winston, 1957.
Rosenman, Samuel I., ed. *The Public Papers and Addresses of Franklin D. Roosevelt* (10 Vols.). Russell & Russell, 1950–1969.
Seymour, Charles, ed. *The Intimate Papers of Colonel House* (4 Vols.). Houghton Mifflin, 1928.
Sherman, Frank. SHERFACS EVENTS DATABASE, American University (1992).
Taylor, Myron C., ed. *Wartime Correspondence Between President Roosevelt and Pope Pius XII*. Macmillan, 1947.

NEWSPAPERS

Christian Science Monitor
Cincinnati Enquirer
The Economist
New York Times
Wall Street Journal
The Washington Post

MEMOIRS AND PARTICIPANT ACCOUNTS

Acheson, Dean. *Present at the Creation*. Norton, 1969.
Adams, Sherwin. *First Hand Report*. Harper & Row, 1961.
Baer, George, ed. *A Question of Trust: Memoirs of Loy W. Henderson*. Hoover Institution, 1986.
Ball, George. *The Past Has Another Pattern: Memoirs*. Norton, 1982.
Bohlen, Charles E. *Witness to History: 1929–1969*. Norton, 1973.
Brezhnev, Leonid. *Peace, Détente, and Soviet-American Relations: A Collection Of Public Statements*. Harcourt Brace Jovanovich, 1979.
Brzezinski, Zbigniew. *Power and Principle*. Farrar, Straus, & Giroux, 1983.
Buckley, William F. *United Nations Journal*. Putnams, 1974.
Bush, George (with Victor Gold). *Looking Forward*. Doubleday, 1987.
Campbell, Thomas M. and George C. Herring, eds. *The Diaries of Edward R. Stettinius, Jr. 1943–1946*. New Viewpoints, 1975.
Carter, James Earl. *Keeping Faith*. Bantam, 1982.

Churchill, Winston S. *The Second World War* (6 Vols.). Bantam, 1962.
Clay, Lucius D. *Decision in Germany*. Doubleday, 1950.
———. *Germany and the Fight for Freedom*. Harvard University Press, 1950.
Cronon, David, ed. *The Cabinet Diaries of Josephus Daniels, 1913-1921*. University of Nebraska Press, 1963.
Davies, Joseph E. *Mission to Moscow*. Simon & Schuster, 1941.
Deane, John R. *The Strange Alliance*. Viking Press, 1947.
Dulles, John Foster. *War or Peace*. Macmillan, 1957.
Eisenhower, Dwight D. *Mandate for Change: 1953-1956*. Doubleday, 1963.
———. *Waging Peace: 1956-1961*. Doubleday, 1965.
Ferrell, Robert H., ed. *The Eisenhower Diaries*. Norton, 1981.
Ford, Gerald R. *A Time to Heal*. Harper & Row, 1979.
Francis, David. *Russia From the American Embassy*. Scribner's, 1921.
Haig, Alexander M. *Caveat*. MacMillan, 1984.
Harriman, W. Averill. *America and Russia in a Changing World*. Doubleday 1971.
———. and Elie Abel. *Special Envoy to Churchill and Stalin*. Random House, 1975.
Hull, Cordell. *Memoirs of Cordell Hull* (2 Vols.). Macmillan, 1948.
Johnson, Lyndon B. *The Vantage Point*. Rinehart & Winston, 1971.
Kennan, George F. *Memoirs*. (2 Vols.). Little, Brown, 1967; 1972.
Kirkpatrick, Jeane. *The Reagan Phenomenon*. AEI, 1983.
Kissinger, Henry. *American Foreign Policy*. 3rd ed. Norton, 1977.
———. *For the Record*. Little, Brown, 1981.
———. *Selected Speeches, 1982-1984*. Little, Brown, 1985.
———. *White House Years*. Little, Brown, 1979.
———. *Years of Upheaval*. Little, Brown, 1982.
Kraus, Sidney, ed. *The Great Debates*. University of Indiana Press, 1979.
Nixon, E., ed. *Franklin D. Roosevelt and Foreign Affairs*. Harvard University Press, 1969.
Nixon, Richard. *RN: Memoirs of Richard Nixon*. Grosset & Dunlap, 1978.
Pribytkov, Victor, ed. *Soviet-U.S. Relations: Selected Writings and Speeches of Konstantine U. Chernenko*. Praeger, 1984.
Reagan, Ronald. *An American Life*. Simon and Schuster, 1990.
Shevardnadze, Eduard. *The Future Belongs to Freedom*. Free Press, 1991.
Smith, Walter Bedell. *My Three Years in Moscow*. J.B. Lippincott, 1950.
Stimson, Henry L. and McGeorge Bundy. *On Active Service in Peace and War*. Harper & Row, 1947.
Truman, Harry S. *Memoirs of Harry S Truman*. (2 Vols.). Da Capo, 1956.
Vance, Cyrus. *Hard Choices*. Simon & Schuster, 1983.
Vandenberg, Arthur Jr., ed. *Private Papers of Senator Vandenberg*. Houghton Mifflin, 1952.
Wilkie, Wendel. *One World*. Simon & Schuster, 1943.

SECONDARY SOURCES

Adler, Selig. *The Isolationist Impulse*. Abelard-Schuman, 1957. Collier, 1961.
———. *Uncertain Giant, 1921-1941*. Macmillan, 1965.
Alexander, C. *Holding the Line: The Eisenhower Era*. University of Indiana Press, 1975.
Ambrose, Stephen. *Eisenhower* (2 Vols.). Simon & Schuster, 1984.

Select Bibliography

Ambrosius, Lloyd. *Wilsonian Statecraft*. Scholarly Resources, 1991.
Americas Watch et al. *Failure: The Reagan Administration's Human Rights Policy in 1983*.
Anschel, Eugene, ed. *American Appraisals of Soviet Russia, 1917–1977*. Scarecrow, 1978.
_____. *The American Image of Russia, 1775–1975*. Ungar, 1975.
Bailey, Thomas A. *America Faces Russia*. Cornell University Press, 1950.
_____. *Diplomatic History of the American People*. Prentice-Hall, 1980.
Baumann, F., ed. *Human Rights and American Foreign Policy*. Kenyon, 1982.
Bell, Coral. *President Carter and Foreign Policy*. Canberra, 1980.
_____. *The Reagan Paradox*. Rutgers University Press, 1990.
Bemis, Samuel Flagg. *American Foreign Policy and the Blessings of Liberty*. Yale University Press, 1962.
Bennet, Edward M. *Franklin D. Roosevelt and the Search for Security: American-Soviet Relations, 1933–1939*. Scholarly Resources, 1985.
_____. *Franklin D. Roosevelt and the Search for Victory: American-Soviet Relations, 1939–1945*. Scholarly Resources, 1990.
_____. *Recognition of Russia*. Blaisdell, 1970.
Bethell, Nicholas. *The Last Secret*. Andre Deutsch, 1974.
Bishop, Donald G. *Roosevelt-Litvinov Agreements*. Syracuse University Press, 1965.
Boaz, David, ed. *Assessing the Reagan Years*. Cato Institute, 1988.
Bradley, John. *Allied Intervention in Russia*. Weidenfeld, 1968.
Brafman, Morris and David Schimel, *Trade for Freedom*. Shengold, 1975.
Brecher, Frank W. *Reluctant Ally*. Greenwood, 1991.
Browder, Robert. *Origins of Soviet-American Diplomacy*. Princeton University Press, 1953.
Brown, Seyom. *The Faces of Power*. Columbia University Press, 1983.
Buehrig, E. *Woodrow Wilson and the Balance of Power*. University of Indiana Press, 1955.
Buergenthal, Thomas. *Human Rights, International Law and the Helsinki Accord*. Allenhead, Osmun, 1977.
Burnham, James. *Containment or Liberation?* John Day, 1952.
Byrnes, Robert, ed. *After Brezhnev*. University of Indiana Press, 1983.
Caldwell, Dan. *American-Soviet Relations*. Greenwood, 1981.
Caldwell, Lawrence T. and William Diebold. *Soviet-American Relations in the 1980s*. McGraw-Hill, 1981.
Carr, E.H. *A History of Soviet Russia* (8 Vols.). Macmillan, 1950–1964.
_____. *The Twenty Years' Crisis*. MacMillan, 1939.
Carynnyk, Marco. *Ukraine and the Helsinki Accords*. Garland, 1988.
Catudal, Honoré. *Kennedy and the Berlin Wall*. Berlin Verlag, 1980.
Claude, Inis. *Swords into Ploughshares*. 4th ed. Random House, 1984.
Clements, Kendrick. *James F. Byrnes and the Origins of the Cold War*. Carolina Academic Press, 1982.
_____. *Woodrow Wilson: World Statesman*. Twayne, 1987.
Cockfield, Jamie, ed. *Dollars and Diplomacy*. Duke University Press, 1981.
Cole, Wayne. *Roosevelt and the Isolationists: 1932–1945*. University of Nebraska Press, 1983.
Conquest, Robert. *The Great Terror: A Reassessment*. Oxford University Press, 1990.
Coombs, Jerald A. *American Diplomatic History*. Berkeley University Press, 1987.

Dallek, Robert. *Franklin D. Roosevelt and American Foreign Policy, 1932–1945.* Oxford University Press, 1979.
Davis, Katheryn W. *The Soviets at Geneva.* Chambery, 1934.
Davis, Lynn E. *The Cold War Begins.* Princeton University Press, 1974.
Dawson, Raymond. *The Decision to Aid Russia.* University of North Carolina Press, 1959.
DeConde, Alexander. *History of American Foreign Policy* (2 Vols.). 3rd ed. Scribner's, 1978.
Divine, Robert. *Eisenhower and the Cold War.* Oxford University Press, 1981.
———. *Foreign Policy and U.S. Presidential Elections: 1952–1960.* New Viewpoints, 1974.
———. *The Johnson Years.* University of Kansas Press, 1990.
———. *The Reluctant Belligerent.* John Wiley, 1965, 1979.
———. *Roosevelt and World War II.* Johns Hopkins University Press, 1969.
———. *Second Chance.* Atheneum, 1967.
Doenecke, Justus. *Not to the Swift.* Bucknell University Press, 1979.
Dowty, Alan. *The Limits of American Isolation.* NYU Press, 1971.
Dulles, Foster Rhea. *Road to Teheran.* Princeton University Press, 1944.
Dumbrell, John. *American Democracy and American Foreign Policy.* St. Martin's Press, 1990.
Ekirch, Arthur. *Ideas, Ideals and American Diplomacy.* Appleton, Century & Crofts, 1966.
Ellis, L. Ethan. *Republican Foreign Policy, 1921–1933.* Rutgers University Press, 1968.
Emhardt, William C. *Religion in Soviet Russia.* Morehouse, 1929.
Farnsworth, B. *William C. Bullitt and the Soviet Union.* University of Indiana Press, 1967.
Feis, Herbert. *Between War and Peace.* Princeton University Press, 1960.
———. *Churchill, Roosevelt, Stalin.* Princeton University Press, 1957.
———. *From Trust to Terror.* Norton, 1970.
Ferrell, Robert H. *American Diplomacy in the Great Depression.* Oxford University Press, 1957.
———. *The American Secretaries of State and Their Diplomacy: Marshall.* Cooper Square, 1966.
———. *Woodrow Wilson and World War I, 1917–1921.* Harper & Row, 1985.
Filene, Peter G. *Americans and the Soviet Experiment, 1917–1933.* Harvard University Press, 1967.
———. *American Views of Soviet Russia, 1917–1965.* Dorsey, 1968.
Fisher, H. *The Famine in Soviet Russia, 1919–1923.* Macmillan, 1927.
———. and Xenia Eudin, eds. *Soviet Russia and the West, 1920–1927.* Stanford University Press, 1957.
FitzGibbon, Louis. *Unpitied and Unknown.* Bachman & Turner, 1975.
Fleming, D. *The Cold War and Its Origins, 1917–1960.* Doubleday, 1961.
Fletcher, W. *The Russian Orthodox Church Underground.* Oxford University Press, 1971.
Flynn, George Q. *Roosevelt and Romanism.* Greenwood, 1976.
Forsythe, David. *Human Rights and U.S. Foreign Policy.* University of Florida Press, 1988.
Fosdick, Dorothy, ed. *Staying the Course: Henry M. Jackson and National Security.* University of Washington Press, 1987.
Fossedal, Gregory. *The Democratic Imperative.* Basic Books, 1989.
Gaddis, John L. *The Long Peace.* Oxford University Press, 1987.
———. *Russia, the Soviet Union, and the U.S.* John Wiley, 1978.

Select Bibliography 279

———. *Strategies of Containment*. Oxford University Press, 1982.
———. *The United States and the End of the Cold War*. Oxford University Press, 1992.
———. *The United States and the Origins of the Cold War, 1941–1947*. Columbia University Press, 1972.
Gardiner. Lloyd C. *A Covenant With Power*. Oxford University Press, 1984.
———. *Safe for Democracy*. Oxford University Press, 1984.
Garrison, Mary, and Abbott Gleason. *Shared Destiny*. Beacon, 1985.
Garthoff, Raymond. *Détente and Confrontation*. Brookings Institute, 1985.
George, Alexander. *Managing U.S.-Soviet Rivalry*. Westview, 1983.
Graber, Doris A. *Crisis Diplomacy*. Public Affairs Press, 1959.
Graebner, Norman. *Age of Global Power*. John Wiley, 1979.
———. *America as a World Power*. Scholarly Resources, 1984.
———. *Foundations of American Foreign Policy*. Scholarly Resources, 1985.
———, ed. *Traditions and Values: 1865–1945*. UPA, 1985.
———, ed. *An Uncertain Tradition*. McGraw-Hill, 1961.
Graves, William S. *America's Siberian Adventure*. Peter Smith, 1931.
Grayson, Benson, ed. *American Image of Russia, 1917–1977*. Ungar, 1978.
———. *Russian-American Relations in World War I*. Ungar, 1979.
Guhin, Michael A. *John Foster Dulles*. Columbia University Press, 1972.
Halle, Louis J. *The Cold War as History*. Challot & Windus, 1967.
Harbutt, Fraser. *The Iron Curtain*. Oxford University Press, 1986.
Hartman, Susan M. *Truman and the 80th Congress*. Columbia University Press, 1971.
Haslam, Jonathan. *Soviet Foreign Policy, 1930–1933*. St. Martin's Press, 1983.
———. *The Soviet Union and the Struggle for Collective Security in Europe, 1933–1939*. St. Martin's Press, 1984.
Henkin, Louis. *The Age of Rights*. Columbia University Press, 1990.
———. *Foreign Affairs and the Constitution*. Norton, 1972.
Herring, George C. *Aid to Russia*. Columbia University Press, 1973.
Hinsley, F.H. *Power and the Pursuit of Peace*. Cambridge University Press, 1963.
Hoffmann, Stanley. *Duties Beyond Borders*. Syracuse University Press, 1981.
Hoff-Wilson, Joan. *Ideology and Economics*. University of Missouri Press, 1974.
Hoopes, T. *The Devil and John Foster Dulles*. Little, Brown, 1973.
Horelick, Arnold. *U.S.-Soviet Relations*. Cornell University Press, 1986.
Hough, Jerry F. *Russia and the West*. Simon & Schuster, 1988.
Humphrey, John P. *Human Rights and the United Nations*. Transnational, 1984.
Hunt, Michael H. *Ideology and U.S. Foreign Policy*. Yale University Press, 1987.
Huntington, Samuel P. *The Dilemma of American Ideals And Institutions in Foreign Policy*. AEI, 1981.
Hyde, Charles C. *International Law Chiefly as Interpreted and Applied by the United States* (2 Vols.). 2nd revised ed. Little, Brown, 1945.
Hyland, William. *Mortal Rivals*. Random House, 1987.
Immerman, Richard, ed. *John Foster Dulles and the Diplomacy of the Cold War*. Princeton University Press, 1990.
Issacson, W. and Evan Thomas. *The Wise Men*. Simon & Schuster, 1986.
Jensen, Kenneth, ed. *Origins of the Cold War*. USIP, 1991.
Jonas, Manfred. *Isolationism in America, 1935–1941*. Cornell University Press, 1966; Imprint 1990.
Jones, Joseph M. *The Fifteen Weeks*. Harcourt, Brace & World, 1955.
Kennan, George F. *American Diplomacy, 1900–1950*. University of Chicago Press, 1951.

_____. *Russia and the West Under Lenin and Stalin*. Little, Brown, 1961.
_____. *Soviet-American Relations, 1917–1920* (2 Vols.). Princeton University Press, 1953.
Kettle, Michael. *The Allies and the Russian Collapse*. University of Minnesota Press, 1981.
Killen, Linda. *The Russian Bureau*. University of Kentucky Press, 1983.
Kimball, Warren F. *The Most Unsordid Act*. Johns Hopkins University Press, 1969.
Kirkpatrick, Jeane. *Dictatorships and Double Standards*. Simon & Schuster, 1982.
Kovrig, Bennett. *The Myth of Liberation*. Johns Hopkins University Press, 1973.
LaFeber, Walter. *The New Empire*. Cornell University Press, 1963.
_____. *America, Russia, and the Cold War*. 3rd ed. John Wiley, 1976.
Lasch, C. *The American Liberals and the Russian Revolution*. Columbia University Press, 1962.
Leffler, Melvyn P. *A Preponderance of Power*. Stanford University Press, 1992.
Levering, Ralph B. *American Opinion and the Russian Alliance, 1939–1945*. North Carolina University Press, 1976.
Levin, N. Gordon. *Woodrow Wilson and World Politics*. Oxford University Press, 1968.
Libbey, James K. *American-Russian Economic Relations, 1790s to 1990s*. Regina, 1989.
Link, Arthur S. *Woodrow Wilson: Revolution, War and Peace*. AHM, 1979.
_____, ed. *Woodrow Wilson and a Revolutionary World: 1913–1921*. North Carolina University Press, 1982.
Liska, George. *Rethinking U.S.-Soviet Relations*. Basil Blackwell, 1987.
Litwak, Robert S. *Détente and the Nixon Doctrine*. Cambridge University Press, 1984.
Lovenstein, M. *American Opinion of Soviet Russia*. Public Affairs, 1941.
Maddox, R. *New Left and the Origins of the Cold War*. Princeton University Press, 1973.
Maddux, Thomas. *Years of Estrangement*. University of Florida Press, 1980.
Manchester, William. *The Glory and the Dream*. Little, Brown, 1974.
Maresca, John. *To Helsinki: The CSCE 1973–1975*. Duke University Press, 1985.
Mayers, David. *George Kennan and the Dilemmas of U.S. Foreign Policy*. Oxford University Press, 1988.
Mazuzan, George. *Warren R. Austin at the U.N., 1946–1953*. Kent State University Press.
Medvedev, Roy. *Let History Judge*. Knopf, 1971.
Melanson, Richard, ed. *Neither Cold War nor Détente?*. University of Virginia Press, 1982.
Mower, A. Glenn. *Human Rights and American Foreign Policy*. Greenwood, 1987.
_____. *The United States, the United Nations, and Human Rights*. Greenwood, 1979.
Muravchik, Joshua. *Uncertain Crusade*. Hamilton Press, 1986.
Nahaylo, B. and Victor Swoboda. *Soviet Disunion*. Free Press, 1990.
Nau, Henry. *The Myth of America's Decline*. Oxford University Press, 1990.
Neal, Stephen. *Dark Horse: Biography of Wendel Wilkie*. University of Kansas Press, 1991.
Newsom, David, ed. *The Diplomacy of Human Rights*. UPA, 1986.
Nichols, Bruce, and G. Loescher, eds. *Moral Nation*. University of Notre Dame Press, 1989.
Nixon, E., ed. *Franklin D. Roosevelt and Foreign Affairs*. Harvard University Press, 1969.
Nye, Joseph. *Bound to Lead*. Basic Books, 1990.
_____, ed. *The Making of America's Soviet Policy*. Yale University Press, 1984.
O'Connor, Timothy. *Diplomacy and Revolution*. Iowa State University Press, 1988.

Select Bibliography

Ognibene, Peter. *Scoop: The Life and Politics of Henry M. Jackson.* Stein and Day, 1975.
Osgood, Robert E. *Ideals and Self-Interest in America's Foreign Relations.* University of Chicago Press, 1953.
Oye, Kenneth et al., eds. *Eagle Defiant.* Little, Brown, 1983.
———— et al., eds. *Eagle Entangled.* Longman, 1979.
———— et al., eds. *Eagle Resurgent?* Little, Brown, 1987.
Pach, Chester and Elmo Richardson. *The Presidency of Dwight D. Eisenhower.* University of Kansas Press, 1991. Revised edition.
Parmet, H. *Eisenhower and the American Crusades.* Macmillan, 1972.
Parrot, Bruce, ed. *Trade, Technology, and Soviet-American Relations.* University of Indiana Press, 1985.
Paterson, Thomas. *Meeting the Communist Threat.* Oxford University Press, 1988.
————, ed. *Kennedy's Quest for Victory.* Oxford University Press, 1989.
Pauly, Karl B. *Bricker of Ohio.* Putnam's, 1944.
Pipes, Daniel and A. Garfinkle. *Friendly Tyrants.* St. Martin's Press, 1990.
Pogue, Forrest. *George C. Marshall* (4 Vols.). Viking, 1963–1985.
Pospielovsky, Dimitry. *The Russian Church Under the Soviet Regime, 1917–1982.* (2 Vols.) St. Vladimir's, 1984.
Purvis, Hoyt and S. Baker. *Legislating Foreign Policy.* Westview, 1984.
Radosh, R. *Prophets on the Right.* Simon & Schuster, 1975.
Rapoport, Louis. *Stalin's War Against the Jews.* Free Press, 1990.
Riasanovsky, Nicholas. *A History of Russia.* Oxford University Press, 1984.
Richman, John. *The United States and the Soviet Union: The Decision to Recognize.* Camberleigh Hall, 1980.
Root, Elihu. *The United States and the War.* Harvard University Press, 1918.
Rosati, Jerel A. *The Carter Administration's Quest for Global Community.* South Carolina University Press, 1987.
Rosenthal, Joel. *Righteous Realists.* University of Louisiana Press, 1991.
Ruddy, Michael. *Cautious Diplomat.* Kent State University Press, 1986.
Russell, Ruth. *History of the United Nations Charter.* Brookings Institute, 1958.
————. *The U.N. and United States Security Policy.* Brookings Institute, 1968.
Schuman, Frederick. *American Policy Toward Russia Since 1917.* International Publishers, 1928.
Schwartz, A. *America and the Russo-Finnish War.* Public Affairs, 1960.
Schwartz, Harry. *Prague's 200 Days.* Praeger, 1969.
Sheldon, Della, ed. *Dimensions of Détente.* Praeger, 1978.
Skilling, H. Gordon. *Czechoslovakia's Interrupted Revolution.* Princeton University Press, 1976.
Smith, Gaddis. *American Diplomacy During the Second World War.* Knopf, 1985.
————. *Dean Acheson.* Cooper Square, 1972.
————. *Morality, Reason, and Power.* Hill & Wang, 1986.
Sodaro, Michael. *Moscow, Germany and the West from Khrushchev to Gorbachev.* Cornell University Press, 1991.
Solzhenitsyn, A. *The Gulag Archipeligo* (3 Vols.). Harper & Row, 1978.
Spargo, John. *Russia as an American Problem.* Harper & Brothers, 1920.
Stern, Paula. *The Water's Edge.* Greenwood, 1979.
Strakhovsky, Leonid. *American Opinion About Russia.* University of Toronto Press, 1961.

Sundquist, James. *Decline and Resurgence of Congress.* Brookings Institute, 1981.
Talbot, Strobe. *The Russians and Reagan.* Vintage, 1984.
Tannanbaum, Duane. *The Bricker Amendment Controversy.* Cornell University Press, 1988.
Taubman, William. *Stalin's American Policy.* Norton, 1982.
Terry, Sarah M., ed. *Soviet Policy in Eastern Europe.* Yale University Press, 1984.
Theoharis, Athan. *The Yalta Myths.* University of Missouri Press, 1970.
Thompkins, Pauline. *American-Russian Relations in the Far East.* Macmillan, 1949.
Thompson, John M. *Russia, Bolshevism and the Versailles Peace.* Princeton University Press, 1966.
Thompson, Kenneth W. *The Moral Imperatives of Human Rights.* UPA, 1980.
_____. *Morality and Foreign Policy.* Louisiana State University Press, 1980.
de Tocqueville, Alexis. *Democracy in America.* Doubleday, 1969.
Tolstoy, Nikolai. *The Minister and the Massacres.* Century Hutchinson, 1986.
_____. *Victims of Yalta.* Hodder & Stoughton, 1977.
Trani, Eugene, *The Treaty of Portsmouth.* University of Kentucky Press, 1969.
Travis, Frederick. *George Kennan and the American-Russian Relationship, 1865–1924.* Ohio State University Press, 1989.
Tucker, Robert W. *The Radical Left and American Foreign Policy.* Johns Hopkins University Press, 1972.
_____ and David C. Hendrickson, *Empire of Liberty.* Oxford University Press, 1990.
Ulam, Adam B. *Expansion and Coexistence.* Praeger, 1974.
_____. *A History of Soviet Russia.* Praeger, 1976.
_____. *The Rivals.* Viking, 1971.
_____. *Russia's Failed Revolutions.* Basic Books, 1981.
Unterberger, Betty Miller. *American Intervention in the Russian Civil War.* Heath, 1969.
_____. *America's Siberian Expedition.* Duke University Press, 1956.
_____. *The United States, Revolutionary Russia, and the Rise of Czechoslovakia.* University of North Carolina Press, 1989.
Van Dyke, V. *Human Rights, the U.S. and World Community.* Oxford University Press, 1970.
Vitas, R. *The U.S. and Lithuania: The Stimson Doctrine.* Praeger, 1990.
Vogelgesang, Sandra. *American Dream, Global Nightmare.* Norton, 1980.
Walsh, Warren B. *Readings in Russian History* (2 Vols.). Syracuse University Press, 1963.
Walton, Richard J. *Cold War and Counterrevolution.* Viking, 1972.
Warth, R. *The Allies and the Russian Revolution.* Russell, 1973.
Weiler, L. and A. Simons. *United States and the U.N.* Manhattan, 1967.
Weissman, Benjamin. *Herbert Hoover and Famine Relief to Soviet Russia: 1921–1923.* Hoover Institution, 1974.
White, Colin. *Russia and America.* Croom Helm, 1987.
Wiarda, Howard, ed. *Human Rights and U.S. Human Rights Policy.* AEI, 1982.
Wieczyniski, Joseph, ed. *Modern Enclyclopedia of Russian and Soviet History.* Academic International, 1984.
Williams, W.A. *American-Russian Relations, 1781–1947.* Rinehart, 1952.
Yergin, Daniel. *Shattered Peace.* Houghton Mifflin, 1977.

INDEX

Abrams, Elliot, 157, 158, 160, 252
Acheson, Dean, 59, 110, 232*n*, 234*n*
Action Program, 227–28
Afghanistan, 136, 146, 147–49, 158, 160, 161, 169, 250
Alliance for Progress, 110
allies, 13, 15–17, 18, 19–25, 37*n*, 57–65, 73, 74–96 *passim*, 181–202. *See also* World War I, World War II
  in World War I, 13, 15–17, 18, 37*n*
  intervention in Russian Civil War, 19–25, 29
  in World War II, 57–65, 73, 74–96 *passim*, 181–202
American Bar Association (ABA), 212, 215, 220–23, 226, 233*n*, 240–41, 247. *See also* Bricker Amendment, Holman
American Relief Administration (ARA), 29–32, 43*n*. *See also* Hoover
Andropov, Yuri, 161
anti-semitism, 13–14, 33–34. *See also* jews
Armenia, 166

arms control, 109–10, 112–13, 116–20, 129, 135, 141–48, 155–73 *passim*, 248–49. *See also* specific treaties
Asia, 6, 13, 26–27, 45–47, 50, 52, 59, 103, 106, 113, 127–28. *See also* specific countries
Atlantic Charter, 63, 70*n*, 74, 75, 82, 182–83, 184, 187, 195, 198. *See also* Roosevelt, United Nations Organization
Austria, 18, 56, 86
Axis alliance, 55, 59, 73, 78, 113, 225, 264
Azerbaijan, 166, 169

Baker, James, 167–73, 255
balance of power, 2, 16, 18, 21, 27, 36, 37*n*, 46, 56, 73, 78, 103–4, 112–14, 120, 127–37, 181–82, 201
Ball, George, 118, 120, 140, 144
Baltic States, 26, 28, 40*n*, 42*n*, 59, 63, 69*n*, 74–96 *passim*, 165–73 *passim*. *See also* Estonia, Latvia, Lithuania, Nazi-Soviet Pact

Belgium, 190
Berle, Adolf, 61
Berlin Wall, 111, 115, 163, 166
Bevin, Ernest, 90
Bill of Rights, of United States, 8, 184, 198–99, 217, 220
blacks, 7, 195, 216. *See also* segregation
Bohlen, Charles, 54, 80, 88–89
Bolshevik Revolution, 17–25, 64. *See also* Soviet Union
bolsheviks, 17, 22–23, 29–32, 34–35, 38*n*, 64. *See also* Soviet Union
Bonner, Yelena, 160, 163, 175*n*, 176*n*
Borah, William, 41–42*n*, 182
Brest-Litovsk, Treaty of (1918), 17–19
Bretton Woods, 103–4
Brezhnev, Leonid, 131, 133, 134, 141, 143–44, 160, 164
Bricker, John, 212–25 *passim*, 244
Bricker Amendment, 9, 61*n*, 108, 212–25, 227, 232*n*, 240, 247, 270
Britain, 8, 13, 15–18, 19–25, 29, 42, 46, 52, 55–67 *passim*, 70*n*, 74–96 *passim*, 181–202. *See also* allies, Churchill, trade, World War I, World War II
  in World War I, 13, 15–17, 18
  and Versailles, 21–25
  intervenes in Russia, 19–25, 29
  interwar diplomacy of, 42, 46, 52, 56
  in World War II, 55–67 *passim*, 70*n*, 74–96 *passim*, 181–202
  and founding of United Nations, 8, 186–202
Brownell, Herbert, 221, 223, 224
Brzezinski, Zbigniew, 141–48
Bukavich, Monsignor, 34–35
Bukhovsky, Vladimir, 142
Bulganin, Nikolai, 109
Bullitt, William C., 22, 49, 53–54, 55, 64–65, 67*n*
Bush, George, 7, 9, 165–73, 176*n*, 253–56, 260*n*
Bylarus (Belorussia), 171–73, 193
Byrnes, James F., 85–89, 90

Cadogan, Alexander, 187–88
Canada, 190, 204*n*, 234*n*

Carter, Jimmy, 6, 139–48, 155–56, 157, 247–49, 251, 258*n*
Carter Doctrine, 155
Castro, Fidel, 111–12
catholics, 4, 47, 57, 59–65, 82
  anti-Soviet views, 4, 47, 57, 59–65, 82
  and Lend-Lease, 59–65
  and Poland, 57, 82
Central Intelligence Agency (CIA), 109, 112, 155
Central Powers, 14, 16
Chamberlain, Neville, 119
Charter of Paris, 10*n*, 170
Cheney, Richard, 167, 169
Chernenko, Constantine, 161
China, 6, 8, 22, 45–46, 104, 106–7, 113, 117, 127–29, 136–37, 166, 181, 184, 227, 269
  at United Nations, 8, 184, 187, 199, 227
  and Soviet-American relations, 104, 117, 136, 166, 181
  Sino-Soviet split, 6, 117
  and rapprochement with United States, 121–29, 137
Churchill, Winston, 22–23, 59, 63, 64, 75–78 *passim*, 82, 183–84
Citizens Democracy Corps, 176, 177*n*
citizenship, disputes over, 4, 36*n*, 50, 51, 56, 67*n*, 70*n*, 80–96, 164. *See also* expatriation
Clark Amendment, 134
Clay, Lucius D., 94
Clemenceau, Georges, 22, 23
Cleveland, Harlan, 207
Colby, Bainbridge, 25
Colby Note, 25–26, 28
Cold War, 1, 4–6, 76–96, 103–20, 128–48, 154–73, 209–30 *passim*, 263–71 *passim*
  and human rights, 5–6, 76–96 *passim*, 103–5, 129–48, 154–73, 209–10, 241–42
  ending of, 2, 3, 6–7, 263–71
collective security, 27, 46–47, 51, 52–53, 56, 103, 182
COMINTERN, 26, 28, 47, 49–53 *passim*
commerce, *see* trade

commercial treaties, of 1832, 13, 36n; of 1935, 51
Commonwealth of Independent States (CIS), 173
communism, 2, 127–28, 160, 165–66
Conference on Security and Cooperation in Europe (CSCE), 137–39, 141, 144, 158, 160, 162, 168
Congress, 5, 9, 28, 30–31, 45–46, 49, 52, 55, 57–58, 59–65 passim, 89–90, 106, 109, 114–15, 129–48 passim, 155–56, 169–71, 182–202 passim, 207–25, 235–56. See also House of Representatives, public opinion, Senate, Soviet Union, United Nations Organization
Connally, Thomas, 194, 197–98, 200
Connally Resolution, 183–84
conservatives, 6, 8–9, 130–37, 142, 143, 158, 166, 171, 212–30, 237–56 passim. See also Bricker Amendment, isolationism, United Nations Organization
Constitution, of the United States, 8, 184, 198–202, 212–25 passim, 237–40, 244–45. See also Bill of Rights, Bricker Amendment
containment, 78, 103–20, 127–48 passim, 157–58, 167–73
Convention Against Torture, 259
Convention on the Elimination of Racial Discrimination, 241
Convention on Religious Tolerance, 241. See also religious freedom
Convention on the Rights of the Child, 254
Conventional Forces in Europe (CFE), 169
Coolidge, Calvin, 26, 28
Covenant on Civil and Political Rights, 208–9, 211–12, 229, 230n, 241–56 passim, 257n
Covenant on Economic, Social, and Cultural Rights, 208–9, 211–25 passim, 230n, 241–56 passim, 257n
Cuba, 110–14 passim, 117, 149–50n, 165, 251
Czechoslovakia, 56, 57, 78, 104, 117–20, 141

Daniels, Josephus, 14, 15, 17
Davies, Joseph C., 54, 55, 64
Deane, John, 81, 82, 84, 98n
Declaration of the Rights of Nationalities (bolshevik, of 1917), 33
Declaration on Liberated Europe, 77
Defense Department, 104
democracy, and international relations, 2, 3, 37n, 56, 60, 80–81, 103–5, 166, 169, 236–71. See also liberal-internationalism
Democratic party, 70n, 107–10, 139–40, 158, 183, 215–16, 252–53. See also elections
Depression, 8, 35, 45, 228, 264–65
détente, 6, 116–20, 127–48, 155, 159–60
dissidents, 132, 134, 141–42, 143, 160, 162–63, 164
Dixiecrats, 216, 228
Dobrynin, Anatoly, 131–34, 138, 141, 149n
Dubcek, Alexander, 117–20
Dulles, John Foster, 8, 107–10, 114, 191, 195, 197–98, 213, 217–30
Dumbarton Oaks, 8, 103, 186–92, 195, 196–97, 202, 204n, 211, 228, 229
Durbrow, Elbridge, 89

Eagleburger, Laurence, 160
East Germany, see German Democratic Republic
eastern Europe, 5, 73, 76–89, 107–10, 114–15, 135–36, 137–39, 140, 165–73, 209–10, 265–66, 269. See also individual countries
Eaton, Charles A., 208
Economic and Social Council (ECOSOC), 189, 194, 204n, 210, 251
Eisenhower, Dwight David, 5, 9, 86, 89, 100n, 107–12, 114–15, 155, 212–30 passim, 234n, 235n, 237–39, 247
elections, and foreign policy, 5, 75, 107–10, 119–20, 132, 138–40, 143, 147–48, 252–53, 253–54, 256
emigration, 4, 7, 46, 74, 130–37, 149n, 160, 164, 169–70. See also commercial treaties, Jackson-Vanik, jews, wives

enlightenment, 2
Entente Powers, 13, 18. *See also* allies, World War I
Estonia, 169–73. *See also* Baltic States, Nazi-Soviet Pact
European Community (EC), 263–71 *passim*
European Status of Forces Agreement, 224
exceptionalism, 96*n*, 113, 129–30, 156–57, 184, 249, 263–65. *See also* isolationism, mission
executive agreements, 14, 48–51, 214–15, 217–18, 221, 224–25, 232*n*. *See also* Bricker Amendment, Roosevelt-Litvinov agreements, Yalta Conference
executive branch, 115, 130–37, 212–30, 237–56
expatriation, 4, 32–33, 80–95, 164. *See also* citizenship

family reunification, 80, 89–91, 95, 160, 163
famine, 29–32, 42*n*, 53. *See also* American Relief Administration
fascist nations, 46, 52, 55, 188. *See also* Axis alliance
Federal Republic of Germany (FRG), *see* Germany
federal state clause, 212, 219, 231*n*
Finland, 14, 26, 42*n*, 57–58, 63, 69*n*, 92
Fish, Hamilton, 53–54
forced labor, 86, 88, 91, 93, 101*n*, 228, 238
Ford, Gerald, 6, 133–37, 140, 143, 145, 246
Forrestal, James, 85, 90
Four Freedoms, 60, 63, 70*n*, 75, 169, 181–84, 199–202
Four Policemen, 181, 201
Four Power Declaration, 184
Fourteen Points, 18, 20, 22
France, 42, 46, 52, 56, 57–58, 70*n*. *See also* allies, World War I, World War II
Francis, David, 14, 20
freedom of information, 209, 227, 236*n*, 251
Fulbright Resolution, 183–84

Gardner, Richard, 238–39, 241–42
Geneva Convention (1929), 84–86, 95, 243
Geneva Disarmament Conference (1935), 52
Geneva Protocol (1924), 27
Genocide Convention, 217–18, 222–23, 227, 243–56 *passim*
George, Walter, 225
German Democratic Republic (GDR), 109, 118. *See also* Berlin Wall
German-Russian Non-Aggression Treaty, *see* Nazi-Soviet Pact
Germany, 5, 13–20, 21–25, 42*n*, 46–47, 52–53, 55–56, 57–65 *passim*, 73, 78, 84, 103–4, 113, 136–37, 166, 169, 193, 239. *See also* Nazi-Soviet Pact, World War I, World War II
  in World War I, 13–21, *passim*, 46
  and Brest-Litovsk, 17–19
  and intervention in Russia, 19–24
  and Versailles Treaty, 21–25
  and interwar diplomacy, 42*n*, 46–47, 52–53, 55–56
  Nazi-Soviet Pact, 40*n*, 57, 59
  in World War II, 5, 57–65 *passim*, 73, 193, 239
  division of, 78, 84, 104
  in Cold War, 103, 113, 136–37
  reunification of, 166, 169
Ginsburg, Aleksandr, 141, 145
Giscard d'Estaing, Valery, 249
glasnost, 161–73
Gorbachev, Mikhail, 6, 7, 161–73, 176*n*
Gorky, Maxim, 30
Grand Alliance, 92*n*. *See also* United Nations Organization
Greece, 78
Grenada, invasion of, 158
Grew, Joesph, 81, 84–85
Gromyko, Andrei, 142, 161, 188
gulag, prison camp system, 74, 80–96 *passim*, 131
Gulf War, 3, 169, 170–71, 255, 268

Hagerty, James, 222, 224–25
Haig, Alexander, 157, 159
Harding, Warren, 26, 27–28, 32, 34–35

Index

Harriman, W. Averill, 43n, 76, 80, 81–89, 99n, 186–87, 193
Helsinki Accords, *see* Conference on Security and Cooperation in Europe
Henderson, Loy, 54
Hiss, Alger, 234n
Hitler, Adolf, 45, 52, 54, 57, 59, 76–77, 95, 121n, 174n, 209, 215
Holman, Frank, 215–25 *passim*
Hoover, Herbert, 26, 29–33, 35–36, 45, 46
House, Colonel Edward, 17, 22
House of Representatives, 53, 57, 132, 183, 208, 237–56 *passim*. See also Congress
Hughes, Charles Evans, 26, 30, 34–35
Hull, Cordell, 47–48, 50, 53, 182, 184–87
human rights, 4–9, 14–17, 27–28, 39n, 47–50, 73–74, 70–96, 104–5, 111, 129–48, 156–65, 168–77 *passim*, 182–202, 208–30, 237–56. *See also* Charter of Paris, Conference on Security and Cooperation in Europe, expatriation, Four Freedoms, Universal Declaration of Human Rights, women
  civil and political, 14, 38n, 184–202, 207–11
  Cold War and, 5–6, 80–96, 104–5, 111, 129–48, 208–30, 247–49
  economic, cultural, and social, 27–28, 184–85, 186–202 *passim*, 204n, 207–11
  and United Nations, 7–9, 182–202, 208–30, 237–56
Humphrey, John P., 190, 196–97, 219–20, 233n
Hungary, 109, 118, 166

India, 7, 10n, 110, 210–11
Intermediate Nuclear Force Agreement (INF), 164
International Bill of Rights, 184–86, 189, 193, 204n, 208–210, 216, 217–18
International Conference on Human Rights (Teheran 1968), 141
International Labor Organization (ILO), 187, 194
Iran, 78, 146–47, 155–56

Iran-Contra, 163
Iron Curtain, 77, 109, 209
isolationism, 6–9, 10n, 17, 26–36, 42n, 47, 51, 52–53, 55, 106, 119–20, 130, 134, 172, 182–83, 191–92, 195–202, 207–11 *passim*, 212–25, 228–30, 246, 263
Israel, 242–43, 246
Italy, 40n, 42n, 55

Jackson, Henry "Scoop," 130–37, 138, 145, 248
Jackson-Vanik (amendment to the 1974 Trade Act), 130–37, 145, 150n, 167, 169–70, 172, 268–69. *See also* Congress, trade
Japan, 7, 10n, 20–27, 29, 45–46, 47, 50–52, 55, 62, 85, 87, 103–4, 113, 134, 165, 187, 264–66
  intervention in Russian Civil War, 20–25, 26, 29
  role in U.S.-Soviet *rapprochement*, 47, 50–52, 55, 85, 87
  in World War II, 62, 85, 87
  in Cold War, 103–4, 113, 134, 165, 264–66
jews, 13–14, 33–34, 37n, 42n, 43n, 51, 130–37, 142–48 *passim*, 155–73, 252–53. *See also* anti-semitism, Jackson-Vanik
  conditions for under the Tsars, 13–14, 37n, 42n, 43n
  conditions for under the Soviets, 130–37, 142–48 *passim*, 155–73 *passim*
Johnson, Lyndon Baines, 108, 116–20, 239–42
Johnson Debt Default Act (1934), 49

Katyn Forest, massacre in, 74–75
Kazakhstan, 171–73
Kennan, George Frost, 31, 50, 54, 63, 76, 80, 105
Kennedy, John Fitzgerald, 110–15, 116, 124n, 135, 237–40
Kerensky, Alexandre, 49
KGB (Committee of State Security), 79, 92, 98n
Khrushchev, Nikita, 109, 111–12

Kirk, Alexander, 88
Kirkpatrick, Jeane, 157, 248, 250
Kissinger, Henry, 127–37, 149, 243, 245–46, 249, 258*n*
Knowland, William, 224, 225
Kohler, Foy, 94–95
Kolchak, Admiral Alexandre, 24, 40*n*
Korea, 78, 106–7, 121*n*, 146, 152*n*, 165, 210–11, 223, 228

Lansing, Robert, 17, 22
Latvia, 169–73. *See also* Baltic States, Nazi-Soviet Pact
League of Nations, 7, 21, 26, 184, 191, 193–94, 200, 204–5*n*
Lefever, Ernest, 157
Lend-Lease, 4, 59–65, 92, 129, 134–35, 182. *See also* Britain, public opinion, Soviet Union
Lenin, Vladimir Illich (Ulianov), 18, 19, 20–21, 22, 29–30, 42*n*, 69
liberal-internationalism, 1–4, 5, 17, 37*n*, 78–79, 80–81, 95–96, 103–5, 106–7, 111–13, 129–30, 135, 138, 184–85, 191–92, 199–202, 209, 223, 246, 253–54, 263–71. *See also* Atlantic Charter, democracy, Four Freedoms, human rights, national security
Lithuania, 59, 169–73. *See also* Baltic States, Nazi-Soviet Pact
Litvinov, Maxim, 26, 32–33, 39*n*, 47–49, 56, 73
Lloyd George, David, 22
London Naval Conference (1930), 27, 46, 117
London Poles, 75, 77
Lublin Poles, 75, 77, 81–84

Manchuria, 13, 88, 95
Mao Tse-Tung, 128
Marshall, George C., 89, 94, 209–10
Marshall Plan (European Recovery Program), 104, 207, 211
McCarthy, Eugene, 119–20
McCarthyism, 220, 234*n*
McCloy, John J., 80

McGovern, George, 132, 139
Minority Treaties, 33
mission, American sense of, 2–3, 98*n*, 113–14, 129–30, 141, 156–57, 173, 264–71. *See also* exceptionalism
Mission To Moscow (Joseph C. Davies), 64
Missouri v. Holland (1920), 213–14
Molotov, Vyacheslav (Skriabin), 75, 81–83, 90, 181, 184, 197–98
Morgenthau, Henry, 48, 62
Moscow Foreign Ministers' Conference, of 1943, 75; of 1945, 90
Most-Favored-Nation (MFN), 52–53, 130–37, 161
Moynihan, Daniel Patrick, 139–40
Munich Agreement, 56, 74, 119
Murphy, Robert, 88

NAACP, 216
national security, 1–2, 3, 45–47, 50–51, 52–65, 103, 109–20, 241–42, 245–46
Navy Department, 55, 56
Nazi-Soviet Pact, 40*n*, 57–59, 61, 74, 92
Neibuhr, Reinhold, 1, 271
NEP (New Economic Policy), 30
Neutrality Acts, 53, 56, 57, 182
New Deal, 9, 46, 193, 194, 213, 215, 264
Nicaragua, 146, 147, 155–56, 188
Nicholas II, 14
Nitze, Paul, 104–6
Nixon, Richard, 109, 120, 122–23*n*, 127–37, 145, 147, 149, 155, 162, 164, 222–23, 242–46, 249
Nixon Doctrine, 128
Non-Governmental Organizations (NGOs), 190, 196–97, 204–5*n*, 243, 252
North Atlantic Treaty Organization (NATO), 10*n*, 98*n*, 107, 127, 138, 160–61, 169, 177*n*, 207, 216, 223, 246
NSC-68, 103–8, 111, 156

Oder-Neisse line, 82
One World (Wendel Wilkie), 65

Open Door, 3, 24, 26–27, 38n, 46. *See also* trade
Orlov, Yuri, 142, 144, 163
orthodox church, 34–35
Oumansky, Constantine, 61

PD-18, 143, 148
Pearl Harbor, 62, 92, 182, 202, 207, 213
perestroika, 7, 161–73 *passim*
Pittman, Key, 50
Poland, 14, 25–26, 33, 40n, 42n, 57, 59, 61–63, 70n, 74–96 *passim*, 109, 115, 118, 161, 166. *See also* London Poles, Lublin Poles, World War I, World War II.
  attacks Soviet Union, 40n
  and Minority Treaties, 33
  as victim of Nazi-Soviet Pact, 57, 59, 61–63, 70n, 74, 92
  and Katyn massacre, 74–75
  Warsaw uprising, 75–76
  POWs in, 81–89
  1956 crisis in, 109, 118
  Solidarity movement 159, 161
  marshal law in, 159
Polish-Americans, 57, 75–76. *See also* catholics, public opinion
Polish-Soviet War (1920), 23, 25
Poole, DeWitt, 21
Pope Pius XI, 35
Pope Pius XII, 60
Potsdam Conference (1945), 79, 87, 108
POWs, 80, 81–89, 95–96, 101n, 129, 243
  forced repatriation of, 80, 81–89, 95–96
  Boris Yeltsin and, 101n
  in Vietnam, 101n, 129, 243
Prinkipo, peace proposal, 22
Protocol on the Status of Refugees, 241
Provisional Government, 14, 15, 38n, 41n, 49
public opinion, 3, 4, 8, 26, 34–35, 47–52, 54–56, 57–58, 59–65, 75–82, 85–95 *passim*, 99n, 115, 132–37, 145–46, 155–56, 161, 182, 191–92, 200–2, 205n, 214–25 *passim*, 226n, 241, 265. *See also* individual ethnic and religious affiliations

Lend-Lease and, 4, 59–65
concerning Poland, 75–77, 85–95 *passim*
and religious liberty, 34–35, 47–50
and United Nations, 9, 182, 205n
purges, 4, 54–55, 63, 67–68n, 75, 91, 98n

Quakers, 29–30
quarantine speech (1937), 55

Rapallo, Treaty of (1922), 42n
Reagan, Ronald, 6, 136, 138–39, 146, 147, 155–56, 170, 249–53, 270
Reagan Doctrine, 158
realpolitik, 23, 76, 78, 80, 105, 111, 113–14, 127–37, 148n, 156–57, 245–46, 249, 263–71 *passim*
recognition, U.S. policy on, 4, 35–36, 37n, 41n, 42n, 46–51, 167, 172–73. *See also* individual countries
Red Army, 5, 20, 54–55, 75, 81–86 *passim*, 88–89, 92, 95, 98n, 169
Red Cross, 88
Red Terror, 20–21, 39n
refuseniks, *see* dissidents
Reid v. Covert (1957), 225, 244
religious freedom, 4, 32–35, 43n, 47–50, 54–56, 59–62, 63, 66n, 189, 197. *See also* Four Freedoms, Roosevelt-Litvinov agreements
Republican party, 8, 26–29, 30–36 *passim*, 107–10, 133–34, 139, 166, 183, 207–30 *passim*, 252–53. *See also* elections
Reykjavik summit (1986), 162–63
"Riga Axioms," 67n
Rights of Man, *see* human rights
Roosevelt, Eleanor, 8, 208, 211–12, 220–21, 231n
Roosevelt, Franklin Delano, 4, 36, 46–65, 73–77, 81–96 *passim*, 169, 181–91, 192–202, 213–14, 228, 255, 269–70. *See also* Atlantic Charter, Dumbarton Oaks, Four Freedoms, human rights, liberal-internationalism, quarantine speech
  and recognition of the Soviet Union, 46–51

Roosevelt, Franklin Delano (continued)
  prewar Soviet policy of, 4, 51–65
  wartime diplomacy, 5–6, 73, 82–96, 228
  views of Soviet Union, 49, 50–51, 54, 64–65
  predilection for personal diplomacy, 46–51, 75
  and United Nations, 181–202, 255, 269–70
Roosevelt-Litvinov agreements, 47–52, 61, 73, 91, 116
Root, Elihu, 38*n*
Rostow, Walt, 113–14
Rumania, 59, 63, 77, 92, 119, 136
Rusk, Dean, 118, 217, 240
Russia, contemporary, 200–2, 263–71 *passim*
Russia, Imperial, 13, 14–19, 32, 33, 79
Russia, Soviet, *see* Soviet Union
Russian Section, 43*n*, 45, 55, 66*n*
Russo-Finnish War, 57–58

Sakharov, Andrei, 132, 135, 141–42, 162, 163, 175*n*, 176*n*
San Francisco, U.N. founding conference, 8, 103, 183, 189–202, 208, 210, 211, 216, 228, 229
Scharansky, Anatoly, 142, 145, 163
Schifter, Richard, 163, 170
Schmidt, Helmut, 249, 257*n*
segregation, 7, 195, 216
self-determination, 18–19, 20, 21–22, 23–24, 73, 75, 77, 113, 118, 227, 231*n*, 239, 249–50
Senate, 9, 41–42*n*, 59, 132–37, 156–57, 170–71, 183–202 *passim*, 205*n*, 209–30 *passim*, 235–56. *See also* Congress
SHAEF (Supreme Headquarters Allied Expeditionary Forces), 85–86, 88
Shevardnadze, Eduard, 163, 168–69, 171–72
Shultz, George, 159, 161–63
Siberia, 19–25 *passim*, 27, 29
Sino-Soviet split, 6, 124*n*, 127–28
Skvirsky, Boris, 35
Smith, Walter Bedell, 88, 90, 94
Solzhenitsyn, Aleksandr, 135, 139

"Sonnenfeldt Doctrine," 138
South Africa, 242–43
Soviet Union, 2–4, 17–25, 29–33, 45–51, 53–55, 56–65, 73–96, 116–20, 127–48, 155–73, 182–202 *passim*, 209–10, 249–50, 252–53, 263–71. *See also* arms control, emigration, gulag, human rights, individual leaders, jews, orthodox church, Russia, wives, World War I, World War II
  Bolshevik Revolution, 4, 17–25, 29
  Civil War, 4, 18–25, 29
  allied intervention, 19–25, 39*n*
  attacked by Poland, 40*n*
  political system of, 36, 53–54, 63–65, 80–96 *passim*
  recognition of by western powers, 25–29, 45–51, 74
  foreign citizens in, 29–33, 47–51, 56, 61, 67*n*, 70*n*, 74, 77–96
  nationalities problem, 43*n*
  purges in, 4, 54–55, 63, 67–68*n*, 75, 91, 98*n*
  and Munich, 56, 74
  and Nazi-Soviet Pact, 40*n*, 57, 59, 61, 74, 92
  attacks Finland, 57–58
  attacked by Nazi Germany, 59
  Lend-Lease to, 4, 59–65, 92, 129, 134–35, 182
  in World War II, 56–65, 73–96
  and Katyn massacre, 74–75
  and repatriation of POWs, 81–89
  and United Nations, 76–77, 182–202 *passim*, 209–10, 249–50, 252–53
  secrecy in, 92
  crushes Hungarian revolt, 108–9
  Sino-Soviet split, 124*n*, 127–28
  invades Czechoslovakia, 117–20
  and *détente*, 127–48
  invades Afghanistan, 136, 147–49, 250
  leadership crisis in, 160–61, 249
  KAL 007 shootdown, 161
  weakness of, 159–73 *passim*
  Union Treaty, 169–72
  end of, 2, 139, 169–72
Spanish Civil War, 54

Index

Stalin, Joseph (Dzhugashvili), 5, 34, 35, 51, 52–57, 58–65 *passim*, 74–96 *passim*, 108, 114, 121*n*, 167, 189, 193
Standley, William, 65
State Department, 34–35, 43*n*, 45, 47, 49, 50, 53–56, 61, 64–65, 74–96 *passim*, 103–6, 113–14, 133–34, 184–202, 208–30 *passim*. *See also* Russian Section
  views on United Nations, 184–202, 208–30 *passim*
  views on Russia, 35, 45, 47, 53–56, 64, 67*n*, 74–96, 103–6, 113–14
states rights, 213–25 *passim*, 237–40, 244–45
Stettinius, Edward, 187–202 *passim*, 214
Stevenson, Adlai, 222, 241
Stevenson, Adlai, Jr., 133, 145, 152*n*
Stevenson Amendment, 133–34
Stimson, Henry L., 45, 66*n*, 79–80
Strategic Arms Limitation Talks (SALT I and II), 117, 129, 135, 142–43, 146
Strategic Defense Initiative (SDI), 159, 161–62, 168
Strategic Arms Reduction Talks (START), 164, 168–69
Supplementary Convention on Slavery, 238, 241

Taft, Robert, 108, 214–15
Taylor, Myron C., 60
Teheran Conference (1943), 75–76, 108, 184
Tikhon, Patriarch, 34
trade, 13–14, 26–29, 45–46, 51, 52–53, 67*n*, 73, 79, 103–4, 115, 128–37, 263, 269. *See also* Congress, Jackson-Vanik, Soviet Union
Treaty on Navigation and Commerce (1832), *see* commercial treaties
Trotsky, Leon, 18, 19, 64
Truman, Harry S, 78–79, 80, 103–8 *passim*, 110, 115, 121*n*, 192–202, 207–12, 213, 228, 232*n*, 255
Truman Doctrine, 103–8, 111, 121*n*
Tunney Amendment, 134
Turkey, 78

Ukraine, 40*n*, 53, 170, 171–73, 193
UNESCO, 251, 254–55, 259*n*, 261*n*
Union Treaty, 169–72
United Kingdom, *see* Britain
United Nations, World War II alliance, *see* allies
United Nations Human Rights Commission, 144, 196, 208, 210, 223, 227, 231*n*
United Nations Human Rights Committee, 250
United Nations Organization, 2, 7–10, 76–77, 91, 101*n*, 103, 129, 181–202, 207–30, 237–56, 263–64
  Charter of, 7, 8–10, 103, 181–202, 207, 216, 227, 242–43, 251, 252, 255, 263–71 *passim*
  General Assembly, 91, 186–88, 195, 209, 227, 239, 241, 242–43, 246, 255
  Security Council, 118, 120, 187, 255, 260*n*
  and collective security, 76–77
  and human rights, 7–10, 91, 101*n*, 129, 181–202, 207–30, 237–56
United States, foreign relations of, 1–9, 13–36, 45–65, 73–96, 103–20, 127–48, 155–73, 181–202, 207–30, 237–56, 263–71. *See also* Conference on Security and Cooperation in Europe, Congress, human rights, individual presidents, Soviet Union, State Department, United Nations
  in World War I, 13–17, 37*n*
  and League of Nations, 7, 21
  and Versailles Treaty, 21–25
  intervention in Russia, 19–25, 39*n*
  recognition policy of, 4, 25–29, 30–36, 37*n*, 41*n*, 42*n*, 46–51, 167, 172–73
  and Lend-Lease, 59–65
  in World War II, 56–63, 73–96
  and founding of United Nations, 8, 181–202
  postwar role in United Nations, 7–10, 103, 118, 207–30, 237–56, 264
  occupation of Germany, 84–89, 93–94, 264

United States, foreign relations of (continued)
  Berlin crises and, 109, 111–12
  Suez and, 109
  Cuba and, 110–14 *passim*, 117, 149–50*n*, 165
  Vietnam and, 78, 106, 111–20, 124*n*, 127–37 *passim*, 141, 183
  Czechoslovakia and, 117–20
  and *détente*, 116–20, 127–48, 155, 159–60
  and arms control, 109–10, 112–13, 116–20, 129, 135, 141–48, 155–73 *passim*
  Watergate and, 132–33, 135, 136, 141
  and dissidents, 132, 134, 141–42, 143, 160, 162–63, 164–73 *passim*
  and Afghanistan, 136, 146, 147–49, 158, 160, 161, 169
  and collapse of Soviet Union, 171–73
  Gulf War leadership, 170–71, 255, 268
  and search for post-Cold War mission, 263–71
Universal Declaration of Human Rights, 7, 8, 141, 208, 226–27, 251–52
U.S. v. Belmont (1937), 66*n*, 214
U.S. v. Pink (1942), 66*n*, 214

Vance, Cyrus, 142–48
Vandenberg, Arthur H., 182–202 *passim*, 208, 216–17, 269–70
Vandenberg Resolution, 216
Vanik, Charles, 130–37 *passim*, 145
Versailles, Conference and Treaty (1919), 21–25, 33, 40*n*, 46, 77, 187, 200, 229
Vietnam, 78, 106, 111–20, 124*n*, 127–37 *passim*, 141, 165, 238, 242, 246, 264
Vlasov, Andrey, 81–82, 86
Vyshinsky, Andrey, 90, 92, 93

war debts, 18, 26, 28, 32, 49–52, 56
War Department, 30, 31, 56
Warsaw Treaty Organization (WTO or Warsaw Pact), 10*n*, 119, 171, 177*n*

Washington Naval Conferences (1921 and 1922), 27, 46, 117
Watergate, impact on foreign policy, 132–33, 135, 136, 141
Weinberger, Caspar, 159, 176*n*
Welles, Sumner, 74, 75
western Europe, 103–4, 113, 116–20, 127–28, 160, 165
whites, in Russian Civil War, 24–25, 29, 39*n*, 40*n*
Wilkie, Wendel, 65
Wilson, Woodrow, 4, 10*n*, 13, 15–26, 37*n*, 38*n*, 39*n*, 64, 113, 158, 181, 191, 208. *See also* Fourteen Points, liberal-internationalism
  view of March Revolution, 14–17
  view of Bolshevik Revolution, 17–19
  and intervention, 19–25, 39*n*
  and Russian Civil War, 4, 19–26
  and League of Nations, 7, 21–26, 191, 208
  at Versailles, 19–25
  and human rights, 7, 10*n*, 38*n*, 113
Winter War, *see* Russo-Finnish War
wives, Soviet, 80, 89–91, 95
women, political and civil rights for, 7, 38*n*, 100*n*, 227, 238
World Court, 26
World War I, 13, 17–25, 27, 29, 37*n*, 264–65
World War II, 8, 34, 56–65, 70*n*, 73–96, 113, 165, 169, 181–202, 264–65

"X" article (George Kennan), 78, 103–4

Yalta Conference (1945), 76–77, 82–96 *passim*, 98*n*, 108, 171, 201, 214, 224–25, 232*n*
Yeltsin, Boris, 101*n*, 171, 172–73
Yost, Charles, 243–44
Yugoslavia, 40*n*, 114–15, 119, 136, 173

zionism, U.N. resolution on, 243, 255, 257*n*, 261*n*

About the Author

CATHAL J. NOLAN, Assistant Professor of Political Science, University of British Columbia, co-edited *Shepherd of Democracy? America and Germany in the Twentieth Century* (Greenwood, 1992). He specializes in U.S. foreign policy and ethics in international affairs.